British Film Culture in the 1970s

The Boundaries of Pleasure

Sue Harper and Justin Smith

with
Dave Allen
Sian Barber
Peri Bradley
Laurie N. Ede
Laurel Foster
Vincent Porter
Sally Shaw

Edinburgh University Press

Edinburgh University Press Ltd
22 George Square, Edinburgh EH8 9LF

First published in hardback by Edinburgh University Press 2012

www.euppublishing.com

Typeset in Monotype Ehrhardt by
Servis Filmsetting Ltd, Stockport, Cheshire, and
printed and bound in Great Britain by
CPI Group (UK) Ltd, Croydon, CR0 4YY

A CIP record for this book is available from the British Library

ISBN 978 0 7486 4078 2 (hardback)
ISBN 978 0 7486 8169 3 (paperback)

Arts & Humanities
Research Council

Contents

List of Illustrations

List of Tables

Acknowledgements

We should like to thank the Arts and Humanities Research Council (www.ahrc.ac.uk) for the research grant which funded the University of Portsmouth's project, *1970s British Cinema, Film and Video: Mainstream and Counter-Culture* (2006–2009), and for their advice and support throughout. We are grateful to Esther Sonnet and colleagues in the School of Creative Arts, Film and Media, and to Simon Claridge, Dean of the Faculty of Creative and Cultural Industries at Portsmouth for their commitment to research.

Librarians at a number of locations have been helpful beyond the call of duty: Greta Friggens at the University of Portsmouth Library, David Sharp, Sarah Currant, Sean Delaney and staff at the British Film Institute Library, Nathalie Morris, Curator of Special Collections at the BFI, and Dylan Cave at the BFI National Archive. Fiona Liddell at the British Board of Film Classification has been incredibly assiduous on our behalf, and we are appreciative of the support of Murray Weston and all at the British Universities Film and Video Council. We should also like to thank the keepers of the BECTU History Project for permitting access to their tapes, the BBC Written Archives at Caversham, and staff at the National Archives, Kew. Special thanks go to Phil Wickham at the Bill Douglas Archive, Exeter University, John Izod and colleagues at the Lindsay Anderson Archive, University of Stirling, the Michael Klinger Archive at the University of the West of England, the Stanley Kubrick Archive at the University of the Arts London, and the Kobal Picture Archive.

We want to record our gratitude to all the interviewees who gave so generously of their time to talk to us about their careers (in person, by letter or email): Don Boyd, David Curtis, Edward Fox, Mamoun Hassan, Glenda Jackson, Malcolm Le Grice, Sandy Lieberson, Ken Russell and Michael Winner. We are especially grateful to Lord Puttnam for allowing us access to his private papers held in the BFI's Special Collections.

We also want to thank those who have given us information, read drafts or helped with the logistical problems of the book: James Chapman, Steve Chibnall, Walter Ditmar, Vicki Donald at Edinburgh University Press, Tony Dunn, Ieuan Franklin, Adrian Garvey, Mark Glancy, Jim Robertson and Andrew Spicer.

Sue Harper, Justin Smith

List of Contributors

Dave Allen is a Visiting Teaching Fellow in the School of Creative Arts, Film and Media at the University of Portsmouth. He is a National Teaching Fellow of the Higher Education Academy and was a Co-investigator on the Arts and Humanities Research Council-funded project *1970s British Cinema, Film and Video: Mainstream and Counter-Culture* (2006–2009). He has written variously on visual arts education, film and popular music, and continues to run a project called 'Pompey Pop', researching popular music in Portsmouth from 1945 to 1969.

Sian Barber is a Postdoctoral Researcher and Lecturer at Royal Holloway, University of London, and was a doctoral student on the 1970s project at Portsmouth. She is currently working on two projects concerning the digitisation of European Television material and the creation of online resources, funded by the European Union and by the Arts and Humanities Research Council. Her research interests are in British cinema and cultural history. She is completing a monograph entitled *Censoring the 1970s: The BBFC and the Decade that Taste Forgot* (Cambridge Scholars, forthcoming 2012).

Peri Bradley is an Associate Lecturer in Film and TV at Southampton Solent University and in Media at Bournemouth University. She was Research Assistant on the Portsmouth project. Her research focuses on the use of the body in cinema, documentary and reality TV.

Laurie N. Ede is a Principal Lecturer in Film and Media at the University of Portsmouth. He has written extensively on issues of film aesthetics, with a particular emphasis on production design. His comprehensive survey of British art direction, *British Film Design: A History*, was published in 2010 by I. B. Tauris.

Laurel Forster is a Senior Lecturer in Media Studies at the University of Portsmouth. Her research interests are in women's writing and women's culture, and she has published widely in this field: on women's work in World War One; housework and reality television; and feminism and science fiction. She has co-edited two collections: *The Recipe Reader* (Ashgate, 2003) and (with Sue Harper) *British Culture and Society in the 1970s: The Lost Decade* (Cambridge Scholars, 2010). She is currently working on a monograph on women's magazines.

Sue Harper is Emeritus Professor of Film History at the University of Portsmouth. She is the author of *Picturing the Past: The Rise and Fall of the British Costume Film* (BFI, 1994), *Women in British Cinema: Mad, Bad and Dangerous to Know* (Continuum, 2000) and (with Vincent Porter) *British Cinema of the 1950s: The Decline of Deference* (Oxford University Press, 2003). She co-edited (with James Chapman and Mark Glancy) *The New Film History* (Palgrave Macmillan, 2007). She was the Principal Investigator on the 1970s project at Portsmouth.

Vincent Porter is Emeritus Professor of Mass Communications at the University of Westminster and Visiting Professor at the University of Portsmouth. His recent publications include 'Alternative film exhibition in the English regions during the 1970s', in Paul Newland (ed.), *Don't Look Now: British Cinema in the 1970s* (Bristol: Intellect, 2010), and 'The exhibition, distribution and reception of French films in Great Britain during the 1930s', in L. Mazdon and C. Wheatley (eds), *Je t'aime . . . moi non plus. Franco-British Cinematic Relations* (Berghahn, 2010).

Sally Shaw is a Lecturer in Sociology and Politics at the University of Portsmouth, where she is completing an Arts and Humanities Research Council-funded doctoral research project on the social and cultural history of black Britain in 1970s film and television. Within the thesis, key emphasis is placed on uncovering 'lost voices', using extensive archival sources and oral testimony.

Justin Smith is a Principal Lecturer in Film Studies at the University of Portsmouth. He is the author of *Withnail and Us: Cult Films and Film Cults in British Cinema* (I. B. Tauris, 2010). He was a Co-investigator on the 1970s project and is the Principal Investigator on the Arts and Humanities Research Council-funded project, 'Channel 4 Television and British Film Culture', www.c4film.co.uk.

Introduction

Sue Harper and Justin Smith

The scope of this book is simultaneously narrow and broad. It aims to draw a map of British film culture in the 1970s. At face value, the title implies one nation, one medium and one decade, but we hope to tease out the complexity of each of these terms. 'British' is understood to mean legislatively and legally British, although such ascriptions have sometimes been problematic. Moreover, the matter of national identity in film was complicated in this decade. 'Film culture' here not only means films shown in cinemas; it also covers the expansion of independent film and video, and television's relationship with cinema. But film culture is not defined solely by its media and practices. We need also to attend to its reception and taste-communities in order to understand its social meaning. 'The 1970s' is a particularly difficult period to conceptualise, but we will come to terms with some of its defining characteristics, while being mindful that neither social nor cultural history is organised in neat decades.

From 2006, the 1970s specifically began to attract the attention of social historians. Before that, there had been studies which located the decade in a twentieth-century context, but because of their range, they did not address the relationship between culture and society in the 1970s.[1] However, these broader histories did analyse the roots of social change in the decade. Marwick, for example, proposed a 'long 1960s', in which the 1970s were seen as a predictable consequence of the innovations of the previous decade. Otherwise, the only dedicated history was Christopher Booker's contemporary, journalistic account, which epitomised the received wisdom of the time about the decade's social gloom and political strife.[2]

The recent cluster of reassessments of the 1970s has been of a different order. It may be fruitful to speculate about the reasons why a decade gains particular currency at specific moments. This may be explained by generational shifts, and by the desire to excavate the recent past by working on the memories it evokes and recovering a sense of its strangeness from its apparent familiarity. New histories of the 1970s have defined the culture/society interface in different ways. Some use a 'snapshot' approach. Howard Sounes, for example, employs a case-study method, but the rationale for selection is personal and there is no coherent attempt to locate cultural events historically.[3] Dave Haslam's account has a similarly episodic structure and he distils the decade into a series of style markers.[4] Francis Wheen also deploys a snapshot approach, but his interpretation is shaped by the invocation of a dominant mood: 'Slice the Seventies where you will, the flavour is unmistakable – a pungent *mélange* of apocalyptic dread and conspiratorial fever.'[5]

Other books survey more diverse social currents. Alwyn Turner highlights specific themes but relates them rather unevenly to cultural forms.[6] Andy Beckett's *When the Lights Went Out* sees the 'long 1970s' as lasting well into the 1980s, with Thatcherism as the apotheosis of the decade.[7] Mark Garnett too presents the decade as the fulcrum of change, accounting for the crises in more recent history.[8] Dominic Sandbrook concentrates on the early years of the decade and identifies 1974 as a cultural end-point. His is also the only recent account to give solid attention to the culture of the period. He argues that it is misleading to interpret plays and films of the period as evidence of national anxiety: 'the fact is that most people found life in Metro-land warm, sociable and thoroughly enjoyable'.[9] Sandbrook's is a scholarly account, and its focus alerts us to important shifts within the decade.

Further evidence of renewed interest in the 1970s came from three academic conferences. The British Academy hosted a symposium on 23 September 2009, which paired contemporary witness accounts with new historical work on the decade, but the focus was squarely on social and economic themes. The Institute of Historical Research mounted a conference in June 2010, which similarly gave a fairly low priority to cultural matters. The Arts and Humanities Research Council (AHRC)-funded research project carried out at the University of Portsmouth, entitled *1970s British Cinema, Film and Video: Mainstream and Counter-Culture* (2006–2009), held its own conference in 2008, which specifically addressed British culture and society. The ensuing collection, edited by Laurel Forster and Sue Harper, suggested that organisational structures in a range of artistic institutions were in flux, and that this coincided with innovation in a range of media.[10] *The Boundaries of Pleasure* is the final outcome of that AHRC project. It aims to build on the broad cultural grounding provided by the conference anthology, to inform our analysis of film culture specifically.

The 1970s has received only limited attention in scholarly histories of British cinema. Three books published in the mid-1980s combined the

1970s with the following decade, thus offering contemporary accounts of a cinema in decline. Alexander Walker's *National Heroes* is the sequel to his study of the 1960s, *Hollywood, England*.[11] Walker's journalistic familiarity with his cast fleshes out many of the important figures in the film industry of the 1970s and his chronology is comprehensive. But his aim that *National Heroes*, like its predecessor, 'will illuminate, even at a lower intensity, the correlation between a society and the films that mirror change', is limited by two difficulties. Firstly, Walker's narrative is driven by his own personal view of a film culture undergoing its death throes. Secondly, compared with the cinema of the 1960s, that of the 1970s proves frustratingly resistant to his reflectionist approach. Similar problems haunt John Walker's *The Once and Future Film*, which provides a useful if selective survey. Another provisional obituary for British cinema, *The Last Picture Show*, laments the demise of cinema-going.[12]

Andrew Higson's contribution to *The Arts in the 1970s: Cultural Closure?* is less valedictory in tone, but Higson has insufficient space in that volume to extend his argument about the fragmentation of visual culture in the decade, and he is hamstrung by his editor's assumption of the idea of 'cultural closure'.[13] Another brief survey is offered by Pamela Church Gibson and Andrew Hill, who use metaphors of 'excess, masquerade and performativity' to interpret the work of the decade's notable *auteurs*.[14] Useful as these concepts may be, the authors fail to identify their cultural roots, or to undertake production history to provide anchorage.

Other kinds of intervention are divided by debates about quality. A number of studies have focused on the exploitation market in the 1970s. Leon Hunt's *British Low Culture: From Safari Suits to Sexploitation* deconstructs the notion of 'the decade which taste forgot'.[15] Others covered similar terrain.[16] Some scholars sought to recover *auteurs* from the morass of 1970s cinema. These include contemporary studies of Ken Russell by Baxter, Gomez and Phillips, and retrospectives on Nicolas Roeg by Sinyard, Izod and Salwolke. Stanley Kubrick received early attention in a 1972 appraisal by Alexander Walker, and has subsequently been the subject of a substantial literature including notable studies by Mario Falsetto.[17] These important accounts of particular film-makers have none the less contributed to the entrenchment of debates about quality in 1970s British cinema, thus inhibiting measured assessment. Film historians have a duty to attend to the whole film culture of a period, irrespective of quality, and to try to account for its variety.

The burgeoning avant-garde in 1970s British film culture has, to date, been the subject of a number of discrete interventions and has featured in longer histories of experimental film-making, including notable studies by A. L. Rees and David Curtis. Margaret Dickinson's anthology, *Rogue Reels*, offers an eclectic selection of primary and secondary sources on this period, while Michael O'Pray's edited volume has a broader scope but includes some important personal testimonies and scholarly essays concerning 1970s practice.[18] This field has also received recent archival attention from a major AHRC-funded project run by Julia Knight at the University of Sunderland: *Artists' Film and Video Database/Digitised Collection Projects: Addressing Sustainability and Historiography* (2007–2009). But, thus far, dedicated work in this area has not been incorporated into a comprehensive survey of 1970s film culture as a whole.

A thoroughgoing reassessment of this period has only really begun in the last five years but has resulted in two important anthologies. Robert Shail's collection contains some significant contributions on hitherto neglected aspects of 1970s film culture, such as James Chapman's work on Amicus's fantasy adventures and Christophe Dupin's study of the British Film Institute. *Don't Look Now*, edited by Paul Newland, arose from a major conference held at Exeter University in 2007, and features, amongst other new work, a chapter on Barney Platts-Mills by James Leggott and Vincent Porter's survey of alternative film exhibition.[19] Contributors to both collections offer an eclectic range of new research drawn from archival and interview sources. Useful though these latest interventions have been, there remains the difficulty of adequately accounting for the fragmentation which Higson noted back in 1994.

This literature survey presents two orders of difficulty to the film historian of the 1970s. Firstly, historical and social analyses seem unable to deal satisfactorily with the place and function of film culture in the period. Secondly, existing work on 1970s British cinema has produced tightly focused anthologies which have not attempted to map the terrain of the film culture as a whole. Our challenges in this book have been to structure an approach which will give a holistic account of the complexity of the film culture, and to provide a model for thinking about the relationship between film culture and society in the 1970s.

The nature of these challenges means that the structure of this book is unusual, but we hope it will go some way towards thinking about cultural history afresh. The book is divided into two halves, which are differently authored and methodologically distinct. The essays in Part I have been contributed by members of the Portsmouth project, and each has a discrete focus and performs a separate task. Sian Barber's two chapters establish the legislative and censorship constraints upon mainstream British cinema in the period. Dave Allen follows these with a survey of independent moving image work, which explores its relationship to the visual arts. In Chapter 4 Laurie Ede considers the field of art direction and production design, addressing the dominant visual discourses in the commercial cinema. Vincent Porter's contribution analyses the way in which film developed a significant place in higher education during the 1970s, and the implications of this for film production and criticism. Sally Shaw's chapter on black film-making offers an example of the intervention of marginalised cultures into commercial cinema and raises issues about ethnic minorities and national identity. Chapter 7 features Laurel Forster's work on the cultural dominance of television in the period and its institutional and aesthetic relationship with the cinema. Another example of cross-media impetus is provided in Chapter 8 by Dave Allen's account of popular music and its influence on moving image culture.

The work completed in Part I illustrates the diversity of the moving image culture of the period. If these essays 'drill down' into discrete areas of the field, then Part II adopts a lateral approach. Here Sue Harper and Justin Smith draw upon the evidence provided in Part I to explore the relations between different aspects of the film culture and to provide reasons for its fragmented nature. Thus Part II functions on a more thematic and speculative level. Chapter 9 identifies the sites of innovation in production, and raises the issue of the relationship of financial to cultural capital. Chapter 10 considers the crisis of permission in British society of the 1970s, and asks how the cinema responded to changes in the sexual landscape. The issue of film style is the business of Chapter 11, which surveys technological developments and explores tone and visual manner. Chapter 12 examines the construction of social space in the cinema, analysing the depiction of geographical space (composition) and personal space (performance style). Any interpretation of the commercial cinema of the decade must take into account its relations with other media, and recognise the cultural function of the burgeoning avant-garde. These 'cross-overs' are the focus of Chapter 13. Finally, Chapter 14 considers issues of reception and taste, and proposes reasons for the segmentation of popular and critical preferences.

In presenting an account of the film culture of the 1970s, we must be alert to the implications of its diversity of output and patterns of consumption. The 1970s was the first decade when the cinema's 'habit audience' no longer existed; it was also the last decade when cinema was the dominant site of film consumption. Falling attendances and cinema closures consigned commercial cinema to the cultural margins, and it thus lost the last vestiges of the hegemonic function it once had. Because of its devalued place, the cinema performed different cultural tasks in the 1970s. The delineation of these tasks is one of the aims of this book. In order to achieve that, we need to be alert to the following questions. Firstly, what are the determinants on artistic innovation in a period of economic uncertainty? Secondly, given its cultural marginality, how does British cinema of the 1970s engage with aspects of social change? Thirdly, what observations can be made about variation and development in film style during the decade? Finally, did the transformations in the cinema's status have an effect upon patterns of audience response and the cultural value ascribed to film?

In finding answers to these questions we have proceeded from the tried and tested methods of revisionist film history. Where possible, we have drawn upon archival sources such as production notes, film scripts, correspondence, publicity materials and official documents. We have also employed the testimonies offered in a range of interviews conducted with key figures from 1970s British film culture. A general analysis of film output has been undertaken which has provided us with an overview of this diverse film culture. Close textual analysis of a range of films has been informed by thorough production history and reception work. This approach has proved fruitful for previous periods in British film history and has been deployed in a mindful way in this study. Its efficacy is rooted in an explanatory model of Marxist cultural criticism in which the cultural superstructure is determined by the economic base in a predictable way. However, in the 1970s, the fragmented nature of the economic base gives rise to an inchoate body of films. This demands an adapted model of artistic agency, which attends to the richness and permeability of the visual discourses of this particular period.

Our research has suggested that there was a radical destabilisation of the systems of meaning across a wide range of cultural forms in the 1970s, and that cinema's uncertain position made it acutely responsive, in a sometimes erratic manner, to these upheavals. This observation also raises questions about our interpretation of cinema's relationship to social change. The established model for thinking through the relationship between film and society has been the reflectionist metaphor: that film art is driven by the desire for mimesis and that it engages directly with the social order. One thing which is noticeable about British cinema of the 1970s is its sheer variety; this is the cinema which produced *A Clockwork Orange* (1971), *Family Life* (1971), *Don't Look Now* (1973), *Confessions of a Window Cleaner* (1974), *Nightcleaners* (1975), *Carry On Emmannuelle* (1978), *Quadrophenia* (1979) and *Scum* (1979). However, such films do not seem to deal with social and sexual transformations of the period in any predictable way, which renders the reflectionist model inadequate.

The 1970s is characterised by unpredictable relations between economic determinants and cultural production, and in the mainstream market, the consensus between film-makers and consumers had broken down. The reason for the proliferation of exploitation cinema in the period is that the pleasures of the audience are consistently met by the formulae of the product. The same might be said of other niche taste-communities like the avant-garde, whose desires were satisfied by the sub-cultural cachet of their product. Thus, pornographic and experimental films, despite their discrete pleasures, share a peculiar similarity: the 'parishes of belief' occupied by their producers and consumers have unusually secure boundaries. Rarely does such consensus obtain anywhere else in this complex film culture.

The subtitle of this book is *The Boundaries of Pleasure*. What do we mean by this? Firstly, we are alluding to the ways in which some films – from *Eskimo Nell* (1974) to *Sebastiane* (1976) – challenged the boundaries of permission. Secondly, we want to suggest that this fragmented film culture was divided by boundaries of taste which were often criticised from outside and defended from within. Thirdly, we want to propose that, during the course of the decade, mainstream cinema retreated from hedonism, and turned back at the borders of the new country. Finally, we want to argue that, in the 1970s, British film culture was preoccupied with the boundaries between public and private pleasures in a way it had never been before.

Part I

CHAPTER 1

Government Aid and Film Legislation: 'An elastoplast to stop a haemorrhage'

Sian Barber

The industrial history of British film in the 1970s has received some critical attention. Betts, Dickinson and Street, and Baillieu and Goodchild all address the legislative and economic problems faced by the industry in the decade.[20] However, the complex relationships between successive governments and the film industry need to be fully explored. Despite the relative prosperity of the British film industry in the 1960s, the early 1970s was a time of great uncertainty. Hollywood companies had been investing heavily in British film, creating an economic and cultural buoyancy which could not be sustained. Dickinson and Street estimate that, by 1968, 90 per cent of British production capital was American, yet by the end of the decade economic retrenchment and new funding strategies caused American companies to withdraw much of their British investment.[21]

While this withdrawal of capital left the industry in a precarious position, it also offered opportunities for rejuvenation. This critical time for the film industry coincided with a period of intense political and economic instability, and with the emergence of a vigorous television culture. In order for the film industry to be revitalised, sympathetic government support was needed. Yet how was this to be achieved and how were existing forms of government support to be deployed? This chapter will consider the strategies employed by successive governments to aid the film industry; it will evaluate initiatives such as the Finance Consortium, European co-production arrangements and the Film Working Party; it will assess the changing roles of the National Film Finance Corporation (NFFC), the Eady levy and the British Film Institute (BFI) Production Board. It will also consider how economic policy helped define the character of the film industry and influenced film production in an unpredictable decade.

The Quota, NFFC and Eady Levy

In 1970 there were three established pillars of government support for the film industry: the Quota, the NFFC and the Eady levy. These were intended to protect the film industry from Hollywood dominance, provide film projects with adequate funding and ensure that profits from successful films were ploughed back into the industry. But why had these measures failed to provide Britain with a financially viable industry?

The Quota was established in 1927, and stipulated that British cinemas must show a specific percentage of British films. It was believed that this would help to protect the domestic industry from domination by foreign film product, and ensure that British-made films found exhibition spaces. As Napper and Chibnall have both shown, although the 'Quota Quickies' were often derided as poor quality, they were an important facet of British film production.[22] The Quota did stimulate film production, and the number of British-made films rose from 34 in 1926 to 131 in 1928.[23] Yet it only managed to promote small-budget British films, and American productions continued to dominate British cinema.

The NFFC worked in a different way. Initially conceived by the then President of the Board of Trade, Harold Wilson, it was formed in 1949 to encourage a competitive domestic industry.[24] Wilson recognised that, although close collaboration with Hollywood was inevitable, the British industry should not be entirely dependent on this relationship. He considered that the best way to ensure independence was through a strong domestic industry. Following its creation, the NFFC was endowed with £6 million from the Government, but was hampered by an early decision to loan over £2 million of its funds to struggling production company British Lion. Between 1949 and 1972, the NFFC played an active part in film production, financing 731 long films and 173 shorts at a cost of £28 million, while continuing to make further payments to British Lion.[25] While the NFFC did fund some important films, many of its investments were small-budget features which had little chance of generating enough profit to pay back the initial loans. It was never clear what the role of the NFFC should be. Should it fund artistic and cultural films, or those with the greatest chance of financial success? Should it act as a bank, primarily concerned with profit, or should it support worthy creative enterprises?

The other pillar of support for the film industry was a tax levied on exhibitors set up in 1954. Named after the Treasury official who implemented it, the Eady levy offered a conduit through which successful companies could channel money back into production. Unfortunately, successful films were the ones that benefited most from the system. Major beneficiaries included the *Carry On* films and the James Bond franchise. Figures from the Film Fund Agency, which administered the Eady money, reveal that American companies were also major beneficiaries of levy finance.[26] Filming in Britain allowed Hollywood subsidiaries to register their films as British and become eligible for the levy. In 1970, United Artists and Columbia took over 40 per cent of the available levy, a total of £1.3 million.[27] In the same year, Anglo-EMI took only 7 per cent, while British Lion received 1.5 per cent. The Rank Organisation did better, with a 16 per cent share during 1970, but this dropped to a mere 2 per cent by 1975.[28]

Another recipient of state aid was the BFI Production Board. In 1966 the Production Board replaced the Experimental Film Fund, which had been created in 1952 to subsidise young film-makers. By the 1970s, the Board was receiving substantial sums from the BFI as well as from the Eady fund, with its total annual income estimated as £120,000 in 1976.[29] However, the purpose of the Production Board fund remained contested. Alan Lovell, writing in 1976, noted the need for the Board to 'decide what kind of role it should play'.[30] Christophe Dupin has subsequently shown how the cultural direction of the Board's funding policy in the 1970s was subject to the vagaries of its leadership and political infighting. None the less, the Production Board was able, for the first time, to support feature-length film projects for commercial release.[31]

The measures set in place by previous governments had not created a stable British film industry. Distributors, producers and exhibitors hoped that the Films Act of 1970 would address contentious issues, including the withdrawal of American money and competition from television. Unfortunately, this Act was a cautious piece of legislation. The Labour Party did not address specific problems, although it promised to provide an additional £5 million to the NFFC, and advanced £1 million before the General Election of 1970. However, this initiative became one of the first casualties of the incoming Conservatives' film policy, and the balance was withheld.

A New Direction?

In an interview in December 1970, the newly appointed Films Minster, Nicholas Ridley, detailed the Government's position: 'We'd like to phase out the injection of public funds . . . I would very much like to see the NFFC giving us a million out of successful trading instead of us giving it a million.'[32] Ridley's remarks outlined the new Government's approach to the film industry and are understandable when considering the chaotic state of the NFFC. In 1971 a new Consortium scheme was announced to encourage city financiers to invest in the film industry. The Government was to give the NFFC £1 million, on the condition that every pound of government money was matched with three pounds from the private sector. Horrified industry figures, including Michael Balcon, Richard Attenborough, Karel Reisz, John Schlesinger, Joseph Losey and Lindsay Anderson, wrote an open letter to *The Times*, arguing that, without operating capital, the NFFC would never be seen as a viable investment opportunity by the private sector.[33] The policy was also challenged in Parliament when Roy Mason MP roundly condemned the shift in policy in July 1971, asking:

> Does the Honourable Gentleman realise where this policy is leading? He must be trying to kill British film production. His impositions on the NFFC and the reduction of its loan making powers, allied to less money from the Levy, are bound to affect production [and] employment . . . and to lessen confidence in the future of the British film industry.[34]

The Consortium scheme was intended to make the film industry economically viable, yet denying it financial autonomy made it structurally weak. Inevitably, only larger projects would attract the backing of city financiers; smaller, independent films would be unlikely to attract private capital. In an era of spiralling costs, the funding possibilities offered by the NFFC were limited.

In its first six years the Consortium financed the production of only nineteen feature films, and city investors contributed only £750,000. The investment was too small to support high-budget features, yet only such films would guarantee the necessary significant returns.[35] One of the first film projects undertaken by the Consortium was Dylan Thomas's *Under Milk Wood* (1972), starring Richard Burton and Peter O'Toole.[36] Investment bank Hill Samuel supplied one-third of the production costs, whilst the NFFC provided the remaining £200,000.[37] Despite optimistic predictions, this film failed to make any significant impact at the British box office.

Many of the projects selected for NFFC funding in the early years of the decade were resolutely populist. These included *A Touch of the Other* (1970), *Up Pompeii* (1971), *I, Monster* (1971), *Ooh . . . You Are Awful* (1972), *Endless Night* (1972), *Steptoe and Son Ride Again* (1973) and *Captain Kronos: Vampire Hunter* (1974). Despite funding sixty-eight film projects between 1969 and 1980, only four made it into the top twenty at the British box office.[38] While the successes of these – *Up Pompeii*, *Stardust* (1974), *At the Earth's Core* (1976) and *Bugsy Malone* (1977) – provided an

Table 1 British film production

Year	Number of British films made	Number of films approved for an NFFC loan	Films funded by NFFC as percentage of British films produced
1969–1970	97	10	10.3
1970–1971	96	15	15.6
1971–1972	104	2	1.9
1972–1973	99	4	4.0
1973–1974	88	1	1.1
1974–1975	81	9	11.1
1975–1976	80	1	1.25
1976–1977	50	5	10.0
1977–1978	54	5	9.2
1978–1979	61	10	16.4
1979–1980	31	6	19.3
Total	841	68	8.7

Source: *NFFC Annual Reports* 1969–1980 and www.screenonline.org.uk

investment return for the NFFC, they also indicated the haphazard nature of the funding policy.[39] The figures in the table demonstrate how marginal the NFFC was in British film production, contributing to only 8.7 per cent of films produced in the 1970s.

In 1973–1974, only one film project was allocated a grant. *Stardust* was the sequel to *That'll Be the Day* (1973), which had been part-funded by EMI and had done well at the British box office. By funding only one film, the NFFC was taking a risk. *Stardust* had to make money, or else be a huge financial embarrassment for all concerned. It was funded in equal parts by EMI and the NFFC, and was chosen for funding because it was considered 'the only project out of 134 submitted to the corporation during the year which was ready to go into commercial production and which seemed to have an outstanding chance of commercial success'.[40] By funding *Stardust*, the NFFC was basing its decision upon the straightforward belief that, if the film did as well as its predecessor, it would make money. This conservative gamble paid off, and *Stardust* featured as one of the top films of both 1974 and 1975.

The NFFC collaborated with David Puttnam beyond *Stardust*, and *Lisztomania* (1975), *Bugsy Malone* and *The Duellists* (1977) forged a mutually beneficial relationship with Goodtimes Enterprises. Collaboration with already successful names became a feature of NFFC investment in the later 1970s, with established directors including Joseph Losey, Ken Russell, Nicolas Roeg and Ken Loach all being granted funding.

By 1977 this change of direction was advanced by the NFFC's decision to become involved with more culturally ambitious projects. After the NFFC declined to part-fund *Carry On England* in 1976, the *Annual Report* for 1977 notes the NFFC's involvement with *Bugsy Malone*, *Black Joy* (1977), *The Shout* (1977) and *The Duellists*, all of which performed well at the Cannes film festival.[41] Involvement with such esteemed projects was a trend which continued, with support for *The Riddle of the Sands* (1979) and *The Europeans* (1979).

An examination of the attitude of the NFFC reveals a great deal about government film policies. Having initially supported a range of low-status features, with unpredictable success, it then chose to support established directors and producers in more ambitious projects. Yet the NFFC was not the only possible source of funding in the decade. Other government policies opened up British film production in new ways.

Co-production and Nationalisation

Britain had established co-production agreements with France in 1965 and Italy in 1967, yet British film-makers were slow to collaborate with their European partners. Britain's co-production agreements were intended to produce films which were 'capable of enhancing the reputation of the film industries of [the] two countries'.[42] In order to ensure the success of these productions in domestic film markets, these films were granted financial concessions by respective governments.[43] It was hoped that, by allowing co-production projects to be registered as 'national films' in two markets, a climate would be created in which European film industries would be relieved of financial and artistic dependence on the American market. However, problems soon became apparent. A guide to co-production published by the Film Producers Association (FPA) in 1971 warned against the production of 'cultural hybrid films' and declared that 'each co-production film should be a reflection of the culture of one of the countries involved'.[44] Despite emphasis on cultural collaboration, co-production agreements were predicated on economic benefit, which produced those very hybrids against which the FPA had warned.

Although the Board of Trade favoured co-production, not everyone in the industry was positive about collaborative film-making. The FPA warned that the British were co-production amateurs when compared to the long-standing arrangements of the French and Italians, and emphasised the need for Britain to establish its own working relationships.[45] The FPA advocated arrangements which would establish Britain as a key player rather than a junior partner, but did not make clear how this should be achieved.[46] Yet there were some supporters of co-production agreements. An article in *The Times* supported the idea of a European film-funding bank which would curb Hollywood's influence.[47] This was a French proposal, which was not received enthusiastically in Britain; the British industry remained closely linked to Hollywood and could not risk alienating such a powerful ally. While European collaborations were potentially rewarding, there were some obvious flaws. A domestic industry which was financially crippled was hardly in a position to establish new partnerships in Europe. Yet this is precisely what the Government advocated through its support for co-production agreements.

The weaknesses of co-production became clear when the much-vaunted schemes failed to produce financially successful films. Only twenty-nine British-European co-production films were made between 1970 and 1980, and only four of these – *Day of the Jackal* (1973), *Lady Caroline Lamb* (1972), *Don't Look Now* and *Moonraker* (1979) – did well at the British box office. The levels of bureaucracy in co-production film-making became increasingly complex, and the FPA recommended the employment of a British accountant to avoid legal and financial problems arising from language difficulties. Even established directors experienced difficulties; Joseph Losey's papers reveal his frustrations at being unable to cast actors of his choice for *The Romantic Englishwoman* (1975) due to the restrictions of co-production agreements.[48] Another problem with co-production was the hostility of the film unions. The FPA suggested that the unions should be involved to smooth over any difficulties regarding working conditions on co-production films.[49] The Government's commitment to co-production was demonstrated by a new treaty established with West Germany in 1975, but the unions' reluctance to support the agreement doomed it to failure.

The Unions and Television

In 1973, the Association of Cinema and Television Technicians (ACTT) published a pamphlet calling for public ownership of the film industry in order to establish a degree of creative competition and to alter the 'financial logic' of the industry.[50] While the ACTT's proposals for nationalisation were never considered seriously, they do highlight the inherent divisions within the industry. In contrast with the views of the ACTT and its focus on a strong domestic industry, both the Cinematograph Films Council (CFC) and the FPA believed that the British industry should have international objectives. The CFC believed that 'the future of the British film industry must continue to be in producing films likely to appeal to a wide audience both at home and abroad'.[51] By 1975, the FPA noted: 'today, more than ever before, Britain needs to be sold abroad and to do this, must have a flourishing film industry'.[52]

The industry was further fragmented by divisions between successful producers of large-budget films and independent producers, for whom funding possibilities were strictly limited. The FPA pinpointed the problem in 1975:

> Independent producers found it increasingly difficult to find financial backing for their films and many who had extended all their resources on the preparation of projects had no more capital to invest in the acquisition of new properties and the preparation of scripts.[53]

In 1976 the Association of Independent Producers (AIP) was formed and directly opposed the pro-union stance of the FPA. Founder-member Don Boyd recalled that the AIP had a radical agenda, including breaking the power of the unions, changing the way money was distributed, altering the Eady levy and, most importantly, ensuring that independent film producers played a pivotal role in the creation of the proposed fourth channel.[54] As well as intensifying the factionalism within the film industry, AIP's demands demonstrated that the film industry faced the same problems in 1976 as it had at the start of the decade. Little had changed and the same problems persisted, most notably the relationship with television.

Despite repeated calls for the Government to intervene in the relationship between the two industries, successive governments were reluctant to legislate. One controversial topic was the sale of films for television broadcast. In January 1974 questions were raised in Parliament about the practice of selling films to television at low prices.[55] Television companies could make a single payment for a film or a collection of films, and then screen them as many times as they chose. Even if the network made a payment every time the film was shown, the payment was usually a token amount and completely disproportionate to the cost of making the film. In 1974, the sale of six James Bond films to ITV for £850,000 prompted new debate. As the average cost of making a film in this period was around £300,000 for a low-budget production and up to £600,000 for a more lavish one, the Bond deal was a bargain for ITV, but a wasted opportunity for the film industry.[56] The five-year delay before films could be shown on television was also reduced to three years, limiting the distribution opportunities for films following their first-run release.

However, despite its prosperity, there were also problems in the television industry. Although it had begun the 1970s stronger than ever before, the television industry was struggling with the policies adopted by successive Labour and Conservative Governments, with frequent union problems, and the dominance of a strong duopoly.[57] Both industries had separate reports commissioned to consider their respective futures, the Terry Report for film in 1976 and the Annan Report for broadcasting in 1977. Yet while the Annan Report eventually led to the creation of Channel 4 in 1982, the findings of the Terry Report were sidelined.

The Working Party and the Terry Report

In May 1975, film industry representatives met the Prime Minister to discuss the future of the British film industry. A month later, in a statement to the House of Commons, Harold Wilson announced the establishment of a working party to 'report back on the future needs of the industry and its relationship with the Government'.[58] The working party was chaired by John Terry of the NFFC, and included Richard Attenborough, Bernard Delfont, John Woolf, Michael Deeley and Alan Sapper. Although hailed as a breakthrough in relations between the film industry and the Labour Government, its disparate constituency made it difficult to agree on a course of action. The debt-ridden NFFC remained optimistic, declaring with palpable relief: 'the Corporation intends to give every support to the Interim Action Committee and to deploy its present resources as effectively as possible.'[59]

When the working party reported in January 1976, its recommendations were extensive and included addressing the relationship with television, the involvement of American companies and co-production agreements. One of its most important proposals was the establishment of a British Film Authority (BFA), which would oversee the Eady levy and incorporate the British Film Fund Agency and the NFFC. The BFA would also take over the role held by the CFC in advising the Government on film policy. Perhaps most significantly, the initial operating expenses of the BFA were to be met by the Government.[60] Further financial recommendations of the report were: investment in the British film industry of £40 million per annum; one-fifth of the Eady fund yield per year to go to the NFFC; additional funds of £5 million to be provided by the Government; and the right for the BFA to call on additional funds of £5 million in subsequent years.[61] It was also proposed that the NFFC be given the balance of the advance which had been made by the Board of Trade in 1970. Other significant items included: finance for feature films to be provided by the BBC and ITV; a three-year statutory time gap before films could be shown on television; and better prices for films offered to UK television.[62]

Responses to the report were mixed. Meeting notes from the CFC highlight the divisions across the British industry.[63] Elizabeth Ackroyd, from the Board of Trade, argued that there was nothing in the committee's findings or the resulting report that made a good case for government funding for the film industry or the NFFC. The producer Lord Brabourne believed the film industry needed to make international pictures which could be marketed abroad and recoup costs. Half the committee insisted that the job of deciding which films the NFFC should fund belonged to a financial decision-maker, whilst others felt it was the job of an artistic director.[64] One suggestion was that the NFFC should operate like an investment bank, while the proposed BFA was securing good projects for investment. This range of views reveals the fundamental rifts within the industry, which prevented fruitful collaboration between the industry and government. Exhibitors and distributors disagreed with producers; small production companies argued against the dominance of Rank and EMI; and everyone objected to the roles played by the NFFC and the Eady levy.

While offering some pragmatic suggestions, the Terry Report inadvertently illuminated industrial divisions. It is doubtful whether its findings could ever have satisfied the varied expectations of such a fragmented industry. There is little evidence to suggest that the intransigence of some factions, notably the unions and the powerful conglomerates, could ever be resolved. However, before any of the proposed changes could be implemented, there was a re-emergence of that political instability which had caused so much variation in policy at the start of the decade.

Missed Opportunities

Wilson's resignation as Prime Minister, barely three months after the publication of the Terry Report, was a catastrophe for an industry which had stood to benefit from his tireless championing. His successor, James Callaghan, appointed Wilson as the chairman of an action committee to follow up on the proposals, and the film industry continued to be cautiously optimistic about its future. In 1978, the Under-Secretary of State for Trade made a landmark statement to the House of Commons, claiming:

> We certainly intend legislation in this Parliament, in the form of a National Film Finance Corporation Bill, because we are committed to ensuring that the NFFC has enough funds for the next five years, or until it is subsumed into the British Film Authority.[65]

When Labour lost the 1979 General Election, the anticipated financial legislation never materialised.

The focus of the new Conservative administration's Films Bill in 1980 was very different.[66] While the £13 million owed by the NFFC to the Government was to be written off, the Government would make a final payment of £1 million to the NFFC.[67] The Bill outlined how funds would be diverted from the Eady levy to support the NFFC, and the opportunity for the Corporation to borrow from non-governmental sources was extended from £2 million to £5 million.[68] These measures signalled that the Government was unwilling to support the NFFC or the film industry any further. The Bill criticised the NFFC's failure to back a blockbuster, stating: 'It is not an activity in which Governments can meddle with any chance of success . . . the government having helped to set the stage in the bill, it will be up to the industry to perform.'[69] This position is strikingly similar to that outlined by Nicholas Ridley in 1971, revealing how Conservative policy toward the film industry remained unchanged, with the emphasis firmly on self-funding rather than government grants. Despite criticisms of the proposed Bill – one MP terming it 'an elastoplast to stop a haemorrhage' – it was subsequently passed, and was unenthusiastically received by the film industry as the best deal they were likely to get.[70]

However, by the end of the decade some aspects of the working party's reforms were beginning to bear fruit. Although the number of films produced was relatively small (only thirty-one in 1980), the films that were being made were of high quality, were often independently funded, and could be sold to other markets. Figures from the Eady fund reveal how changes in the apportioning of the monies meant that more recently established companies were taking smaller chunks of the levy. British film production had diversified to such an extent that smaller companies now proliferated. This ad hoc, entrepreneurial spirit of small-scale film production is indicative of the demise of conventional funding frameworks, and is evidence that the larger conglomerates no longer held sway over the industry. In 1979, the independent company Tigon received more than 1.2 per cent of the available levy fund (over £66,000), Rank took nearly 12 per cent and Anglo-EMI drew 5 per cent, while the major beneficiaries from previous years had substantially reduced sums, Columbia receiving 7 per cent and United Artists 17 per cent.[71] Although still significant shares, both of these figures are lower than at the start of the decade, despite the resurgence of an American presence within British production. The number of companies claiming money from the levy indicates that the money was trickling down though smaller production and distribution outlets in the way that the fund was initially intended to function. Despite these developments, political imperatives ensured that the NFFC's days were numbered. Even the arrival in 1979 of Mamoun Hassan as the head of the Corporation was not enough to save it. Hassan's previous positions at the BFI Production Board and the National Film School reflected his involvement with the film industry and, along with his film-making credentials, offered the promise of a compromise between business acumen and creative flair. However, succeeding governments had ensured that, by this time, the NFFC was superfluous to British film finance and it was wound up, along with the Eady levy, in the Films Act of 1985. The era of direct government funding through the NFFC and the Eady levy was over.

Conclusion

The 1970s is notable for the inconsistency of government policy towards an ailing industry. Throughout the decade, the Conservatives favoured subsidising the non-commercial sector, choosing to fund regional film theatres and the BFI Production Board rather than the debt-ridden NFFC. Yet the threat to dismantle the NFFC mooted at the start of the decade was not carried out until the Films Act of 1985. By contrast, Labour remained committed to state support through the NFFC in order to sustain the domestic film industry, but its efforts rarely achieved success. While Labour established the working party and commissioned the Terry Report, little solid achievement was forthcoming. Ultimately, neither the sympathy of the Labour administration nor the economic pragmatism of the Conservatives offered a real solution for the British film industry's insuperable difficulties. The industry's own lack of cohesion and clear objectives, the intransigence of the film unions, and the factionalism of such groups as the AIP, FPA and CFC, thwarted progress in a period of economic crisis. Perhaps it was not so much that governments refused to help, but that the film industry did not help itself.

CHAPTER 2

British Film Censorship and the BBFC in the 1970s

Sian Barber

The 1970s has been considered a contentious period for film censorship in Britain. *The Devils* (1971) and *A Clockwork Orange* have been established as *causes célèbres*, and a great deal of work has been carried out on these films, notably by James Robertson.[72] The scrutiny accorded these well-known cases often obscures the broader issues of censorship, classification and control. These are revealed in the archives of the British Board of Film Censorship (BBFC), which provide important detail about the everyday work of the Board. This material is also useful in illustrating the different approaches of BBFC Secretaries of the decade: John Trevelyan (1958–1971), Stephen Murphy (1971–1975) and James Ferman (1975–1999). Their decisions and observations provide insights into the Board's changes in policy and strategy.

The censorship debate

Debates about film censorship intensified in the 1960s. Films such as *Saturday Night and Sunday Morning* (1960), *Darling* (1965) and *Alfie* (1966) stimulated debate about censorship, and they anticipated legislation which ushered in a more permissive society. Abortion was legalised in 1967 and in 1968 homosexual behaviour was decriminalised. The landmark legal case about *Lady Chatterley's Lover* in 1960 had led to a relaxation of censorship in literature, while theatre censorship was formally abolished in 1968. The abolition of the Lord Chamberlain's office was an indication that the middle classes were empowered to make their own decisions about what to see on stage, but the mass audience for cinema was not. The discrepancies between film and stage censorship have been usefully examined by Aldgate and Robertson in their comparative analysis.[73]

In 1969 the number of films passed by the BBFC with an 'X' certificate exceeded the total passed in all the other categories combined. The

Table 2 Number of cut films and 'X'-rated films submitted to the BBFC

Year	Number of films submitted	Number of films categorised 'X'	Number of films refused certificate	Number of films cut	Number of cut films as percentage of total films submitted
1969	643	215	21	166	25.8
1970	715	217	23	180	25.2
1971	690	264	28	142	20.6
1972	662	258	35	190	28.7
1973	721	299	36	221	30.7
1974	708	319	27	240	33.9
1975	550	190	21	167	30.4
1976	614	239	23	179	29.2
1977	543	223	12	151	27.8
1978	458	156	4	94	20.5
1979	480	142	2	96	20.0
1980	464	148	6	75	16.2
1981	400	127	6	69	17.3

Source: www.bbfc.co.uk

necessity of dealing with a proliferation of adult material continued into the 1970s. The table illustrates the increasing number of films which were passed with an 'X' certificate. To some extent, the preponderance of 'X' films, the significant proportion of films cut, and the higher number of films refused certificates in the first half of the decade can be attributed to the large numbers of European pornographic films which flooded the British market. After 1974 the number of 'X'-rated films began to fall sharply, as did the proportion of films which were cut.

Censorship was frequently debated in Parliament throughout the 1970s, with regular calls for more stringent legislation.[74] Since 1912 the BBFC had been an independent body funded by the film industry, acting on behalf of local authorities and free from overt state control. By the early 1970s the BBFC's institutional guardianship was being widely challenged; questions were raised in some quarters as to whether the BBFC still had a valid role as an institutional arbiter of patterns of behaviour and taste. Evidence from the National Archives reveals the extent of government concerns:

> Censorship is a problem where the spectrum of public opinion is wide and views are held with equal strength and sincerity on all sides. Although the existing laws may not be ideal in all respects, the difficulty would be to find any generally acceptable way of improving them.[75]

Such even-handedness can be interpreted as the impetus for the Government to constitute a Committee on Obscenity and Film Censorship under Lord Williams in 1977. Along with submissions from pressure groups, local councils and the general public, the BBFC submitted a seventy-page report to the Committee on its function and objectives, and a further seventy pages of supporting material.[76] Yet well before the Williams Report, the BBFC files reveal that the Board was acutely aware of prevailing tensions in public opinion and government response. It is instructive to examine the ways in which successive Secretaries responded to challenges from the public, politicians and film culture at large.

Personnel, policy and approach

From 1958 to 1971, the BBFC Secretary was the consummate diplomat John Trevelyan, who handled the media and the film industry with adroitness. Trevelyan frequently advised on scripts and casting, and altered categories for films when appealed to by directors with whom he was friendly. This mode of operation, which had relied on patronage and personal contacts, made life difficult for his successor, Stephen Murphy. Murphy had previously worked for the British Broadcasting Corporation (BBC) and the Independent Television Commission, and was familiar with television censorship. However, he was unprepared for the publicity that accompanied his new role at the BBFC. Murphy was reluctant to adopt the grace-and-favour approach of his predecessor; he was also unlucky to preside over decisions in a number of extreme cases presented for classification while he was still new to the position. It was not only specific films which proved challenging for Murphy, but also the intensification of public debates about the function of the Board itself.

Trevelyan, perhaps more than any other BBFC Secretary, had understood the precarious position of the Board. He trod a careful path of collusion with the establishment, collaboration with film-makers, and sympathy with the so-called permissive society. Murphy, by contrast, was in a much more vulnerable position. He was acutely aware of the debate raging in the press about his suitability for the job: 'I'm just a failure. (This I gather is a majority view!),' he quipped in a letter to James Carreras.[77] As well as attacks from the press and audiences, he also came under fire from industry insiders. In an extraordinary attack, Kenneth Rive, Chairman of the Film Distributors Association, claimed in 1972, 'I believe we have got the wrong man in the job. I don't honestly believe you or I want to get rid of censorship. But I do believe we want to get rid of the present censor.'[78] This candid statement forced Lord Harlech, the President of the BBFC, to declare complete faith in Murphy and call on other industry figures to do the same. Murphy's supporters included John Trevelyan, who spoke at a meeting of film-makers in London, urging them to support the current system and the current censor.[79] Despite his determination to remain unaffected by the public calls for his resignation, following almost constant vilification by the tabloid press, Murphy left the BBFC in 1975.

Murphy's successor, James Ferman, called for greater transparency in censorship practices; he issued written monthly bulletins which detailed censorship decisions in a bid to avoid accusations of inconsistency and secrecy. Perhaps Ferman's greatest achievement, however, was in securing film's inclusion in the Obscene Publications Act (OPA) in 1977. The extension of the OPA removed the risk of private prosecutions, by ensuring that none of the films the BBFC certificated contained material that could fall foul of the 'deprave and corrupt' test. This policy achievement must be considered alongside Ferman's broadly conservative approach to censorship practice.

Challenges to authority

As Aldgate and Robertson suggest, the BBFC acknowledged prevailing social attitudes and public opinion in its decision-making.[80] The problem for the Board was that public opinion was extremely volatile in the decade which followed the social transformations of the 1960s. Under these circumstances, the idiosyncratic structure of the BBFC presented it with particular difficulties. For example, local authorities had the power to overrule the Board's decisions and prevent specific films from gaining exhibition licences in their local areas. This gave considerable power to the local Watch Committees, most of which were ill equipped to exercise this responsibility and often treated films with a combination of censoriousness and prurience. Local bans were imposed on extreme films like *Straw Dogs* (1971) and *The Devils*, and also on others in the 'X' category such as *Soldier Blue* (1970), *Love Variations* (1970), *I am a Nymphomaniac* (1970) and *Oh Calcutta!* (1972).

In 1972, the Greater London Council (GLC) inspected all films passed by the BBFC which it perceived to be controversial, and altered categories accordingly. Enid Wistrich, the Chairman of the Film Viewing Board at the GLC between 1973 and 1975, claimed that the GLC relied on the decisions of the BBFC '99% of the time', yet such public questioning of its authority severely damaged the credibility of the Board.[81] Following the GLC's lead, other local councils began to review controversial films, thus creating a situation in which a film could be banned in one area but shown in another. Absurdities abounded. In Portsmouth the Fire Services and Public Control Committee spent Wednesday afternoons inspecting all films denied a BBFC certificate, to decide if they could be screened in the city.[82] It was only after a personal visit from Stephen Murphy to discuss the intricacies of local censorship that the Committee decided to grant film licences in line with the decisions of the BBFC.[83]

Often the BBFC worked in collaboration with directors and producers, to ease a film through the difficult phases from completion to certification and to negotiate an acceptable outcome.[84] Films were cut at the request of the Board, but not by the Board themselves. The archival files show the Board offering shrewd and pertinent comments on the films that were submitted for classification. A useful example is the archival material for the film *Straw Dogs*. *Evening Standard* critic Alexander Walker termed the film 'vicious and degrading', while *The Sun* labelled it 'a mindlessly revolting pornography of violence'.[85] This extreme reaction was completely at odds with the BBFC readers' reports on this film: 'We were all agreed upon the massive impact of this film and we were equally agreed that it is tremendously enjoyable for the most part and compulsive viewing.'[86] Though they appreciated the quality of the film, they had concerns about the rape scene and it was duly cut. In response to a letter of complaint about the 'bestiality' in the film, Murphy outlined the Board's position:

> There are none of the 'blood shots' – blood spurting, bodies twitching etc that one finds in exploitative films. We at the Board will do all we can to stop filmmakers exploiting violence, but when a serious filmmaker makes a serious film about violence, I think we would be failing in our public duty if we prevented people from seeing it – however unpopular our decision may be.[87]

Murphy was clearly drawing a line between serious films which tackled serious issues, and those which sought to exploit to achieve cheap thrills. If screen violence was portrayed with honourable intent, then it was permitted within reason; excessive sensationalism of the kind seen in *The Abominable Dr. Phibes* (1971) or *House of Whipcord* (1974) was not permitted without cuts and restrictions.[88]

The BBFC and the Film Industry

Collaboration between producers, directors and the BBFC was a fundamental part of the Board's operation. However, sometimes it was not a case of the producer pleading for a family certificate, but rather of him requesting higher certification in the hope of attracting a greater audience. In this way the 'X' certificate became a badge of honour for some

Figure 1 *Confessions From a Holiday Camp*

low-budget companies, notably Amicus and Tigon.[89] The *Confessions* romps were raunchier than the *Carry On* films, but were still characterised by slapstick and innuendo rather than eroticism. In response to recommendations from the BBFC examiners for cuts to *Confessions of a Window Cleaner*, Stephen Murphy objected: 'I find it difficult to take very seriously . . . this is pure farce and I cannot accept that anyone will believe that we are showing more than slithery buttocks and some grotesque farcical leg-waving.'[90]

By the time the final instalment of the series came to be classified, the examiners debated the need to award an 'X' certificate to *Confessions from a Holiday Camp* (1977). One examiner reported: 'we did question whether the sexual antics, parodied rather than simulated, really demanded the shield of an X certificate.' Another noted: 'we had some discussion as to whether the film should be AA since there was nothing in the second half to justify the X . . . it was decided to go along with the company's request for an X.'[91] This was a case of the market being the prime motivator in determining classification. In more general terms, the changing social climate ensured that sex films now had to be more explicit or violent in order to be granted the highest certificate with all its attendant connotations. But the Board was reluctant to attribute any serious cultural significance to sex comedies.[92]

Horror film producers were also struggling to retain the shock factor amidst changing notions of acceptability. In the Amicus film, *The Beast Must Die* (1974), the examiners considered the company's desire for an 'X' to be laughable. The examiners felt, 'this really isn't an X . . . it's a good scary story for 14 year olds . . . obviously they want the X to make it appear a stronger horror than it is, but do we risk credibility?'[93] Murphy agreed with the decision, noting, 'the film is really so mild that we would look ridiculous.'[94] After conversations with the producer, Murphy agreed to reconsider the film once additional material had been shot and inserted to make it more shocking. This shows that the Board was concerned with the credibility of its categorisations in a period when boundaries were shifting rapidly. Certainly a comparison of the readers' reactions to *Countess Dracula* (1970), when they were shocked at the excessive scenes of incest and gore, with the liberal treatment accorded Pete Walker's *Frightmare* (1974) effectively illustrates how attitudes had changed. *Frightmare* included graphic scenes of cannibalism and mutilation, but was granted its 'X' certificate with minimal cuts and amiable collaboration between Murphy and Walker.

Such co-operation with exploitation film-makers is an indication of the good relations between the Board and the industry in this challenging period. After requesting cuts to *Vampire Circus* (1971), Murphy wrote personally to James Carreras apologising for 'murdering the film' and for not attending the studio party to celebrate the film's release.[95] Both John Trevelyan and Stephen Murphy collaborated with key industry players, including some of the more autocratic directors. The file for *The Go-Between* (1971) reveals letters between Trevelyan and Joseph Losey, discussing their recent meetings and quibbling familiarly over who should have paid for dinner.[96] In a letter from the file for *Stardust*, producer David Puttnam wrote earnestly to Murphy, 'thank you most sincerely for the enormous amount of energy, enthusiasm and the very real help you have put into the problem of finding the most suitable rating for the film'.[97]

According to Trevelyan, positive working relationships with individuals within the industry were of the utmost importance.[98] Peter Rogers, producer of the *Carry On* films, had an excellent relationship with both Trevelyan and Murphy. Often jokes were cut from the *Carry On* films with the agreement that similar lines would remain; the smutty innuendo of this series ensured that each new film release tested the boundaries of permission.[99] The series foundered with *Carry On Emmannuelle* when examiners were unable to classify it 'A' because of its content. The film was certificated 'AA', with one examiner acidly observing, 'it's not a question of cutting, since blue is the pervading shade'.[100] This film demonstrates an unsuccessful change of approach for a series which had relied heavily upon what was said and implied, rather than what was seen. It was not felt, even in the changing climate of permission, that it was acceptable for a film which was 'one long sex joke' to be classified in the family category of the 'A' certificate.[101] Moreover, this film was also felt to be of a lower standard than previous films in the series and was labelled 'plotless parody' and 'retrogressive sex-stereotyped leering', once again indicating that the BBFC was making judgements based upon quality.[102]

Changing Times

The principal position of the BBFC was that they refused to pass anything violent which could be easily imitated.[103] Along with concerns about the growth of sexual violence, this was one of their chief worries. However, in considering violent films, the issue of quality reappears once again. When *The Long Good Friday* (1979) was submitted to the BBFC for certification, James Ferman publicly promised that he would not cut a single frame from such a high-quality British film. However, there were concerns about the violence, the political narrative and the language. One examiner commented: 'an extremely well made British thriller with an exciting and different story. In a lesser film these [scenes of violence] might well have been cut. But within the context of this excellent film, they are acceptable.'[104]

At the end of the decade, distinctions were still being made between quality films and those less well made or less well intentioned. The second examiner for *The Long Good Friday* echoed this unwritten policy, but also sounded a note of caution:

> We should be aware that we are passing here material we would certainly have cut, even at 'X', from a film made with less skill and directional flair, and we could also be laying ourselves open to accusations of xenophobic prejudice since comparable material would be cut from films originating in Hong Kong, Italy or perhaps the USA.[105]

The examiners were aware that they were granting this film extra licence on the grounds of its quality, but also on the grounds of its provenance. An independent report on the file recommended: 'all dialogue referring to the IRA should be deleted otherwise exhibitors will no doubt be wary of taking this because of its political nature.'[106] Clearly, the film was addressing sensitive political issues and would undoubtedly provoke a reaction. Yet to its credit, the BBFC stood firm; it felt that the public could accept a well-made film treating serious themes and addressing them in a non-moralistic way.

The latitude granted to *The Long Good Friday* illustrates the flexible approach of the Board under successive Secretaries during the 1970s. For example, in 1972 Murphy had refused to certificate the film version of the popular musical review *Oh Calcutta!*, as he feared it would cause offence and provide further evidence of his own incapability. In the file Murphy noted: 'I cannot think that it would be wise at this stage for the Board to offer certification for this film . . . there could not be a worse time than this to put pressure on. The film might be subject to a private prosecution.'[107] However, he reserved judgement and agreed to re-view the film 'when things have quietened down a bit'.[108] This example reveals that Murphy thought it expedient to defer certification because of the volatile social climate and the furore which would ensue. Such examples reveal the Board's measured responses to the pressure that it was under to make difficult decisions. In 1972, a beleaguered Board was feeling the pressure of public opinion; by 1979, it enjoyed the partial protection of the OPA, which enabled it to act with more confidence.

In arriving at decisions during the 1970s, the BBFC was unable to ignore press and public response to a film entirely. One case which caused a massive amount of press controversy was *Monty Python's Life of Brian* (1979). The BBFC's view was that:

> Dialogue and some nudity . . . make the AA appropriate. Perhaps the real problem is that it is the gullible crowd who are made to look ridiculous and the devout may find the jokes too close to home, though I think they would have to be pretty humourless to infer that deliberate offence was intended.[109]

The Renters' Association presciently considered, 'controversy will only lead to the film being seen by more people'.[110] The BBFC were well aware that the controversy created by the advance release in America made their job harder, as they had to make the appropriate categorisation while being scrutinised by the media. The decision finally taken to classify the film was carefully considered, and a cautious BBFC, drawing on previous experience of the private prosecution over *The Language of Love* (1970), took legal advice over whether the film could be considered blasphemous and if they could be prosecuted for granting it a certificate.[111] Here, the attitude of the BBFC also demonstrates an increased awareness of the way in which the legal mechanisms and the protection offered by the OPA could be utilised to their advantage.

Towards the end of the decade, James Ferman was under pressure to allow increasingly explicit material that targeted the under-eighteens. Films including *Saturday Night Fever* (1977) and *Quadrophenia* had the BBFC in a quandary. One of the examiners of *Quadrophenia* regretfully commented:

> Had we a category that admitted 16 year olds I hope we could consider this for it, despite the violence of both action and language, the brief and unsatisfactory sexual encounters and the reliance on drugs for escapism, particularly since the tragedy to which this last in particular contributes is so clearly defined. As things stand however, these are the factors that must confine the film to the X category.[112]

The BBFC faced the difficulty of classifying films aimed at teenagers that included sex, violence, drugs and extreme language. Sometimes producers of such films who were keen to target the teenage audience arrived at novel ways of exerting pressure on the Board. In the unusual case of *Stardust*, this is exactly what happened.

Stardust: Collaborative Classification

Stardust was funded by the NFFC and was the sequel to *That'll Be the Day*, which had been a commercial hit the previous year. Unfortunately, despite the undoubted teenage appeal, *Stardust* was considered by the BBFC to contain: 'a couple of sex scenes and some dialogue that would certainly have to come out for "AA"'.[113] To have the film classified as an 'X' would have prevented it from reaching the intended audience and making significant profit. Unhappy with the BBFC recommendation, a meeting was arranged between producer David Puttnam, Stephen Murphy and John Terry of the NFFC. Following this meeting, Murphy noted that:

> We are not luckily in any sort of confrontational situation . . . I asked them to resubmit the film in September to see whether the social climate had changed. The language, pot-smoking and sex combine to make it an extremely difficult offering at the AA level.[114]

Puttnam, and the film's production company Goodtimes Enterprises, decided to tackle the problem by arranging a public screening and requesting feedback. Adverts subsequently ran in *The Guardian* and *Time Out*, and a London screening was duly organised so that selected respondents (including teachers, social workers, youth leaders and parents) might offer their opinions. In addition to the screening in London, Murphy arranged another in Reading, in order to add weight to the data collected.

Murphy further requested that the results be examined by an independent researcher. The audience responses were duly analysed, and showed overwhelmingly that the respondents deemed the film suitable for the 'AA' category due to the morality of the story, the integrity with which it was made and its highlighting of a current social problem. These conclusions were presented to the BBFC, who relented and awarded the film an 'AA'.[115]

In a letter to Mary Whitehouse, who objected to the film, Stephen Murphy defended the Board's approach to this compromise:

> We thought that this might be an opportunity to test our judgement making against that of interested members of the public . . . I have to tell you that the results from the two audiences were considerably more liberal than our own thinking had been. I hope you will agree that to test our judgement against intelligent representative public opinion is a worthwhile exercise. If however, you can suggest any way in which we could have taken more time, more trouble in arriving at this decision, I'd be glad to hear from you.[116]

Murphy clearly saw collaboration with producers and the public as a positive step forward in the operation of film censorship.

Conclusion

The archival material illustrates the close collaboration between the BBFC, film directors and producers, and demonstrates that the Board was committed to classifying films responsibly and finding the most suitable rating for work of quality and integrity. However, they did make judgements based upon their own definitions of quality and cultural value. The BBFC examiners often failed to take seriously genres they did not deem culturally worthwhile, such as the sex-comedy or horror. Although the significant number of exploitation films presented to the Board during the 1970s were perceived to have little cultural value, these films were popular with audiences and met a particular cultural need. Audiences enjoyed films such as *Confessions of a Window Cleaner* and *Vampire Circus*, and their treatment by the BBFC reveals how the censors themselves were not exempt from cultural and aesthetic snobbery.

As well as these issues of quality, the personalities of Trevelyan, Murphy and Ferman also directly affected how decisions at the BBFC were made. There was a continuation of liberal policy throughout the decade, and the different leadership styles contributed to the maintenance of the BBFC's role. Trevelyan's contacts and methods of working, Murphy's stoicism and refusal to be bullied over controversial material, and Ferman's public declarations of support for seminal films demonstrate the continued efforts of the BBFC to champion and defend the work of the British film industry. In an unenviable position of independent but non-statutory authority, the Board had to tread carefully in responding to changing patterns of consumption and levels of permission; it also had to deal with vilification from the tabloid press and right-wing pressure groups. While some dubious decisions may have been made in the 1970s, the BBFC championed hundreds of films to be shown without cuts or with only minor cuts. Despite criticism on many fronts, the BBFC carefully ensured that British cinema in the 1970s was more controversial, intelligent and innovative than it otherwise might have been.

CHAPTER 3

Moving Images and the Visual Arts in 1970s Britain

Dave Allen

This chapter will focus on 'experimental' moving image work that often developed from the visual arts in 1970s Britain. Before this, the visual arts were principally drawings, paintings, sculptures and prints, but a new generation of artists became increasingly interested in film (and subsequently video) from the mid-1960s onwards.

Arguably, the 1960s was the last decade in which British fine art – galleries, dealers and teachers – was dominated by the great traditions of painting and sculpture. By the end of that 'swinging' decade, graphics and fashion occupied a more powerful position, while fine art included painting and sculpture but also screen prints, photography, verbal texts, philosophy, installations, performances and moving images. If mainstream British cinema was in decline in the 1970s, a generation of young artists, who had grown up with the 'movies' and television, developed innovative ways of working in moving image media.

In 1970, most of the great painters and sculptors of early British modernism – Nicholson, Moore, Sutherland, Hepworth, Piper and Bacon – were still alive. Younger artists, including Caro, Hamilton, Paolozzi, Hockney, Blake and Riley, had made their presence felt, but even those newcomers, with their vibrant colours, sharp shapes and increasingly urban subjects, were still principally painters and sculptors. While Britain had never been at the heart of international modernism, it now produced artists who embraced newer approaches including moving images – although not for mainstream television and cinema. Much work was supported wholly or partly by public funding and labelled 'avant-garde', 'underground' or 'experimental', although debates about this nomenclature have never been entirely resolved. For example, Wollen wrote about two 'avant-gardes', Sitney 'visionary', Le Grice 'abstract', the Hayward Gallery 'Film as Film', and Gidal 'materialist'. Subsequently MacDonald and O'Pray both used the term 'avant-garde' and Rees preferred 'experimental' (and now attached to film and video), whereas Dixon and Foster edited an anthology on experimental *cinema* (my emphasis).[117]

Most of these authors sought precise terms because their focus was specific and differentiated aesthetically, economically, politically and/or institutionally. The terms were often in deliberate opposition to other ideas; Le Grice, for example, excluded many of the North American films considered 'visionary' by Sitney. This chapter, while limited to Britain, seeks a broad survey and any simple unifying term may be elusive, except that our subject is generally outside the conventions of mainstream production, distribution and exhibition in film and television. For brevity I shall occasionally employ the term 'experimental' but with the reservations as stated. Similarly, I will generally use 'film' generically, while recognising that there were varieties of gauge (notably 8mm, 16mm and 35mm), that some films manipulated found footage without employing a camera, that they were projected in different ways and that through the 1970s videotape became a significant (and economical) option both in mainstream television and in experimental work. Today, video productions are often called 'films'.

This work demanded some special effort to distribute and exhibit, and for spectators to find the rare, localised screenings. Most British people could choose easily enough to watch or ignore mainstream work but the same could not be said of most of the 'films' I am concerned with here. This was not, then, merely a question of aesthetics.

Relatively small audiences accessed the work that is central to this chapter, while its representation and critical evaluation were frequently confined to specialist publications with small circulations. None the less I will suggest that the 'long' 1970s (beginning around 1968) were an extraordinarily varied and fertile period for these new approaches to moving images and laid the foundations for important developments in the following decades.

The London Film Makers' Co-operative

A key figure was the film-maker, historian, theorist, polemicist and teacher, Malcolm Le Grice. In 1979, he distinguished between 'what constitutes the mainstream of commercial narrative cinema' – most obviously the majority of Hollywood's output – and 'the progressive exploration of the potentialities of the medium in its own terms'.[118] These two categories were respectively the 'negative and positive' elements of an enterprise that helped inform a major Hayward Gallery exhibition focusing wholly on the latter. In 1979 he identified three major areas of interest: the material of film as its 'content', the 'primary reality' of the screening in time and space, and the problematising of 'reproduction, documentation and the representation of "incident"'. His over-riding concern was to challenge the illusory nature of dominant cinema.[119]

This chapter will broaden and develop Le Grice's identification of alternatives to the mainstream and its preoccupation with commerce and story-telling – including television. Le Grice argued that 'most attempts to develop film art have followed the pattern which applies principles from the theatre or novel,' adding that this had become a deeply established norm. In commercial cinema he suggested 'no alternative is known,' and he did not restrict himself to fiction since documentaries also sought 'to tell stories'.[120] But for Le Grice this had never been inevitable because cinema might have chosen to draw more on the innovations of twentieth-century art and music. It did not, at least in its commercial or mainstream sectors, developing instead the conventions of nineteenth-century literary and theatrical narrative. Perhaps these were predominantly commercial decisions, but the distinction between theatre/literature as the influential model, and art/music as the 'alternative' can be taken as a starting point for understanding the work described here. However, even this distinction does not mean that all 1970s non-mainstream work pursued a mid-century visual modernist aesthetic. During the 1970s and increasingly beyond, some experimental work engaged with a more Romantic sensibility.

There were other common elements beyond the films themselves. Many were produced with support from public funds, principally through the BFI, Arts Council of Great Britain (ACGB), Regional Arts Associations or formal education – especially the art colleges, which in the 1970s often joined local polytechnics. Many of these films were made by individuals or small groups working in artisanal ways, unlike industrial and highly structured mainstream cinema and television.

Experimental film-makers took advantage of new, lighter and cheaper film and video equipment and, however pragmatic, these new ways of working became matters of principle, related to broader political issues. The counter-culture, feminism, gay rights, black issues, and the complex politics of the left in the early 1970s contributed to the production and reception of this work to a far greater extent than was the case in the mainstream. This may have been because the work was economically modest and therefore not subject to the laws of the marketplace, but equally the central practitioners generally emerged from institutions (not least higher education) where radical ideas had a strong hold – especially the art colleges of the late 1960s.

The London Film Makers' Co-operative (LFMC) was a key initiative and its history, and the broader British underground film scene, is well documented by London's Study Collection.[121] Rees has described how the LFMC emerged in the late 1960s,[122] partly influenced by the New York co-operatives, as American film-makers like Peter Gidal and Steve Dwoskin, and films by Warhol and others, arrived in London. The sound poet Bob Cobbing managed Better Books in London's Charing Cross Road and provided space for experimental theatre and other arts from the mid-1960s, including underground film. The LFMC was officially founded on 13 October 1966 and soon added production and publishing (*Cinim* magazine) to exhibition and distribution.

The next venue for the development of the LFMC was the Arts Laboratory in Covent Garden, established by Jim Haynes in the fabled Summer of 1967. Miles describes the basement cinema where David Curtis programmed 'underground cult and classic movies'[123] and Le Grice met Curtis when showing his loop film, *Little Dog for Roger* there in 1967.[124] To some extent, this early 'underground' phase brought together varied media, practices and practitioners. Miles calls it a 'community centre for creative individuals', but like so many elements of the British (London) underground and counter-culture, it fell prey to serious operational and ideological disagreements. In November 1968, the majority of the Arts Laboratory staff (including Curtis) resigned in protest at Haynes's operating manner, and it closed a few months later.[125]

In the Summer of 1969, the former staff opened a New Arts Lab (the Institute for Research in Art and Technology) on the Hampstead Road. Curtis and John Hopkins (a leading innovator in community video) were among the directors, and Curtis ran the cinema on the ground floor, projecting 8 and 16mm films – including evenings devoted to the LFMC. Carla Liss and Le Grice ran the LFMC distribution office from the building and a donation enabled film-makers to process films on the premises – a crucial development. The building also housed facilities for screen-printing, a photographic darkroom, a theatre, a macrobiotic café, experimental workshops and a meeting room. For Miles, 'their approach was very different to Haynes . . . the New Arts Lab was community-based and saw itself as providing a service to the arts community in a very real way.'[126] The London underground at this time attracted a range of people, from the frivolous to the deeply serious. There were swinging fashion-followers, stoned hippies, sexual adventurers, a variety of Marxists and anarchists, inter-disciplinary artists, single-minded film-makers and cultural tourists. Many would have come from art colleges or higher education, but it must not be assumed that everyone was well versed in complex semiotic or aesthetic analysis of experimental films. What is important about this early phase is that so many screenings were part of multi-disciplinary venues or projects.

Outside London 'radical film collectives . . . began to flourish'[127] and art colleges showed films from the historic avant-garde, while Warhol's broader fame drew attention to his films. Some independent cinemas might show Warhol interspersed with a programme of art-house films, especially the Paul Morrisey productions starring Joe Dallesandro, although even these were not unproblematic. In February 1970, police invaded a screening of *Flesh* (1968) in Soho and a prosecution was threatened under obscenity laws. In the House of Commons, Home Secretary James Callaghan supported the police but eventually the case was dropped. The publicity meant that, when *Flesh* returned to the screen, attendances improved considerably.[128]

Like London's Arts Lab and similar projects, Warhol's New York Factory had explored a range of arts practice, but by the early 1970s many groups and practitioners went their separate ways, defined generally by medium or art form and seeking greater organisational stability. However, it would be wrong to suppose that the experimental film-makers were one coherent group – indeed, the recollections of Dwoskin, Gidal, Le Grice, critic Ray Durgnat and others suggest serious ideological and operational disagreements. According to Durgnat: 'Things are getting so personal. There is a highly emotional meeting between highly emotional people and one person just says three long sentences and they become enemies for life.'[129] Bob Cobbing was treasurer but resigned over a matter of decision-making, and by the end of the 1960s all the original members of the LFMC had left. The study collection commentary suggests that Le Grice was one of those on the 'winning side', and he became a key figure as a film-maker but also as a teacher, writer and theoretician, and by 1979 a major exhibition organiser. The winners' focus became more singular and probably more productive, but perhaps something was lost with fewer exchanges between artists, musicians, film-makers, poets and activists.

At the LFMC, Le Grice and Gidal led one approach concerned with structure and material – Structural Materialism. Through advocacy, publications and teaching, they became the best-known group and disputed fiercely with others, notably the American critic Sitney, over the precise use of terms. Leighton suggests that: 'particular emphasis has been placed upon the legacy of "Structural film" (or "Structural Materialist film") in recent re-examinations' of the work of this period.[130] He was referring in particular to their work on the contexts and ways in which their films were shown – one of the important aspects that challenged the conventions of the mainstream. Their screenings often involved multiple projections or live performances by the film-makers, who intervened in the projection of the films. Le Grice, for example, would stand in front of the screened image in some of his work or project the same film twice, simultaneously, side by side.

Not everyone outside the industrial and commercial mainstream took this approach however. For example, British films like *Pressure* (1975) by Horace Ové or Derek Jarman's *Jubilee* (1977) were projected conventionally, and watched by spectators as they might see a feature film in the local Odeon cinema. Le Grice and his colleagues made a very important contribution to moving image culture but others attempted different 'progressive' explorations, which often led to disagreements between the various makers and distinct interest groups.

The Origins of Experimental Film in Britain

Compared with North America and other European countries there was no well-established tradition of experimental film in Britain. In Europe, the Futurists had led the way before the First World War, while individual artists like Léger, Picasso, Moholy-Nagy and Duchamp had experimented with film in the 1920s. Dusinberre has suggested that 'Britain claimed no avant-garde cinema prior to 1966',[131] and in many histories, British film is absent or trailing behind work from Russia, France, Germany and elsewhere. None the less, in the 1970s a considerable variety of non-mainstream film and video work was produced in Britain.

Despite Dusinberre's assertion, there was some experiment in British moving images prior to 1966. Most notably, perhaps, for some decades the British had contributed internationally to the development of 'documentary' cinema and there was a legacy of important work – especially in terms of the link between sound and image (music and art). This can be traced back to modernist influences in British documentaries like *Coal Face* (1935), *Night Mail* (1936) or *Listen to Britain* (1942), as well as Len Lye's experiments with a kind of abstraction such as *Colour Box* (1935). By the 1950s, film-makers like Lindsay Anderson and Karel Reisz were among British documentary-makers who were perhaps less monolithic than the title 'Free Cinema' suggests. Responding partly to budget restrictions and the limitations of equipment, they developed a new image/sound aesthetic and their documentaries were shown either as supporting features in cinemas or to much smaller audiences in film societies or special screenings. The rapid spread of television in the following decades offered a broader range of documentary opportunities to makers and spectators.

British television grew rapidly through the 1950s and 1960s, offering occasional challenges to the narrative conventions or 'safe' story-telling. In 1959, the BBC series *Art-Anti-Art* considered the links between the British Independent Group and the Futurists, and three years later Ken Russell's film *Pop Goes the Easel* (1962), for the arts series *Monitor* (BBC), depicted four young 'Pop' artists from the Royal College of Art (RCA). The televisual depiction of these new artists was not entirely conventional – particularly perhaps the sequence on the one woman, Pauline Boty, which seemed to owe something to Polanski, and the artists were shown engaging with mass culture.

In 1969, Christopher Finch identified a number of contemporary British artists who were preoccupied with 'the media landscape'. He suggested that the artists in Russell's film, and Richard Hamilton, Eduardo Paolozzi and Richard Smith were 'greatly concerned with breaking the communication codes employed by the ad-mass world'. While they were not making moving images, their work drew upon the increasing impact of film and television, helping to legitimise its presence in the art gallery alongside painting and sculpture. As members of the Independent Group (IG) at the Institute of Contemporary Arts in 1950s London, Hamilton, Paolozzi and others displayed a common interest in 'urban . . . mass-produced' and 'vernacular culture', including movies, advertising, science fiction and pop music.[132] In such ways, the British artistic 'avant-garde' began to legitimise an engagement with the subject matter and media of film and television. Materials became cheaper and more accessible, and some young artists and students began to work with them in the normal experimental ways. As a consequence, in at least one corner of British artistic life, experimentation became more common with and around the increasingly influential moving image culture.

During the 1960s, key British work that preceded the formation of the LFMC included Jeff Keen's 8mm films using collage, live action and animation, John Latham's coloured 'abstract' film, *Talk* and films by Richard Smith, Robert Freeman, Bruce Lacey and Eduardo Paolozzi. Le Grice began studying at the Slade School of Fine Art, followed two years later by Derek Jarman, while Steve Dwoskin arrived from the USA to teach at the London College of Printing. In 1964, Sitney organised an ICA show, the 'International Exposition of the New American Cinema', and in 1965 the poetry event at the Royal Albert Hall, with Allen Ginsberg and a host of British performers, was taken to be the first public statement of the British 'underground' or burgeoning counter-culture. The Beatles' films often included the input of British artists such as Robert Freeman and Stuart Brisley; their television film to accompany 'Strawberry Fields Forever' (1967) had echoes of Surrealist film, while *Yellow Submarine*

(1968) involved innovative work by a number of animators. Here was a foundation for the growth of experimental film and video in Britain in the 1970s.

The Mainstream and Avant-Garde

While most 1960s and 1970s British television was mainstream in production and style, we have noted Ken Russell's innovative arts documentaries at the BBC. In 1967, the arts series *Tempo* ran for one year under the guidance of Mike Hodges (who later directed *Get Carter*), and included a visually innovative episode, directed by Dick Fontaine and called 'Noise', with contributions from John Cage and the jazz multi-instrumentalist Roland Kirk. In 1972 the seminal series *Ways of Seeing*, presented by John Berger, developed the recent British publication of major work by Walter Benjamin, offering new approaches to visual literacy and a new way of saying this on television and in the accompanying book. Initiatives such as these reflected and influenced new approaches to moving image arts in Britain, which were increasingly (although not exclusively) visual. Importantly, they also encouraged the spread of various kinds of film and later video production in Britain's art colleges.

By the 1970s these developments grew into a broad range of practices outside mainstream, commercial, narrative cinema. Structural Materialism was important in this film-making in the 1970s, but it was too precise a term to be applied to everything outside mainstream cinema and television. Despite some concerns with the term 'avant-garde', the film-maker and theoretician Peter Wollen used it in an important paper.[133] He took a historical view covering some fifty years to offer his definition of the 'two avant gardes' and, drawing on another essay by Gidal, offered a distinction between visually experimental film produced in artists' co-operatives in the USA and Britain, and the 'political' and cinematic avant-garde of European film-makers like Godard or Straub-Huillet.

Leighton records that Wollen believed the gap between his two 'avant gardes' to be 'unbridgeable', but she also considered a third area of practice which emerged from the art colleges and the world of fine art in the late 1960s.[134] None the less, she added that Wollen and like-minded film-makers were suspicious of moving image work that was shown in art gallery spaces. Given their shared roots in visual modernism and the art colleges, such suspicion was perhaps surprising. Le Grice's important history *Abstract Film and Beyond* paid considerable attention to the modernist changes in painting from Monet and Cézanne through the Cubists to the Futurists and Surrealists. He reported Richter's view that 'problems in modern art lead directly into film,' adding that during the development of modernism in the early twentieth century, 'it is difficult to imagine that most artists . . . did not talk about the possibilities for film'.[135]

With similar concerns, Walley offered 'a model' for distinguishing 'avant-garde cinema proper' from 'artists' film . . . especially in installation formats'.[136] He drew upon the ideas of Bordwell, Staiger and Thompson on the classical Hollywood cinema to examine film production, distribution, exhibition and viewing strategies (reception) further. He seemed to use the terms cinema and film interchangeably, which is not unproblematic since his definition of avant-garde cinema seems, unlike Wollen's, not to include film-makers like Godard, who made feature-length films. None the less, he suggested that, because his 'two modes . . . share aesthetic preoccupations and personnel', that may be a reason '*not* to distinguish between the two groups of film artists'.

If we consider these analyses by Wollen, Leighton and Walley together, we might identify three groups of film-makers who, in the 1970s, stand outside the industrial practices that supported mainstream cinema and television and were working and/or showing in Britain:

1. the experimental ('co-op') avant-garde
2. artists using film/video in gallery contexts
3. political film-makers working often in 35mm, sometimes in narrative films.

The third group was perhaps least visible in Britain, except through screenings by film-makers from other countries (especially Godard), but the first two are clearly significant in the emerging British practices of the 1970s. However, even this does not tell the whole story. In 1999 A. L. Rees published *A History of Experimental Film and Video*, ranging broadly from the 'canonical avant-garde' to 'contemporary British practice', featuring work from 1970s Britain that included the Structural Materialists alongside the emerging video art, early initiatives by Jarman and Greenaway (the 'odd couple'), the first shoots of black British film and other practices – indicating the diversity of practices in that period. To these we might add the political documentary films of the Berwick Street Collective or Amber Films, the 'art' cinema of Russell, Roeg and others, and the early work of Peter Greenaway, who, like Jarman, also emerged from an art college education.

There was also a growing group of women artists, many of whom identified themselves collectively in a dispute around the selection of artists for the 1979 Hayward Gallery exhibition, including Annabel Nicolson,

Felicity Sparrow and Lis Rhodes. All three were involved in the exhibition committee, but eventually published a statement in which they described being 'continually undermined by the lack of understanding and respect for their research, by the Arts Council's committee'.[137]

Poetry and Romanticism

Most of those women were working in or from London and some were members of the LFMC. Far away from that world, Margaret Tait was working in film and presented her experimental film, *One is One*, as early as 1951. Tait studied film in Italy (1950–1952) and thereafter lived in Scotland – mostly on Orkney. Her work developed in relative isolation and she was rarely included in surveys of experimental film – neither Curtis nor Rees mentions her at all and she was not one of the eight signatories to the statement by women in the *Film as Film* catalogue. None the less, she made films from 1951 to 1998 and said of them, 'the kind of cinema I care about is at the level of poetry – in fact – it has been in a way my life's work, making film poems.'[138]

Le Grice has suggested that there was a distance between Europe and the USA because in Europe 'a-political Romanticism holds singularly little intellectual credence' and that some of the post-war experimental European work 'was strongly anti-Romantic'.[139] Writing of contemporary practice with polemical purpose, it is perhaps unsurprising that Le Grice offered a rationale for non- (anti-?) romantic practice, and it may be that he was seeking specifically to distance his work from ('a-political') sentimental mainstream fiction.

But the question of how art(s)/film are 'political' is complex and there is a very strong and intellectually respectable tradition of Romantic visual art in Britain that stretches back centuries, is not necessarily 'a-political' and, at least since William Blake, can be very much the opposite.[140] Perhaps in the spirit of his 'new' generation, Le Grice was distancing himself from some major figures and dominant practices in British post-war art and art teaching. Artists like Michael Ayrton, Prunella Clough, Robert Colquhoun, John Craxton, Robert MacBryde, John Minton, John Piper, Ceri Richards, Graham Sutherland and Keith Vaughan might all be considered 'Romantic' and serious/respectable artists, while Ackroyd has identified the importance of 'inner spirit' in British Romanticism in comparison with Catholic Europe, which 'became elaborate and symbolic, clothed in allegory and invaded by intimations of strange sins'.[141] In that sense, British and European Romanticism may not be one and the same.[142]

In film, a return to the 'image', the self, mythology, ecology and similar 'romantic' concerns is often identified with the 1980s, but film-makers like Tait, Ian Breakwell, B. S. Johnson (also a novelist and poet), Derek Jarman and others were always producing work which might be seen as more personal, poetic or Romantic than the work of (say) the Structural Materialists. This different approach was not necessarily confined to the films. In the Arts Council's Hayward Gallery exhibition, 'Perspectives on British Avant Garde Film', Annabel Nicolson began a catalogue piece on 'Expanded Cinema' in a manner very different from the writing of Le Grice, Rees, Gidal and others: 'Yesterday I was walking in Crowlink Downs with a drummer. The birds moved along the air current provided by the swooping downs.'[143] It is important to stress that, while this brief section begins and ends with two women film-makers, no gender-specific point is being sought – many of the 'romantic' artists identified are men, while there were certainly women film-makers whose work could not be described as 'romantic' or 'poetic'. To a large extent, this experimental work was certainly different from abstract or Structural Materialist film and attracted greater attention in the following decade – its presence here is to emphasise that it is part of a continuous thread in British creativity and, more recently, in British experimental film.

Reception/Audiences

This distinction between Romantic and Materialist film-makers is one example of the different ideological positions held by film-makers and theorists in Britain through the 1970s. In most cases, these differences were derived from aesthetic or political convictions and the search for a kind of purity or authenticity. In some cases they were both aesthetic and political but we must also ask whether these differences were more pronounced among the makers and theorists at the heart of this practice (and often earning money from the work). Were the audiences equally split or (more probably) were many of those who watched one type of 'film' also interested in some/many/all of the others?

Through the 1970s, experimental film came to be shown around Britain but often in art colleges and galleries, polytechnics, arts centres and film co-operatives. More people studied film formally as theorists, historians and/or practitioners and this specialisation meant that, while there was a larger audience for experimental film across Britain, it was increasingly one that had been educated – formally or informally – to engage with the work. None the less, we can ask whether some spectators who attended screenings by Le Grice or Godard also watched film and video in art galleries as part of a broad interest in experimental film. And did they also go to their local cinemas and at home watch *Play for Today*, *Top of the Pops* or *Coronation Street*? Who was watching what, where were they watching it and what else did they watch?

In one sense, the role of the spectator was seen to be increasingly central to understanding, as Barthes's 'Death of the Author' and similar ideas became more prevalent in 1970s British intellectual life. In 1977 Rees suggested that, in the new work, 'the perceiver rather than the artist is made responsible for the production of meaning'.[144] Meanwhile, Le Grice insisted that his history was for 'the involved practitioner, filmmaker or theorist so committed as to be illiberal about films or their presentation'.[145] Lis Rhodes contributed a paper to the same catalogue which implicitly responded to Le Grice by asking 'Whose History?'[146] Perhaps it is now appropriate to ask much broader and more 'liberal' questions about viewing habits at this time.

I have been emphasising difference and diversity in this 1970s British work, with clear distinctions between many practitioners, but I wish to suggest, too, that many spectators would have been open to most or all of the variety – and probably watched the mainstream too, even if that was with a new critical perspective. While there is a paucity of historical evidence, fine distinctions are generally clearer when applied to practitioners, artefacts and organisations than to spectators.

Fine Art Film

We now take for granted the presence of moving images in art galleries, but Dodd suggests that, in the early 1970s, the art world feared film as an 'alien force supplanting painting and sculpture'. His short chapter traversed the terrain of film and art imaginatively, referring to relevant British work by a range of British artists across much of the twentieth century.[147] Dodd also suggested that visual culture in Britain is 'ready to try anything new'.[148] Modernist it may not have often been, but modernising it has been.

One of the critics interested in innovative work was Richard Cork, who wrote for two very different constituencies in the 1970s. He addressed a mass audience in his role as the leading reviewer for London's *Evening Standard* but also edited the influential *Studio International*, which supported much of the most innovative visual art. For example, in 1976 *Studio International* published themed editions on avant-garde film in England and Europe, performance, video art, experimental music and, in the following year, women's art.

An anthology of Cork's 1970s reviews and articles includes few about painting or (conventional) sculpture.[149] It reveals his interest in minimalism, conceptualism, artists' video, performance art, art education, the galleries, televising art and the Arts Council, yet there is no reference to the work of experimental film-makers like Gidal or Le Grice, who were exhibiting outside the gallery context – thereby adding to the view that, despite their origins in and links with art colleges, their work was considered to be separate from the art world. None the less, Cork's 1972 review of William Wegman observed that for some time artists had been turning to film 'as an alternative to physical objects on the one hand and written statements on the other'.[150] Similarly, Cork felt David Dye's work showed 'one way in which an artist's mind can conduct an enquiry into the nature and potential of film'.[151]

Cork also reviewed video work by David Hall, Victor Burgin's image/text critical 'adverts', a tape/slide show by Dennis Oppenheim, Susan Hiller's postcard 'storyboards', John Latham's retrospective at the Tate Gallery and, in June 1976, the Tate Gallery's first show of (British) video art. He saw the latter as a positive development but expressed concern that it had not arrived as part of the main exhibitions policy but through initiatives by the Education Department and was 'tucked away downstairs'. He described funding difficulties, since 'neither' of the main funders of video work, the BFI Production Board and the Arts Council's Community Arts Committee, had provided any money to support the Association of Video Workers.[152]

He suggested that, without adequate funding, this artists' video work 'will virtually cease to exist', although with the benefit of hindsight we know that nothing of the kind occurred. Technological advances in video production and exhibition have transformed that world, and we now take for granted video installations in major contemporary exhibitions or events like the Turner Prize. And while it is clear that in the mid-1970s video art was very much a minority practice, in 1977 the Arts Council and British Council sent an exhibition, 'Perspectives on English Avant-Garde Film', around thirty countries.[153] Its specific purpose was to survey the films that it had funded (with the British Council) and to place them appropriately in the 'context of avant-garde film practice'.[154] In the version of the show at the Hayward Gallery, historical and contemporary films were shown from the USA and Europe, as well as the British work. Richard Cork contributed notes on David Dye and there was a crossing-over in this show with work by Le Grice, Nicholson and others.

In his reviews, Cork noted 'video art's relationship with television', which was by then available to most British people. He hoped this might enable engagement with the work of artists, 'even [by] people unversed in the language of painting and sculpture', although he regretted that the (three) channels had not yet shown any interest in video art.[155]

The organisation of the 1976 video show was interesting. None of the artists was presenting documentation or representation of previous work (for example, performance); everything was made as video art. Only eight paired artists, including Tamara Krikorian, Brian Hoey, Stuart Marshall, Steve Partridge and David Hall, were featured, each pair for a one-week show. Cork noted that the majority used multi-monitor projections and 'demanded an active questioning response to the monitor'.[156] Roger Barnard used a real-time camera to show spectators themselves juxtaposed with others who had just passed through the space, which Cork suggested was typical of the way the artists 'managed to provoke a heightened consciousness of what is involved in being both the observer and the observed, manipulated by the faithful yet endlessly deceptive video screen'.[157]

While this links with the everyday experience of watching television or being watched by security cameras, in each case Cork reviewed shows in art galleries or similar locations with all those conventions and expectations. He added that they would probably only be seen by those 'who make it their business to keep up' with the art world, which takes us back again to the matter of the spectators and the extent to which they did or did not access avant-garde film, artists' film and video, commercial cinema and broadcast television.

There was a shift away from the dominance of painting and sculpture during the 1970s but this was not the 'end' of those traditional practices – indeed, they were accorded a critical revival in the following decade. None the less, other visual practices began to stand alongside them, and in some exhibitions and publications they took precedence or were integrated 'naturally' as a part of a show of varied media and materials. An important example was the Hayward Gallery's 'The New Art' exhibition (1972) – not because it showed these new approaches for the first time but because it brought these new artists together in a well-publicised context which reached a wider public.

Anne Seymour curated the show and resisted the Arts Council's desire for a more catholic survey in favour of innovative young artists. Among the fourteen, some are familiar names today, including Gilbert & George and Richard Long. In the introduction to the catalogue, Seymour suggested that the 'single attitude' among the artists 'was their ability to look reality in the eye', which might mean an artist working in 'areas in which he is interested – philosophy, photography, landscape etc. without being tied to a host of aesthetic discomforts which he personally does not appreciate'.[158] Most of these artists (generally young, all male) seemed to have broken wholly with

Figure 2 *Radio On*

the traditions of painting, drawing and sculpture – with the possible exception of a huge charcoal drawing by Gilbert & George, and even they were also recording events like their 'Singing Sculpture' on film by 1970.

Elsewhere, David Dye presented film works using loops and 'moved' projectors, Keith Arnatt combined photographs and words much as film storyboards might do, while Victor Burgin began visual work, which would lead later to the reworking of signifying images and texts which seemed to have been extracted from narrative films and advertising. Michael Craig-Martin created individual booths with lights and mirrors reminiscent of the fairground origins of cinema, while Richard Long and Hamish Fulton travelled the landscape so that their photo/text pieces were again time-based, as were John Hilliard's photo storyboards of different events and camera settings and Gerald Newman's duration pieces. David Tremlett included references to an audio-tape piece and a film 'Non Improvisation', including the soundtrack of a tree creaking.

Unlike the Pop Artists of a decade earlier, the new conceptual work could hardly have been further from the world of the mass media or the Hollywood star industry – in style or intention. None the less, it too used photographic images and words, duration and time sequences, and occasionally even film or video. In following years, multiple images continue to be a part of some artists' work – for example, Susan Hiller's mid-1970s installation of panels of up to thirty-six postcards, each showing a storm-battered seafront entitled *Dedicated to the Unknown Artists*. Hiller would soon turn to video as a new medium, and continues to show various kinds of photographic images in her work.

Conclusion

My focus has been on moving images and their broader link to the visual arts in Britain. I have sought to show the varied and complex cultural roots of this practice while stressing the contributions from a range of practitioners who emerged from (and sometimes returned to) Britain's art colleges, including Le Grice, Jarman, Greenaway and Hall. Even so, and with brief mentions of Amber Films, Berwick Street Collective, Lis Rhodes, Ken Russell, Peter Greenaway, Horace Ové and others, this is not the whole story of an extraordinarily varied decade of British films that stood outside mainstream commercial film and television. We might equally well consider Bill Douglas's autobiographical trilogy (1972, 1973, 1978), Terence Davies's *Children* (1976), funded by the BFI Production Fund, Chris Petit's 1979 film *Radio On*, and other women film-makers like Sally Potter and Laura Mulvey. In some cases (especially Jarman, Greenaway, Russell, Davies and Potter), this work became increasingly well known, often finding its way into more mainstream contexts over following decades. In addition, the theoretical and historical work of others like Le Grice and Mulvey has continued to exert an influence while, as I have suggested, moving images are now common in contemporary art contexts.

CHAPTER 4

British Film Design in the 1970s

Laurie N. Ede

Film design, in the 1970s or any other epoch, should be thought of as an applied art form. The film designer attempts to satisfy the vision of the director and other senior figures on a given film project; he or she endeavours also to meet the expectations of the audience with regard to the visual fabric of the film. But, of course, such determinants shift over time. In 1974, the serving President of the [British] Guild of Film Art Directors, Michael Stringer, wrote that the designer should 'make the imagination soar to seemingly impossible heights within a practical and economic framework'.[159] During the 1970s, that framework was determined by the reduction of American capital. In addition, the British designer's task was affected by a range of factors, including the rise of a new generation of art directors; new patterns of directorial authorship; changing practices within the major studios; and influence felt from television production. For a time, the long-running brands – Hammer, the *Carry Ons* and the Bond films – helped to preserve a sense of continuity with British film culture. Otherwise, aesthetically speaking, most things were up for grabs in the 1970s and, as Stringer implied, British designers had to adjust to local determinants of production.

State of the Craft

Writing in 1969, *The Times*'s film critic, John Russell Taylor, noted the emergence of a group of British film designers who had brought 'background to the fore', and even challenged the assumption that 'the "author" of a film need . . . necessarily be the director'.[160] Certainly, the 1960s established a design elite formed around practitioners such as Ken Adam, John Box and Assheton Gorton; these designers continued to enjoy major mid-Atlantic assignments throughout the 1970s. Over time, further American money would promote the careers of Michael Seymour and, in particular, John Barry. But the 1970s also witnessed the decline of the 'British art department' – the technicians who had developed studio design since the 1930s. Pinewood veterans such as Stringer, Carmen Dillon and Lionel Couch continued, but the decade also saw the retirements of three representatives of the influential 'Gainsborough school': Alex Vetchinsky, Maurice Carter and Cedric Dawe. The decline of British 'hothouse' design was symbolised further by the closure of the MGM studios in 1970. Its art department chief, Eliot Scott, had encouraged methods of design that he learned from his mentor (and predecessor at MGM), Alfred Junge. The closure of the MGM studios drew a line under German-influenced methods of design that had travelled, over 60 years, from Tempelhof to Shepherd's Bush and Denham, through to Borehamwood.

The decline of the studio design tradition brought particular problems to the Guild of Film Art Directors (GFAD). The GFAD had existed since 1946 as a specialist forum for British film designers, and its rhetoric had remained largely unchanged over the decades. In 1973, Michael Stringer wrote of the need for the Guild to function 'for the betterment of Design in films',[161] but the GFAD faced some trenchant difficulties by the start of the 1970s. The decline of the British studio system dispersed design activity. The modern film designer worked equally on location and in the studio, and that studio was often a comparatively modest facility or built on location. Consequently, the GFAD could no longer draw its members from the long-standing British studios and it felt obliged also to assume a larger function as an agency for designers. Of greater consequence was the increasing threat from television. For a long time, the Guild resisted taking in members who worked exclusively for the domestic medium, but by 1973 the pressures were irresistible. The directory of members for that year was presented 'primarily . . . to assist in the selection of members for Art Departments for both Films and Television'.[162]

Television also exerted a marked aesthetic influence on British film design during the 1970s. This phenomenon was traceable to the previous decade and, in particular, to the progressive art departments at the BBC and Associated Television (ATV). The BBC's design wing was managed by Richard Levin, who influenced Natasha Kroll, Luciana Arrighi and others with his non-representational approach to screen design. Levin believed designers should abandon their futile quest for realism in order to 'create a significant visual pattern to which an audience can respond'.[163] The design regime at ATV was equally forward-looking, headed by the former theatre designer Tim O'Brien. He felt that television settings should draw attention to their essential unreality and he gave his design tyros latitude to create studio scenery which made 'an apt and parallel comment of its own'.[164] Inevitably, designers such as Brian Eatwell and Philip Harrison extended this attitude into their subsequent work for films.

Naturally, all British film designers of the 1970s were compelled by the prevailing economic and aesthetic trends. Throughout the decade, these factors combined to encourage location shooting. Since the end of 1950s, and particularly in the wake of the seminal films of the New Wave, British designers had grown accustomed to regarding locations as a fundamental design element; even the veteran Vetchinsky conceded that his job was 'primarily to visualise the background . . . and then search for suitable locations'.[165] During the 1970s, locations were used in variety of ways. Sometimes, their use was expedient, as British producers continued to save money by staying away from the studio. The *Carry On* and Hammer films were conspicuous examples of the cheapjack location approach, but many low-budget features were shot in real places. As ever, the best location-led work occurred when the designer was permitted to select and adapt the environments. David Lean's *Ryan's Daughter* (1970) was a jewel. It was designed by the extraordinary artist Stephen Grimes and the sets, built over eight months on the Dunquin Peninsula in Ireland, expressed the elemental passion of Grimes's original oil colours.

No less extraordinary in its way was *Get Carter* (1971). This was designed by Antonioni's former collaborator, Assheton Gorton, the self-described 'half painter, half architect', who deemed the choice of built environments to be as important as the selection of colours from a palette.[166] The environment of *Get Carter* made imaginative use of a range of locations, found largely within a fifteen-mile radius of Newcastle; these included the incongruously named La Dolce Vita pub and a betting shop in Hebburn. As with Gorton's most famous previous credit, *Blow-Up* (1966), everything was shot on location, but the design sensibility was quite different. Antonioni had urged a semiotic approach to design, to reconceive the shapes and colours of the built world (even to the extent of painting streets and houses). In contrast, *Get Carter* made straight presentation of some stark modern settings, such as the Brutalist Trinity Centre multi-storey car park in Newcastle and Blackhall Colliery near Hartlepool. Such godless places performed an essentially sociological function for a key film of the post-New Wave era, hinting at the environmental influences on ugly human behaviour.

Designing the Leading Brands: *Carry On*, Hammer and James Bond

The *Carry Ons*, Hammer horrors and James Bond films have functioned like the veins in the sandy rock of British film culture. These series, in their different ways, have imparted a sense of continuity to a perennially fragile industry. This was as true of the 1970s as any other era, although the decade saw a decline in all three of the leading brands.

The designers of the *Carry On* films and Hammer horrors were in the business of providing cheap laughs and cheap thrills. The design ethos in both cases was set, in the first instance, by one designer; the *Carry On* method was initiated by Alex Vetchinsky, the Hammer approach by Bernard Robinson. During the 1970s, the Vetchinsky tradition was more easily maintained. He designed one final title, *Carry On Up the Jungle* (1970), and the series continued to be produced at Pinewood by the duo of Peter Rogers and Gerald Thomas. By contrast, Hammer functioned as a tenant producer in a variety of studios, and the production values suffered accordingly.

The eleven *Carry Ons* of the 1970s were designed by four different art directors: Vetchinsky, Robert Jones, Jack Shampan and Lionel Couch. Of course, the films were scarcely moments of *auteur* design. Every designer was constrained by the modest ambitions of the series; Rogers had long maintained that he would not 'work on a precarious balance', making big pictures for international audiences.[167] In addition, each designer knew that the sets should never draw attention to themselves. This ethos was summed up by Rogers towards the end of his life: 'We put stupid people in respectable surroundings then let them make fools of themselves.'[168] 'Respectable' was *Carry On* speak for 'inconspicuous' and it determined that the art direction should never detract from the stars and the scripts. Throughout the 1970s, this followed Vetchinsky's formula of building only what was necessary, using stock pieces wherever possible, recycling existing sets at Pinewood and shooting extensively in nearby locations. The *Carry On* locations were invariably within a fifteen- to twenty-mile radius of Pinewood, and they included such over-familiar places as Burnham Beeches in *Behind* (1975) and *England*, the shops and buildings of Windsor in *Loving* (1970), and the studio buildings themselves. The gardens of Heatherden Hall, Pinewood, were used for the army headquarters of *England* and *Henry* (1971); remarkably, the car park at Pinewood was covered with sand to form the beach of Elsbels for *Abroad* (1972). *Carry On*'s *objet trouvé* style of design extended also to the use of standing sets at Pinewood. The familiar 'Italian Village' at Pinewood was re-dressed for a number of films and some bespoke sets were recycled; the computer system of Gerry Anderson's TV series *UFO* was reused for the 'love-match computer' of *Loving*. Elsewhere, Rogers made extensive use of Europe's largest scene dock.[169]

The Rogers/Vetchinsky method ensured that the *Carry Ons* of the 1970s looked much the same as those of the previous decades. By contrast, the visual style of the Hammers was much degraded in the 1970s. The best Hammer horrors were made when the company had a stable studio base at Bray, and a stable group of technicians. This was not the case during the 1970s. In the early part of the decade, the company's relationship with Seven Arts-Warner Bros. obliged Hammer to shoot at the Warner-owned Elstree studios. Thereafter, the company engaged in short-term deals with a range of companies, including Rank, EMI, Twentieth Century Fox, the German company Terra Filmkunst and the Hong Kong-based Shaw Brothers. At the same time, the early 1970s saw some important changes in the senior management of Hammer. The producer Anthony Hinds left the company in 1970 (after 34 years) and founder James Carreras quit film production in 1971. The appointment of Carreras's son, Michael, as Chairman in 1972 brought some continuity, but the Hammer bureaucracy was relatively weak. The accountant Roy Skeggs assumed increased significance within the company, as did outside producers such as Harry Fine and Michael Styles.[170]

During the 1970s, Hammer films continued to be economically made – typically on budgets of between £200,000 and £250,000 – but the art directors now struggled to conceal the low costs. The Hammer films of the post-Bray period tended to rely on locations; Black Park was extensively used on at least seven occasions and the Don Picton-designed *To the Devil a Daughter* (1976) was 95 per cent shot on London streets. The Hammer 'look' was depleted by its move to the outdoors. Its visuals also suffered from designers' ad hoc recycling of sets and pieces found in rented studios. Philip Harrison achieved wonders on *Countess Dracula* by his recycling of Maurice Carter's sets from *Anne of the Thousand Days* (1969). Working for the sensitive director Peter Sasdy, Harrison was able to create an historical dreamscape from wildly out-of-period sets – a relative of the real Countess Bathory declared the décor to be 'as good as film convenience can contrive'.[171] Otherwise, Hammer's recycling practice led to arbitrary effects, on films such as *Twins of Evil* (1971) and *Vampire Circus*.

Broadly, the Hammers were burdened by a lack of imagination. This was demonstrated by the £220,000 production of *Dracula A.D. 1972* (1972). The film was designed by Robinson's assistant, Don Mingaye, and it aimed, as the press materials averred, to relocate the vampire from Transylvania to the 'trendy areas of London's Kings Road . . . ranging from frenetic discotheques to late night laundrettes'.[172] The results were a visual muddle. Johnny Alucard's flat (which cost £3,750 to produce) had some architectural interest – a basement pad, it was entered via a kitchen and a flight of stairs – but Mingaye's 'Pop Art' motifs did not work. The

Cavern Disco Bar also looked poorly finished, despite its intriguing plastic 'spider's web' decorations.

Of course, the Bond films had higher ambitions than the other leading British brands and they had more expensive sets. By the 1970s, these were a core element of the franchise, as the director Guy Hamilton suggested in 1974: 'Audiences go to the annual pantomime and they say, "what have you got for us this time?" We say, "well children, we've got some goodies for you which you haven't seen on television or in other pictures".'[173]

Five Bonds were made during the 1970s and these were designed by three art directors. As in the previous decade, the most imaginative designs came from Ken Adam. Adam designed *Diamonds Are Forever* (1971), *The Spy Who Loved Me* (1977) and *Moonraker*. The brand values were so well established by the 1970s, and the tone of self-mockery so well engrained, that Adam felt obliged to quote his own work. He conceded that he was aiming at 'absurdist reality' by the time of *Moonraker*, particularly in the moonscape and lunar vehicle chase sequences (although these used some NASA references).[174] Elsewhere, Adam made ever more audacious use of his characteristic circles set against strong, straight lines. These had been seen first in Adam's sets for *Dr No* (1962), specifically the 'tarantula room', and his war room for Kubrick's *Dr Strangelove* (1963). During the 1970s, strict geometry governed Adam's 'Atlantis' set of *The Spy Who Loved Me*. This was based on the look of mass-produced plastic furniture, but it took on a sinister air thanks to Adam's rigorous contrasts between curved and straight elements. Most memorable of all was Adam's Pyramid Control Room of *Moonraker*. Designed in Mayan style, the fierce slopes of the walls also carried echoes of the town scenes of *The Cabinet of Dr Caligari* (1920). Typically, Adam softened the effect by introducing some muted curved elements (here in the modernist furniture and glass decorations).

For the Bonds of the 1970s, Adam continued to practise his quirky form of expressionism. Inevitably, the self-quotation could only go on for so long; Adam admitted that the space settings of *Moonraker* took his ideas as far as they could go. In this context, Adam's most enduring achievement of the 1970s was probably his creation of the new 007 stage at Pinewood. This was built in 1977 to house the 5/8 scale set for the super tanker of *The Spy Who Loved Me* and its walls were incorporated into the setting. Adam felt that the results gave the film 'beauty of the structural line'.[175] The stage was created just as a fresh wave of 'runaway' American production finance was arriving in Britain, and it symbolised the relationship between the internationalist Bond series and the emerging idea of the blockbuster. As Adam observed, 'they [American producers] found out that we could do big pictures. Big, special effects, important pictures. You know, we weren't just the poor cousins on the other side of the Atlantic . . . the Bonds were very important.'[176]

Pictorialist design

The modification of the leading brands of British cinema during the 1970s was clearly linked to the economic troubles faced by the film industry; the sets of the Hammers, in particular, revealed the strains. But this period of austerity brought some benefits to the national film culture through the emergence of new *auteur* directors. To some extent, the previous decade had kept directors hostage either to brand values (who recalled the directors of the Bonds?) or to prevailing fashions ('Swinging London'). Though finances were tight in the 1970s, certain producers were prepared to speculate on new *auteurs*. Some of these were directors of *mise en scène*, pictorialists who asserted their authorship via the visual elements in the frame. Two directors, Ken Russell and Robert Fuest, fulfilled Robin Wood's requirement of the *auteur*, 'to place the actors significantly within the décor, so that the décor itself becomes an actor'.[177] This had significant implications for designers such as Luciana Arrighi, Brian Eatwell, Philip Harrison, Derek Jarman and Natasha Kroll.

Robert Fuest's *œuvre* is small (he made only eight films between 1968 and 1982), but it is remarkable for its pictorialist intent. Molly Plowright's observation about his first film, *Just Like a Woman* (1968), held good for the rest: 'it's the frame that counts . . . Each frame has been composed for colour as well as shape'.[178] Fuest's best films – *The Abominable Dr. Phibes*, *Dr. Phibes Rises Again* (1972) and *The Final Programme* (1973) – expressed the new connections between film and TV design. Moreover, they referenced the 'nostalgia craze' in British visual culture, that period between 1966 and 1973 when, according to Bevis Hillier, first Art Nouveau and then Art Deco became fashionable with British youth. Fuest came from an art and design background, and had started his screen career as a designer for television. His mid-budget features brought modishly 1930s design values to the fore. The press materials for *Dr. Phibes* emphasised that 'particular attention was given to designing sets that emphasise the [Deco] period.' Fuest himself recalled that, for the *Phibes* films, he and his designer Brian Eatwell were 'like two art directors on heat!'.[179] Their use of Deco was instinctive – conflating early Parisian motifs with late-period *streamline moderne* ideas – but it was also considered. Fuest said that his own Deco revival commented on the similarities between the 1930s and the 1970s: two 'tense ages trying to wipe away the past'.[180] In the event, he and Eatwell produced dizzy pastiches of the 1930s, which seemed gloriously of the moment.

Fuest's films were hothouse productions; the key settings were contrived within the studio. In contrast, and often through financial necessity, Ken Russell frequently took his small crews out on location. Throughout his nine films of the period, Russell developed a distinctive visual style which was based on mobile design and the metaphorical use of props.

Russell's style of location adaptation became a design trademark of his desire to 'mingle reality and fantasy'. Russell saw no conflict between realism and surrealism. He spoke of the need to recreate historical settings with care, as a means of *feeling* the past.[181] At the same time, he referred frequently to the dreamscape of cinema and the need to keep audiences 'on their toes, alive'.[182] His heroes – Mahler, Tchaikovsky, Gaudier-Brzeska – lived in the material world, but they sought to transcend it and they came alive in the world of the imagination. Russell's symbolic *mise en scène* worked best in the films about artists. For *The Music Lovers* (1970), Natasha Kroll staged a wondrous recreation of Swan Lake in the grounds of West Wycombe House using sparse pieces of stage scenery. In *Mahler* (1974), Ian Whittaker created some memorable moments with his cruelly attractive crematorium sets and also his large busts of the composer (symbolising Mahler's earth-bound vanity). But Russell's symbolic approach to design worked less well on the films rooted in popular culture. *Tommy* (1975) was particularly erratic. Paul Dufficey's spare props imparted a striking, cartoon-like sensibility to the early holiday camp scenes, filmed on Hayling Island. Elsewhere, the musical suffered from some clumsy scenic gestures. These included the large ball bearings (signifying the pinball wizardry of the eponymous hero and the RAF/munitions backgrounds of his parents) and the huge statue of Marilyn Monroe (symbolising the false idols of popular culture). Russell claimed that such props allowed him to 'introduce symbolism into scenes of reality [to] say two things at once', but the symbols were sometimes obtuse.[183]

The highest flowering of Russell's expansive approach to *mise en scène* remains *The Devils,* for which Derek Jarman designed the sets. *The Devils* charts the events leading up to the destruction of Loudon in France in 1634, and the execution of its maverick religious leader, Father Urban Grandier. Its themes struck a chord with both Jarman and Russell. By 1971, the director already had a sense of his outsider status in British films and he readily identified with Grandier; Russell said that the film was about 'the lasting impact the individual has, even when he loses'.[184] Jarman, who was introduced to Russell by a mutual friend, was simultaneously creating an art project on themes of religious hypocrisy. The design of the film was a meeting of minds.

Jarman had an unhappy time during his eighteen weeks at Pinewood; he felt marginalised within the studio bureaucracy, and some veterans mockingly referred to him as 'the artist'.[185] None the less, he produced some astounding sets. His references were diverse, ranging from the familiar (Fritz Lang's *Metropolis* and Piranesi's seventeenth-century *Carceri* engravings) to the obscure (the French neo-classical architects Ledoux and Boullée). Jarman also incorporated some set dressings which seemed straight out of Bosch. The production notes described one scene as 'a crazy clutter of the medieval mind. Horses' hooves, human bones, the foetus of a whale'.[186]

Notably, Jarman and Russell responded to a line from Aldous Huxley's *The Devils of Loudon*, in which he wrote that the 'exorcism of Sister Jeanne was equivalent to a rape in a public lavatory'.[187] Jarman's Loudon was consequently built from faux white-glazed bricks of the kind favoured by Victorian sanitary architects, and they created an atmosphere which was at once clinical and modern. Elsewhere Jarman brought an acute architectural sensibility to bear. The Loudon exteriors were strong and forbidding, rendered impregnable by centuries of god-fearing. By contrast, Jarman created a modern apartment for Grandier (Oliver Reed), built around a circular staircase and dressed with indulgent items such as furs, flowers and secular statues.

Design of the Times: *A Clockwork Orange*

It is impossible to select one film to represent film design during Britain's rag-bag era of the 1970s, but Stanley Kubrick's *A Clockwork Orange* set the tone of art direction for the decade. Kubrick led the move towards pictorialism and no one theorised as deeply about *mise en scène*. For several reasons, *A Clockwork Orange* may be considered to represent the 'design of the times'. Like Russell's films, it took a mobile approach to design, its sets built either on location or within an improvised studio. In addition, Kubrick's use of locations was modishly sociological. Ostensibly, *A Clockwork Orange* was a sci-fi film, but everyone knew that Kubrick wished to comment on contemporary society. He and his production designer John Barry produced an ugly vision of the future, which was terrifyingly rooted in the present.

John Barry (or 'Jonathan' as he called himself at the time to avoid confusion with the Bond composer) was not a front-ranking designer at the time of *A Clockwork Orange*. Following architectural training, he

Figure 3 *A Clockwork Orange*

had entered the film industry in 1961 as a draughtsman at Pinewood. Subsequently, he became Elliot Scott's assistant at Borehamwood and attained two minor design credits. The $2.5 million Kubrick assignment was a major boost to his career and, like the director's previous design collaborators, Barry found it to be an arduous rite of passage. At the time, Kubrick was entering his 'fictional documentary' phase and he ordered Barry to scour hundreds of possible locations. Barry's task was then made more complex by Kubrick's decision to shoot in an improvised studio, which Barry had to convert from a disused factory. The locations, props and fixtures were subject to Kubrick's dickering. Barry presented hundreds of photographs of council flats as Kubrick searched for the perfect home for Alex (Malcolm McDowell). The interiors of the Korova milk bar were created from moveable blocks, designed by Barry to comprise a 'big Meccano set' that Kubrick could play with at will.[188] The director demanded numerous permutations in props, only to feel hamstrung by the burden of choice. During the shoot Barry made the mistake of presenting Kubrick with a catalogue for a modern furniture exhibition. This led to a nationwide goose-chase after exhibits from a recently dismantled show, as Barry and his colleagues endeavoured to find the perfect items to adorn the ultra-modern home of Mr Alexander (Patrick Magee).[189]

Barry said that the design of *A Clockwork Orange* was complicated in any case by the absence of visual detail in Anthony Burgess's source novel. In addition, the book's first-person narrative meant that Alex's personal set dressings had to be conceived from scratch. Although Barry and Kubrick had great visual latitude, they used it to depressingly conservative ends. Conventionally, *A Clockwork Orange* is thought of as a radical moment in British film history – a film that was just too challenging for its times and which therefore became embroiled in contemporary moral panics. Actually, *A Clockwork Orange* was the product of a purely personal panic, and Barry's sets assisted in cementing Kubrick's dyspeptic vision. The futuristic new Thamesmead development, where Alex lives, is depicted as not just Brutalist but brutal: a dreadful carbuncle *avant la lettre*, festooned with classical murals which were defaced by local roughs. The interior of Alex's flat is equally dismissive of working-class culture: a mess of clashing colours (silver, blue, yellow, black). The rooms are filled with awful items – mass art prints, a Bontempi organ, a corner bar – and Barry was explicit about the set's meaning:

> We tried to project the degeneration of modern design to a further degeneracy in the near future . . . It was an effort to design the ill-informed taste of intellectually deprived people who rely on commercial interest to form their tastes.[190]

But the film lacks a coherent vision of the workings of hegemony. Consequently, the proletariat are depicted as benighted dupes who clutter their lives with kitsch. Elsewhere, the 'not-too-distant' world is characterised by the demise of old high-cultural standards. The Cat Lady's house, as Barry conceded, was described neutrally in the book as 'a rather shabby old house'. But he and Kubrick transformed it to include pornographic prints and a large ceramic phallus. The latter is described by the owner (Miriam Karlin) as 'a very important art work'; as such, it characterises a heathen society wherein pornography is passed off as art, to everyone's detriment. The decline of old standards can only bring chaos.[191]

This message is rammed home in the film's most famous set. The lurid set for the Korova includes statues of naked women on lighted plinths, based on Barry's photographs of actual models. Presented, blankly, as if for sex, these four women speak powerfully of Kubrick's fears. He claimed that *A Clockwork Orange* was not 'primarily or even significantly, a topical, social story' but about 'an aspect of human personality' (as represented by Alex). He also observed that films provided a forum 'where you can explore things without any responsibility or conscious ego or conscience'.[192] In the end, the film amounted to a critique of the modern world based on original sin. The vivid sets were a fundamental part of the horrid fabric and Barry followed his director's visions to the letter. Everything was horribly effective.

Conclusion

The collapse of film finance at the start of the decade meant that everyone involved in British films had to apply themselves to new times. This had two major – and related – consequences for British art direction. Firstly, the collapse of the British film economy drew a line under old studio practices and the surviving production centres became home to the products of the 'fourth wave' of American film finance; blockbusters such as *Star Wars* (1977) and *Superman* (1978) filled the stages at Pinewood and Shepperton. In this way, British studio set techniques adapted to new, globalised film practices. Secondly, British film design was dominated by the creative adaptation of real places and things. The films of the New Wave and later 'Swinging London' had shown what could be achieved (and saved, financially) by shooting on location. The best of them gained scenic value from having their sets designed and built on location: for example, *A Taste of Honey* (1961), which was designed by Ralph Brinton, or *Blow-Up*, designed by Assheton Gorton. Location shooting became such a dominant practice during the 1970s that it became common for the word 'set' to be applied to any dramatic environment, studio-built or otherwise. Over time, the work of Russell and Kubrick, and films from *Ryan's Daughter* to *The Wicker Man* (1973) challenged the old designer's orthodoxy that expressive work could only be achieved in the controlled environment of the studio.

The 1970s marked a transitional phase in British film design. It was not the case that the sets of the period lacked character; rather the reverse. The unpredictable financial climate produced surprising variety in British film design and some notable examples of innovation.

CHAPTER 5

Film Education during the 1970s

Vincent Porter

The 1970s was a seminal decade for film education. Initially, it appeared to be struggling to survive, but by its end, film education was flourishing both in schools and in higher education. It developed along three paths: film-making as a profession, film as a medium of personal expression, and the study of film as a medium of communication.

The two key players were initially Anthony Crosland, who was Secretary of State for Education and Science between 1964 and 1967, and Jennie Lee, who was Minister for the Arts between 1964 and 1970. The two did not get on personally; the Oxford-educated economics don had no interest in art, whereas the widow of Nye Bevan and daughter of a dissenting Scottish miner believed that everything in Government should be subservient to the arts. In her view, the latter were about life-enhancing things, such as fun, festival and community. Relations between the two worsened in 1965, when Wilson moved Lee into the Department of Education and Science. Although still only a Parliamentary Secretary, Lee insisted, in her *grande dame* manner, that Crosland's Department should provide her with her own personal toilet.[193]

Crosland's achievement was to change the face of British higher education by establishing a binary policy in order to democratise it. In so doing, he undermined the dominance of the elitist attitudes enshrined in the Robbins Report. By 1966, Crosland had established a chain of thirty polytechnics, which would be related to the needs of technology and industry, and would stand alongside the universities. Although different, they would not be inferior.[194]

Film-making as a Profession

Jennie Lee did not initially include film in her panoply of the arts. But Stanley Reed, the new Director of the British Film Institute, lobbied Lee, criticising her for not mentioning film in her 1965 White Paper. In

August, Lee announced that she was setting up a committee of inquiry into establishing a national film school.[195] It would be chaired by Lord Lloyd of Hampstead, a governor of the BFI, who had recently been given a peerage.[196] Other members of Lloyd's committee included film producer Carl Foreman, director Karel Reisz, Chairman of the BFI Sir William Coldstream, John Terry, and George Elvin, the General Secretary of ACTT.

In April 1967, the Lloyd Committee recommended that a national film school should be established as an autonomous institution. There should be a three-year course, with an annual intake of forty UK film-making students.[197] Most members of the Committee wanted this expensive initiative to be paid for by the British Film Fund, but George Singleton, for the cinema exhibitors, opposed it outright, while another eight members considered that the Fund should contribute a smaller proportion of the school's annual costs.[198]

The educational establishment also opposed the proposal, objecting to public money being diverted from existing film courses at several art schools. Locating the new school within an existing institution would be better value for money. The colleges objected strenuously to the idea of union cards going automatically to National Film School (NFS) graduates, when their own film graduates were scrambling for work. A new school could also poach their best students and staff.[199] Sir Robin Darwin, the Rector of the RCA, which had an established film and television department, was especially trenchant. There was, he warned, a danger of overproduction of trained personnel, and it was short-sighted of the Lloyd Committee to have disregarded the interests of television.[200]

It took Lee two years to persuade the Cabinet to accept the Lloyd Committee's proposals. By then, there were fifteen film schools in the UK, all of which had built up their student numbers, many with courses similar to the proposed NFS, and some in receipt of funds from regional television companies. 'What do you want a film school for?' Lee's civil servants asked her; 'it is a declining industry and they are all unemployed anyway'.[201] By now, Crosland had moved to the Board of Trade, but for once she had his support. The 1970 Films Act duly included a provision that, with the approval of the Board of Trade, and following consultation with the Cinematograph Films Council, the NFS could receive support from the British Film Fund.[202]

In March 1970, the National Film School Planning Committee, under Lloyd's chairmanship, invited Colin Young to become the first director of the NFS. A key intermediary in the appointment was the producer Carl Foreman, a retrospective of whose films Young had recently mounted at the Los Angeles Film Museum.[203] Together with the planning committee, Young became responsible for developing a curriculum and finding suitable premises.[204]

One of Lee's last acts as Minister, before she lost her seat in the 1970 General Election, had been to register the putative NFS as a company.[205] But when the Conservatives won the election, Paymaster-General Sir David Eccles assumed responsibility for the arts. He was sceptical about the need for a national film school. He summoned Young and gave him half an hour to justify the need to fund a separate institution.[206] Although Young succeeded in convincing Eccles, Labour's policies on film education fell foul of the law of unintended consequences.

The Lloyd Committee had rejected any suggestion that the proposed school could exist within an established institution. The London School of Film Technique was unsatisfactory because it was run as a private company, and depended on fees paid by students, many of whom came from the United States. The Committee did not feel that 'it provided the sort of foundation from which could best stem a National Film School'.[207] Moreover, although the Regent Street Polytechnic School of Photography had recently introduced a three-year diploma course in cinematography, 'its developments were hampered by uncertainty as to the future plans for a National Film School'.[208]

The advent of the NFS undermined film education in both institutions. The Regent Street Polytechnic (renamed the Polytechnic of Central London [PCL]), which recognised that it would never get official approval to establish its own film course, converted its Diploma into a Degree Course in Photographic Arts. This offered students a combination of practice and theory, and the opportunity to study film exclusively during their second and third years.[209]

The London School of Film Technique (renamed the London Film School) suffered severely and in June 1974 its director, Robert Dunbar, had to put the company into liquidation. But the students and staff refused to let the school die, and it was resurrected as the London International Film School (LIFS). Students manned offices, established an ad hoc curriculum, and raised a hardship fund to help staff members. A benefit première raised enough money to buy the assets of the old school, and to rent premises from the Covent Garden Market Authority.[210]

Meanwhile, the NFS was established at the empty Beaconsfield Film Studios. Young planned 'to work as much as possible as an operating studio, with general training at first, and then gradually build on the competence of each person'.[211] After the first year, he would form small production companies, each of which would 'undertake a programme of pictures designed to stretch or otherwise develop existing talents'. He aimed to foster good practice 'by making strategic appointments to the staff and by encouraging close dialogue with outside professionals'.[212]

By 1975, there was a striking contrast between the finances of the NFS and those of the LIFS. Each of the 108 LIFS students paid £240 per term, while the 75 NFS students were charged only £400 per annum. The NFS also received a further £420,000, of which about £250,000 came from the taxpayer, £120,000 from the British Film Fund, and the remainder from television.[213] There was a similar contrast in the availability of equipment; whereas the NFS possessed one 16mm facility for every five students, the LIFS had to hire in most of its equipment.

There were also differences in teaching philosophy. Young had modified his curriculum into one that was learning-based, rather than teaching-based. He envisaged '75 film schools for 75 students, and an assumption that the curriculum must enable and support the development of individual or group initiative'.[214] By contrast, the curriculum at the LIFS was, in Young's terms, strictly 'passive'. Students were required to take all parts of the school's highly structured syllabus. The LIFS Diploma course was 'designed to give all students a wide knowledge of all aspects of film-making, encouraging them to learn not only how, but why, a job should be done and where it fits into the film as a whole'.[215] Some of the school's alumni soon backed up this comprehensive approach, with its concentration on co-operative practical skills, with a series of 'Screen Textbooks'.

Young's expansive – and expensive – vision for the NFS gradually began to bear fruit. When the Labour Government returned to power in 1974, Hugh Jenkins, Lee's successor as Minister for the Arts, considered that the NFS had become 'a workman-like outfit existing on a shoestring without excessive complaint, no grand buildings, just a grotty collection of huts inhabited by people who knew what they were about and loved it'.[216] And even though the British film industry was still in decline, by the end of the decade the NFS was receiving £215,000 from the British Film Fund, almost double the amount it had received in 1975.[217]

Initially, it seemed that the NFS was developing into a stronghold of political cinema. The student films screened at the 1974 Edinburgh Film Festival had titles such as *Behind the Rent Strike*, *Miner's Film* and *Free the Six*.[218] Three months later, however, the NFS unveiled a wider variety of work in a season at the National Film Theatre. This included Ben Lewin's *Dear Mr. Barber I'd Like to Swim the Channel* and *Horse-boy*.[219] In February 1975, the Institute of Contemporary Art (ICA) cinema's season of animated films included two films by NFS students: *Puttin' on the Ritz*, an Art Deco romp by Antoinette Starkiewicz, and Thelma Goldman's

Green Men, Yellow Woman, a rude and angry parable of woman's disenchantment with men who only want to finger her flower.[220] The School's films also began to appear on late-night television, with screenings of *Mr. Barber I'd Like to Swim the Channel* on ITV, and *War* on BBC2. But it was not until 1977 that the School's new screenwriting department fostered an increased emphasis on dramatic films. The most successful of these was James O'Brien's adaptation of Doris Lessing's *Woman on a Roof*.[221]

In Autumn 1977, Young published the testaments of five of the school's successful graduates who were struggling to make their way in the industry. Although they had all found work, it was mainly in television – the original choice of only one of them.[222] In the Parliamentary debate on the 1980 Films Bill, Labour's Bob Cryer argued that the Independent Television companies should make a contribution to the NFS.[223] By 1982, since most of its graduates were actually working in television, the NFS changed its name to the National Film and Television School.

Film as a Medium of Personal Expression

The art colleges were profoundly concerned about Crosland's plan to integrate sixteen of them into his new polytechnics. There was a clash between the specialists who were primarily concerned to develop individual artistic skills, and the generalists who recognised that designers had to be conscious of the industrial and cultural environments in which they would have to work.[224] *The Times* considered, however, that judgement had to be suspended until there could be further reflection on the nature and purpose of the advanced further education system.[225] Nevertheless, in October 1971, led by the painter and art critic Patrick Heron, 22 out of the 24 members of the National Council for the Award of Diplomas in Art and Design (NCADAD) resigned in protest against what they considered to be a government 'diktat' to integrate them into institutions led by scientists, engineers and technologists. By June 1973, the hostility to the planned merger between the National Council for Diplomas in Art (NCDA) and the Council for National Academic Awards (CNAA) had become so intense that Dr Edwin Kerr, the Chief Officer of the CNAA, was forced to declare publicly that fears that the quality of art education would suffer were 'a lot of nonsense'. 'This is a merger,' he said, 'not a takeover.'[226]

Film education was also caught in the cross-currents which arose from these institutional mergers; mainstream film-making had always been a collective industrialised activity as well as an art form. The managerial structures of the major British and American film companies were carefully designed to locate both the industrial and the creative control of the film-making process in the hands of senior producers. At the other end of the consumption chain, most film critics knew little, if anything, about the process of film-making, and often asserted that the film director was the sole creative individual who was responsible for the artistic elements in a film.

At the start of the 1970s, film-making was still a cumbersome business, which required expensive equipment, technical knowledge and the co-operative collaboration of several film technicians. Images were still recorded on 16mm film stock, and could not be viewed until the next day, after they had been processed by a commercial laboratory. The cameras themselves had to be 'blimped' to prevent the noise of the motor from being picked up by the sound recording equipment, and complex links had to be established to ensure that the camera images and the sounds recorded remained in synchronisation. Beyond this, students had to work in small groups in order to operate the camera and the sound recorder simultaneously. The organisational arrangements quickly became even more complicated if the students wanted to light scenes indoors, construct background sets in a studio, or work with actors. Finally, any aspiring film-maker still had to follow a series of complex technical procedures in order to edit a series of camera shots into a narrative sequence, and to construct and mix a series of parallel soundtracks for voice, background sound and music, before finally sending both the cutting copy and the dubbed track back to the film laboratory to produce the final married print.

These technological and organisational facts of life accorded ill with the individualist models of art education, and of educational assessment generally. The Lloyd Committee even questioned whether art college film departments were 'an appropriate environment for a National Film School'.[227] However, the PCL, which did not have an art department, tackled the challenge of organising group work head-on. Although its staff set the framework of the projects during the first two years of its broad-based undergraduate programme, the ideas were always generated by the students. Moreover, since creative group work could be difficult, staff were prepared to bring in a psychologist to work with the students on decision-making exercises. On the PCL course, getting the best out of a 'film crew' was as important as knowing how to operate a Nagra tape recorder.[228]

Film lecturers in many art colleges saw these technological and organisational issues as barriers to individual creative expression. They were ready to explore alternative approaches to film production. One way was to allow a student to make an animated film to focus their attention on creating atmosphere and the illusion of movement by drawing and painting sequences of individual cells. This could be shot silent to a pre-recorded soundtrack. In 1971, Keith Lucas, a painter who had become Head of the Film and Television Department at the RCA, allowed Vera Neubauer to transfer from the Department of Print-making in order to make two one-minute animation films, *Cannon Fodder* (1971) and *Genetics* (1972).[229] He also permitted the Quay Brothers to transfer from the Illustration Department.[230]

The following year, Lucas resigned from the RCA to become the Director of the BFI. His successor was Stuart Hood, who had been Controller of Programmes at the BBC, and Head of Programmes at Associated Rediffusion. He too placed greater emphasis on individual work than on links with industry, and during his tenure much experimental work emerged, reflecting his interest in political, structural work and semiotics.[231]

The RCA's emphasis on individual expression drew its inspiration from a number of sources. One was the advocacy during the 1960s by the 'New American Cinema Group' of an artisanal tradition. This promoted a cinema of personal vision, and encouraged film-makers to deploy their private language to convey a personal fantasy. This required film-makers to organise their own finance, often by private patronage or grants from public institutions, and thus to control the film at all stages, including its distribution and exhibition. Within the UK, an entrepreneurial student could sometimes persuade an acquiescent art college to provide the finance.

But the artisanal mode of production came under theoretical attack from two directions. The first was from Marxists, for whom artisanal production was conceptually based on bourgeois individualism. The second came from 'structural' film-makers who wanted to explore the formalist relations between the 'content' of a film and the manner in which it was made. Both critiques sought to change the 'politics of perception' by simultaneously exposing the dominant ideology implicit in capitalist film production, and the illusory transparency of conventional film narrative, which the dominant film industry had spent some seventy years seeking to perfect.

The prominent activists in the UK art schools were Peter Gidal, a former student and member of staff at the RCA; Malcolm Le Grice, who taught at St Martin's College of Art; and David Curtis, who taught at Croydon College of Art. Curtis also wrote a history of experimental cinema and Gidal edited a collection of essays about Structural Materialist films,[232] while Le Grice played a central role in the development of the LFMC.

Other art schools played a prominent role in developing the artists' film movement, at Brighton, Coventry, Maidstone and Wolverhampton. As the 1970s progressed, art colleges gradually became the foundation for the artists' film and video movement. Students became tutors, who in turn spawned new students who themselves became tutors.[233]

The Arts Council also played a key role in supporting these developments. In 1970, Rodney Wilson initiated a new programme at the Arts Council for funding artists' films, while the BFI tried to acquire the distribution rights to LFMC films. By late 1972, the Arts Council had created an artists' films sub-committee, which became their principal source of funding. In the following year, the Council's Film Committee of Enquiry recommended that the Arts Council should give financial support to non-narrative films. The grants allocated for production alone rose from £6,000 in 1972 to £150,000 in 1999, and between 1972 and 1980, some 263 film projects received grants.[234] But by the mid-1980s, the self-perpetuating movement shuddered to a halt. The lack of other professional opportunities for film and video artists, combined with Margaret Thatcher's restructuring of higher education, caused many art departments to close.

Film as a Medium of Communication

In 1963, the Newsom Report had noted the failure of education to pay attention to 'the degree to which film and television enter into and influence the lives of our pupils and to those media as legitimate means for the communication of personal experience alongside literature and painting'.[235] Some education colleges therefore sought to use the widespread popularity of cinema films as a springboard to encourage trainee teachers to inspire children in secondary modern schools. Pioneering work by Roy Knight at Bede College, Durham, and by Roger Watkins at Bulmershe College of Education led to teacher training courses in which film became the main subject of study.[236] In Hammersmith, teachers working in further education sought to encourage 16- to 18-year-old working-class students to express their feelings by encouraging them to write about realist feature films.[237]

But success was limited. The Bede experiment was short-lived because of the difficulty of seconding teachers to it.[238] Many practising teachers resisted examinations in film, film appreciation or screen education, partly because they viewed it as a relatively immature area of study, and partly because they considered that it might inhibit the growth and consolidation of the fifth year of a pupil's development in secondary school. Teachers wishing to offer Film at CSE level were faced with two alternatives. Either they had to work within the syllabus of an orthodox subject whose examinations were set and moderated by the appropriate Regional Examinations Board (Mode I); or they had to present an entirely separate syllabus for approval by the Board and prepare pupils for examinations set either by the Board (Mode II) or by the teacher (Mode III).[239] The English and Art Panels of the Metropolitan Regional Board had encouraged Mode I examination, whereas the English syllabuses of the Southern and Welsh Boards had proved most suitable for assessment in Modes II and III.[240] This had permitted valuable initiatives by individual teachers, such as that at Blackwell Secondary Modern School, where some twenty students of average and above-average ability were able to study Film as an alternative to French.[241]

These worthy efforts suffered from two sets of problems, however. Firstly, there was a lack of documentation, limited training facilities, problems of film availability and costs. Secondly, there was the theoretical issue of defining the content of the subject, and reaching agreement about appropriate methods of study.[242] Moreover, the Department of Education and Science had neither an Inspector for film study, nor any organisers at county level. Decisions about film courses were quite frequently made by those already overloaded by the problems of educational technology.[243] For Paddy Whannel, the BFI's Head of Film Education, it was important for teachers to realise that film, like literature, had its different forms and genres, its authors, and its texts. He therefore advocated a threefold approach to film study: firstly, film criticism, which emphasised description and elucidation rather than evaluation; secondly, film theory, which might be developed from recent work in the field of semiotics; thirdly, contextual studies, in which a director's work could be examined within the structure of the film industry.[244]

The BFI Governors disagreed. Early in 1970, a Governors' subcommittee, chaired by Professor Asa Briggs, the Vice-Chancellor of the University of Sussex, concluded that rather than pursuing research and theoretical analysis, the function of the Education Department should be to support teachers in schools.[245] Led by Whannel, six members of the Education Department resigned. However, a compromise emerged; the BFI agreed to give an annual grant-in-aid to the Society for Education in Film and Television (SEFT), which was an autonomous part of its Education Department. This allowed SEFT's Secretary, Sam Rohdie, to spend most of the BFI's grant-in-aid in revamping its journal, *Screen*, in which he sought to develop a Marxist-inspired theoretical analysis of film – and later television – culture. 'Above all,' the *Screen* Editorial Board asserted, 'film must be studied as a new medium, a product of this century and the machine, and which as a new medium and a mode of expression challenges traditional notions of art and criticism and the system of education which is still in part tied to these notions.'[246]

Rohdie commissioned, or republished, English-language translations of theoretical papers written during the 1920s and the 1930s in the debates between formalists and socialist realists in Russia, along with contemporary semiological and structuralist essays which came mainly from France. Implicitly or explicitly, most of these articles questioned the manner in which the capitalist film industry mediated the real world. The essays of Roland Barthes, Claude Lévi-Strauss and Christian Metz questioned the reproductive capacity of cinema at three levels: the capacity of the film camera to reproduce an image of the real world; the ability of the film editor to create an illusion of narrative space, or the passage of a real event, by editing together a sequence of individual shots; and finally, the similarity between the narrative structures of Hollywood films and those of primitive folk-tales. Another strand of *Screen* drew on the work of French Marxist philosopher Louis Althusser, and the post-1968 critical work of the French film magazines *Cinéthique* and *Cahiers du cinéma*, in order to analyse the interplay between the economic, political and social forces which underpinned the emergence of ideology in capitalist society, and its impact on film criticism.[247]

Although this body of intellectual work proved valuable in analysing the production of film texts, disagreements soon emerged within the *Screen* Editorial Board about the intellectual influence and the emotional impact of films upon their audiences. Resignations followed. For some members of the Board, psychoanalytic theories propounded by Freud and Lacan provided adequate answers. But for others, film audiences brought more complex social and emotional histories into the cinema. They therefore looked for more empirical proof of the determining power of film in mediating the audience's world-view and its social and cultural values.

The polytechnics and the universities responded to *Screen*'s new intellectual agenda in different ways. Post-war changes to the higher education system had left traditional interests untouched by the creation of a parallel system of 'new universities', 'technological universities' and 'polytechnics' alongside the existing categories of 'Oxbridge', 'London', 'Redbrick' and 'ex-University colleges' – terms which were more ideological than descriptive.[248] For a while, the university sector was reluctant to acknowledge SEFT's pioneering work. By 1974, however, the PCL had integrated many of the new intellectual developments into a two-year part-time evening course which led to a CNAA Postgraduate Diploma in Film Studies. Indeed, the PCL course was 'a response to the unsatisfactoriness [sic] of the scheme of study and structure of the University [of London's] certificate classes'.[249] Its organising principle, which was primarily designed for practising and aspiring film teachers, was to give students 'a knowledge of the most important film styles, of the relations between systems of production, ideology and films, and of the current debates and experiments and practices in film-making, film theory and film criticism'.[250] The BFI also incorporated *Screen*'s new approach to the study of film, and in 1977, Colin McArthur revamped the film catalogue of the BFI Distribution Library, so that it could function as a critical work as well as a source of information on the Library's holdings.[251] As one reviewer observed, however, the problem for the catalogue was to establish a productive relationship with readerships from the film society movement and from education, which had traditionally come to the catalogue for basic information.[252]

In an attempt to stimulate film study in universities, the BFI also decided to pump-prime a series of university lectureships in film, as a result of which, between 1973 and 1976, appointments were made at the universities of Warwick, Keele, Essex and East Anglia. By 1979 over fifty institutions of higher education were offering courses involving film studies. Fourteen were in colleges and university departments of education, twenty-two in universities, and seventeen in polytechnics.[253] Even so, there was still uncertainty in many higher education institutions 'about what constituted an acceptable body of knowledge' and about methodology.[254] The most common location for film courses within universities was within French Language Departments, closely followed by English, or English and American Studies. Drama and History Departments also offered film courses.[255] The danger was that, in order to be legitimised as a university-level subject, film studies in some institutions would lose its radical edge, possibly becoming indistinguishable from more traditional subjects.[256]

The leading role played by the School of Communication in the Polytechnic of Central London in developing film study during the 1970s, and in linking it to the development of media studies, became clear in 1979 at a conference on Film and Media Studies in Higher Education. Four of the twelve papers were authored by members of that establishment,[257] while a fifth explicitly acknowledged the influence of the original PCL postgraduate syllabus on the undergraduate film studies programme at the University of Kent.[258] The PCL had also pioneered a way of integrating some of *Screen*'s new theoretical insights into its undergraduate course in Film and Photographic Arts, although the course team was conscious of 'the dangers of inflicting a theoretical "line" on its students, without allowing them access to the knowledge which would allow them to develop a critical understanding of it'.[259]

Despite the elitism of some universities, the growing convergence between the study of film as a medium of communication and the emerging discipline of media studies reinforced the tendency to treat film as a medium to be studied, rather than as a window on the world, or as a branch of high art. By 1985, encouraged both by the BFI and by SEFT, there had been a startling increase in 16+ media-related syllabuses. Between them, the twelve regional examination boards in England and Wales offered over seventy Mode III CSE syllabuses in Communications, Media and Television Studies as well as in Film. Moreover, three CSE Boards and two 'O' Level Boards had banded together to establish a joint GCE 'O' Level/CSE syllabus in Communications.[260]

Conclusion

During the 1970s, therefore, film education expanded rapidly. The causes are not hard to discern. The university sector had largely ignored the concerns of the Newsom Report by failing to develop a means whereby teachers could analyse the manner in which film and television influenced teenagers' lives. Moreover, new academic developments in film education and new forms of cultural expression were able to flourish, precisely because the growth of the polytechnics coincided with the decline of the British film industry, and because of the closed nature of the television industry. The media were unable to employ the graduates from those educational institutions that Crosland had originally launched to serve industry's needs, but their unremitting output still demanded an academic analysis of how the media influenced people's lives and behaviour.

The new educational developments unpicked the double meaning of the word 'screen'. Both in the cinema and on television, the screen was the surface on which viewers watched, enjoyed, and frequently wanted to study the images and sounds produced by the audiovisual industries. But a screen was also a filter, or a veil, which separated the informed viewer from the events and the emotions which the audiovisual industries portrayed. The cover of *Screen* deftly captured this double meaning. The six letters of the word itself were composed into a vertical lattice, which occupied the middle third of the journal's front cover.

The dominant mode of film criticism also changed during the decade. In 1972, V. F. Perkins, a member of the editorial board of *Movie,* a journal which had challenged the values of the BFI-published *Sight and Sound*, set out 'to present criteria for our judgments of movies'; and he wrote his book, *Film as Film*, 'in the belief that film criticism becomes rational, if not "objective", when it displays and inspects the nature of its evidence and the bases of its arguments'.[261] But although Perkins succeeded in his aim, he only drew his evidence from the movie text. His arguments relied upon the first meaning of the word 'screen', rather than the second. Although *Film as Film* was initially very popular, it was overtaken by the changes which took place in film study and later in media studies. Studies of stardom, genre, narrative structure and ideology were all incorporated into academic film criticism. By the end of the decade, both scholars and students had come to realise that, for good or ill, all audiovisual media – including movies – carry messages, which are carefully constructed both socially and industrially.

CHAPTER 6

'Picking up the Tab' for the Whole Black Community?: Industrial, Social and Institutional Challenges as Exemplified in *Babylon* (1980)

Sally Shaw

Only three feature films made in the 1970s dealt explicitly with black British experience. These were *Pressure*, *Black Joy* and *Babylon*.[262] Apart from current affairs documentaries and the odd one-off play, television offered reactionary entertainments such as *Love Thy Neighbour* (Thames, 1972–1976) and *The Black and White Minstrel Show* (BBC1, 1958–1978), and only engaged more sympathetically with black British life in *The Fosters* (LWT, 1976–1977), *Empire Road* (BBC Birmingham, 1978–1979) and *Mixed Blessings* (LWT, 1978–1980). Thus, both progressive and reactionary texts existed cheek by jowl, with some actors, writers and directors working in both types. For example, Rudolph Walker had lead roles in the black soap opera *Empire Road* as well as in *Love Thy Neighbour*. The directors Franco Rosso and Horace Ové worked in both film and television. Rosso assisted Ové on his documentary *Reggae* (1970), and directed the controversial BBC *Omnibus* documentary *Dread, Beat an' Blood* (1979), before making *Babylon*.[263] Likewise, Ové's credits included two episodes of BBC2's documentary series *The World About Us* (1972 and 1978), *Pressure*, episodes of *Empire Road* and the *Play for Today* 'A Hole in Babylon' (BBC1, 1979).[264] In interview Ové recalled crewing 'A Hole in Babylon': 'I had lots of guys who were good at their jobs . . . they went for it because they were interested in my film and my style of filmmaking . . . so they came and worked for me.'[265] So, although in the 1970s no broadcasters actively promoted opportunities for black directors, actors and writers, informal networks grew whereby black and white practitioners worked together on more progressive films and television programmes, sometimes for free.

As Medhurst notes, the 1970s was a period of 'expansion and development for British television', which allowed some limited opportunity for black practitioners.[266] But the financial crisis which beset the British film industry militated against risky investment in independent black film, so it was difficult for black creative workers to work in film alone. The collaborative nature of film and television agency was further tested when it was overlaid with race politics. In television the institutional pressures were considerable. Norman Beaton, writing about the first episode of *The Fosters*, observed that any new programme concerned with black communities in the 1970s would come under intense scrutiny:

> If we blew it, the possibility existed that there would be little justification for giving other Blacks a break for God knows how much longer. We all knew this was a searching test. As the studio countdown began . . . I thought to myself, *We're picking up the tab here for a whole community, a whole generation, please God don't let us fail.* [original emphasis][267]

The responsibility felt by those few black workers in film and television to 'tell it like it is' was profound, but frequently their voices were compromised by commercial, institutional and political constraints. *Babylon*, which was made at the end of the decade, provides an exemplary case study.

Babylon: A case study

Filmed on location in South London in 1979, *Babylon* tells the story of a young black man, Blue (played by Brinsley Forde), and his friends. The film focuses on the lives of the young men and vividly exposes the racism that they are subjected to on a daily basis from hostile members of the community, the National Front and the police. *Babylon* was made against a backdrop of rising racial tension in Britain and, as such, was politically sensitive. Producer Gavrik Losey was forced to balance the commercial requirements of *Babylon* (such as the promotion of its reggae soundtrack) with the edicts of the BBFC and the NFFC. Both agencies became increasingly concerned about the contentious content of the film during its making. Losey's papers at the Bill Douglas Centre reveal his deft handling of the project, representing it variously as 'youth film' or 'black street movie', in dealing with censors and sponsors alike.

Andrew Spicer notes that the role of the film producer has been neglected in academic literature.[268] He suggests two key reasons for this. Firstly, the producer is associated with the commercial aspect of film-making, rather than with its creative authorship, which may lead him to be regarded as a somewhat shady figure, one who is perhaps devoid of 'cultural capital'.[269] Secondly, there is confusion about what a producer actually does. Spicer argues that when a producer is written about, he is

Figure 4 *Babylon*

often disparagingly characterised as an amateur 'trimmer, pursuing not an artistic vision, but a saleable product'. However, as Spicer asserts, such views are simplistic; in reality a producer must not only negotiate the hinterland 'between commerce and creativity' but also retain 'an overview of the whole film-making process'.[270] Gavrik Losey was well placed to undertake this complex role. The son of director Joseph Losey, he had a thorough film apprenticeship, having worked as assistant film editor to several directors including Lindsay Anderson, and as a cameraman for Granada Television. Furthermore, his experience of working with David Puttnam and Sandy Lieberson as associate producer on *That'll Be the Day* and *Stardust* had given him a good insight into the flexible approach to film-production necessary for survival in times of economic difficulty. This would prove invaluable when it came to producing *Babylon*.

Babylon's history is complicated in terms of creative agency. Indeed, Sean Burke's question concerning authorship, '*who* is speaking?', is particularly interesting in this case.[271] *Babylon*'s screenplay was written by two white men, Franco Rosso and Martin Stellman. Losey, too, was white, as were the majority of the film crew.[272] However, as he acknowledged, Rosso's Italian immigrant background gave him an insight into the 'pressures' experienced by his characters in *Babylon*:

> A lot of the film is close to autobiographical . . . there's a very natural sympathy, because a lot of my experiences are very similar, even though they may not be the same – visually *I'm* not that different from English people for example . . . So I suppose that must have been one of the reasons why sub-consciously I wanted to do the film.[273]

Furthermore, by the time that he directed *Babylon*, Rosso had spent a decade working on films and documentaries concerned with London's black community. Again, the personnel that Rosso was involved with in the 1970s reinforces the idea of informal networks of practitioners working in black film and television. As mentioned above, Rosso had worked as an editor with Horace Ové and he had directed a play for television, *The Mangrove Nine* (1973). Perhaps most importantly, in 1979, Rosso made *Dread, Beat an' Blood*.[274] This featured the Jamaican dub poet Linton Kwesi Johnson, who had become famous amongst London's black community for his radical political poetry documenting the 'pressures' faced by black British youth. Some scenes in *Babylon* echo those in *Dread, Beat an' Blood*, such as when the film's main protagonists drive through Deptford, in an open-backed lorry, clutching their sound equipment. *Dread, Beat an' Blood* was due to be aired in 1979 but it was controversially rescheduled by the BBC, who deemed it too politically sensitive to be shown prior to a General Election.[275]

At the end of a turbulent decade, race relations in Britain were approaching their nadir; this is a theme which underpins *Babylon*. In London, from around 1974 onwards, a 'paramilitary' wing of the Metropolitan Police, the Special Patrol Group (SPG), stopped and searched (and sometimes physically assaulted) large numbers of the black population, especially young men.[276] Indeed, by 1977, the authors of the Commission for Racial Equality's annual report were moved to comment that they were 'concerned with the disproportionate number of black youths . . . arrested in suspicion, the now well known "sus" charge'.[277] The SPG was also used to police increasingly frequent demonstrations by members of the disenfranchised black community.[278] A few months before the filming of *Babylon* commenced, some 2,756 officers, including the SPG, forcibly broke up a crowd of people who had gathered to demonstrate against a National Front campaign meeting in Southall – an area which housed a high proportion of black and Asian people. Eye witnesses later described the way in which the police had set their dogs on the demonstrators, had driven their vans into sections of the crowd and had indiscriminately 'bludgeoned people at random as they scattered and ran'.[279] A few days later, the Metropolitan Police Commissioner is reported to have told London's black community 'if you keep off the streets . . . and behave yourselves you won't have the SPG to worry about'.[280] *Babylon* deals explicitly with the SPG's brutality. In a shocking scene, two men in an unmarked police car chase Blue (who has merely been taking a late-night walk) through the Deptford streets. When they catch up with him, one man violently assaults him and spits out racist abuse while his colleague coolly radios the police station to report on the 'suspect' that they have arrested.

Seemingly, as the 1970s progressed, there was little practical support from either of the major political parties for black people living in Britain.[281] The Labour Government had implemented a new Race Relations Act in 1976, which looked at both direct and indirect racial discrimination and extended to areas such as 'employment, housing [and] the provision to the public of goods, facilities and services'. However, the terms of the Act did not cover the police and other public authorities such as the National Health Service.[282] Such legislation inadvertently enabled police brutality and corrupt behaviour to go unchallenged in the courts. Additionally, the stemming of (black) immigration was advocated by both Labour and the Conservatives throughout the decade.[283] As Sivanandan, writing in the radical journal *Race and Class*, noted: 'Both [parties] hold the view that to improve race relations, to make things better for the "coloureds" you must first restrict their numbers.'[284] Such sentiments were voiced by Margaret Thatcher in January 1978. In a television interview for Granada's *World in Action* to promote her election campaign, she commented:

> A committee which looked at . . . [immigration] said that if we went on as we are then by the end of the century there would be 4 million people of the new Commonwealth or Pakistan here. Now that is an awful lot and I think it means that people are really rather afraid that this country might rather be *swamped* by people with a different culture.[285]

In May 1979, some five months before filming on *Babylon* began, Mrs. Thatcher was elected. Black communities, already disadvantaged by tough immigration laws and the negative discourses which surrounded them, now also had to contend with New Right policies on the inner cities (where a large proportion lived). Under the auspices of the Conservative Government, public money was diverted away from areas such as Deptford and emphasis was placed on private investment.[286] In theory, this was to encourage the 'working of market forces'. [287] But in reality, these so-called 'enterprise zones' became further impoverished and dilapidated, arguably contributing to the sense of anger and alienation already felt by many of the black population. Perhaps race relations in Britain were never as strained as at this time.

It is in this social and political context that *Babylon* went into production. Filming took place over a six-week period in November and December 1979, on location in the Deptford area of South London.[288] For Gavrik Losey, the project was a challenge in this climate of racial tension. The producer's tasks of financing, scheduling, completing and selling the film were made doubly difficult when one of its central characters answers a resounding 'YES!' to the question 'Do you want a race war?' Indeed, it became necessary to close the film set to all but crew and actors 'because of the film's sensitive subject matter' and the fact that shooting 'was taking place in an area of London' known for its 'racial tension'.[289]

Controversy also surrounded the use of black 'extras' in the film. Franco Rosso, Martin Stellman and the film's casting director, Sheila Trezise, had contacts in South London's black community. It appears that they used a snowballing technique to recruit scores of extras, 'the vast majority' of whom were 'West Indians living around the Deptford, Lewisham, Peckham and Croydon area'.[290] A memo from Martin Stellman to Franco Rosso, written during filming in December 1979, demonstrates the way in which both men relied on informal networks to ensure that they would have fifty black 'extras' for the scene concerning Lover's engagement party: '3 Notting Hill mums and 6 kids c/o Brinsley Forde . . . Aswad (5

+ 3 women) c/o Mikey . . . Archie Pool will bring two women [,] Brian Bovell will bring 3 people of unknown sex'.[291] All the personnel listed here are either actors in the film (such as Brinsley Forde) or musicians involved in the film's soundtrack. Stellman goes on to list other people who are friends and relatives of others involved in the film and who have agreed to bring 'extras' along with them. This approach to recruiting extras was deeply frowned upon by the Extras' Union, who threatened action on the grounds that only their members should be used for filming.[292] It was only after being shown the script that the Union realised that they did not have sufficient numbers of black paid-up members to take part in *Babylon*'s large set pieces, such as the 'Blues dance'. The fact that the Union was forced to capitulate on these terms is, perhaps, indicative of the marginalised nature of black British film in the 1970s.

Even in the context of a cash-strapped 1970s British film industry, *Babylon* was a low-budget film. The film cost only £360,000 and some 87 per cent of the budget was provided by the NFFC.[293] Mamoun Hassan (former Head of Production at the BFI) had taken over as Managing Director of the NFFC in the Spring of 1979 and had initially found it hard to persuade the NFFC to finance *Babylon*. He later recalled that several members of the Board had asked, 'Who wants to see films about black people?'[294] Although the NFFC eventually agreed to provide money for *Babylon*, the Board remained cautious. In a letter written a month before filming commenced, Mamoun Hassan confided to Franco Rosso and Martin Stellman that, having read the script, the Board had misgivings about the project:

> [the NFFC]. . . is worried that the film will be incomprehensible because of the use of patois or ethnic slang. Authenticity is an essential element in the film . . . but if we do not understand what people are saying then we are going to be irritated and alienated.[295]

It seems doubtful that the issue at stake was the 'incomprehensible' nature of the dialogue alone. Jamaican patois had become widely appropriated by second-generation black youths as a signifier of resistance and black power, especially among those who identified with the Rastafarian movement.[296] In the final cut of *Babylon*, the authentic patois remained, although Losey was forced to have the film subtitled. This concession infuriated Eden Charles of the radical magazine, *Race Today*, who commented that subtitles lent the film 'a ridiculous, almost Monty Python' element.[297]

Perhaps this early reaction to *Babylon* from the NFFC, allied with the knowledge that even the act of filming black people in Deptford could be seen by some to be a politically provocative act, suggested to Losey that he should proceed with caution when promoting the completed film. In an article for *Films and Filming* in May 1980, Losey told the interviewer Jenny Craven that *Babylon* was a 'youth movie' and went on to suggest that, whilst it contained a black cast, this did not 'separate it from other stories about poor kids pouring their hearts and souls into making music as a way out of the slums . . . the colour is different; the dreams are just the same'.[298] It could be argued that by describing the film in this way, Losey was attempting to align *Babylon* with the more politically anodyne youth films on which he had previously worked. *Time Out* carried a two-page feature about *Babylon* in November 1980. The journalist Vivien Goldman spoke to members of the cast, and to Franco Rosso and Gavrik Losey about the film. Whilst Rosso and cast members such as Beverley Michaels were keen to promote the authenticity of the film's depiction of the privations faced by black people, Losey himself made the following comments about *Babylon*:

> It's about blacks, but it's not a black movie. I didn't want a polemic movie, I wanted a movie that people could sympathise with and understand. It's a look at the potential situation arising out of the treatment of a minority – it could be Swedes or Italians. It's a peace and love movie, really.[299]

It is interesting to note that Losey was not always so cautious about the way that he 'sold' *Babylon* to others. In terms of the music used in the film, Losey recognised that black 'authenticity' was of paramount importance both to the film's financial backers and to a burgeoning youth market. Thirteen per cent of *Babylon*'s budget had come from the music company Chrysalis, who were keen to replicate the success of other record labels in exploiting soundtracks from youth-oriented films. Furthermore, dub reggae, the music genre used throughout *Babylon*, was enjoying high levels of popularity among both black and white youths in Britain. This was partly due to the fact that the punk movement of a few years earlier had provided some white youths with widespread exposure to dub reggae. Mindful of the commercial importance of *Babylon*'s soundtrack, in correspondence with those in the music industry Losey showed none of his previous reticence about the film's racial content, but instead was keen to emphasise its 'edgy' nature. In a private letter to Don Smith of the Musicians' Union, Losey described *Babylon* as 'a black British street movie made on a shoestring'.[300] In this way, Losey demonstrated a high level of awareness of niche taste-communities in which 'authentic' music played a highly important role.

Perhaps mindful that a proposed *Play for Today* version of *Babylon* had been abandoned by the BBC five years earlier, allegedly due to its inflammatory content, and of the concerns expressed by the NFFC, Gavrik Losey appears to have been worried about how the film would be received by the censors.[301] Once again, he argued that whilst the film was about black people, its primary focus was youth in general. Moreover, he was keen for the film to receive an 'AA' certificate, which would make it available to the lucrative 'younger teenager' market. In June 1980 Losey wrote a circumspect letter to James Ferman, the Secretary of the BBFC:

> This is the first submission that I have made to you as a Producer for my own company. I thought that it might be helpful to you in considering our picture to know that we regard it as being concerned with the general problem of youth today although it is ethnically orientated around British West Indians in South London.[302]

Despite his letter to James Ferman, the BBFC took a hard line with *Babylon* when it came to its classification and awarded it an 'X' certificate. The BBFC were clearly worried about the politically contentious nature of the film's content and, in an unprecedented move, they invited seven members of the Commission for Racial Equality to view and discuss *Babylon* with the Board.[303] Ferman later recounted the discussion to Losey in a private correspondence:

> [the Commission for Racial Equality] thought that the film, although truthful, was potentially inflammatory in its reinforcement of racial stereotypes, and they ended up voting five to two to recommend the 'X'. This very much reflected the . . . opinion . . . of the British Board of Film Censors.[304]

It is instructive to note that, in terms of visual content, the scene which drew the most concern from the BBFC, in which Blue stabs his racist neighbour, was fairly muted. The scene does not happen in close-up, the viewer does not see the knife enter the body and no blood is shown. Neither does the camera linger on the injured man. Visually, then, *Babylon* is much less explicitly visceral than many other films that were given an 'X' certificate in the 1970s, such as *Straw Dogs* or *Scum*. Indeed, it would seem that *Babylon*'s 'X' certificate had much more to do with the difficult socio-political climate in which it was made and released, rather than its actual pictorial content; this is an idea reinforced in Ferman's letter to Losey justifying the certification: 'Young teenagers would be . . . attracted by the music and perhaps confused and troubled by the message.'[305]

Whilst data concerning cinema audiences for British films during the 1970s are notoriously patchy, a contemporaneous review in *Race Today* perhaps gives some indication of the film's resonance for a particular audience:

> I saw the film on a Saturday night in Brixton. The audience largely comprised the living models from which the celluloid characters were cast. They had come to see themselves and they were not disappointed as a certain walk, a facial expression . . . generated cheers of recognition and appreciation. The audience roared their approval at the drop of a 'raasclatt' [Jamaican expletive]. Throughout, there was a virtual love affair between the audience and the film characters.[306]

Obviously, this one example cannot be used to generalise about black audience response to *Babylon*. However, the example is useful in so far as it gives an indication of the film being a fairly accurate representation of life for young black Londoners in the late 1970s, as evidenced by the 'cheers of recognition and appreciation' of the audience.

Conclusion

In the case of Gavrik Losey and *Babylon*, the role of the producer extended far beyond the 'shadowy realm of business interests'.[307] Losey's role in *Babylon* can be regarded as that of a mediator and broker whose vision influenced and shaped the completed film. In this way, Losey used skills honed on previous productions to help to position the film as a 'youth movie' in a politically complex market, and also to negotiate finance from the recording company, Chrysalis, on the back of the commercial viability of the film's soundtrack. He also took steps to defend and protect *Babylon*'s creative integrity. This can be seen in his refusal to 'tone down' the patois used throughout *Babylon* despite market and NFFC pressure. *Babylon* has much to say about the collaborative nature of film-making and the struggles and negotiations that are an integral part of it. But perhaps more importantly, it sheds light on the creative skills of the producer in a way that has not, hitherto, been properly recognised. Arguably, it was only his considerable expertise, creativity and knowledge of *all* areas of the film-making process that enabled Losey to produce *Babylon* at a time when the British film industry was in commercial decline and British race relations were at their most turbulent.

CHAPTER 7

1970s Television: A Self-conscious Decade

Laurel Forster

> As I have said before, we are not making films and this must be brought home to the writer. Our facilities are bursting at the seams and editing must be kept down.[308]

These sentences in a 1968 memo from Gerald Savoy, Head of Plays at the BBC, to producers and story editors in the Plays Department, speak to the heart of the relationship between television and film in the 1970s. It was not the only attempt to control a burgeoning development in television: the one-off play. Fortunately, for television viewers of that decade, the plea seems to have gone unheeded. Managerial edicts did not impede the impressive output of writers and producers, who developed rapidly, revelling in the knowledge that their work was being widely appreciated by viewers. The memo also calls to mind the fact that television's internal working practices in the 1970s were often constrained, in this militant decade, by unionisation and control of productivity by the workforce. Furthermore, it highlights tensions between industry guidelines and enthused creative workers who consciously transgressed the boundaries of the medium, and even competed with film. The *Play for Today* strand (BBC1, 1970–1984), discussed later, epitomised these tensions.

This chapter considers the ways in which television matured in the 1970s to achieve a self-conscious status, and how this in turn empowered the medium to communicate the political to the individual. The chapter addresses two important questions. Firstly, how did British television develop in the 1970s? And secondly, what was the relationship between film and television in the decade? The overlap between film and television needs to be seen in a number of different contexts of industry and practices. Compared to film, television was a relatively new medium and, as Raymond Williams has persuasively argued, its origins were 'dependent on a complex of inventions and developments' in related communication technologies.[309] Williams further suggests that 'the development of a new technology of social communication' emerged out of the limitations of other media forms in relating new social perspectives and orientations.[310] The breadth of interests served by television explains the procrastinations in the official scrutiny and regulation of the medium.

As television in the 1970s became more self-conscious through regulation and debate, it also became increasingly aware of its power as a means of communication between society and the individual. Televisual technologies continued to develop; programming matured into a variety of genres; audiences were high; and perhaps most importantly for this discussion, television increasingly understood its influence on public opinion as well as on an individual's engagement with the world. In short, television in the 1970s became the dominant medium and a forceful presence in the lives of the British public.

It had long been understood that television was an important social influence. Lord Reith (BBC Director General, 1927–1938) had insisted on the moral obligation of public service broadcasting to educate, inform and entertain. His influence can be detected in television regulation throughout the 1970s. The Pilkington Report (1962) had praised the responsible approach of the BBC, but was extremely critical of the populist tone of commercial television. It recommended that the third television channel should be given to the BBC, and BBC2 started transmission in 1964. The Television Act (1964) permitted the Independent Television Authority (ITA) to 'mandate "serious" programmes' to independent television providers.[311] As a result of this, it has been argued that an entertainment culture on ITV in the 1950s and early 1960s was replaced by a journalistic culture a decade later. This new emphasis was significant in shaping the output and influence of television in the 1970s.

However, the Pilkington Report had also suggested a fourth channel, which would be allotted to independent television. Mention was made of 'ITA2' (later ITV2, then TV4) being licensed within two years, but in fact this debate continued throughout the 1970s, raising issues of quality and 'narrowcasting' to specialised publics. The Annan Committee produced its wide-ranging report in 1977, arguing for minority programming and paving the way for Channel 4, which, after the 1980 Broadcasting Act, began in late 1982.[312] The debates of the 1970s raised some profound questions about control of this powerful medium, the purpose of programmes and the needs of viewers.

The Britain of the 1970s witnessed political, social and personal dislocations which provided much controversial material. On the world stage, wars and dictatorships, the nuclear threat and oil crises, and the European Union caused tensions. At home, terrorism in Northern Ireland, shifts in party politics and militancy in the workplace created an unsettled Britain. Questions about race and gender relations were being raised in many ways. There was domestic unease, with increasing divorce rates and women reassessing their roles. Personal and political protest was expressed in marches, demonstrations and strikes. Oppositional currents, such as Marxism, feminism, ecology, communal living and self-sufficiency, impinged upon public consciousness. This troubled decade was blighted by electricity black-outs, food shortages, rising unemployment and widespread dissatisfaction.

Film and Television

Television, more than film, was able to engage these social changes and so influence a changing Britain. It was better able to mediate between the threatening, outside world and the unsettling domestic one. By dealing with contemporary ideas and radical developments, television responded with more variety and sensitivity to changes in British daily life. ITV's journalistic style was appropriate to the task. Many pressing social and political concerns were addressed only on television, because of the risks taken by those ambitious to present their views of contemporary society. Wheatley suggests that this was a period when 'programme-makers began to respond more ingeniously to the requirements of the medium' and to the ideas of the 'reception context' of television.[313] Behind this increasing integration was a developing intellectual engagement with the social significance and even power of the medium of television. Broadcasters manifested the ability to communicate political ideas and social shifts to the individual in the private sphere. Their acknowledgement of television's domestic function influenced both the subject matter and the type of programme offered to viewers. ITV's commitment to the soap opera has been seen as 'evidence of this response'.[314] There was an almost continuous and often rigorous debate in this period about the 'quality' of television programming, and the capability of different parties to provide appropriate televisual content. And as the understanding of the dynamics of domestic viewing evolved, so television subject matter was fine-tuned to fit that viewing experience.

Television's potential to negotiate complex issues at global and personal levels attracted talent from the film industry. Guarantees of large audiences and rapid production schedules meant that many writers and directors brought their skills to the television industry. Others brought organisational skills and financial backing. These included Lew Grade, who invested in British television with money from his entertainment concerns, and John Woolf, whose experience of the British film industry led him to diversify, becoming a founder-director of Anglia Television. The film industry seemed dolorous, while television manifested variety, creativity and innovation. The two industries had always been separate, and in the 1970s there was only limited co-operation between the two. This was largely due to the film industry's fear of competition from television. Before the Second World War, film companies had been 'loath to sell their wares to television', and the only films made available were either European or Disney shorts.[315] After the war the film industry 'closed ranks to prevent television using its own product against it'.[316] Broadcasters needed films to help fill schedules, but until the early 1970s these had been expensive and restricted. From the early 1970s, Hollywood back catalogues started to be sold more cheaply to the BBC, to the annoyance of the FPA, who campaigned for a broadcast levy. It was not until 1964, after boycotts, and removal of films from the market by the Film Industry Defence Organisation (FIDO), alongside sweeping claims by the BBC for the moral high ground, and by film-makers for a superior product, that British films were screened regularly on British television at all. Although the five-year restriction was reduced to three, the embargo on film transmission remained. Consequently, in the 1970s, a recent British film screened on television was still an event, and some achieved very high ratings: for example, *633 Squadron* (1964), shown by the BBC in 1970, and *Goldfinger* (1964), shown on ITV in 1976.

Made-for-television films had been more common in the United States and were disparaged for their limited casts and production values, but their increased prominence on British television was evidence of the appetite for feature-length dramas. Those made in Britain in the 1970s included *Dracula* (1974) and *Rogue Male* (1976). Further evidence of the currency of film culture on television is the emergence of magazine programmes about film, such as Barry Norman's relaxed and incisive *Film* (BBC1, 1972–1998). Others included film as part of larger cultural debates, as in *Late Night Line-Up* (BBC2, 1964–1972) with Joan Bakewell, presenting provocative arts-based discussions. From the mid-seventies onwards there were two further reasons that encouraged viewing of films in the home environment; from 1976 more homes had colour sets than black-and-white, and in 1974 feature films began to be released on video cassette for domestic viewing. However, British television in the

1970s was not dependent for its fictional output upon the feature film; it produced a rich seam of drama in its own right.

Television Drama Series

Many television dramas of the decade were based on historical periods. British history was often approached through the monarchy: for instance, *Edward the Seventh* (ATV, 1975), *The Six Wives of Henry VIII* (BBC2, 1970), *Elizabeth R* (BBC2, 1971) and *Edward and Mrs. Simpson* (Thames, 1978). Ancient Rome was another period of interest represented by *I, Claudius* (BBC2, 1976), adapted from the two novels by Robert Graves. Eighteenth-century Cornwall featured in *Poldark* (BBC1, 1975–1977), and *The Onedin Line* (BBC1, 1971–1980), about nineteenth-century commercial seafaring, was a particularly long-running series. Recent war history was also addressed in the series *Colditz* (BBC1, 1972–1974) and *Secret Army* (BBC1, 1977–1979).

Many canonical authors were adapted for the television screen at this time, including Jane Austen, Balzac, Dickens, Thackeray, Shakespeare, Hardy, Tolstoy and Arnold Bennett. Many of these had already been adapted for the cinema, but television allowed different aspects of their work to be brought to the fore. Original period dramas on television also made good use of the medium's intimate scale. *Elizabeth R*, for instance, starring Glenda Jackson, made much play of private conversations in enclosed rooms, as did *I, Claudius*. Political intrigue was particularly suited to the static studio set. Costume adaptations in the 1970s earned television a reputation for quality drama.

Dramas focused heavily on the late-Victorian and Edwardian eras, and there were several long-running serials, such as *Upstairs, Downstairs* (LWT, 1971–1975), *The Pallisers* (BBC2, 1974) and *The Duchess of Duke Street* (BBC1, 1976–1977). Recourse to these periods helped a fragmented Britain to believe in its past. Portrayals of Edwardianism leaned heavily on an imagined social order. These dramas depicted England's 'halcyon days' with unchallenged social hierarchies, individual purpose and optimistic outlook, and permitted viewers a nostalgic envelopment in a seemingly confident time. Thus television offered a differently textured viewing experience from film, certainly by offering escapism, but also by bolstering security in heritage. McArthur interprets this as an ideological choice for a post-war Britain, faced with mediocrity and fragmentation, 'to return to the period of the zenith of bourgeois and imperial power'.[317]

Contemporary drama was equally innovative at this time and brought television further riches in its programme development. Although ITV's screenings of single studio-based plays reduced in the 1970s, it did augur the start of films for television. *Armchair Theatre* ceased in 1974; however, Euston films brought out dramas on film, called *Armchair Cinema* (ITV, 1974–1975). Some of these television films piloted successful police series. *Regan*, for instance, was the genesis of the long-running and hugely popular *The Sweeney* (ITV, 1975–1978), which in turn spawned two feature films. This revival of the police genre included other series such as *Special Branch* (Thames, 1969–1974), *New Scotland Yard* (LWT, 1972–1974) and *Target* (BBC1, 1977–1978). The police genre developed a harder-hitting approach to law and order, befitting a country of more frequent violent crimes and greater unruliness. Some of the series were based on the concepts and even the names of actual special police departments being set up to deal with a more disruptive Britain. Controversy was sparked over the dramatisation of police procedure. Lez Cooke has argued that, as crime dramas progressed through the decade, they were not 'merely "reflecting" what was going on in society at the time but contributing to the formation of ideas about, and attitudes towards, law and order in 1970s Britain'.[318]

In terms of cost-effectiveness, the drama series was favoured over the one-off play, especially by the commercial imperatives of ITV. The series offered more broadcast output and guaranteed work for the same studio space and set-dressing, and economies of scale could be achieved in personnel. Potential for overseas sales also made drama series lucrative properties. Advertisers welcomed their formal structure since they could be scripted to allow sensible narrative breaks. In addition, their command of regular audiences made them an attractive format, even though advertising was limited to six minutes per hour. Although it was considered that advertisers merely bought their spots and had no association with, or influence over, schedules, their interests were clearly served by programme design.[319] Television advertising, especially in food, drink and domestic goods, expanded considerably over the decade, with expenditure on advertising increasing threefold.[320] Inflation in prices kept both consumer expenditure and company profits high. Adverts became increasingly sophisticated, displaying innovation, creativity and flair. Some campaigns won major awards for products such as Smirnoff vodka and Benson and Hedges cigarettes.[321] The effectiveness of direct selling to a captive and differentiated television audience in their homes had been established.

The commercial underpinnings and accommodations of the television series did not hinder innovation. It not only remained popular, but also became increasingly sophisticated across numerous genres. For instance, it proved a productive format for comedy. There were many memorable comedy series in this period, such as *Rising Damp* (Yorkshire Television, 1974–1978), *Citizen Smith* (BBC1, 1977–1980), *The Fall and Rise of Reginald Perrin* (BBC, 1976–1979), *Fawlty Towers* (BBC, 1975–1979) and *The Good Life* (BBC1, 1975–1977). Many of these have proved enduring in British cultural memory. These comedies referred to contemporary issues of power struggles between landlords and tenants, husbands and wives, managers and workers. They gave the British public permission to laugh at others and at themselves regarding politics, class divisions, sexism, work-shy attitudes and, controversially with *Love Thy Neighbour* (Thames, 1972–1976), at racism. The troubled politics of the domestic sphere was addressed in a number of situation comedies. These addressed the peculiar nature of English marriage, home customs and traditions, elaborating upon the power plays between men and women. They revealed both the tenacity and tenderness of the British subject. In particular *Man About the House* (Thames, 1973–1976) and *George and Mildred* (Thames, 1976–1979) made play on the sceptical attitudes towards marriage and the family so prevalent in this decade.

Comedy series encouraged audiences to laugh at elements of this contradictory decade. Satire, however, which also grew rapidly in the 1970s, stimulated a subversive attitude towards an increasingly mistrusted and disrespected system. The diversification and shift in comedic tone across the decade points to this change. The domestic privacy of the viewer of television, as opposed to film, meant that a potentially subversive humour could play directly into private views. Long-running favourites like *The Benny Hill Show* (Thames, 1969–1989) drew on bawdy traditions, while anti-establishment cynicism and surrealism characterised *Monty Python's Flying Circus* (BBC, 1969–1974), Spike Milligan's *Q* series (BBC, 1969–1982), *The Kenny Everett Video Show* (Thames, 1978–1981) and *Not the Nine O'clock News* (BBC, 1979–1982).

The success of television sitcoms in the 1970s spawned a number of feature-length spin-offs for cinema. *On the Buses* (LWT, 1969–1973) is one example. Its humour is derived from its workplace hierarchies and battles. The bus depot becomes a contested site of work-shy antics and sexism, drawing on at least two of the contemporary concerns of the 1970s. The ailing Hammer Film Productions sponsored three films: *On the Buses* (1971), *Mutiny on the Buses* (1972) and *Holiday on the Buses* (1973). Only the first achieved any box-office success. The comedy spin-off film exploited the television popularity of a familiar product and attempted to extend the domestic space, characters and concerns of the sitcoms to the

Figure 5 *On the Buses*

broader one of the cinema, at a time when British film production was at a low ebb.

Realism

It was not only the limitations of British film that accounted for the increased importance of television fiction in this decade. Television had, by the 1970s, appropriated the major discourses and modes of address. Realism, or television naturalism, was the dominant visual style on television.[322] The impact of the realist documentary-dramas of the 1960s, and the tradition of theatrical plays, led 1970s television towards naturalism. One of the most celebrated television plays of the era, *Abigail's Party* (BBC1, 1977), had been adapted from the stage. The stasis of a cramped sitting-room provides a perfect backdrop to its theme of suburban suffocation. This was a mode of domestic naturalism which underpinned a range of television genres: sitcoms, historical dramas, comedy series and even science fiction narratives. The emphases of such naturalism were character, interaction, dialogue and ideas. The most radical aspects of television resided in scripts, narrative structure and cultural reference of dramas, rather than in experimental formal techniques. Although the BBC Radiophonic Workshop (1958–1995) produced remarkable special effects for some programmes, its work remained within the overall mode of television naturalism.

There were some exceptions to the realist mode in the 1970s, and some one-off plays have been noted for their 'compositional complexity', echoing Czech and Italian neo-realist cinema.[323] A notable example was *The Cheviot, the Stag and the Black, Black Oil* (BBC1, 1974), whose radical political agenda is expressed through numerous devices. This is particularly evident in the opening, which uses a montage sequence to compress 200 years of history.[324] The play weaves a varied texture of theatrical sequences, historically reconstructed scenes, narration, documentary material and song. These combine to stimulate an understanding of the political issues at stake in a manner which has been termed 'Brechtian Television'.[325]

Current Affairs

Documentary reportage became established as the dominant non-fictional mode of address in television of the period. Until after the Second World War, visual news had been provided for cinema by the Wardour Street newsreel companies, but once again in a spirit of hardened competition, they declined to sell their product to television, so television companies in the 1950s had organised their own news programmes and documentaries. This refusal to co-operate with television led the decline of cinema newsreels.

By the 1970s, news had become one of the ways in which television demonstrated its capacity for social communication. It could disseminate information immediately and imply truthfulness through the visual image. As television became the dominant medium for understanding the world, so world events became mediated through television. This symbiotic development fostered an assumption of the authority of television news. Current affairs programmes, such as *World in Action* (Granada, 1963–1998), *Panorama* (BBC1, 1953–) and *Weekend World* (LWT, 1972–1988), covered a whole host of issues on the world stage of politics, wars, famines and dictatorships, as well as cultural and social issues in Britain.[326] Some politically ambitious individuals on their way to fame understood the power of television from an early point in their careers, whilst politicised groups such as terrorists and feminists exploited television as a protest medium. This range of politicised messages reached out to individuals all over the country who, in their private homes, were left to their own thoughts and opinions and were not obliged to adhere to mass opinion.

By the 1970s, the familiarity of a range of current affairs, news, documentary and discussion programmes permitted a show like *Nationwide* (BBC1, 1969–1983) to eschew serious news in favour of quirky and improbable stories. *Nationwide* proved popular. Its format, and the variety of audience response it generated, made it fruitful for academic study. David Morley's ground-breaking research on *Nationwide* asked questions about hegemony, the making of meaning on television, and the ways in which audiences responded.[327] His findings about the cultural competence of the viewer helped to dispel the myth of a monolithic viewing public.

Television Markets

Diversification of the audience through the 1970s became evident as new markets were developed. Children's television was extended by new puppet characters like *Bagpuss* (BBC1, 1974) and *The Wombles* (BBC1, 1973–1975). This sector was further expanded through innovative actuality programmes such as *John Craven's Newsround* (BBC1, 1972–1989), which enabled children to engage in news of the world around them.[328] The children's market was better understood in this decade; for example, the teenage audience was targeted specifically with programmes such as *Swap Shop* (BBC1, 1976–1982) and *Tiswas* (ATV, 1974–1982) to revitalise Saturday mornings.

Different kinds of appeal were made to female audiences. 'Second wave feminism' was pointedly asking serious and far-reaching questions about contraception, sex, work and home, all issues important to women. One televisual response was that the domestic location became a contested space in many genres in this decade, and was represented in intriguing ways. Directors recognised that the set of a kitchen, sitting room or bedroom lends itself superbly to the dimensions of the 'small screen', and the physical presence of the small screen in the family living room seems a natural place from which to muse upon on other, reflected, family groups in their imaginary homes too. Soap operas, such as *Coronation Street* (Granada, 1960–) and *Crossroads* (ATV, 1964–1988), offered particular pleasures to female audiences. With domestic and localised settings, interrupted progress and never-ending narratives, it is here that 1970s television most closely addresses female audiences' lived experiences. In this decade, feminist television critics began to acknowledge the important influence of soap operas and family melodramas on women.[329] It was understood that these programmes operated ideologically, 'working with other social and cultural institutions to reflect, reinforce and mediate existing power-relations and ideas about how gender is and should be lived'.[330]

Domestic life was represented in other ways through daytime programmes and cookery shows targeted specifically at women. For example, *Houseparty* (Southern, 1972–1980) was a magazine programme simulating a drop-in coffee morning, and there were a number of cookery shows from TV chefs such as Delia Smith and Madhur Jaffrey. New programmes offering innovation in subject matter, form or texture were transmitted in this decade to expanding and diversifying audiences.

The Single Play

By the 1970s, television drama was well established and recognised by both critics and the broadcasting authorities as an area of innovation. Commercial television's substantial contribution was *Armchair Theatre* (ABC, 1956–1969; Thames, 1970–1974), which had been started by Sydney Newman before he transferred to the BBC in 1962. Thereafter, the BBC dominated in this field with serious drama strands such as *Play for Today: Theatre Six Two Five* (BBC2, 1964–1968), *Play of the Month* (BBC1, 1965–1983) and *Thirty Minute Theatre* (BBC2, 1966–1973). In turning dramatic attention to the issues of the decade, plays became both personal and political, and moreover, often controversial.

To return to the memo which opened this chapter, one of the reasons why Gerald Savoy felt compelled to remind staff that they were not making films was because, in fact, many of them were doing just that. And if television dramas were not shot exclusively on location, production was shifting from tape to film. Editors were improving their cutting skills on tape for out-of-sequence shots or splicing studio-set sequences, and directors were encouraging actors away from a theatrical to a filmic mode of performance. Not all these practices accorded with company policy, but as Savoy's warning indicated, these changes in drama departments were widespread.

Both the BBC and ITV had made significant investment in studio facilities, and wanted that investment to be fully utilised.[331] Consequently, filming on location was supposed to be a sparsely used luxury for scenes which could not be managed in a studio. Irene Shubik (BBC drama producer) recalls that she felt faint when confronted with the first draft of *Edna the Inebriate Woman* (BBC1, 1971), where 'almost every scene took place in a different location'.[332] And yet these new practices persisted. The single play held a position of privilege in the 1970s and, as Cooke argues, 'was not yet subject to the commercial pressures to attract mass audiences that the series and serial drama were subject to'.[333] Even though some plays attracted in excess of five million viewers, the remit of the individual play was to fulfil a need for quality programming. This public service imperative was more important to the BBC than to ITV, and it was the *Play for Today* strand, which took over from *The Wednesday Play* (1965–1970), that earned the BBC its outstanding reputation for challenging drama in the 1970s.

As the decade progressed, more and more plays were made on film, although innovative directors like Ken Loach had been surreptitiously incorporating much more film into their plays than the BBC sanctioned, at least since *Up the Junction* in 1965, even though he knew that 'it was totally breaking the rules'.[334] This exciting air of experimentation in practice, pushing the boundaries of creative freedoms, attracted talented writers and directors to the television play. The 'theatrical' play was now firmly in decline. As Irene Shubik notes, the writer had to be a 'very careful craftsman' in order to incorporate 'filler' scenes when actors needed to switch sets or change clothes.[335] And she commented prophetically: 'The plotless "slice of life" play could not really be made to work in a studio set-up without the surrounding documentary images of film.'[336] Dennis Potter, however, lamented the shift to film for the television play, arguing that 'it'll be a director's medium like the cinema', because of the inevitable demise of the writer's skills in favour of the director's or editor's.[337]

The vogue for real-life dramas about ordinary people continued in television plays of the 1970s. This encouraged techniques and practices best suited to its representation. For instance, instead of the theatrical mode of one actor speaking at a time, the filmic mode of multiple voices and layered sound was adopted. The use of static cameras in studios and the technique of long shots gave way to rapid cutting and psychologically revealing close-ups. The power of variation in film apparatus and materials was understood from early on, when equation was made between the grainy quality of 16mm film and the gritty realism and documentary quality necessary when portraying the daily grind. The play *Kisses at Fifty* (BBC1, 1973) has been noted for its effective mixture of video recording under studio lights juxtaposed with film location shooting, and for the way these different modes represent domestic entrapment and the rougher workplace respectively.[338] Work on location meant a truer-to-life portrayal of surroundings and atmosphere, and the use of improved film and more portable cameras made this possible. Such was the extent of this shift that one critic argued, 'Many "plays" could equally well have been labelled "films".'[339]

Although film and television may have shared some common approaches, the 1970s was a decade of restrictive industrial practices and strict unionisation. This resulted in many technical and artistic personnel not being permitted to work for both and, if they did, their work often went unacknowledged. Some directors developed their craft in television before making films for cinema; they include Philip Saville, Michael Apted, Stephen Frears, Mike Newell, Alan Clarke, Ken Loach and Mike Leigh. Mike Leigh, for instance, lamented the time it took to get his work out to the world and so worked mainly in television and only managed one film for cinema in the 1970s.[340] Ken Loach, having become 'frustrated by the bureaucratic procedures of the BBC', started making films in the late 1960s, but problems with finance, distribution and British politics led to his disillusionment. By the time of Channel 4 feature films in the early eighties, Loach did not even apply.[341]

The excitement of television at the time was driven in part by audience reaction. Watching in their millions and vastly outstripping cinema audiences, television audiences were important to the success of plays. Audiences expected controversial material in these regular slots. These same audiences, whether members of the general public or the establishment, were not shy of writing to the BBC to express their outrage. For example, Ken Loach's twice-postponed drama-documentary about dockers' strikes and Trotskyite workers' control, *The Big Flame* (BBC1, 1969), received complaints from Mary Whitehouse and the trade unions, other letters which engaged politically with the arguments, and internal memos.[342] Television magazine programmes held discussions about controversial plays, and so circulated their cultural significance. Irene Shubik wrote that she 'would prefer not to be offered up as a human sacrifice' on *Late Night Line-Up* (BBC, 1965–1972).[343] Writers and directors were only spurred on by these controversies, gratified that their work provoked debate.

Play for Today has been described as the true national cinema in a period when British film was bogged down in 'sitcom spin-off hell'.[344] This sense of national address was rooted in the subject matter, which engaged with current events and movements. Plays often raised challenges for institutions and individuals. Institutionally-based plays revealed large-scale bureaucratic corruption or disillusionment with agencies supposedly working for the people. Some raised concerns about forms of governance, such as *All Good Men* (BBC1, 1974), which looks critically at the parliamentary Labour movement, and *Leeds – United!* (BBC1, 1974), where the trade union betrays the loyalty of women textile workers. In *The Stone Tape* (BBC1, 1972) the march of scientific progress was subject to scrutiny, while *The Cheviot, the Stag and the Black, Black Oil* and *Days of Hope* (BBC1, 1975) investigate an unjust and divided British history.

Representations of individual experiences focused on gender, families, the domestic, and the working environment – prominent themes in real-life 1970s Britain. A number of plays took the theme of disaffected individuals: for instance, *Penda's Fen* (BBC1, 1974), which addresses a young boy's discovery of his homosexuality. It uses the Malvern landscape to produce dream and supernatural sequences. *Edna the Inebriate Woman* examines society's treatment of the poor and dispossessed. Other plays cast a critical gaze on the family and class, such as Mike Leigh's *Hard Labour* (BBC1, 1973), which portrays the modest, working-class Mrs Thornham, and enters the frame of second-wave feminist debates about family, marriage and domesticity. Writers and directors often engaged their viewers in complex and subtle ways, rather than imposing polemical views. Dramas as nuanced and relevant as these prompted the studio play to be pronounced a 'dead art' in 1983, and there was the great hope that Channel 4's *Film on Four* banner would provide a 'belated fusing' of the television play and the film.[345] Indeed, when Channel 4 broadcast re-runs of some dramas from the *Play for Today* strand, they were introduced as *Film 4 Today*. In this final renaming of the plays as films, we see an industry sufficiently confident of its product and its standing to call its more sophisticated dramas what they really were: films.

Conclusion

In the 1970s, a number of different factors contributed to the relationship between television and film in terms of industries and practices, and audiences and society. Television grew in confidence as a medium throughout the decade, and became self-consciousness about its social role. Television drama and journalism had important functions in confirming the medium's responsiveness to contemporary change. As the viewing circumstances of television came to be understood as a domestic and often individual or familial mode of consumption, this encouraged examinations of the relations between the individual, the family and society, and a permanent relationship was established between television and the British viewing public. Greater understanding of consumer tastes and constituencies led programme-makers to target specific audiences in this decade. The variety of material from real life assisted television drama and journalism in cementing this cultural significance, not least because of the immediacy and specificity with which television, unlike film, could respond to those events. These factors combined to make television viewing in the 1970s a quantifiably different experience, with different expectations and tempo, from the mass consumption of film. As television came to understand the importance of its social role, there developed a broader exchange of source material, technologies, personnel and practices between both industries. Television drama and journalism led the way in establishing television, not film, as the giant of British culture in the 1970s.

CHAPTER 8

British Graffiti: Popular Music and Film in the 1970s

Dave Allen

In 1969, Nik Cohn published a book subtitled *Pop from the Beginning*.[346] Cohn was a young man, from a generation that included an increasing numbers of musicians, promoters, media presenters, producers or, in his case, commentators. His first chapter examined the 'roots' of what he called 'modern pop', recounting its familiar origins in 'Negro rhythm 'n' blues and white romantic crooning; coloured beat and white sentiment'. He stressed the significance of beat, amplification, sexuality, aggression and 'sheer noise', which had replaced the 'soft, warm, sentimental' music of the dance bands and crooners.[347]

Cohn concluded (lovingly) that pop's 'first mindless explosion' was finished by 1969: 'Pop has gotten complicated . . . split itself into factions and turned sophisticated. Part of it has a mind now, makes fine music. The other part is purely industrial, a bored and boring business like any other.'[348] He did not anticipate the full variety of popular music over the next decade, although he was right about the growing significance of the industry that surrounded, drove and exploited it, and about 'factions'. The popular music of the 1970s entertained an increasingly diverse audience with a broader age range, demanding variously familiarity, nostalgia, novelty and new idols. Meanwhile, the industry 'colonised' new territories in the search for innovation, including Jamaica (reggae) and Germany (electronica), and these new sounds would influence younger musicians and fans in Britain and elsewhere.

Diversity and Fragmentation in the 1970s

At the start of the 1970s, as a new generation of glittering pop stars emerged, the excesses of psychedelic rock gave way to a return to the roots of American country and British folk; the growing 'student' audience embraced Cohn's 'sophisticated' rock ('prog'), while later in the decade the punks spat and swore at them. Glitter and disco, although despised for lacking 'authenticity', were sexy options in a somewhat earnest period. By the late 1970s, disco was big business, including films like *Car Wash* (1976) and *Saturday Night Fever*. Increasingly, there was something for everyone, and something for everyone to despise. Diversity was also a consequence of this 'sophisticated' attitude – which for followers of Adorno would necessarily have been pseudo-sophistication.[349]

One indicator of this sophistication was that, from the mid-1960s, led by the Beatles, more and more popular musicians wrote and performed their own material. Previously, most professional singers performed materials written by professional songwriters, backed by professional (session musicians). The key influences were a few performer-writers like Chuck Berry and Buddy Holly, and by the mid-1960s major British groups like the Beatles, the Kinks, the Rolling Stones and the Who were writing their own songs. While this can be seen as a kind of artistic 'sophistication', it was encouraged equally for economic reasons by an industry recognising that signing three or four musicians, who were self-contained as writers and performers, would both save and make money. So it was that, talented or not, aspiring musicians in the late 1960s would have a better chance of being 'signed' if they could write, play their instruments and sing their songs. One such man was Pete Townshend, who developed from the guitarist in just another R&B 'covers' band to a writer of notable pop singles and then longer 'concept' albums, two of which became significant British films: *Tommy* and *Quadrophenia*.

The previous limited canon of popular songs interpreted by individual singers and arrangers was being replaced by more original songs – another kind of pseudo-individuality which accelerated the sense of diversity and fragmentation of styles and audiences. This chapter will examine the extent to which that shift in popular music was reflected in visual representations – particularly in British cinemas and to a lesser degree on our television screens. I will argue that, while pop's endless search for novelty remained in 1970s popular music, a growing nostalgic impulse developed alongside it – a desire perhaps to recover the innocence and excitement of pop's 'first mindless explosion'. We shall find the latter tendency in films like *American Graffiti* (1973), *That'll Be the Day*, *Grease* (1978) and *Quadrophenia*; I am including some major films from the USA because they were shown in British cinemas and had a significant impact on British audiences and popular culture – just as American performers like Frank Sinatra, Elvis Presley or Bob Dylan had in previous decades.

Rock Displaces Pop

As the 1970s arrived, British cinemas found themselves able to exploit the growing audience for rock music and the counter-culture. This audience was still relatively youthful but was often more sophisticated cinematically and musically than their predecessors, who had watched 'variety' films like *Rock Around the Clock* (1956) or *It's Trad Dad* (1962) and playful star vehicles for Elvis or Cliff Richard. *Easy Rider* (1969) offered a rock (rather than pop) soundtrack, a counter-cultural representation throughout and a pessimistic ('we blew it') ending. In 1970 came the delayed release of *Performance*, starring Mick Jagger as a rock star in decline, and three documentaries: *Woodstock*; *Let It Be*, documenting the end of the Beatles; and *Gimme Shelter*, depicting the chaos of the Rolling Stones' free festival in Altamont, California. These films offered images, issues and representations of greater sophistication than earlier pop movies and this was reflected in the quality of film and music reviews in counter-cultural publications like *International Times* or *Rolling Stone*, although only *Woodstock* offered any optimism about this 'new' world. The films emerged in the months following the Los Angeles murders committed by the gang of failed pop musician Charles Manson, and whenever his victims were mentioned, two names stood out – the murdered actress, Sharon Tate, and her husband, director Roman Polanski. It was their cinematic connections that gave them particular significance.

Taken together, these events, occurring over a short period of time, link popular music (more specifically, rock) to the cinema. They are cited frequently as signifiers of the end of the sixties dream, although they were nothing of the sort because the more substantial ideas about society, community, health, ecology, equality, spirituality and education needed time to develop. In addition, while the films may have had greater impact in the USA, only *Performance* and *Let It Be* were set in British contexts and explored worlds outside most people's direct experiences – gangsters and rock superstars.

But this particular reading of 'The End' – accompanied by the superstar deaths of Hendrix, Jones, Morrison and Joplin that have also been represented on film – was convenient precisely because the events were represented in the mass media and remain available for mass consumption in publications and on film. Even the fictional *Easy Rider* and *Performance* were taken to exemplify the dangers of hedonistic, self-serving behaviour by young people who had rejected 'normal' life. In each of these representations excess was the enemy – whether drugs, sex, violence or social experimentation.

Get Back

One response to the growing pessimism around 1970 was to look backwards. Woodstock wished to 'get back to the garden',[350] whereas the Beatles just wanted to 'get back' to good old rock & roll. Popular music in song and on film responded to this search for greater innocence, simplicity and familiarity in two different ways: offering either the comfort of nostalgia, or the earnestness of 'authenticity' in the roots of American blues and country or British folk.

We can find examples of this throughout the decade and across all the commercial artefacts of popular music. But the cinema also exploited and perhaps encouraged this backwards look because feature-film production is a lengthy process – especially compared with popular music. Films which tried to keep pace with new fashions often fell flat – in the world of pop, to be six months out of date is to be dead – whereas to reminisce about earlier periods can be successful. The Beatles' *A Hard Day's Night* (1964) just 'made it' but was shot rapidly in documentary fashion, while accounts of festivals at Monterey (in 1967) and Woodstock (1970) were popular cinema screen documentaries. But the Monterey film did not appear for two years while *Dont Look Back* (sic), the revered record of Bob Dylan in Britain, ignored its own advice, looking back from its release date of 1967 to the pre-electric Bob Dylan of 1965.

Popular music had always recycled the past but from the 1970s it did so increasingly knowingly, not merely re-presenting old songs to new audiences but deliberately celebrating, revisiting and reconstructing the past – for young and old alike. This tendency has grown ever since so, while this is a chapter about the 1970s, we must ask precisely when (or whether?) that decade ended. For example, as 2008 drew to a close, there seemed to be many reminders of the 1970s – not merely and predictably with the increasingly gloomy news on the economy and accompanying industrial unrest, but also in popular entertainment and more particularly through popular music as represented by television, DVD and cinema.

This included the BBC's resurrection of *Top of the Pops* over the holiday period, while ITV's *X Factor* propelled Leonard Cohen's 'Hallelujah' to the top of the Christmas charts. BBC's *The Culture Show* celebrated the fiftieth anniversary of *Tamla Motown* records and, blessed mainly with footage from the late 1960s and 1970s (especially of the Jackson 5), stressed that period more than the early years. One notable economic success was the musical/soundtrack/film and DVD of *Mamma Mia!* (2008). On 1 January 2009, *The Times* reported that, in just five weeks, it had outsold any other DVD since that format's introduction ten years previously and in the process became the first DVD to pass five million sales in Britain. On the same day, *The Guardian* reported that British people had spent £69 million on watching the film, making it the biggest-grossing film ever in Britain. *Mamma Mia!* was a twenty-first century success but it was based on the songs of ABBA, one of the biggest 1970s pop acts. Simultaneously, a BBC4 season examined 'prog' rock, the much-maligned 1970s genre, with hours devoted to the music of Yes, Genesis, Emerson, Lake & Palmer and lesser-known exponents of the very British style. Then in the following Summer of 2009, we had the fortieth anniversary of the Woodstock Festival, with extended box sets of the 1970 movie and album – accompanied by new publications from participants and television programmes about the event.[351] In January 2011 the counter-culture's archetypal rock band, the Grateful Dead, issued the largest ever CD box set – sixty CDs of every minute of their 1972 European tour. The album was issued only after fans pre-ordered in sufficient numbers at $450 each set and it sold out in four days.[352]

For the entertainment industry and its consumers, the 1970s (and other decades) remain a part of the present. There is an audience for Cohn's 'modern pop' which encompasses most generations and which has continued to exploit the commercial potential of the many new formats since the 'early' days of 45 rpm singles, cinema visits and grainy TV shows at Saturday teatime. We can all access and/or own the history of modern pop, while the mass media and entertainment industries collaborate in the commercial exploitation of nostalgia and a 'popular' history of sorts.

Sub-cultures in the 1970s

One sign of audience fragmentation as modern pop matured was through the various sub-cultures, often more apparent in British youth culture than in other countries. The first British teddy boys, mods, rockers and skinheads were largely self-defining and self-regulating, while providing occasional, lurid headlines in the popular press. But increasingly, the fashion and music industries recognised that these highly motivated groups might be exploited commercially as much as the larger but less clearly defined mass audience of 'pop' fans.

In the 1970s skinheads, punks, casuals and new romantics succeeded their older brothers and sisters while popular music and British youth sub-cultures became serious areas of academic enquiry.[353] In 1979 *Quadrophenia* triggered a mod revival. This was another sentimental memory of a 'factional' past and it persists in the specialist mod (retro) boutiques, or the characterisation of 'the Modfather' Paul Weller – even though Weller was too young to have been 'there' in the early (authentic?) 1960s. In September 2010, *The Times* ran a major supplement on mod styles, 'scooting back into style' – as though they had ever been away.[354] They suggested that part of this latest resurgence was the result of 1980s mods 'growing nostalgic' and passing their 'passion . . . to their children'. It wasn't quite like that between parents and their offspring in 1963.

These new sub-cultures changed looks, fashions, musical tastes and behaviours, but through the 1970s they also sustained the tribal mentality and associations between specific music and fashions and encouraged contemporary popular culture's links to the past. This began perhaps with British teddy boys exploiting upper-class Edwardian fashions while jiving to the new rock & roll; however, the teddy boys had attracted attention from the press in the early 1950s when the (new) British charts were still full of music that we now characterise as 'easy listening'. Bill Haley first 'charted' in Britain at Christmas 1954 but without reaching the Top Ten. The teddy boys picked up on rock & roll, but in Britain their fashions preceded it.

In 2011 the British remake of *Brighton Rock* shifted the story's period and subject from 1930s gangsters to mid-1960s mods and rockers. The ongoing popularity of *Quadrophenia*, and of mod sub-culture more broadly, is intriguing, precisely because in the early 1960s these 'modernists' had little interest in nostalgia of any kind. The simultaneous fashion explosion known as the 'swinging sixties'[355] was similarly concerned with today and tomorrow. In the mid-1960s, miniskirts, plastic materials, Pop Art designs and futuristic styles blew away tradition but, just when the search for novelty seemed likely to exhaust itself, the fashion industry of the late 1960s turned back to the past. On the city streets and council estates that had been home to the teddy boys and mods, skinheads stripped everything down to a pessimistic acceptance of working-class cultural poverty, but elsewhere, young people were being sold a range of images of a more romantic past in the guise of a dream for the future. Fashion drew upon Victorian military uniforms, rural peasant styles, the 'Wild West', Bonnie and Clyde gangsters, the Biba-led exotic excesses of Art Nouveau, cool 1920s sophistication and the romantic imagination of the tragic Ossie Clark. Suddenly, everywhere you looked, the past seemed to have become the present. This was propelled and reflected in films such as *Bonnie and Clyde* (1967), *Far From the Madding Crowd* (1967), *Charge of the Light Brigade* (1968), *Witchfinder General* (1968), *The Sting* (1973) and *The Great Gatsby* (1974).

Rural Retreats or Glittering Futures?

Musically, the 'sheer noise' of Cohn's pop's first phase was sometimes countered by a search for peace in rural environments and gentler sounds. It can be seen in *Woodstock* despite the mud and the chaos, and I have argued elsewhere that the film presents acoustic music as an equal partner with amplified rock in a way that has now vanished.[356] Acoustic 'folk' musicians and singer-songwriters may still contribute to the broad sweep of popular music but rock and hip-hop dominate in almost every context. In the *Woodstock* film, even more than the actual event, acoustic performers like Joan Baez, Crosby, Stills & Nash, Richie Havens, John Sebastian, Country Joe McDonald, Arlo Guthrie and Tim Hardin provide a significant and perhaps aesthetically appropriate contribution to this return to nature.

Young has traced the similar upsurge of interest in British folk music at the time, not least in the new approach of young musicians like Fairport Convention, Incredible String Band, Pentangle, Donovan, Steeleye Span and others.[357] Pentangle's 'Light Flight' provided the theme tune to the television series *Take Three Girls*, starring Joanna Lumley (BBC1, 1969–1971), and Donovan starred as the eponymous *Pied Piper* in Jacques Demy's 1971 film, writing songs for that and for Zeffirelli's *Brother Sun, Sister Moon* (1972). 'Traditional'-sounding, acoustic music also plays an important role in the cult film *The Wicker Man*. Although it is composed and mainly sung by American Paul Giovanni, his fellow British musicians used traditional instruments to create a soundtrack, which Young describes as 'very much in keeping with the prevailing early-1970s climate of rural acoustic folk'.[358] The dramatic conclusion shows the doomed policeman singing the 23rd Psalm while the islanders dance around to the traditional song 'Sumer is A-Cumen In'. In the same year, BBC's *Play for Today* series offered *Penda's Fen*, directed by Alan Clarke; it is another exploration of paganism, focused on Elgar's musical visions of England.

But alongside this romantic nostalgia of older rock fans, the charts became dominated by the superficial glitz and glamour of new pop acts like the Osmonds, Sweet, Slade, Gary Glitter, Suzi Quatro and David Cassidy. More futuristically, Roxy Music enjoyed chart success, while David Bowie's album, *The Rise and Fall of Ziggy Stardust and the Spiders from Mars*, stayed in the charts throughout 1973. In the same year, David Essex topped the charts with 'Rock On' and starred in Claude Whatham's British film, *That'll Be the Day*, alongside older British pop stars Ringo Starr and Billy Fury.

Figure 6 *That'll Be the Day*

Those Were the Days?

That'll Be the Day examined the impact of rock & roll on 1950s British teenagers, with Jim McLaine (Essex) rejecting the advantages of his grammar school education in favour of a life of fairgrounds, sex and rock & roll. In one revealing scene, Essex, with quiff and tight jeans, reconnects with his closest sixth-form friend at a university dance where the students, in college scarves and duffle coats, are entertained by a typically British 'trad' jazz band. The attitudinal differences are magnified as Essex, equally bright, is shown as contemptuous, ungenerous and surly but he is right to describe as 'bollocks' his pal's view that rock & roll is dead and 'trad' is the thing. By the 1970s most 1950s rock & roll stars were still performing and younger British acts like Gary Glitter, Showaddywaddy, the Rubettes and Mud were reworking rock & roll – albeit in a fairly anaemic style. Meanwhile, 'trad' and its typical instruments (trombone, clarinet, banjo and so on) were nowhere to be seen.

The cinema played its part in sustaining rock & roll as British audiences welcomed George Lucas's nostalgic movie, *American Graffiti*, a 'rites-of-passage' tale with a soundtrack, which took chronological poetic licence to evoke the spirit of late Summer 1959/60/61. Many of the recordings were introduced by a real American radio DJ, Wolfman Jack, and Lucas explored class differences and (white) adolescent cultures playfully and with a poignant conclusion implying that formal education might be the best course. This was less clear at the conclusion of *That'll Be the Day*, but in its sequel, *Stardust*, Essex initially enjoys the fruits of his decisions as a rich and famous rock star. However, as with Turner (Mick Jagger) in *Performance*, these rewards turn to dust through excess and over-indulgence, and 'moral' tales about the dangers of hedonism in popular music became increasingly prevalent. In 1972, director Sidney Furie, who had given us the innocent *Young Ones*, directed Diana Ross in the Billie Holiday biopic, *Lady Sings the Blues*, while in 1979 Mark Rydell directed Bette Midler in *The Rose*, a fictional version of the life (and death) of Janis Joplin. These were precedents for recent biopics of damaged and doomed stars like Ray Charles, Johnny Cash, John Lennon, Jim Morrison and Brian Jones. They allow cinema to recreate the past at its leisure, packing it around a series of warnings and moral lessons – where, by contrast, are the cheery tales of Cliff Richard or Paul McCartney?

Documenting the Present

This period offered a number of styles that mined the popular past but, alongside pop's growing nostalgia, there was its persistent craving for the next thing – not least from a younger 'pop' audience, the first that had been born after rock & roll emerged in Britain. Under the guise of self-expression, individuality and innovation, the pop industry pursued a burgeoning and broadening market.

Variety and fragmentation were key elements of the 1970s popular music scene and British television contributed – for example, through highly contrasting programmes like *Top of the Pops*, which was determined almost entirely by the sales of 'singles', and the album-/festival-/club-driven rock show, *The Old Grey Whistle Test*. There were other significant moments on British television, including the controversial behaviour of the Sex Pistols and followers on Thames Television's teatime *Today* programme in December 1976. For interviewer Bill Grundy it was the end of his career while Johnny Rotten remains a media star.

That'll Be the Day and *American Graffiti* were fictions that exploited the recent past. In 1976, Thames Television screened the series *Rock Follies*, about a contemporary female rock vocal trio, which attracted attention for its use of experimental visual and theatre effects. The second series (1977) offered visual images which, alongside videos like 'Bohemian Rhapsody', pointed the way to the next decade and the launch of MTV.

All this contributed to the variety of visual styles accompanying popular music in the period. We have considered the counter-culture and the burgeoning festival scene, rock & roll nostalgia movies, the experimental excesses of *Tommy*, and the folk revival on screen. Many of the major British acts, including the Beatles, Rolling Stones, Pink Floyd and Led Zeppelin, appeared in documentary films in the 1970s. *The Harder They Come* (1972), starring singer Jimmy Cliff, brought reggae to our screens; *Wattstax* (1973) was a black 'Woodstock'; 'Blaxploitation' movies offered soundtracks by Curtis Mayfield, Isaac Hayes and Melvin van Peebles; while *Foxy Brown* (1970) drew on the *Tamla Motown* back catalogue.

David Essex was the first of a number of new British stars to appear in films, while his co-star, Ringo Starr, directed Marc Bolan and Elton John in *Born to Boogie* (1972). Slade starred in the rock drama *Flame* (1974) and the Bee Gees' career enjoyed a new life through their contribution to the disco hit, *Saturday Night Fever*, which, as with *Easy Rider*, led to a series of inferior copies. It also reminds us of the increasing importance of the soundtrack album and other commercial 'tie-ins'. Pop music may have once centred on selling records and live shows but through the 1970s new formats and outlets, including audio cassettes, videotapes and music videos, pointed towards a future of product diversity and profit. In 1973, *American Graffiti* and *That'll Be the Day* had enabled the commercially successful repackaging of hits from the past on double 'soundtrack' albums – at minimal cost and maximum profit.

A certain kind of 'pop' also surfaced in theatrical musicals and cinematic adaptations like *Godspell* (1973), *Jesus Christ Superstar* (1973), *The Rocky Horror Picture Show* (1975), *Catch My Soul* (1976) and *Hair* (1979). Most were of limited interest to the growing rock audience but they had a broader appeal and *The Rocky Horror Picture Show* now enjoys cult status.

In the 1950s, cinema exploited Elvis Presley's musical success, as it had with stars like Bing Crosby, Frank Sinatra and Doris Day, and in Britain the same happened with Tommy Steele and Cliff Richard. But by 1970, they had diminishing box-office appeal. Elvis appeared in a dramatic screen role (*Change of Habit*) for the last time, although documentaries of his live performances in 1970 – *Elvis, That's the Way It Is* – and 1972 – *Elvis on Tour* – compensated fans unable to see him live in Britain.

Mick Jagger was successful in *Performance*, thanks partly to a 'natural' role, but it is harder to be positive about his appearance as *Ned Kelly* (1970). This also reflected attempts by the film industry to exploit the box-office potential of rock stars as 'outsiders'. David Bowie appeared in *The Man Who Fell To Earth* (1976), while Martin Scorsese, who had worked on the *Woodstock* film, pursued his interest in popular music through discerning soundtracks and the documenting of the Band's farewell show, *The Last Waltz* (1978). Other documentaries featuring British acts included *Mad Dogs and Englishmen* with Joe Cocker (1971), *Concert for Bangladesh* with Bob Dylan, Eric Clapton and George Harrison (1972), *Jimi Hendrix* (1973) and *The Kids Are Alright* with the Who (1979). In part – and in Britain in particular – these screen appearances compensated for the top acts' growing preference for fewer large-scale live gigs instead of constant touring and smaller venues.

Rock, Film Genres and Commercial Exploitation

Bowie's appearance as an alien in a 'sci-fi' film raises one interesting issue – the strange lack of cross-over between that genre and modern pop, given the obvious overlap in audiences since the mid-1950s.[359] Through the 1950s' first flowering of the cinematic genre, only *Forbidden Planet* (1956) deviated from conventional cinematic orchestrations, although a few pop hits reflected the growing interesting in outer space – in Britain most obviously 'Telstar'. The soundtrack album for Kubrick's *2001* (1968) enjoyed popularity with the psychedelic generation but through the 1970s neither the dystopian first phase of movies nor the return to innocence and wonder in the films of Lucas and Spielberg linked significantly with modern pop.

Instead, many American films associated with modern pop and rock seem to have been a desperate attempt to cash in by any means. Woodstock star Country Joe McDonald's appearances in films like *Gas-s-s-s* (1970), *Zachariah* (1971) and *More American Graffiti* (1979) are best forgotten and the same might be said about Frank Zappa's *200 Motels* (1971) and Bob Dylan's lengthy *Renaldo and Clara* (1977). These were 'star' vehicles or indulgent projects, which were shown in cinemas and/or became available on video in Britain but have left little lasting impression.

Even the demise of the Beatles did not deter the film industry. In 1976 Susan Winslow directed *All This and World War II*, a documentary montage of the war with a soundtrack of Beatles covers by Elton John, the Bee Gees, Rod Stewart, Bryan Ferry, David Essex and others. If that was mediocre, *Sgt Pepper's Lonely Hearts Club Band* (Michael Schultz) two years later was more expensive and worse. It starred the now ubiquitous Bee Gees, Peter Frampton, Aerosmith, Earth, Wind & Fire and performers like Frankie Howerd, Paul Nicholas and Donald Pleasence in a visual updating of the 1967 album. The director, who had shown promise with the black disco-oriented comedy *Car Wash,* came out of this project with little credit – but as with Winslow's effort, there was the inevitable (and awful) soundtrack album. In 1978 Robert Zemeckis's *I Wanna Hold Your Hand* provided a fictional narrative about four young Beatles fans with a soundtrack from the group's recordings, and in 1979 came the first cinematic biography of the Beatles, the made-for-TV *Birth of the Beatles* (Richard Marquand).

The gradual disappearance of American funding from the British film industry in the 1970s encouraged cheap television spin-offs or comedy series. The *Carry On* series ignored pop but Norman Cohen directed *Confessions of a Pop Performer* (1975), which was everything you might fear from that series, while in 1971, the Kinks provided the soundtrack to *Percy* – a man who undergoes a penis transplant. Musicians also made more serious contributions to higher-status films – for example, Alan Price's performances in *O Lucky Man!* (1973) – which provide a kind of Brechtian disruption to the narrative structure. Warner Bros. hoped that Price would help to popularise the film but his main chart successes had come in the previous decade – once again cinema was playing 'catch-up' with pop music.

Experimental Film

There were some experimental films with links to popular music. Peter Whitehead revisited earlier footage, including the Rolling Stones and Jimi Hendrix, in a meditation on film construction in *Fire in the Water* (1977). *The Body* (1971) included a soundtrack by Ron Geesin and Pink Floyd's Roger Waters, and in 1979 Derek Jarman made the short *Broken English: Three Songs by Marianne Faithfull.* Jarman also responded to the punk moment with his film *Jubilee*. *Jubilee* sought partly to invoke the spirit of Britain's first Elizabethan period and many punks dismissed it as failing to represent their world accurately[360] while others identified the emergence of an important new British film-maker. Jarman came to it from the relative success of his homo-erotic *Sebastiane* and began *Jubilee* as a series of 8mm recordings of punk artist Jordan – indeed, the film draws attention to the role of young women in British punk, which was more significant than previous sub-cultures. The punks preferred *The Punk Rock Movie* (1977) by West Indian DJ Don Letts but Miles suggests that, while *Jubilee* was never conceived as documentary, 'it is now considered to be the best film about British punk . . . It captured the punk sensibility of the time, albeit in a highly romanticised art film format.'[361] In 1977 German director Wolfgang Buld offered the documentary *Punk in London*, and two years later Julien Temple produced his 100-minute montage on the Sex Pistols,

The Great Rock 'n' Roll Swindle (1979), which, in visual style, reflected the energies of that British punk period.

From the 1960s black British film-makers began to make films about their experiences. This grew through following decades, and the films often displayed a distinct relationship with black musical styles, especially reggae – the dub aesthetic was significant in the editing of some more experimental films. In 1970, Horace Ové directed an hour-long documentary of a Wembley concert of some of Jamaica's finest acts in *Reggae*. Black British poet Linton Kwesi Johnson was portrayed in the 1979 documentary *Dread, Beat an' Blood* by Franco Rosso, whose film *Babylon* featured music by British reggae group Aswad. Similarly, in 1978, *Blacks Britannia* (David Koff) offered an account of black life in Britain with a soundtrack by Steel Pulse. In the 1980s the films of Horace Ové, Black Audio & Video Collective, Sankofa and their member Isaac Julien would extend these representations of black British culture – usually with significant soundtracks in films like *Handsworth Songs* (1986) and *Looking for Langston* (1989).

As the 1970s drew to a close, *Radio On* and *Quadrophenia* both featured Sting and, with their considerations of youth cultures, 'book-ended' the 1970s with *Bronco Bullfrog* (1970), which had opened the decade in the tradition of British dramatic realism. Barney Platts-Mills's low-budget, independent film was developed in a project for young people from London's East End at Joan Littlewood's Theatre Workshop and was semi-improvised by non-professional performers. The score was by Audience, a folk/prog-rock band of that time. It was an extraordinary start to the decade in British cinema – but what followed in popular music and the films that linked to it was also remarkable in range and variety, if not always in creative ambition or achievement.

Conclusion

I have argued that the film industry had a varied relationship to popular music in the 1970s. The popular music styles of the period were eclectic, innovatory and nostalgic in turn, and the film and television industries responded in a piecemeal and often partisan fashion to the richness of popular music culture, offering limited opportunities to some performers and substantial ones to others. While it appears that the relationship between popular music and film in this period was one of casual interdependence and economic expedience, it is clear that film had a crucial role to play in the commodification and recycling of youth sub-cultures and their musical tastes, to an unprecedented extent.

Part II

CHAPTER 9

Key Players

The film policies of successive governments failed to address the major economic crisis which faced the industry in the 1970s. As Barber argued in Chapter 1, the long-established mechanisms of state support – the Quota, the Eady levy and the NFFC – were inconsistent in their effects, and did not proceed from a coherent policy. Government innovations, with the exception of the abortive National Film Finance Consortium, were largely directed at promoting the independent sector, which resulted in a reconfiguration of the fields of power. As Porter has shown in Chapter 5, the National Film School and the BFI Production Board were instrumental in developing new talents.

In this chapter we shall examine the effects of the economic crisis upon the film culture at large, surveying the work of significant film-makers and speculating about the sources of their originality. The first issue we need to raise is whether the old conglomerates were able to draw on any substantially new cultural materials in order to reinvigorate the commercial film culture. Our second concern is to assess the scope and degree of innovation which independent producers were able to adduce. The third issue is the extent to which the unstable film market affected the creative autonomy of directors in this period. In addressing these central questions, this chapter will offer an interpretation of the relationship between capital, culture and creativity in this fragmented film culture.

Producers I – The Conglomerates

The old institutions had been the mainstay of the British industry in the 1960s: Rank, Anglo-Amalgamated, Associated British Picture Corporation (ABPC) and British Lion. These companies were affected firstly by the influx of American capital during that decade and its withdrawal thereafter, and secondly by their agglomeration of non-film business assets. Both Rank and ABPC retained their exhibition duopoly but, by the end of the 1960s, the EMI recording business had subsumed ABPC and Anglo-Amalgamated. The Rank Organisation, meanwhile, had acquired the office equipment firm Xerox. By the end of the 1970s, both Rank's Xerox arm and EMI's alliance with Thorn Electrical would be more significant to both businesses than cinema.[362] During the decade EMI also took over the remaining independent distributor British Lion. We need to establish the effects of these commercial changes on the roles of producers and the kinds of film that they were able to make.

In the 1970s Rank scaled back its production activities. By mid-decade Sir John Davis had sacked the Head of Production at Pinewood, Edmond Chilton, with the clear intention 'to withdraw Rank entirely from active film production'.[363] In the interim, there was an increasing distance between management and film-makers. Rank's only significant production franchise remained the *Carry On* films, which it had taken over in 1963. However, by the 1970s the *Carry Ons* were a spent force, culturally speaking. As Ede relates in Chapter 4, the series' low production values made it increasingly formulaic. The long-standing partnership of Gerald Thomas and Peter Rogers now produced films which were both opportunistic and conservative.[364] This attitude is most obvious with *Carry On Emmannuelle*, which is a flagrant attempt to jump on the soft-porn bandwagon. The team's customary *élan* is lacking, and candid sex – as opposed to their familiar picture-postcard type – seems a furtive disappointment. It is clear that Rank was unable to adapt to changes in the sexual landscape.

EMI took over ABPC and Anglo-Amalgamated in 1969. Bernard Delfont, Head of EMI's Film Division, appointed Bryan Forbes as Head of Production. However, Forbes's discontents with EMI were legendary, and he described his experiences there as 'watching a deformed dog urinate on yesterday's sandcastles'.[365] In his brief tenure Forbes directed only one picture, *The Raging Moon* (1970), but was midwife to the formation of a short-lived partnership between EMI and MGM (who had pulled out of Borehamwood) at Elstree studios, where *The Railway Children* (1970), *Tales of Beatrix Potter* (1971), *Get Carter*, *Villain* (1971) and Losey's *The Go-Between* and Patrick Garland's *A Doll's House* (1973) were made.[366] But EMI, under Forbes's principled conservatism, lacked both the confidence to specialise in any one area, and the pragmatism to cut its coat according to its cloth.

In 1973, Nat Cohen, who had run Anglo-Amalgamated, assumed overall control of production at EMI. Cohen was a canny entrepreneur, with a reputation for backing safe and predictable films like Frankie Howerd's *Up* series (1971–1972) and the *Steptoe and Son* (1972 and 1973) TV spin-offs. A brief partnership with James Carreras at Hammer produced three features from *On the Buses*. Cohen put up half the funding for Goodtimes' *That'll Be the Day*, and eagerly supported its sequel, *Stardust*, with assistance from the NFFC, where his credit proved durable. He also financed bigger genre projects such as *The Boy Friend* (1971), *Fear is the Key* (1972) and *The Final Programme*. Deeply competitive, Cohen was one of the few producers from an earlier period who managed to retain a foothold in the precarious film business in the first half of the 1970s. Despite his ambitious support for John Brabourne's lavish and lucrative *Murder on the Orient Express* (1974), by mid-decade Cohen and Carreras were looking increasingly like yesterday's men, lacking the vision to lead EMI in the international market. Although, in Michael Deeley's words, 'Bernard Delfont knew little about films, he realised none the less that . . . EMI's film management was over the hill'.[367] A shrewd businessman, if nothing else, Delfont saw the energetic partnership of Deeley and Barry Spikings at the financially crippled British Lion as a takeover opportunity with mutual benefits.

British Lion was the sole surviving independent studio at the beginning of the 1970s. In 1964, their principal shareholders (the Boultings, Sidney Launder, Frank Gilliat and David Kingsley) had been bought out by the NFFC, who had in turn, after much protracted deliberation, passed control to a consortium called Star Associated led by Michael Balcon for £1.6 million.[368] Yet British Lion Films Limited suffered from the company's historical difficulties: expensive studio assets at Shepperton, lack of an exhibition circuit, and unreliable relations with independent producers at home and distributors abroad. It was also exceptionally exposed to the effects of the reduction of American investment in British 'runaway' production at the end of the 1960s. According to Alexander Walker, the newly floated British Lion was losing '£12,000 a week by the start of 1972', and reduced to producing low-budget fare such as *I, Monster* for Amicus, and *Fright* (1971) and *Endless Night* for EMI-MGM at Elstree.[369] As Barber noted, the NFFC added its name and money to this ignoble list, which was rounded off by the lame Dick Emery comedy *Ooh . . . You Are Awful*. And indeed, it was.

In April 1972 British Lion was sold by Star Associated to the tycoon John Bentley, whose Barclay Securities invested £7.5 million, apparently on the strength of the development potential of Lion's Shepperton Studios.[370] To appease union fears of site development Bentley appointed Canadian producer Peter Snell in July 1972, quickly promoting him from Head of Production to Managing Director. At the time Nicolas Roeg's *Don't Look Now* was being shot on location in Venice, and Snell brought with him playwright Anthony Shaffer's script of *The Wicker Man*.

Bentley, knowing little about film and caring even less, backed the project with Snell as producer and Shaffer's advertising partner, Robin Hardy, as first-time director, according it a modest £420,000 budget and an on-location shoot that, like Roeg's film, would return to Shepperton only for post-production. British Lion's precarious finances, its eccentric management structure, its ignorant executives (compared with its predecessors Boulting, Launder and Gilliat), and the distance between studio backers and film-makers on location created the conditions whereby its recent lame titles could be overturned by audacious work such as *Don't Look Now* and *The Wicker Man*. But while both were still in post-production, Barclay Securities sold a 23 per cent stake in British Lion to the business partnership of producer Michael Deeley, journalist Barry Spikings and actor Stanley Baker.

Within three months Deeley, who had cut his teeth at Tony Richardson's Woodfall, had replaced Snell as Managing Director. Meanwhile, John Bentley sold his controlling share in the business to the financial services group J. H. Vavasseur, who formed Lion International as a holding company. These machinations enabled Deeley to forge ahead with production, notwithstanding a stock market collapse during the Winter of 1973–1974.[371] Within two years Deeley was using his American studio contacts to steer British Lion towards international genre pictures. Although Stanley Baker was a casualty of his own prescient assessment of Deeley and Spikings' ambition,[372] their business acumen was not lost on Bernard Delfont at EMI, who 'initiated acquisition talks at the 1975 Cannes Film Festival'.[373]

By the time the takeover was completed, Deeley had relocated to California, and he embarked upon an ambitious programme of six big-budget features: *Death on the Nile* (1978) for Paramount, *Warlords of Atlantis* (1978) and *Arabian Adventure* (1979) for Columbia, *Convoy* with United Artists, *The Deer Hunter* with Universal, and *The Driver* for Twentieth Century Fox (all 1978). As Deeley explained:

> If I could not get from a US major a guarantee yielding 50% of the budget plus a commitment to provide the full costs of prints and advertising in their territory we would not produce the picture . . . This method allowed EMI to produce much bigger pictures at almost no risk, provided we had the discipline to stick to the rules.[374]

Deeley's 'stop-loss' financing technique at EMI proved successful, until it was challenged from an unexpected quarter.

In 1978 Deeley received a call from Bernard Delfont's brother, Lew Grade, who had himself entered international film production, establishing ACC (Associated Communication Company) on the back of his ATV television ownership. Grade had successfully persuaded director Blake Edwards to revive his partnership with Peter Sellers, who played the hapless French detective Inspector Clouseau. Three very popular and lucrative features ensued: *Return of the Pink Panther* (1974), *The Pink Panther Strikes Again* (1976) and *Revenge of the Pink Panther* (1978). Made at the newly branded Shepperton Studio Centre, sold off when British Lion was absorbed by EMI, the series enjoyed continuity of personnel, a familiar formula based upon slapstick and European stereotypes, and international distribution from United Artists. Grade was flattered by this notable success and launched a programme of big-budget productions, which included *The Eagle Has Landed* (1976). However, ACC were unable to sustain this costly programme without guaranteed distribution. Grade's suggestion to Deeley was that EMI should set up its own US distribution network, 'then we would not only keep all the profits but also make money from the distributor's fee, currently being nabbed by the major'.[375] But this was a high-risk strategy which Deeley rebuffed.

In 1979, Delfont told Deeley that EMI's financial difficulties (in other sectors of the recently formed Thorn–EMI conglomerate) meant that it could no longer sustain film production, despite recent successes.[376] For Deeley, this was a smokescreen to cloak EMI's investment in Grade's US distribution interests. He left the company, although Spikings remained; EMI and ACC set up a joint international sales division, under Grade's chairmanship, called Associated Film Distribution Inc. This proved to be the recipe for the financial disaster that Deeley had predicted. It not only promoted British films of indifferent quality, such as John Schlesinger's lamentable *Honky Tonk Freeway* (1981), but also incurred the wrath of the US majors and fractured the beneficial business relations which Deeley had done much to foster.

The survival of the old integrated combines as modern conglomerates clearly depended on the entrepreneurial instincts and flexibility of those executives who had enough presence of mind, independence and guile to steer their organisations effectively. And while the large conglomerates, sustained by non-film interests, did subsidise cinema, their executives lacked the imagination of independent producers.

Producers II – The Independents

The notion of independence in 1970s British cinema is a complex one. We need to delineate the character and operational approach of different film-makers in order to understand the film culture. Two points are important here. Firstly, production arrangements were ad hoc and not (apart from union agreements) subject to established practices or formal chains of command; many film deals were negotiated on a one-off basis. Secondly, the 'old guard' and newcomers alike shared an unprecedented lack of confidence about the market in which they were operating. These circumstances marked a breach with the established continuities of film-making practice, which forced some to return to residual forms, and led others to push the boundaries of imagination or taste. So this was a cinema polarised between extreme conservatism and often haphazard innovation.

The commercial film industry's difficulties opened up a space for creative independents, working in different contexts and with a range of methods. As mentioned in Part I, the BFI Production Board deployed its new-found affluence to sponsor feature-length films for cinema release, which altered the complexion of the independent production sector. In assessing the roles of independent producers operating within the commercial industry, Walker rightly foregrounds the emergent careers of David Puttnam and Don Boyd.[377] It is instructive to observe their entrepreneurial behaviour and to consider their handling of finance and collaborators, in order to account for the films they made.

Sandy Lieberson, who had arrived in Europe from his native Los Angeles in the early 1960s, was, by 1965, working for the Creative Management Agency in London.[378] He discovered Warner Bros.' interest in casting his client Mick Jagger in a feature film, and acquired the rights to Donald Cammell's script for *Performance*. Lieberson met Puttnam, who was running a photographic agency, and their shared ambitions resulted in two fledging companies: Goodtimes Enterprises (to make feature films) and Visual Programmes Systems (to exploit the nascent technology in video recording equipment). The latter initiative found financial backing from the bankers Rothschild.

Puttnam's suburban, grammar-school background gave him a keen edge to prove himself, tempered with a highly moral social attitude amidst times of hedonistic excess.[379] He also had level-headed business acumen, and a canny sense of how to exploit new opportunities in the creative industries of the late 1960s. However, between the innovation of *Performance* (which launched Goodtimes) and the excesses of *Lisztomania* and *Trick or Treat* (which effectively sank them), their film output was remarkably cautious. In Chapter 8 Allen explains the context in which popular music became ripe for cinematic exploitation. Goodtimes launched a series of films which would mine this profitable seam: *Memory* (1971), *The Pied Piper*, *That'll Be the Day*, *Stardust*, *Flame* and *Bugsy Malone*. There are several aspects of their business practices which brought these projects to fruition, and advanced the careers of some notable new talents.

Firstly, they were flexible in their roles on each new project. For example, Puttnam worked closely with screenwriter Ray Connolly on the autobiographical script of *That'll Be the Day*, while Lieberson brokered the innovatory deal with Ronco records to supply half the budget on the advice of a music publishing lawyer. As Lieberson notes, 'we were the first . . . to get a record company to help finance the movie, [and] to release the soundtrack simultaneously'.[380] The willingness of each partner to perform a range of tasks in promoting their work was the key to their success; they paid attention to each element in a project and left nothing to chance. And, as Barber demonstrated in Chapter 2, their handling of the censorship of *Stardust* revealed their pragmatism.

Secondly, Puttnam openly courted the film unions, the NFFC, and Nat Cohen at EMI. Of the forty-eight British long films which received support from the NFFC during the 1970s, eight were Puttnam/Lieberson pictures, and as many again had backing from EMI. But adept as he was in the boardroom, Puttnam was not above touring first-run West End cinemas where his films were showing, in order to buy up unsold seats which would generate a street placard announcing 'SOLD OUT'.[381] Lieberson supported new directors like Michael Apted and Richard Loncraine, encouraged producers like Gavrik Losey, and pursued documentary and television projects.[382]

Thirdly, Puttnam and Lieberson spread their risk across a variety of different subjects. Although shrewd in tapping into the youth market, they did not pander to it; as Allen noted in Chapter 8, *That'll Be the Day* and *Stardust* remain cautionary tales. They also backed Robert Fuest's sci-fi thriller, *The Final Programme*, and in 1973 made two documentaries, *Swastika* and *The Double-Headed Eagle*, based upon original Nazi film footage recovered from the archives of Albert Speer, Hitler's architect.

By mid-decade Goodtimes was sufficiently confident to sign a three-picture deal with Ken Russell to make *Mahler* and *Lisztomania* and a biopic of George Gershwin. The second film ran into difficulties (which were largely the result of Russell's unbridled indulgences) and they pulled out.[383] Following this, another débâcle ensued on the abortive *Trick or Treat*, financed by EMI and *Playboy* magazine, and starring a truculent Bianca Jagger.[384] During the shoot Jagger broke the terms of her contract by refusing to perform in the scripted bedroom scenes, and director Michael Apted was forced to consider hiring body doubles. Lieberson recalls:

> there was a lot of hesitation. It's going to get out that it was doubles and things like that . . . And then EMI got cold feet over the whole thing. They said, 'Pull the plug.' So then we had a huge fight, because we said 'Fine, well then we're going to sue Jagger.' She'd refused to perform under a contract, and had approved the script and everything. And EMI and *Playboy* said, 'Well no, we don't want to get involved in a law suit; it might look bad for us.'[385]

This time Puttnam and Lieberson fell out over the question of whether to pursue litigation. Lieberson was determined, but Puttnam was hesitant, perhaps because 'there was a view that this was a weird sex film,'[386] or perhaps because he feared souring relations with EMI. He refused. Puttnam and Lieberson parted company, the former going on to produce *The Duellists*, the latter backing *Jabberwocky* (1977). Both producers were subsequently courted by Hollywood.

The partnership of Puttnam and Lieberson was ultimately wrong-footed by the very excesses of 1970s independent film-making which they had tried so cautiously to avoid. Their independent productions establish, therefore, that there is no obvious link between independence, radicalism and risk in 1970s British cinema. Indeed, in another era Puttnam would doubtless, like his hero Michael Balcon, have run a tight studio ship.[387]

Don Boyd was another key producer to emerge in the 1970s. A graduate of the London Film School, he consistently refused to define himself solely as a producer. Rather he saw himself as a director *manqué* – in his own phrase, a 'director-oriented audience-conscious film-marketing editor'.[388] Boyd wanted to make artistically ambitious films which held their own at the box office.

Boyd established an innovatory way of sourcing and spending money. He financed a raft of seven features in a single year by cultivating patrons like Roy Tucker, whose Rossminster group assembled investment portfolios from private donors to provide development money for BoydsCo's projects: *The Tempest*, *The Great Rock 'n' Roll Swindle*, *Hussy*, *Scum* and *Sweet William* (all 1979). The central point here is the distance between the sources of capital and the creative use to which it was put.[389] This was a high-risk strategy, but it encouraged considerable creative freedom.

Once the money was raised, Boyd worked on one film at a time and was very intimately involved at the production level. He insisted on a degree of authorship on Alan Clarke's *Scum*:

> I had complete artistic and commercial control over every element of the film from the day I decided to produce to the day it was released . . . I monitored every version of the script, and all the details of casting. I saw every frame of the rushes . . . and intervened on Alan's behalf when the line producers tried to soften the rape scene.[390]

Boyd was careful in interview to accord some artistic autonomy to the director and other workers on the film, but attention to his papers make it clear that he viewed *Scum* as his film, and that its bleakness and radicalism came from him:

> Our film attempted to show that the penal system here continues to fail. It also attempts to mirror some aspects of contemporary British society . . . The film has helped to adjust the authorities' opinions about Borstal.[391]

The sheer range and audaciousness of Boyd's output can be seen by contrasting *Scum* with Derek Jarman's *The Tempest*. The first was realist and confrontational; the second was visually audacious. On *The Tempest* Boyd again claimed a degree of control over the film; he was involved 'in every millimetre from the conception, casting, rushes, editing and mix'.[392] He had a realistic sense of what the film would cost and earn; he advanced £150,000 and all he hoped for was that 'Derek's audience would cover its costs'.[393] He clearly trusted that the art-house market would respond just enough to support this risk-taking film. Boyd's combination of financial flair and cultural competence make him an unusual yet key figure in 1970s film production.

Gavrik Losey was another independent producer to come to prominence during the 1970s. Puttnam and Lieberson gave him his first major production credit on *Flame*, and he went on to produce *Little Malcolm and His Struggle Against the Eunuchs* (1974), *Agatha* (1978) and *Babylon*. As Shaw has shown in Chapter 6, Losey was a flexible producer. However, he sometimes neglected, or sought to evade, the protocols of contract negotiation and the finer points of budget accounts in his desire to support the vision of a particular film-maker. This was evident on the chaotic production of *Agatha*.[394]

The *jeunes premiers* Puttnam, Lieberson, Boyd and Losey can be characterised as a new breed of independent producers who shared a serious intent about producing quality cinema for mainstream audiences. Some established independents – conservative by background as much as instinct – were also able to adapt to the prevailing conditions. John Knatchbull, seventh Baron Brabourne, is a good example. From the upper reaches of the aristocracy and married to Lord Mountbatten's daughter, Brabourne demonstrates that 1970s film culture was catholic in the range of people it could accommodate. Diffident in manner, but powerful in social connections which he did not scruple to use, Brabourne was a producer who saw his job as choosing the initial story, finalising the script, and fine-tuning the personnel so that the project ran smoothly.[395] He worked closely with his production manager, Richard Goodwin, throughout the 1970s, and together they made *Murder on the Orient Express* and *Death on the Nile*. The first film attracted an international cast, because UK tax laws then offered a good deal for foreign actors.[396] The tax situation had changed by the time Brabourne and Goodwin made *Death on the Nile*, so the cast was less illustrious but the performances were equally stylised.

Sir John Woolf was another producer with a long pedigree in the film industry, who managed to adapt to circumstances in the 1970s. Woolf thought that financial success in films depended on having the right distribution arrangements as well as the right script.[397] His 1970s career showed the risks he was capable of taking. He set up an investment trust to house his film profits, and was adept at exploiting the Anglo-European co-production treaties, producing *Day of the Jackal* and *The Odessa File* (1974).[398]

Other important producers hailed from rather different backgrounds, and exploited very different niches in the film market. Michael Klinger was the son of a Polish immigrant Londoner who graduated into the film business in partnership with Tony Tenser, having run Soho strip clubs in the late 1950s. He attempted to engage with new economic conditions, while appearing old-fashioned; Sheridan Morley described him as resembling 'Nothing so much as a flamboyant character actor doing impressions of Louis B. Mayer'.[399] He was willing to take enormous risks and produced films for varying markets, but found extraordinary problems bringing many of his projects to the screen. In the 1960s, Klinger and Tenser's Compton-Tekli had produced some high-status films such as *Repulsion* (1965) and *Cul-de-Sac* (1966). Klinger then left Tenser to set up his own company, Avton Films, where he was able to procure American finance for *Get Carter* and *Pulp* (1972). By mid-decade it looked as though Klinger had hit his stride with his backing of the *Confessions* series, but he kept changing his tack. Sometimes he would intervene in the scripts and the minutiae of performance, and sometimes he would hold himself aloof from the details and pay attention to issues of distribution.[400]

Klinger also made international action pictures including *Gold* (1974) and *Shout at the Devil* (1976), but acute funding difficulties beset him in this volatile market, and wrangles with British distributors like Hemdale thwarted his progress.[401] Klinger's difficulties can also be interpreted as a consequence of his particular attitude to agency; wanting to be everywhere and to do everything can have a limiting effect.

When Klinger left Compton in 1966, Tenser set up Tony Tenser Films Ltd. as an independent distributor, taking his associate Laurie Marsh with him. Tenser backed Michael Reeves's *The Sorcerers* (1967) and *Witchfinder General* (1968); on the strength of their success he launched

Tigon Pictures as a distributor and Tigon British Film Productions Ltd. While exploitation remained the mainstay of Tigon's product, there was a shift away from standard low-budget horror – *The Beast in the Cellar* (1970) and *Blood on Satan's Claw* (1971) – to a wider variety. Tigon made the children's adventure, *Black Beauty* (1971); a Raquel Welch western, *Hannie Caulder* (1971); comedies, *The Magnificent Seven Deadly Sins* (1971) and *Not Now Darling* (1972); a sci-fi TV spin-off, *Doomwatch* (1972); the contemporary drama, *Neither the Sea nor the Sand* (1972); and a Royal Shakespeare Company adaptation of Strindberg's *Miss Julie* (1972).

Laurie Marsh attracted the attention of new City investors Batavia (who dealt in rubber); their financial commitment enabled the Tigon Group to acquire the Classic and Essoldo cinema chains in 1971. In a year, Marsh had enlarged Tigon's asset value from an estimated £250,000 to an extraordinary £15 million.[402] There was even talk of an amalgamation with Hammer as the exploitation market (including newcomers Amicus and Tyburn) became overcrowded. But Tigon's production success was short-lived. None of its major features (apart from *Black Beauty*) made money, and they failed in the American market. Faced with the 1973 downturn that affected the whole industry, they were obliged to cease production and concentrate their business in distribution and exhibition, which remained lucrative. Tenser's business sense, marketing flair and successful partnerships had ensured Tigon's transition from exploitation to mainstream and its corporate position as a third major behind Rank and EMI. But arguably, the further he moved away from the formula product he understood, the less successful he was in the fickle climate of 1970s British cinema.

Pete Walker is probably the most excoriated producer/director of the 1970s. However, he repays attention because of his authorial control. His production and distribution company, Heritage Films, specialised in short sex films in the 1960s.[403] In the 1970s, he used the sale of its home movie distribution business to finance feature films, which he both produced and directed.[404] Walker had alternated sexploitation with horror in the late 1960s, but in the 1970s judged it advantageous to develop horror films exclusively.[405] Most remarkable in his extensive output was the trilogy *House of Whipcord*, *Frightmare* and *House of Mortal Sin* (1975), which exemplified Walker's customary tight hold over the production process.

Walker's success in comprehensively transforming the now moribund gothic horror into the contemporary, American-influenced, gory shocker eclipsed a number of other exploitation producers of the period. And his example shows how certain kinds of entrepreneurial creativity could flourish in the fragmented market of 1970s film production, irrespective of cultural respectability. As a producer/director, Walker embodied that successful mix.

Other incursions into film production were made by diverse business interests. Hemdale Corporation was set up by John Daly and David Hemmings in 1967 and pursued a range of showbusiness activities.[406] Some were flamboyant, such as the hire of Wembley Stadium for an Evel Knievel show; others were specifically film-oriented, such as the attempt to buy Isleworth Studios for their own film productions.[407] In 1970 they acquired and rapidly re-sold the Tigon Group; in the same year Hemmings left the company after a board-room wrangle, and Hemdale merged, briefly, with Equity Enterprises.[408] They produced Jean Anouilh's *Time for Loving* (1971), *The Triple Echo* (1972), Robert Enders's ghost story, *Voices* (1973), and J. Lee Thompson's wartime adventure *The Passage* (1978). But as the decade progressed Hemdale International concentrated more on distribution. They handled, amongst others, Goodtimes' *Melody* (1971) and *Tommy*, and Michael Klinger's *Gold* and *Rachel's Man* (1975). For financial reasons Daly relocated to the USA at the end of the 1970s.[409]

Brent Walker, like Hemdale, was a broad-based entertainments and leisure concern. By the mid-1970s George Walker's company had acquired a number of cinemas totalling twenty-four screens nationwide and moved into distribution with business partner Alan Kean (who had worked for the ABC circuit and in rentals at British Lion and MGM-EMI).[410] They specialised in distributing independent American films in the UK, including *Foxy Brown* and *Death Race 2000*, and in 1976 agreed a deal with AIP.[411] They produced a number of British features, including *Tower of Evil* (1972), *Satan's Slave* (1976), *The Stud* (1978), *The Bitch* (1979) and *Quadrophenia*. The key to their success was an eye for unusual exploitation product and vigorous marketing campaigns.[412]

Jake Eberts was a stockbroker in the mid-1970s. As Managing Director of Oppenheimer, he was able to access a range of venture capitalists and take advantage of tax shelter incentives to acquire development money for feature films. To begin with, he knew nothing about films except how deals were brokered, but in 1977 launched Goldcrest in partnership with Michael Stoddart of Electra Investment Trust and the publisher Longman Pearson's Chief Executive Officer, Roger Brooke. They helped producer/director Martin Rosen to raise funds for the animated adaptation of *Watership Down* (1978), and also backed Stuart Cooper's *The Disappearance* (1977) and Ken Loach's *Black Jack* (1979), and persuaded Dodi Fayed to invest in *Breaking Glass* (1980). By the end of the decade

Goldcrest had formed what would become a successful, if short-lived, alliance with David Puttnam.[413]

We have detailed in this section the nature of the transformation in the landscape of 1970s British film production. Specifically, we have shown how the centralised power of the old conglomerates had given way to looser corporate structures. In addition, new independent producers demonstrated a range of innovative financial and production arrangements. Significantly, the effect was to create further distance between funding sources and creative agency, and it allowed free rein to a new breed of producers who were less fettered by the cultural hierarchies of previous periods. These changes had consequences for the type of films directors were able to make and there was a radical shake-up in the range of directorial autonomy.

Directors

Some directors whose careers had flourished in earlier periods were still making films in the 1970s. Often their modes of operation replicated those of their heyday, and their patterns of delegation were ill suited to the film culture of the 1970s. David Lean made only one film in the decade, the remarkable *Ryan's Daughter*. He was marketable due to his earlier successes, and set up funding with MGM for *Ryan's Daughter*, a project which he had conceived after reading *Madame Bovary*. Lean's mode of procedure on the film was as before: a haughty attitude to his sponsors, and the exclusive trust of a small group of familiars. He had always had an inspirational approach to actors, and in *Ryan's Daughter* he deployed this to full effect. But the film's romantic seriousness was fatally out of joint with the critical taste of the period; masterpiece though it was, it was excoriated, and Lean did not make another film for fifteen years.

A sense of hubris soured some other established directors. Veteran Carol Reed, who had made crucial films in the 1940s, fared ill. He felt creatively vulnerable as an independent director and made only one film in the decade: *Follow Me!* (1972). This was dominated by his own sense of artistic bankruptcy:

> I had nothing on my plate when Hal Wallis offered this. That's the value of producers. As an independent, from finding the story, to finding the money, to casting, you've spent two years before you can start shooting. If you like making pictures, you've got to go from one to the other – within reason. It's just like a boxer – there's no good just sitting down.[414]

Someone like Reed, who had spent too long 'sitting down', could not muster the fleet-footedness that was required in the 1970s. Neither could the Boultings nor Launder and Gilliat. Both these producer/director pairs, who had had such productive careers, made few films in the 1970s.

Launder and Gilliat's earlier St Trinian's films had offered a terrified homage to female energy. *The Wildcats of St. Trinian's* (1980) was their last film, and it showed a coarsening of their former flair, with characters called 'Big Frieda' and 'Butch'. Their other film of the period, *Endless Night*, is an interesting attempt to render the plot complexity of Agatha Christie. It successfully deploys the first-person narrative, and underpins the protagonist's ambiguity by the editing, music and décor; it is interesting to compare it with the denser texture of *Murder on the Orient Express* and *Death on the Nile*.[415] Gilliat's minimalist approach to Christie was an innovation in terms of his own practice, but audiences preferred a more luxuriant version.

The Boulting Brothers, those bilious satirists who had taken the Establishment to task in the 1950s and 1960s, made their last films in the 1970s: *There's a Girl in My Soup* (1970) and *Soft Beds, Hard Battles* (1973). Both of these starred Peter Sellers, and although the first did fairly well at the box office, both films lacked the Boultings' customary bite, and the saucy elements were uncertainly handled.[416]

Alexander MacKendrick made his name working at Ealing Studios in the 1950s, and successfully transferred to Hollywood during the 1960s. His attempt to return to British production in 1970 to make *Mary, Queen of Scots* (1971) was plagued by difficulties, and Hal Wallis employed Charles Jarrott to direct instead.[417] MacKendrick returned to the United States to teach and abandoned film-making entirely. Jarrott, by contrast, pursued a successful career in Hollywood, working for many of the major studios. Other older directors remained in America for most of their careers in the 1970s, and only made the occasional foray into British production. J. Lee Thompson's only British film, *The Passage*, drew together various themes in his previous films, but was marred by his inability to control Malcolm McDowell's performance as a psychopathic SS officer, wild-eyed and sporting a swastika jockstrap.[418]

A contrast may be drawn between older directors who could not adapt, and directors of the New Wave who still had creative energy. Tony Richardson had directed a range of key films of the 1960s for his own company, Woodfall, which had financial support from United Artists. But in the 1970s, Richardson's two absolutes – location shooting and improvisation – were viewed with some suspicion by American backers, and he had problems obtaining finance. Richardson directed *A Delicate Balance* (1973) and *Dead Cert* (1974). He followed these with the risk-taking *Joseph Andrews* (1976), in which the structure, tone and performative styles should be attributed to him. Richardson had a major hand in adapting the script, and was responsible for the outright paganism of the country scenes; his left-wing materialism was combined with a rigorous attention to period detail, which was challenged by the extravagant costumes and hairstyles. This all produced a problematically mixed text, in which the *picaro* figure (Jim Dale), invented by Richardson, sets the whole plot in motion. Richardson's confident deployment of residual cultural motifs, combined with his political and sexual radicalism, made *Joseph Andrews* an important but neglected film of the period.

John Schlesinger had had a distinguished British career in the 1960s, which led to opportunities in Hollywood such as *Midnight Cowboy* (1969). Schlesinger found it hard to thrive in Britain in the 1970s, directing only *Sunday Bloody Sunday* (1971) and *Yanks* (1979). However, the quality and inventiveness of the first film outweighs the paucity of the overall output. Schlesinger's established partnership with Joseph Janni underpinned the success of *Sunday Bloody Sunday*. This relationship worked because of clearly defined areas of expertise.[419] The film, which deals with homosexuality and its emotional discontents, was innovatory in its combination of a calm demeanour with an intense emotionality of tone. Schlesinger himself argued that his own Jewishness and sexual orientation fed into the subject in a particularly poignant way.[420] Struggles with Penelope Gilliat over the script meant that every word was contested, until the resultant treatment was hammered into rigorous shape.[421] *Sunday Bloody Sunday* was that *rara avis* in British film culture, a liberal film which was well received by both critics and audiences.

Besides those who were from the radical edge of 1960s cinema, there were directors from earlier mainstream cinema who managed to adapt to the new circumstances. Don Sharp, for example, had directed a varied range of films, including several Hammer horrors, and never claimed *auteur* standing.[422] His pragmatism meant that he could work confidently with substandard material. *Psychomania* (1972) in particular, in spite of the absurdity of its plot, is thoroughly convincing due to its textural coherence. Even the spectacle of Beryl Reid being turned into a frog is accorded the seriousness of grand myth. That is the mark of a good commercial artist: to be able to pick up on those popular motifs that hold the culture together. Sharp's remakes of earlier film classics, *The Thirty Nine Steps* (1978) and *The Four Feathers* (1978), are remarkable in the way they pay visual homage to their progenitors, while explicitly crafting them for a new age. The Big Ben sequence in *The Thirty Nine Steps* is an inspired example of how a small idea can carry enormous narrative weight – turning back time and yearning for the past, while simultaneously displaying an athletic masculinity. And the pace of *The Four Feathers* owes much to an awareness of the attractions of the themes of disguise and gentry culture. Sharp made one really remarkable film in the decade, *Hennessy* (1975). This is a rare example of a film made about the 'troubles' in Northern Ireland. It had a stellar cast and a tight script, but sank without trace, probably because it touched too many raw nerves.

Unlike Sharp, the majority of established directors who survived in the 1970s were journeymen. Val Guest, for example, had cut his teeth at Gainsborough in the 1930s, and was prolific thereafter. He directed one of the most popular films of the 1970s, *Confessions of a Window Cleaner*. Guest had a sure sense of how the story should be nuanced for the mass audience, but made no claim to be anything other than efficient.[423] A comparable figure is Ken Annakin. Despite his long track record, it is hard to trace any consistent theme throughout his films. In the 1970s he made co-productions *The Call of the Wild* (1972), *Paper Tiger* (1974) and *The Fifth Musketeer* (1977), and directed television films in the USA. On reflection, he rather lamely ventured that his *œuvre* was held together by 'a fascination with human beings and their endless variations of behaviour in different settings'.[424]

Some older directors managed to profit from the surge of sex films in the 1970s. Sidney Hayers made films which inserted violent scenes into otherwise traditional narratives: *Assault* (1970), *Revenge* (1971) and *All Coppers Are . . .* (1971). Gerry O'Hara, who had been given his directorial break with Compton-Tekli in the 1960s, directed *The Brute* (1976), *The Bitch* and others. These were glossy soft-porn, and had a sly knowingness and an implicit critique of the sexual market. O'Hara also directed *Feelings* (1974), an opportunistic piece about test-tube babies. Playing both sides against the middle in typical 1970s manner, he also directed for the Children's Film Foundation. The readiness to turn one's hand to anything was a very useful skill for some directors. James Hill, who had directed *Born Free* (1966), made a range of animal films in the 1970s such as *Black Beauty* and *The Belstone Fox* (1973), but also had recourse to a sex spoof with *The Man From O.R.G.Y.* (1970).

Other directors, who had been solid performers rather than high fliers, were unable to continue at their peak under the new conditions. Lewis Gilbert had specialised in war films in the 1950s, and his opus was emotionally restrained. But this quality was not required for the Bond films that Gilbert directed: *The Spy Who Loved Me* and *Moonraker*. Guy Hamilton, by contrast, made the earlier Bond films – *Diamonds Are Forever*, *Live and Let Die* (1973), *The Man with the Golden Gun* (1974) – but his temperament was quite different. He had made a series of action films in the 1960s, and was unworried by the issues of motivation that preoccupied Gilbert. That may be one way of accounting for the greater artistic coherence and deftness of touch which characterise Gilbert's 1970s Bond films.

Some directors managed to make a living by their very flexibility. Peter Collinson, for example, had had experience with co-production from his work on *The Italian Job* (1969) and so was able to direct a clutch of international co-productions, including the Agatha Christie adaptation *And Then There Were None* (1974). Claude Whatham had directed in television, and his *That'll Be the Day* and *Swallows and Amazons* (1974) were competent but stylistically orthodox. Middle-of-the-road directors who wished neither to be compliant nor to make soft porn went under.

Michael Tuchner was another example of a director who was flexible in his methods and eclectic in his manner, though he worked best within the realist mode. After directing some successful TV plays, his first film *Villain*, was tautly constructed and shot, with a proliferation of tight close-ups and bleak location shots. *Villain* was scripted by Dick Clement and Ian La Fresnais, and Tuchner clearly accorded well with their world-view, as there are stylistic similarities between this and his film of *The Likely Lads* (1976), which they also scripted.[425] Tuchner directed a slick version of Alistair McLean's *Fear is the Key* for American producers, and *Mister Quilp* (1975), a musical version of Dickens's *The Old Curiosity Shop*, in which he abandoned his customary soberness of style. He subsequently worked as a director for American television.

Michael Apted also entered film from television directing, and had a varied career in the 1970s. His films were all precisely structured and showed strong empathy for the female characters. *The Triple Echo* (1972) identifies the pain of being both a 'real' woman and a 'masquerade'. *Stardust* focuses on the struggles of the abandoned wife and the dignified mistress. *The Squeeze* (1977) is a violent thriller, but gives narrative and emotional space to the ex-wife. *Agatha* was an account of Agatha Christie's disappearance in 1926, and again gave the heroine space to breathe.[426] The abortive *Trick or Treat* project has been mentioned before, but it provides evidence of Apted's extraordinary ability to empathise with female characters. Ray Connolly's account of the script meetings in a restaurant is expressed as high comedy, but stresses Apted's temporary assumption of female identity.[427]

Ken Hughes was less versatile than Apted, and his 1970s career was uneven. *Cromwell* (1970) was slow-moving, though imaginatively conceived, and performed well at the box office. Hughes then made *Alfie Darling* (1975), which was critically slated but which had an inventive take on troubled masculinity. Hughes then declared himself bankrupt, and claimed to have lived for a year on beans on toast. His was an admirably complex sensibility, but he was unable either to compromise with the new conditions, or to be confident about his vision, and consequently ceased to direct.

All the above directors worked in a range of genres. The fantasy mode, in particular, enabled many directors in the 1970s to flourish. Fantasy has its roots deep in Romanticism; it abandons straightforward dialectic juxtapositions, and proceeds instead from the idea of subjective transformation and the law of desire. As a mode, fantasy released many directors from what they perceived as the straitjacket of naturalism.

Ken Russell's 1970s work confirms his place in the Romantic canon, but he required discipline to produce his best work. Judging by *The Boy Friend*, *The Devils* and *Tommy*, it looks as though Russell worked best as an adaptor. *The Boy Friend* is a sustained pastiche of the 1930s. *The Devils* was based on Aldous Huxley's novel, and makes a swingeing attack on established religion and celibacy, presenting both as a prisonhouse of the spirit. *Tommy* was a cinematic version of the Who's 'rock opera', which presented a stylised recreation of 1950s popular culture.

Russell's imaginative collaborations with costume designer Shirley Russell, and artists Derek Jarman (on *The Devils* and *Savage Messiah*) and Paul Dufficey (on *Tommy*) created a coherent visual symbolism. Sadly, his three composer 'biopics', *The Music Lovers*, *Mahler* and *Lisztomania*, failed due to their visual and financial excesses. By the time of *Valentino* (1977), Russell was quoting from, rather than transforming, the materials of the past. None the less, Russell's 1970s work is remarkable for his insistence on the triumph of the imagination; at every stage his work engages critically with realism.

John Boorman made more pragmatic choices in order to free himself to dabble in the fantastic. Following the success of *Point Blank* (1967), his American projects were *Hell in the Pacific* (1968), *Deliverance* (1972) and *Exorcist II* (1977) – all slick enough. But they were interspersed by two extraordinary British-made films: *Leo the Last* (1970), which was an uneasy meditation on charisma and urban masculinities, and *Zardoz* (1973). The latter plays with ideas of culture and female power, and ultimately takes a conservative line on both. The intensity of Boorman's two British films show that they allude to something personal. This 'jagged' quality is missing from his American films. A comparison can be made here with the films of Michael Winner. His Hollywood films of the 1970s, such as *Scorpio* (1972), *The Sentinel* (1976) and the *Death Wish* series, are exactly the same as his British ones, *Chato's Land* (1971), *The Nightcomers* (1972) and *The Big Sleep* (1978). These are devoid of any patina, save that derived from luxury and pain. The fantasy/reality dyad, which stimulated so many innovatory directors of the 1970s, was irrelevant to Winner.

Nicolas Roeg had certain similarities to Russell. He too was a maverick, a fantasist, and an unknown quantity, as far as studio backers were concerned. But he had served a long apprenticeship and was a well-respected cinematographer long before gaining his own directorial credit on *Performance*. Roeg directed *Walkabout* (1970), which nuanced the adventure story by concentrating on subjectivity and desire. He then made the Italian co-production *Don't Look Now*. Unlike Russell, Roeg utilised his creative freedom in a thoroughly disciplined way, though with equally unconventional results. *Don't Look Now* is justly celebrated for its love-making scene (its ecstasies tempered by the inserts of the recovered lovers dressing, afterwards), but it should also be seen as a contribution to debates about the life of the spirit. By the time Roeg came to make his next location film, his exploration of the theme of alienation had acquired a new level of fantasy expression. *The Man Who Fell To Earth* alarmed its US backers Paramount as much for the liberties it took with linear narrative as for the startling revelations about the instability of masculinity. But it gained a cult following among youth audiences.

Other directors who flourished in the fantasy mode may not have been prolific, but they produced some of their best work within it. Stanley Kubrick, of course, was American, but worked and lived in Britain throughout the 1970s, and arguably his two films of the period, *A Clockwork Orange* and *Barry Lyndon* (1975), were a sustained meditation on what he saw as the best and worst of its culture. Kubrick had challenged realism in a radical manner in his earlier films, and *Dr Strangelove* (1964) and *2001: A Space Odyssey* (1968) presented sets and performances which ushered the viewer into possible rather than actual worlds. His 1970s films took this a stage further. *A Clockwork Orange*'s verbal and visual registers invite audiences to imagine the unspeakable – that to live without desire is as dangerous as to live with and by it. *Barry Lyndon*' s visual sophistication belies its radical questioning of the consensual codes by which everyone lives, and which make no one content. It is not a realist film, but a hyper-real one in which the obsessive attention to detail forces the imagination out of its commonsense boundaries.

Lindsay Anderson had also had a radical career in the 1960s, and he too had made films which radically deconstructed the language of realism in favour of a Brechtian structure and mood – *If. . .* (1968), for example. The problem with Anderson was that his famously choleric temperament was particularly unsuited to the cinema, in which the capacity for guile and double-dealing was profitable. He made only two films in the 1970s,

O Lucky Man! and *In Celebration* (1974). The first is a bricolage of mixed tones and styles, held together by an over-riding belief in the supremacy of the individual imagination. Through songs which punctuate it and appear to instruct the audience how to respond to the picaresque hero, the film provides a Brechtian critique of institutional constraints and textual traditions. The second film is an adaptation of David Storey's play, which Anderson had already produced in the theatre. The film version, by a subtle management of mood and tone, picks away at the surface of everyday life and insists on the vitality of the outsider's imagination.

Other directors in the fantasy field had more patchy careers. Don Chaffey had had a solid reputation with *Jason and the Argonauts* (1963) and others, and continued with fantasy in *Creatures the World Forgot* (1971), a film with sub-standard visuals. Chaffey was unable to maintain his profile, and ended the decade by making *The Magic of Lassie* (1978) in Hollywood. Another patchy 'fantasist' was Robert Fuest who, as Ede has shown, had a distinct stylistic repertoire. *The Abominable Dr. Phibes* had a marvellously coherent visual style, which Fuest attempted to replicate in *Dr. Phibes Rises Again*. But his backers, AIP, re-edited the film without Fuest's permission, and when he made *The Devil's Rain* (1975) for them, they arbitrarily changed the shooting schedule.[428] The exasperated Fuest abandoned film-making to teach at the LIFS.

Richard Lester was another director who eschewed realism. An expatriate American, the director of the Beatles films and *The Knack* (1965), Lester specialised in historical adventure films during the 1970s. He made *The Three Musketeers* (1973), *The Four Musketeers* (1974) and *Royal Flash* (1975). In these films history is replete with double-entendres, changes of mood, and a poignant sense of the parallels between the present and the past. The fast cutting and camera movement intensify the ironic tone. In all Lester's films of this period, the characters are simultaneously recognisable and strange. And this holds good for his American films of the decade, *Robin and Marian* (1976) and *Butch and Sundance: the Early Days* (1979). Only one of his films differs markedly from this avoidance of realism. *Juggernaut* (1974) was unusual in addressing, albeit symbolically, contemporary concerns. This thriller about the liner *Britannia*, held to ransom by terrorists, clearly works as a state-of-the-nation commentary.[429]

So far, we have argued that fantasy was an important mode in 1970s British cinema, which had a liberating effect on a number of film-makers. In contrast to earlier periods of British cinema, realism was in decline and was a minority mode. As Forster has shown in Chapter 7, realism remained the dominant language in television, where generic specialisms and programming imperatives ensured that realism retained its discursive consonance; great care was taken to ensure that its visual and aural codes were consistent with each other. Moreover, televisual realism in the 1970s was, for the first time, predominantly in colour. Realism's documentary authority was adopted by a handful of emergent film-makers who worked outside (and in some cases in opposition to) the dominant ideology of television culture, and who worked primarily in monochrome. Some of these were graduates of film schools, and several of them attracted support from the BFI Production Board to develop personal projects. In his survey of radical film-makers, Allen has noted the contributions of Bill Douglas, Terence Davies and Chris Petit. To these we might add Kevin Brownlow and Andrew Mollo, Barney Platts-Mills, David Gladwell and Stuart Cooper. Their films shared a rigorous attention to the everyday and to the minutiae of male subjectivity.

Ken Loach was another film-maker of the period whose uncompromising personal approach to screen realism made him an outsider in British film culture of the 1970s. In the 1960s, Loach had established himself in television, where his success enabled a move into feature films with *Poor Cow* (1967) and *Kes* (1969). His adaptation of David Mercer's TV play, *In Two Minds*, was retitled *Family Life* and was stolid, despite excellent performances from the cast. Thereafter, as Forster has noted, Loach found it difficult to advance his cinema career and returned to television. It was not until 1979 that Loach was able to make another feature film. *Black Jack* was a period drama adapted from a children's story by Leon Garfield. It was part-funded by the NFFC, but its small-scale production values and Loach's idiosyncratic use of amateur child actors was out of keeping with the bold narratives and strong characterisation of costume films at this time.

Another realist film-maker who was able to sustain work in both media was Jack Gold, whose style was rigorously naturalist, whatever his theme. His break into international pictures came with *Man Friday* (1975). Here there is a careful balance between shots, and also between foreground and background, with the whole overlaid by a sober liberalism.[430] As with Loach, Gold's cinematic realism was identical to his television work such as *The Naked Civil Servant* (1975).

This broad contrast between fantasy and realism, useful though it is, cannot account for all innovatory direction in the 1970s. Two notable directors, Ridley Scott and Derek Jarman, were at the beginning of their film careers in this period, but opened up cinema in a new way. They were able to refashion concepts of social space and history by calling into question established notions of the hierarchies of matter and form.

Ridley Scott's first feature, *The Duellists*, was shot on location in the

French Dordogne and is, visually, an extraordinarily assured debut. Trained as an artist, Scott's reliance on natural lighting conditions and dramatic seasonal weather imbued this tale of a relentless Napoleonic feud with the look of a Géricault or Vermeer.[431] It is significant that on his first feature Scott insisted on operating as well as directing.[432] His control over visual style was, therefore, absolute. Following *The Duellists*' winning the Special Jury Prize at Cannes, Scott was offered the script that would become *Alien* (1979), and he subsequently worked in Hollywood. But *The Duellists*' elaborate fetishisation of the past may be seen in the work of Merchant/Ivory and influenced the British 'heritage school' well into the 1980s.

Scott was ambitious to create a sort of *Gesamtkunstwerk* in which he alone combined visual discourses with the acting style and narrative structure. He had this precisely in common with Derek Jarman, whose commitments were also to the visual arts and to the construction of films which evoked an entirely new sense of historical and mythical space. Both directors were able to transcend the structuring antinomies of realism and fantasy which dominated, determined and sometimes limited their peers.

During the 1970s, Jarman directed three features: *Sebastiane*, *Jubilee* and *The Tempest*. In all of them, he achieved a great measure of artistic control. *Sebastiane* is an extremely audacious film, which completely redrafts the costume film, *Jubilee* confers a resonant historical perspective on to an analysis of punk culture, and *The Tempest* provides an extraordinarily imaginative reading of Shakespeare's play, rethinking key scenes such as The Masque and key players such as Caliban. There is a freshness and audacity about Jarman's work in this decade, which is derived from his ability to combine visual pleasure with revolutionary analysis.

Conclusion

In this chapter we have established that changes in the economic structure of the film industry in the 1970s led to a bifurcation of production styles. The old conglomerates were sustained by the influx of new entrepreneurial talent, but their managerial difficulties and their unwieldy corporate structures meant that they were not sufficiently responsive to the vagaries of the film market and popular tastes. Some of the new, independent production regimes were able to benefit from unconventional sources of funding, both public and private. These arrangements enabled fresh thinking in the realm of creative autonomy, and promoted flexibility, cultural eclecticism and a degree of risk-taking. As new production circumstances overcame earlier studio practices, established cultural hierarchies were challenged by the imaginative freedom of the newcomers.

We have argued that these changes in the field of production resulted in a diffusion of directors' creative practices. In surveying the key players, we have made a distinction between those who were unable to adapt to the changing circumstances and went under, and those who could adapt, but remained journeymen. A third category of directors, however, were able to be more creative. Their innovations in subject matter and film style may be interpreted as a consequence of a shift in the dynamic relations between realism and fantasy. In locating this changing relationship, it would be tempting to reduce the field of direction into two schools of realism and of fantasy, by contrasting the work, for example, of Bill Douglas and Ken Russell. However, it looks as if the emergent talents of Derek Jarman and Ridley Scott disrupt such neat distinctions, because they invested film culture with a new visual sensibility derived from their respective art practices. They reconfigured the imaginative landscape of cinema in radical ways, which had profound and far-reaching effects.

CHAPTER 10

Boundaries and Taboos

In the previous chapter we suggested that economic changes to the structure of the film industry had a profound effect on working relations and artistic autonomy. We now want to turn our attention to films themselves and examine the ways in which specific texts of the 1970s engaged with aspects of social change. In this period film culture had a vital task to perform, in interpreting shifts in the boundaries between the sacred and profane. Ever since its inception, the medium of film has had a unique function in negotiating the relations between social morality and the emotional hinterland of psycho-sexual life. Film thus has a particularly conspicuous role to play in periods when notions of boundary and taboo are unstable. In the 1970s such boundaries were acutely at issue and film had to deal, on the one hand, with regulatory crises and, on the other hand, with the transformation of the landscape of desire. And this held good for films right across the spectrum, from popular low-brow texts to the higher uplands of the avant-garde.

In Chapter 2 Barber demonstrated how the institutional position of the BBFC placed it under unprecedented and acute pressure in a period of massive social change. In this chapter we will survey transformations brought about by the 1960s' 'permissive society' and 'the sexual revolution', and consider how these changes were addressed in film culture. The 1970s witnessed a particularly public debate about gender, sexuality, reproduction and the family. Greater freedoms in bodily display in films of the period should be seen as part of the more widespread visibility of sexuality in media culture. This includes the advent of Page Three topless models in *The Sun* from 1969 onwards and the prominence of *The Guardian*'s 'Women's Page'. It can be measured by the growth in sales of soft-porn magazines, and features and discussions about female sexual desire in popular journals like *Cosmopolitan*.[433] And it is evident in television and radio documentaries, dramas and sitcoms, and in the widespread exploitation of sex in TV and print advertising.[434] Tabloid newspaper editors and advertising executives alike worked on the premise that sex sells. And the link between sex as a commodity and the sexualisation of material goods was made explicit as never before, especially in film.

The transformation of sexual behaviour which took place in the 1970s had its origins in the legislation of the 1960s. The Sexual Offences Act, legalising some aspects of homosexual behaviour, was passed in 1967, as was the Abortion Act. However, it was not until the 1970s that the effects of such laws were filtered down into the broader population. The National Abortion Campaign was founded in 1975 to defend the 1967 Act. Although the Family Planning Act had been passed in 1967 (giving state commitment to contraception), it was not until the early 1970s that the Pill became easily available; it was not free until 1974.[435] Other events which affected the moral landscape were the blasphemy cases of *Oz* in 1971 and *Gay News* in 1977.

Sexual attitudes were changing in the 1970s, but less quickly among the older generation. Geoffrey Gorer noted that tolerance of extramarital sex and homosexuality in the decade was markedly more prevalent among the younger generation.[436] There certainly was a liberalisation in sexual thinking which increased throughout the decade. The percentage of people who believed premarital sex was wrong dropped from 63 per cent in 1963 to 10 per cent in 1973, and 70 per cent of a fairly large sample thought that pornography should be freely available.[437]

During the 1970s, two important movements made these changes in the sexual landscape more visible. The Women's Movement, though informally constructed, had a high public profile. Caricatures of bra-burning 'Women's Libbers' preoccupied many media commentators and featured prominently in popular cultural texts. But there was a real transformation in the way women thought about themselves and their bodies. This was evident from the range of feminist texts which were published in Britain in the early 1970s.[438] But we should not assume that it was a top-down movement led by academic thought alone. Consciousness-raising groups flourished throughout the decade, and non-academic feminist magazines had a wide circulation; *Spare Rib* sold all 20,000 copies of its first number.[439] Women's Liberation, until the latter part of the decade, was a broad church, in which radical feminists, lesbians and worried heterosexuals questioned the unequal operations of patriarchy and linked those to parenting, sexual pleasure and professional opportunity.

The other active movement of the period was Gay Liberation, whose first demonstration was in November 1970. *Gay News* was first published in 1971, and the first Gay Pride march took place in 1972. Although its campaigns were equally radical, the Gay Liberation Movement did not have such a high public profile as the Women's Movement; neither did it feature so prominently in popular cultural texts. However, Beckett comments that both movements were 'theatrical, ambitious and sometimes utopian' in their approaches and methods.[440] Certainly, both groups were perceived by sceptics as being as interested in style as in substance. But both demonstrated their commitment to combining political beliefs with new modes of dress and interpersonal behaviour. The idea was bruited that the intimate, personal life could be turned inside out and enter the public domain. The slogan 'the personal is political' meant that the concepts of privacy and decorum would never be the same again.

Liberal ideas about sexuality and pleasure were not confined to radical groups in the 1970s. One of the best-sellers of the decade was Alex Comfort's *The Joy of Sex* (1972), with the telling sub-title: *A Gourmet Guide to Love-Making*. The book is structured around Starters, Mains and Sweets, and, with a range of drawings, presents sexual activity not as a life-changing cataclysm, but as a matter of choice. Thus the primal scene was transformed into a matter of consumption. Indeed, the idea of sexual pleasure as a mere lifestyle choice was a potent one in the decade, which may account for the increase in the variety and consumption of pornography.

Lord Longford's independent inquiry into the pornographic industry produced a report which became an accidental best-seller in 1972.[441] A right-wing Christian alliance was established between Longford's campaign and Mary Whitehouse's National Viewers and Listeners Association: the Nationwide Festival of Light. This is evidence that there was a serious moral panic among cultural conservatives, fuelled by the tabloid press and the supposed excesses of the liberationists. In July 1977, Mrs Whitehouse became the first person in half a century to sue successfully for blasphemous libel, in a case against *Gay News*, which had published a poem about a Roman centurion's love for Jesus. The journal's editor, Denis Lemon, received a suspended sentence, which was later quashed on appeal, but the Establishment's willingness to give credence to Whitehouse's zealous campaigning was clear.[442]

One of the major targets for the Festival of Light's campaign was the BBFC and its perceived laxity in dealing with the huge increase in sexually explicit films in the 1970s. The extent of the growth in the pornographic film market during the decade meant that a good deal of the work of the Board was preoccupied with policing this area. As Barber argued, successive Secretaries of the Board were under acute pressure to make difficult decisions in a climate of public anxiety about censorship practices and codes of sexual permission. The Board's ambiguous position – as the guardians of public morality and the paid servants of the film industry – called into question its very existence at a time when some film-makers were challenging the boundaries of sexual taboo. Chapter 2 has drawn attention to a number of *causes célèbres* for the BBFC. This has provided us with evidence about the politics of regulation and splits in public opinion. Now we want to explore the ways in which the film culture responded to the sexual transformations we have set out above.

Let us, for the purposes of argument, group films which can be seen to share similar preoccupations and approaches. We can thus delineate different kinds of textual function. In exploring the ways in which cultural forms deal with attitudes to sexual freedom and its boundaries, we want to argue that three positions are possible. Firstly, conservative cultural texts can support and rigorously police traditional notions of difference and permission. Secondly, transgressive texts can challenge and effectively deconstruct those notions. Thirdly, what we shall call 'boundary-walkers' can hedge their bets in adopting ambivalent attitudes to change. Let us explore each category in turn.

Conservative

In the 1970s there are many popular films which are conservative in their attitudes to changes initiated in the 1960s. There is a strand of nostalgia for Edwardiana and the idyll of the family in *The Railway Children*. Here the merits of the traditional order provide the narrative impetus, which is only resolved by the return of the father. Although *The Go-Between* appears to present more complex possibilities of personal memory and social transgression, it ultimately reinforces a morally conservative position in undermining its central protagonists. Nostalgia for a less troubled childhood is evident in *Swallows and Amazons*, where the absent father provides the motivation for the children's adventures; these require their adherence to traditional gender distinctions. Even *Bugsy Malone*, in which children play adults in a fantasy recreation of 1920s New York, celebrates the durability of prescribed gender differences. The Agatha Christie adaptations, *Murder on the Orient Express* and *Death on the Nile*, also share traditional values which cannot be shaken loose by either the exoticism of foreign travel or the corruption of criminal intent.

Conservatism, however, is not the preserve of period drama. Such values are reinforced with equal vigour in other genres. Small-scale domestic films, notably the raft of TV comedy spin-offs, are equally conservative. From *On the Buses* to *Porridge* (1979), these televisual productions pad out their familiar formulae without ambiguity.

In crime films of the decade, such as *Get Carter*, *Villain*, *The Squeeze* and *Scum*, the narratives endorse patriarchy and punish sexual deviance violently. The same can be said of the international thriller. In *Diamonds Are Forever*, the two gay criminals, Mr Wint (Bruce Glover) and Mr Kidd (Putter Smith), are summarily despatched. The Roger Moore Bonds of the 1970s are more conservative than their 1960s predecessors, although their tone is more ironic. Other thrillers, such as *Day of the Jackal*, *Caravan to Vaccares* (1974), *Gold* and *The Eagle Has Landed*, present derring-do as scarcely troubled by interventions from dewy-eyed females.

As we suggested in the previous chapter, the dynamic relations between realism and fantasy were undergoing a profound refurbishment in the film culture of this period. Arguably, the fantasy mode allows greater latitude for the exploration of moral boundaries and issues of transgression. In Chapter 4, Ede charted the decline in Hammer's imaginative repertoire in the 1970s. However, the studio maintained its conservative position on female sexuality. Some Hammer films of the 1960s had been concerned with the polluting effects of female blood (*Plague of the Zombies* [1965]) and with the horrors of the ageing female body (*She* [1965]). In *Countess Dracula*, these themes of repression were united to powerful effect. This film deals with the ageing Elizabeth Bathory (Ingrid Pitt), who falls in love with a young soldier (Sandor Elès) and discovers that the blood of virgins will temporarily restore her beauty and facilitate her desires. She daubs herself with the blood of her victims and masquerades as her own daughter. The narrative swings from enjoying the beauty of the young Elizabeth into loathing the sagging, carbuncled flesh of her ageing incarnation. In a scene of particular *frisson*, Elizabeth reverts to her old self and cradles her lover's head in her lap, crooning that he is her 'son'.

Countess Dracula was directed by Peter Sasdy, whose films were preoccupied by patriarchal issues and physical excess: *Taste the Blood of Dracula* (1970), *Hands of the Ripper* (1971), *I Don't Want to Be Born* (1975). Sasdy was quite enterprising in his work on *Countess Dracula*. He approached John Trevelyan personally, requesting his comments on the pre-production script. Trevelyan prompted Sasdy to make it 'more convincing and more reflecting of historical fact' than other Hammer horrors. The censor stressed that he thought Sasdy's work was superior, but warned him that he should tread a fine line between sex and horror: 'To have a naked girl in a bath of blood is an unpleasant idea and in this we have a closer association with sex and violence than anywhere else in the film. I do not like this at all.'[443] The reader's report had also disliked the bloodbath, since 'it is one thing to be made to shudder with fright and another to be made to vomit in a public place'.[444] None the less, Trevelyan decided to pass the film uncut.[445]

What is significant is that the BBFC were concerned about the blood taboo, but not about that of ageing female desire. The film does not distinguish between the sacred and profane body – between virginal and menopausal flesh – but reinforces it with rigour. *Countess Dracula* argues the reactionary case powerfully: that the political and social power that older women may accrue must on no account extend into the sexual arena. The broaching of the incest taboo is unambiguously condemned, and the desire of the old woman for the young man is punished by the narrative structure, and also by the *mise en scène*. Thus the film reinforces accepted taboos about gender and generational difference.

Science fiction in the 1970s is preoccupied with ideas about alternative ways of living which have their roots in 1960s counter-cultural aspirations. A very conservative response to such ideas is to be found in *Zardoz*. This deals with a world divided into Brutals, who police the Outlands, and the everlasting Eternals, who inhabit the Vortex. Insulated from time and pain, the Eternals are a matriarchy which has lost the will to procreate. Their chant is that 'the penis is evil'. Brutal Zed (Sean Connery) bursts into the Vortex and brings death, but he also paradoxically brings life. The latter is defined in specifically heterosexual terms; the warrior princess is vigorously returned to a proper role of mother and wife.

One scene is of particular interest. While Zed is the object of the Eternals' scientific enquiries, they ascertain that he, unlike they, is capable of erection. It is the presence of Consuela (Charlotte Rampling) which stimulates this, and not the rape film which they show him. Zed looks down at his erection, then at Consuela, then repeats the sequence, but this time with a rueful, half-apologetic expression. It is this capacity for irony and self-mockery which marks him out as a superior being. Zed is able to usher Consuela into orgasm, childbirth, motherhood and death, and Boorman uses Beethoven's Seventh Symphony to confer a benison upon the 'natural' cycle.

Boorman preferred to make films which were not anchored in, but were critical of, contemporary life. He had earlier tried to make a film of Tolkien's *Lord of the Rings*, and was aware of his own mythopoeic tendencies. He conceived *Zardoz*, like the Tolkien film, as full of Jungian archetypes and Grail symbols: 'In the pagan version [of the Grail] he had to achieve his knowledge carnally. He learned from a series of women, who allowed him to find the Grail. And that's the way it happens in *Zardoz*.'[446]

Boorman knew that the film could be interpreted as patriarchal and, in a 1974 interview, defended himself vigorously:

> The Women's Lib people think that the film is saying that male virility is the only answer, which is a bit of a misreading, because after all the women are the dominant people in the film. Somebody said to me that what it comes down to in the end is that Zed has to bang some sense into these women, which is the exact opposite of what happens, because actually they bang sense into him, don't they? In the scene in which they give him their knowledge, they are the sexual aggressors and he's totally passive.[447]

Arguably, this is a case where we should trust not the teller but the tale, since the textual evidence is clearly that women should be repositioned back into the patriarchal order, forcibly if necessary, until they learn to enjoy it.

But more is at issue here. This is a case where we should pay particular attention to the date of an interview. By 1986, Boorman was arguing that the Eternals had committed the worst sin of all in that they had denied sexual difference: 'Both men and women have become very delicate creatures, finally resembling each other and wearing the same clothes.'[448] In this later interview, he bewails experiments in which, living in ideal stress-free conditions, female mice came to dominate the males, who simply 'played all day long' (instead, presumably, of being Real Mice).[449] Boorman here presents the lesbian relationship between Consuela and May as something that they grow out of, once a proper man appears on the horizon.[450]

Certainly, *Zardoz* is the film which, more intensely than any other in the decade, presents extreme sexual difference positively, but only as long as it is situated within the patriarchal order.

Transgressive

Let us now consider those films texts which challenge traditional attitudes and present the breaking of taboos as either positive or pleasurable. Such films occupy the polar extremes of the film culture of the period. On the one hand, sexploitation films like *Confessions of a Window Cleaner* and *Eskimo Nell* engage in bawdy celebrations of heterosexual pleasure. On the other hand, some independent films are transgressive in both political and gender terms. These include: Peter Whitehead's *Daddy* (1973), Laura Mulvey and Peter Wollen's *The Riddles of the Sphinx* (1977) and Ron Peck's *Nighthawks* (1978). Such films argue that a social transformation also involves a restructuring of the patriarchal order, and they use polemical modes of address. *The Riddles of the Sphinx* was preoccupied by ancient history and myth. The script foregrounded challenges to the symbolic order, through radical deconstructions of narrative:

> We live in a society ruled by the father, in which the mother is suppressed. Motherhood, and how to live it, or not to live it, lies at the root of the dilemma. And meanwhile the Sphinx can only speak with a voice apart.[451]

Few radical films in this category are preoccupied with visual pleasure and they make little attempt to provide it.

Some low-budget comedies display a new liberalism in their espousal of sexual freedom. *Confessions of a Window Cleaner* was the first in a series about a young male initiate abroad in a world of libidinous females. Their scripts and visual style owe much to a vernacular tradition in British comedy derived from the music hall and saucy seaside postcards; in this sense they are thoroughly residual in their values. Yet the ways in which such elements are nuanced here is significant. The *Confessions* films addressed a young, working-class audience. With their pop soundtracks and denim fashions, the adventures of Timmy Lea (Robin Askwith) chart the initiation of a young man into the world of adult sexual pleasure. In *Confessions of a Window Cleaner*, an encounter with a bored housewife of insatiable appetites ends up with limbs flailing and buttocks thrusting in a foam of detergent bubbles. It may be clumsy, but it's all good clean fun.

The *Confessions* films propose, without hint of irony, that sexual freedom can be available to all, regardless of gender or class. In all the sexploitation films of the 1970s, the provision of pleasure is presented as a straightforward matter. But they deal with it in different ways. *The Ups and Down of a Handyman* (1975), for example, is located in a familiar landscape. The handy hero, Bob (Barry Stokes), lives in a village inhabited by fossilised characters: the Wife of Bath, the flagellating Squire, the tumescent policeman. These prisoners from the past are released into a joyously libidinous future. By contrast, in *Eskimo Nell* pleasure is experienced as if for the first time, but with the addition of an excoriating irony.

Eskimo Nell is extremely self-reflexive. It deals with a portly pornographer (Roy Kinnear), who persuades three fledgling film graduates to make a porn movie. He persuades a hard-core American producer, a gay entrepreneur with a karate-soprano protégée, and a 'Festival of Light' group to back him. The graduates are forced to make different films for their sponsors and they get mixed up, to disastrous effect. The film is remarkable for its frankness about the financial imperatives of cultural production, and the vast distance between the world of the critics' cinema and the producers' cinema. In one memorable scene, the young director waxes lyrical about film theory, displaying a range of fashionable *auteur* books, and he asks the producer what is his favourite genre. 'Genre? GENRE?' shouts the producer, making an unambiguous gesture, 'I like them with GREAT BIG genres.'

But in spite of all, *Eskimo Nell* is on the side of pleasure. The virgin penguin fancier (Christopher Timothy) learns that sex is easy; the nubile girls and boys take their happiness, unperturbed by onlookers; the gay cowboys get their moment of joy. Even Kinnear's Benny Murdoch finds someone to love his paunch. The irony and cynicism of the film give an edge to its generosity and permissiveness, which might otherwise make it seem sloppy.

Such films made a passionate espousal of heterosexual pleasure. Other films of the period address homosexual pleasure with equal candour. Derek Jarman's *Sebastiane* dealt with homosexual love in ancient Rome. The film presented one of the first Christian martyrs as fuelled by erotic love. Jarman was imaginative with funding, raising money from the Marquis of Dufferin and Ava, David Hockney, Lord Kenilworth and others. The film was conceived as a co-operative venture.[452] It was Jarman's decision to script it in Latin rather than English, 'in order to eliminate the horrors of the normal English historical film'.[453]

The film was made on a three-week shoot in Sardinia, and with a very economical budget.[454] The research was provided by a Benedictine monk, Dom Sylvestre Houédard, who created a solid imaginary world in the document *Sebastiane in History*, with maps, mythologies and a study of Diocletian's empire.[455] There was considerable historical verisimilitude, with circular cloaks from unbleached oatmeal and original implements.[456] However, there were heated debates on set about whether the collaborative team was making a Steve Reeves gay porn movie or a serious art-house text, while Jarman wanted 'a poetic film full of mystery'.[457]

The film had a remarkably positive response from the BBFC. It was passed without cuts for an 'X' certificate. Although there were scenes with erections, and mock-ejaculations during the court scenes, no objections were made:

> This is a very beautiful and remarkable film . . . No one in this film is effeminate or camp. This is about sexuality not so much as about homosexuality. And I think this is the first of its kind in this respect . . . here we have allowed pretty intimate shots of mens' genitals, of the scrotum seen between legs as from behind and an erection. But we must be careful that the natural gaity of the two men in their water frolics is not used as a precedent for all sorts of gay lib monkey tricks.[458]

Clearly, for the BBFC examiner, the film draws an acceptable line between effeminacy and manliness, and all is permitted so long as the film avoids any hint of gay propagandism.

The film's use of Latin, of course, restricts its impact for a popular market – no exception is taken to calling a beetle Mrs Whitehouse as long as she is called 'Maria Domus Alba' – but Jarman has taken care to avoid possible offence by using two tactics. Firstly, the most explicit sex scene takes place in water, always a purifying medium. Secondly, it is in slow motion, which confers a dignity on most actions. The most erotic displays of the male body take place in the bath-house, with close-ups of dirt being scraped off by the strigil, revealing the wholesome skin beneath. And great care is taken to distinguish the 'pure' homosexual desire of the lovers for each other from the 'profane' one of the captain for Sebastiane, which is tortured and torturing. Potentially the most radical images are the close-ups of Sebastiane in the sun, hymning Jesus as the young God of the Sun. In time-honoured manner, Sebastiane's Christian passion is stimulated and fuelled by erotic desire. But the charge – and any sense of culpable danger – is defused by the outright lyricism of the scene, and by the fact that the object of the young man's love, though male, is invisible.

Boundary-walkers

Our third category includes films which express a tension between the desire for freedom and fear of its consequences. Such films display the utmost anxiety about transformations in the sexual and social landscape, and they walk the boundaries between the sacred and profane. They do not police those boundaries in any proscriptive sense, but they display an awareness of the power of taboo and the dangerous exaltations which ensue from its destruction.

This is a useful way of assessing the cultural tasks being undertaken by films as different as *The Romantic Englishwoman* and *The Bitch*. Both films are preoccupied with changes wrought by the Women's Movement, but they arrange their anxieties in contrasting ways. The first rehearses, with some hesitancy, the pains caused when the old habits of female deference are shed; the second presents a new order in which women invent a more ruthless system than patriarchy. The latter film falls into the boundary-walker rather than the transgressive category because it is clearly worried by the excess, and the unease betrays itself in the details of the *mise en scène*.

Other films are preoccupied by transformations in masculinity. They are often set in the past, where anxieties can be dealt with in a more direct manner. Thus *Royal Flash* intensifies the themes of disguise and dishonesty contained in the original novel, and makes an uneasy settlement with the Flashman character (Malcolm McDowell). His iconoclastic energy is admired, but the chaos he brings is not. Similarly, *Barry Lyndon* is attracted by the entrepreneurial hero (Ryan O'Neal) but there is also distaste for his feckless self-destructiveness. And *The Devils* can be interpreted on one level as a film torn between admiration for the coherence of the old order and an admiration for the energy of the new.

Many films are riven by the pains of sexual difference; they look back with longing to a time when men and women inhabited separate countries, but they also anticipate a world where they might live together. This anticipation is a mixture of terror and desire, because it involves rethinking masculinity and its relationship to the woman as both mother and lover. This is manifest in a film built on a small scale, such as *The Triple Echo*, as well one with more generous proportions such as *Tommy*. Films as various as *A Clockwork Orange*, *The Wicker Man*, *That'll Be the Day*, *Alfie Darling* and *Stardust* are preoccupied by what men are or might be, how they should behave, and what is involved in the gradual transmission of power.

Codes of masculinity are conspicuously to the fore in *Conduct Unbecoming* (1975). This was the adaptation by American screenwriter, Robert Enders, of Barry England's late-1960s stage success. England's story exposes hypocrisy and misogyny beneath the veneer of regimental honour in the British Army of the late nineteenth century serving on the North-Western Frontier. But the scripting process, which involved a brief intervention by Terence Rattigan, was vexed. The removal of Rattigan from the project (Enders alone is credited as screenwriter) cost the production an estimated £250,000.[459] *Cinema TV Today* reported that pre-production costs had escalated to 'as much as $800,000'.[460] This was a considerable slice of a modest shooting budget which allowed only for a brief second-unit location shoot in Pakistan and an intensive five weeks at Shepperton Studios. Therefore the film's economy of style, and almost unrelievedly claustrophobic interiors, are a tribute to Michael Anderson's experienced directorial efficiency, rather than any investment of creative flair.

The film's preoccupations with gender and codes of masculinity are extremely prominent. The theme of public duty versus private principle is examined via the new recruit, Drake (Michael York), stoically defending his fellow probationer Millington (James Faulkner), who is wrongly accused of having assaulted the widow of the regimental hero, Captain John Scarlett (Susannah York). In a mock trial, convened in order to avoid a humiliating public court martial, Drake's 'bourgeois morality' in achieving justice for Millington is overshadowed by the sexual corruption in which the regiment has become mired. The dark centre of this scandal is discovered in a violent re-enactment of a game of 'sticking-the-pig', in which the regiment's errant wives are substituted for a stuffed pig on wheels, in an act of ritual vengeance for a bloody massacre in which John Scarlett was castrated and butchered. As Major Wimbourne (Christopher Plummer) explains to the incredulous Drake: 'For all of us, who saw John that day, the memory was a recurring nightmare. He felt his own sex had been destroyed. From that moment, he was numbed, impotent.' When Drake asks: 'Why should these women be attacked in this manner?', Wimbourne replies: 'Because in his mind their infidelity to regimental heroes had made them pigs – and that's how we treat pigs in this regiment.'

The weight of this revelation, and the confession of the ringleader Major Roach (Richard Attenborough), takes the drama beyond a critique of military duplicity. It is figured rather as clandestine, ritualistic male abuse in which the wounded females are complicit victims who undergo symbolic 'correction' in acts of vengeful compensation for male impotence. Ultimately, the tension between this psycho-sexual violence and the codes of military honour destabilises the whole narrative, for it reveals a deep-seated anxiety about the potential of female sexual power to undermine male camaraderie. The film is ambivalent in the conflict it presents between regret for the passing of the old order and fear of the female principle which threatens it.

Extreme anxiety about empowered women is also a recurrent preoccupation in the films of Pete Walker. His 1970s films constitute a sustained meditation on the abuses of power by those in authority. *House of Whipcord* deals with a private prison run by an unbalanced wardress and a feeble judge, who punish young girls for their lax sexual behaviour. *Frightmare* deals with a family for whom 'dysfunctional' would be a mild term: cannibalistic, murderous and incestuous. *House of Mortal Sin* deals with a priest obsessed with the sexual peccadilloes of his female parishioners, one of whom he persecutes and murders. The films arraign, in an explicit way which is entirely new, the institutions of judiciary, family and church, push them to their limits and display them as terminally corrupt. What holds the trilogy together is not just the coherence of its forthright attitudes, but also that of its manner. The performance style of the protagonist in all three films, Sheila Keith, is deliberately overblown, with a repertoire of sideways glances and staccato movements, and this is intensified by a varied cinematography, where angles and shot length are always unexpected. This gives it a throwaway, ironic air markedly different from

Figure 7 *House of Whipcord*

other films of its type. This Walker trilogy, unsavoury though its subject matter is, shows that a small-scale operation and unfettered control can have some innovatory effects.

Walker's contrary attitudes to the contemporary public discourses about sexual morality and generational rifts dominate his work:

> *Whipcord* particularly was sort of tongue-in-cheek really. I mean, I was sort of on the side of Mrs. Wakehurst and Justice Bailey . . . So you had to be very careful not to get

> into that area. In fact, this was something that older statesman Freddy Shaughnessy always used to lecture me on. 'Be very careful about that otherwise, if you've got to do it, you've got to do it so they don't know which side you're on.' I thought Mary Whitehouse had got a point. I just thought she did not sell it very well . . . and set herself up to be ridiculed.[461]

This revealing commentary shows his underlying sympathy for conservative morality and, at the same time, his awareness of the benefits of exploiting contemporary moral panics. But Walker also acknowledges his consistent practice of presenting graphic violence in a playful manner without seeming to impose moral judgement. His ambivalent attitude to the subject matter affirms his marginal position; he gives equal weight to both liberal licence and conservative prurience.

Nicolas Roeg's *The Man Who Fell To Earth* drew on Paul Mayersberg's adaptation of Walter Tevis's sci-fi novel to explore sexual boundaries and taboos within an alien explanatory model. Alienation is evoked in three aspects of the film's construction: in the photography of the desert landscape of New Mexico and its 'Land of Enchantment'; in a disruptive, non-linear mode of editing; and in the performance of David Bowie as the alien Thomas Jerome Newton. Newton has left his family and come to Earth to find a solution to the environmental disaster which threatens the life of his planet, Anthea.

Newton appears physically frail and juvenile in his green dufflecoat. The film's costume designer, May Routh, said she 'wanted to have a feeling like a sort of school uniform'.[462] This decision is telling, for school uniform is both pre-pubescent and codified, and thus obscures both sexual difference and individual personality. Roeg himself cast the pop star for his non-professional acting abilities as much as for the sci-fi androgeny associated with his stage persona, Ziggy Stardust. The director explained: 'Actors play alien people, alien from themselves. It's a very highly skilled and brilliant actor that can get rid of that performance.'[463] Elsewhere he has paid tribute to Bowie's on-screen charisma:

> He may have been slightly clumsy, and somebody else might have been more together but training would have stopped it. It wouldn't have had the authenticity of the alien, without anything except who he was . . . So the throwing away of the alien disguise was rather like exposing yourself emotionally.[464]

This scene of emotional exposure is at the heart of Newton's relationship with the 'girl next door', Mary Lou (Candy Clark). At its climax, Bowie's emasculated alien represents the terrifying other in a rehearsal of the primal scene. Roeg explains:

> In that scene, Mary Lou and Mr. Newton had been together for a while, and though she thought that he was a bit strange and odd, she had no idea where he came from. Sure he was an alien, but he wasn't a monster. She didn't know that on his planet, it had been planned that he would come to Earth and be among humans, but that they didn't get things quite right with his body. And so when she says that he can tell her anything, which in the human context means 'You can tell me anything and I'll still love you,' and he shows her his method of making love – by exchanging bodily fluids on a grand scale – of course she recoils.[465]

The ultimate strangeness of sexual difference is revealed in this act of sexual initiation. A contemporary fan response suggests that the awkwardness of this scene provided stimulation and reassurance for some:

> When I saw *The Man Who Fell To Earth* I got influenced by the idea of skins peeling and the fact that skin can be taken away and produce juices of a kind that can reveal themselves at the height of sexuality.
>
> So that when you make love you actually destroy certain layers of skin and form a liquid mass together.
>
> It was incredibly sensuous and very wild at the same time.[466]

Sexual mystery and ambiguity in the film are figured both as an emancipatory field in which to explore new possibilities, and as a site of problematic uncertainty haunted by the fear of the forever unknown. In this way,

Figure 8 *The Man Who Fell To Earth*

The Man Who Fell To Earth may be read as an ambivalent commentary on changing attitudes to sexuality in the 1970s.

Conclusion

In this chapter we have addressed the ways in which British film culture of the 1970s engaged with transformations consequent upon the sexual revolution of the 1960s. We have acknowledged the intensity of public debates about sexual freedom, equality and censorship, and have highlighted the difficult role of the BBFC in policing shifting boundaries of taste. We have argued that the whole film culture was coloured by these debates and therefore we needed to devise a model for analysing a broader range of responses, beyond that of a handful of controversial test cases. We proposed three categories – conservative, transgressive and boundary-walkers – which would enable us to characterise groups of films according to their attitude and manner in addressing sexuality. Firstly, each category includes a variety of film types, such that no simple conclusions can be drawn along genre lines. Secondly, each category includes films which reveal a range of production backgrounds, such that straightforward explanations about agency will not suffice. Thirdly, none of the categories has a predictable relationship to hierarchies of taste; low-brow, middle-brow and high-brow films appear across all three.

A considerable number of films fall into the 'conservative' category. Such films imply a morally centrist position and infer a consensual response. Whilst many of these are prepared to deal with sex with a new frankness, they attempt to impose order upon the boundaries of pleasure. The 'transgressive' category appears to be the least populous. These films, whether low-brow or avant-garde, manifest a directness of tone and a self-aware manner. The populist texts tend to be candid and 'knowing', while the radical ones are assertive and propagandist. Both types share a confidence about their terms of reference. The films that we have designated as 'boundary-walkers' – those which express anxiety about the new sexual order – are those whose attitudes are more ambivalent. These unresolved texts are often composed of a number of competing discourses which infer contradictory or confused responses.

However, this model of analysis as an index of attitudes to sexuality in the film culture can only be taken so far. We must not forget that the idea of sexual pleasure as a commodity, and sexual preference as a lifestyle choice, pervades almost the entire film culture, regardless of politics. And it is also possible to discern, across the range of films surveyed, some similarities in mood or tone; irony and disavowal seem to prevail. These qualities can be located predominantly at the level of visual and performance style, and these will be the subjects of the next two chapters.

CHAPTER 11

Technology and Visual Style

Visual style can be interpreted as an expression of the creativity of workers in various areas – cinematography, art direction, costume design, editing – and film style may also be interpreted as a consequence of the director's ability to coordinate those contributions into a coherent whole. But in the commercial cinema, visual style cannot simply be attributed to the free spirit of artists. Rather, it must be seen through constraints – financial, managerial and technical – which affect the autonomy of creative artists.

As explained in Chapter 9, by the 1970s the old relationships between production, distribution and exhibition were irretrievably fractured, and power was structured around more individualistic, entrepreneurial models. The old studio system had ensured a security of tenure for production teams, and a continuity of tone in films made under stable conditions. This stylistic coherence gave way to a new heterogeneity. On the face of it, 1970s British cinema can be characterised as one of unresolved conflicts – between different colour palettes, different formal proportions, and different foreground/background ratios. And it seems like a cinema which is characterised by visual excess.

But there is more to it than that. Many producers, as we have shown, had considerable cultural literacy and *nous*; others worked within the stylistic parameters of popular culture. Crucially, some directors gained a new confidence in the 1970s, and intervened directly in matters of visual style. To be sure, there were older cinematographers such as Walter Lassally and Geoffrey Unsworth who argued powerfully for their own autonomy.[467] But more commonly, innovative directors took control of the camera and dominated the 'look' of their films. John Boorman intervened powerfully in the cinematography and lighting of *Zardoz*, insisting on a diffused pastel effect to offset the violence concealed within the narrative,[468] and Ridley Scott was responsible for the aesthetic effects of *The Duellists*.

Ken Russell is another example of this shift in the balance of creative power. Peter Suschitzky, cameraman for most of his major films, asserted that Russell organised all the compositions and framing himself and occasionally operated the second camera on set. Such were the controls imposed by Russell on *Lisztomania* and other films that the only tiny area of autonomy Suschitzky had left was the lighting, and even that was quite rigorously policed.[469] The same obtained for *Valentino*.[470] Russell, of course, claimed authorship for the way in which the past was portrayed in *The Devils*, in the sets as well as in the camerawork.[471] He characterised his own formal procedures as varied and eclectic:

> I try to match the style to the subject. For example, in a film I did for television about Rousseau, the primitive painter, I employed a very primitive style – shot everything dead centre, with people just walking through the frame, and no camera movement. *The Boy Friend* was a pastiche of 1930s films, and so it had that sort of style. *Tommy* had a definite rough style about it that sort of suited the modern idiom. And now in *Valentino*, the thing about it is that every sequence has its own style.[472]

It is clear that in this period artisanal methods were on the decline, and the newer methods were more instinctive, inspirational and personal. The codes and symbols which some directors deployed related directly to the transformations in cultural forms outside the cinema; others were more firmly embedded within it. But in order to assess how ideas about form and style were transmitted on to film, we need to take into account the key technological developments in the cinema of the period.

Technological Developments

The relationship between technical innovation and film style is unpredictable. Some periods in cinema history witness technical innovations in the film process which improve quality and make efficiency savings, yet their effects upon film style are negligible. Furthermore, some film-makers embrace the latest technology for reasons of economy, rather than stylistic innovation.

In the realm of cinematography, cameras and lighting equipment became more versatile, lighter and more compact. Major camera developments were dominated by the new Panaflex generation available from 1973,[473] and the Arriflex 35BL model which was particularly suited to handheld work.[474] Cameras sported motor-driven focusing, aperture stopping, and synchronisation, yet their mechanisms were quieter and, in the case of the Panaflex, nothing required blimping. Digital read-outs and flexible viewfinders also became standard. Canon, Panavision, and

Zeiss developed lenses which were more refined than their predecessors, and Stanley Kubrick had Ed DiGiulio of Cinema Products Corporation specially modify a range of Zeiss lenses and design an entirely new one for *A Clockwork Orange* and *Barry Lyndon*.[475] Yet such innovations aside, the general trend in cinematography in the 1970s was towards a greater flexibility for film-makers working on location. Life on the road was catered for by a specially adapted Land Rover, and 1970 saw the arrival of the Samcine Rain Deflector, which saved hours of shooting time that would otherwise have been lost on *When Eight Bells Toll* (1971).[476] A new generation of CdS (cadmium sulphide) exposure meters known as Spotmeters also promised the ability to 'measure lower light levels and far more selective parts of the subject'.[477] Meanwhile, lighting itself was improved by two innovations from Thorn; their compact source iodine (CSI) lamps, first introduced in 1970, were feted as the smallest arc lamps in the world, and their special control gear units which followed promised 'flicker-free filming'.[478]

In terms of film stock and processing, the new-generation Eastman colour (35mm type 5247 and 16mm type 7247) was faster than its predecessors and offered reduced grain, increased sharpness and better colour resolution (especially in greens). This development was driven by the television industry for 16mm location work, but a 35mm version followed, which was available in both negative and colour reversal form. New high-temperature processing techniques were also introduced by Kodak to handle the Eastman colour film.[479] Indeed, the film laboratory sector was particularly responsive to the changing demands of the market. For example, they had an important creative role in optical printing (matte work and special effects) and, in the second half of the decade, pioneered film transfer to the new medium of commercial videotape.[480] Greater flexibility and improvements in quality, speed and efficiency were the watchwords of the British film processing industry in the 1970s. The results, on film, are particularly noticeable in colour resolution and contrast.

Film editing was influenced in the 1970s more by creative fashion and economy than by technological change. At the beginning of the decade, Moviola's 'Anniversary Series' of horizontal editing desks created some consternation, despite their avowed speed and mastery of control.[481] But by 1975, their addition of a 'hollow prism' to their range of flatbed machines promised 'absolutely flickerless images' even when fully lit, again improving speed and accuracy.

Cinematography

Economic uncertainty made it difficult for lighting-cameramen to produce consistent work in this period. There are only two popular genres which manifest coherence in cinematography: international thrillers and TV spin-offs. This can be explained by the economic imperative of brand identity, rather than consistency of personnel or artistic ambition. In the thriller, photography tends to be plot-driven and focused upon action, with little attention to character motivation or *mise en scène*. TV spin-offs restrict camera movement to the requirements of performance and the domestic sphere, and rely on their audience's familiarity with the dependable reality of the world beyond the frame.

Aside from these examples, there is little evidence of a coherent cinematographic style during the period. Freddie Young's Academy Award-winning work on *Ryan's Daughter* was a rare example of bravura in the classical mode, contrasting lingering close-ups with sweeping panoramic shots which took in the whole social and natural landscape. By contrast, Billy Williams's photography on *Sunday Bloody Sunday* presents a culture of entrapment by restrictive master shots and an avoidance of pans and dollies. Wolfgang Suschitzky's mobile camerawork in *Get Carter* encompasses the austerity of the Tyneside skyline and his varied lighting regime is alienating in its effects. In *The Go-Between*, Gerry Fisher's lingering mastershots and sober framing call attention to the static ambience of Edwardian society. One of the most striking images in 1970s British cinema, the final shot of *The Wicker Man*, was photographed by veteran Harry Waxman, who used framing and scale inventively to lend a mythic quality to an unremarkable coastline. The sheer variety of these examples demonstrates the difficulty of ascribing a dominant 'look' to the cinematography of the decade.

Some experienced cinematographers were able to sustain their careers by being flexible. The former natural history documentarist John Coquillon was able to respond to Don Sharp's lively direction on remakes of *The Thirty Nine Steps* and *The Four Feathers*, lending these period adventures a vitality in their natural landscapes and social interiors. Coquillon also reproduced the same kind of haunted landscape he had created for *Witchfinder General* and *Straw Dogs* when he shot *The Triple Echo*. Clearly, an experienced and adaptable cinematographer could find some expressive space when working to the demands of different directors. Coquillon is an example of the kind of expertise which was able to adapt to the limited opportunities available.

A few leading directors of photography managed to maintain their profiles across a variety of films. John Alcott's best work was done for

Stanley Kubrick on *A Clockwork Orange*, *Barry Lyndon* and *The Shining* (1980). His other work in the decade, notably for Stuart Cooper on *Little Malcolm and His Struggle Against the Eunuchs*, *Overlord* (1975) and *The Disappearance* offered less scope for virtuoso style. David Watkin also worked with a number of important directors during the 1970s. His cinematography for Ken Russell on *The Boy Friend* and *The Devils* was vibrant and beautifully lit. He continued his association with Richard Lester, photographing *The Three Musketeers*, *The Four Musketeers* and *Robin and Marian*. Further evidence of Watkin's flexible management of lighting and colour palette is provided by two other films he shot in 1976: Tony Richardson's *Joseph Andrews* and the Hammer horror *To the Devil a Daughter*. Ossie Morris was another established British cinematographer who managed to develop a consistent style across a wide variety of projects. He followed his Oscar-winning photography on *Fiddler on the Roof* (1971) with other Hollywood successes: *Sleuth* (1972), *The Man Who Would be King* (1975) and *Equus* (1977), but he was also Director of Photography on the British co-productions, *Lady Caroline Lamb* and *The Odessa File*, and shot the Bond adventure, *The Man with the Golden Gun*. Throughout his career Morris was open to technical experimentation; for example, he was the first to use the new silent Panaflex on *The Odessa File*.[482]

We have established that production teams faced a number of challenges in the changing climate of the British film industry in the 1970s. Economic constraints made it difficult to sustain momentum and personnel across projects. The reduction in studio space appeared to afford directors more flexibility to shoot on location, but in practice this freedom was often restricted by tight budgets. These circumstances meant that the creative relationships between key personnel, especially the director and cinematographer, were put under new pressure. There was more responsibility on the shoulders of younger directors working on location, and this had an impact on shooting practices. One example is worth examining in detail: Ridley Scott's *The Duellists*.

Ridley Scott had worked as a designer at the BBC before establishing his own commercial advertising company. He had directed almost 2,000 television commercials before making his first feature film. Adapted from a story by Conrad, it charts the prolonged and senseless duel between two rival French hussars against the backdrop of Napoleon's imperial decline. The £900,000 budget, put up by Paramount, necessitated a location shoot which offered little scope for an epic treatment. Following an intensive three-week recce, Scott found an appropriate setting in the Sarlat area of the French Dordogne. He identified exterior locations and carefully storyboarded every scene by walking through each site with a stopwatch. His choices and labours were rewarded by the progress of the seasons. When his small, mobile crew began shooting in November 1976, the trees were denuded, the skies overcast and the landscape saturated – qualities which were 'an advantage because it was so beautiful . . . because it was more austere'.[483]

Scott's art training informed his sensitive response to the vagaries of the environment, while he maintained tight control over every aspect of the filming. All the exteriors were shot using natural light, which, in the short days of Winter, added an extra urgency to the process. He employed the latest Panaflex S.35 and Arriflex cameras, and shot on the new Eastmancolor II 5247 stock, making the best of the overcast conditions with the addition of Tiffin low-contrast filters to add 'mood and a certain coldness'.[484] Against the advice of his producer David Puttnam, Scott had recruited colleagues from commercial advertising. His cinematographer Frank Tidy had shot 200 commercials for Scott's company. When it came to lighting the interiors, Tidy's familiarity with Scott's approach enabled them to push the boundaries visually. Scott recalled: 'He would let shadow fall off, or didn't fill it in . . . Frank knew that this was what I liked . . . I don't mind if windows are burnt out . . . I don't mind if sometimes it goes totally dark . . . Frank knew how far to go.'[485] Yet despite Tidy's understanding of the director's requirements, after only five days Scott insisted (again against the advice of Puttnam) on operating himself, 'because I wasn't really getting what I wanted, pictorially, and I wasn't concentrating on the actors'.[486]

Scott's vision was meticulously planned and powerfully conceived. His approach, honed over years of commercial practice, was both economically efficient and visually coherent. It determined the precision of each set-up, positioning minor characters and minimal extras so as to make the frame look full. It extended to shooting certain set-ups from both directions to save time and money. 'What I learnt from commercials is to do what looks right,' he recalls:

> Making commercials had been my school and refinement process in the use of lensing and working on celluloid. [Now] I was surrounded with people I was comfortable with, and I was involved with Frank in terms of the lighting and the camera which, of course, was my forte at this moment in time. That's why I was so successful as a commercial maker – because it's nearly all visual.[487]

Scott explains this painterly preoccupation:

> I'd started to adopt the idea of transitions . . . the still lifes. I took them from paintings I'd seen as I was planning the film. That became a stylistic approach to the film: why not adopt almost painterly views of certain moments or scenes or transitions?[488]

Figure 9 *The Duellists*

He studied painters and engravers of the period, noting especially the 'importance of corners of pictures. The *mise en scène* tells you a lot about how people lived'. Such attention to authentic period detail creates the sense that 'you're watching a pictorial essay of that particular period'.[489]

The cinematography is the most striking quality of *The Duellists*. The interiors combine seductive shadows, sensuous fabrics and fetishised objects, and the dramatic landscapes offer impassive commentary upon the futile human struggle. At the time, Scott's refined photographic manner – lingering upon details, cutting in close-ups, sustaining establishing shots with the musical score – attracted some criticism.[490]

Stanley Kubrick's *Barry Lyndon* was Scott's inspiration for *The Duellists* in breaking 'the constipation of the costume drama':

> *Barry Lyndon* attempted to do that. I admire what Kubrick did, but because I'm very visual, I know he got bogged down in his own visuals. And in a funny sort of way, once you do that, you can't get out of it again. I'm very much aware of the problems.[491]

But in paying tribute to Kubrick, Scott was also acknowledging his own visual style. His art education and his commercial training liberated him from any reverence for cultural hierarchies beyond the imperative of period authenticity, visual texture and narrative coherence. This freedom to render the past as an imaginative landscape which offers visual pleasure for its own sake transformed the field of costume drama from the 1970s. Reflecting upon his innovation in pictorialism, Scott commented: 'Commercial film-making caused a whole reappraisal of feature film over this twenty year period. It made us re-examine how quickly we communicate, our cutting processes, and certainly lighting processes.'[492] *The Duellists* is an example of the way in which some enterprising new directors could exploit the limited opportunities offered by location shooting, in order to take creative control of the cinematography and pursue their own visual style.

Set design

Location shooting became increasingly common in 1970s British cinema. In Chapter 4 Ede argued that this practice had a significant impact on the role of the production designer. He showed that Hammer Studios, the *Carry Ons* and the Bond films were the only examples of consistent set design. From the increase in location work, we might expect that realism predominated in the period, as had been the case with the New Wave in the 1960s. Not so. British cinema of the 1970s was predominantly a pictorialist and fantastic cinema, and even those films which deployed realist discourses tended to do so self-consciously.

The sets and locations in many 1970s films can be interpreted as an index of the cultural competence of their authors, and they should be judged by the coherence and efficacy of their symbolic systems. In a range of films of the period, such as *The Final Programme*, *The Wicker Man*, *Get Carter*, *Something to Hide* (1971), *Monty Python and the Holy Grail*, *Mahler* and *The Tempest*, the locations are unusually motivated by narrative concerns. Bearing this in mind, our analysis of set design must take into account their locations, texture, composition and colouring. The role of the art director in the decade encompassed the adaptation of the 'found' environment to a greater extent than before, but location shooting also meant that directors could exert more control over production design. We observed this in the case of *The Duellists.*

It is instructive to pursue the comparison made by Scott himself with Kubrick's *Barry Lyndon*. Kubrick based the film on the novel by Thackeray, and his script constructed it with a voice-over instead of the bland first-person narrative of the original, arguing that this provided 'an ironic counter-point to what you see portrayed by the actors in the scene'.[493] Kubrick, having total control over Warners' generous budget, decided to eschew sets altogether and to film exclusively on location. Any personnel showing even a residual interest in studio shooting were

Figure 10 *Barry Lyndon*

weeded out.[494] Production designer Ken Adam was artistically drawn to expressionist *mise en scène*. In his set work for the Bond films and in his previous work for Kubrick, Adam had constructed an autonomous world out of kilter with reality. Kubrick's project with *Barry Lyndon* was to open up the past in a radically democratic manner: to make it live and glow by situating modern actors in historical locations. This gave Adam problems on both aesthetic and practical levels.[495] He regretted that *Barry Lyndon* called for his work to be 'much more reproductive than imaginative . . . We did enormous amounts of research. That's why it was never that exciting to me as a designer, even though I won an Academy Award for it.'[496] In the end, poor Adam was so distraught with the location demands that he tried to light a chocolate biscuit in his mouth, thinking that it was a cigar.[497]

Kubrick was obsessively thorough, and Adam's location notes reveal that he was sent on searches for suitable houses, which he clearly considered to be wild-goose chases. In quick succession, Adam was bitten by canine and human inhabitants on his travels.[498] He compiled a list of possible fronts, backs and interiors of houses across a swathe of countryside. The resulting selection was so complex that only Kubrick could hold the patchwork in his head. A ceiling from one location, a staircase from another, a door-jamb from one place, a garden wall from another – all were melded together with more extensive selections from Castle Howard, Wilton House, Longleat and others. The eighteenth-century interiors were both a simulacrum and a stylisation. In the breakdown pages for the filming in Ireland, there were 110 different houses used alone.[499] What is remarkable in the finished film is the solidity of the imagined world. This is a place which never was, but Kubrick took such care to back-fill the ages and temperaments of the inhabitants of that world that its emotional veracity is never questioned.[500] And the inhabitants' accoutrements were painstakingly selected and arranged; the Chevalier de Balibari's coach had to have at least one mare, as an index of his personality.[501]

Kubrick's choices of lighting and lenses profoundly affected the composition. The candle-lit scenes were shot without any artificial light, and cinematographer John Alcott had to be extremely inventive in his use of daylight sources. The problem was that using real locations in stately homes meant that very large rostrums had to be constructed inside the rooms themselves, limiting the crew's freedom to manœuvre.[502] Kubrick's custom-made lenses had little depth of field, and this meant that the actors too had restricted movement in the settings.[503] Kubrick had to use closed-circuit video on set in order to map the actors' limited range. The technical inventiveness occasioned by the location shooting, and the painstaking set dressing created a number of visual tensions which were only defused by the consistency of the compositions. In image after image, Kubrick centres the composition with a rigorous symmetry. With very few exceptions, the focus of interest is placed at the very centre of the screen. This gives a balance and a coolness to the film, and is a sort of visual correlative of the urbane sophistication of high Augustanism.

According to Adam, Kubrick also immersed himself in the paintings of the period – Gainsborough and Reynolds, in particular.[504] These painters are essentially critical of the values of Augustan culture. They adumbrate an emergent Romanticism, a definitive break with rationality and *sang-froid*. The subjects of their paintings look out with quizzical desire and unanswerable questions, and this look is often reproduced in the pose and gaze of the film's protagonists, particularly Lady Lyndon (Marisa Berenson). And so the visual texture of *Barry Lyndon* displays a mixed aesthetic. The rigour of the symmetrical compositions, which are most often evident in the interiors, conflicts with the undisciplined emotions experienced within them. The emotions are often carried by the set dressing or the costumes, even though both bear the patina of verisimilitude. Thus, compositional and design features are all incorporated within an overarching vision of the past in which no possibility is refused and no closure achieved.

Costume design

Costume design is a means of signifying, at a subliminal level, hints about class, politics and sexuality. A covert 'costume narrative' within film texts is an economical way of signalling messages which have been either ignored by, or repressed within, the script.

In the 1970s, costume designers, like other creative personnel, found it difficult to take risks due to market unpredictability and job insecurity. Emma Porteus is a case in point. The designs for her British films – *Swallows and Amazons* and *The Lady Vanishes* (1979) – were succinct and witty, but unambitious. But when she moved to America to design the costumes in such films as *The Island of Dr. Moreau* (1977) and *The Clash of the Titans* (1981), she developed innovatory methods and imagery, which she found impossible in a British context.[505]

As with other creative personnel, the costume designer's relationship with the director was also intensified in this period. Jocelyn Rickards, who had done such sublime work in *The Knack* (1965) and *Alfred the Great* (1969), had a real struggle with David Lean on *Ryan's Daughter*. Lean's inability to read a costume drawing meant that Rickards had to work against the grain, and she created the fairy-like yellow dress and the scarlet petticoat only with difficulty; the authentic Kinsale cloaks were included via a sort of subterfuge.[506] John Boorman, a very hands-on director, had a major input into the costumes designed by his wife (Christel Kruse Boorman) in *Zardoz*. Similarly, Shirley Russell shared with her husband a taste for 'fantasticated gear' and produced a range of clothes which were extravagant and risk-taking: the keyboard-lapel jacket and Bo-Peep dress in *Lisztomania*, and the Acid Queen's costume in *Tommy*.[507] But Russell was also capable of subtle designs, as attested by her work in *Savage Messiah* (1972) and *Valentino*.

When the work of the costume designer was thoroughly integrated into the ensemble, then remarkable things could be achieved. A good example of this is *Don't Look Now*. The costumes were designed by Andrea Galer and Marit Lieberson, who had a close working relationship with director Nicolas Roeg. The film constructs a formal unity of texture and colour in order to break the firm boundaries between the seen and the unseen, the known and the unknown. The hero John Baxter (Donald Sutherland) has, unbeknown to himself, psychic abilities, and this is expressed through his unconscious recognition of patterns: between the textures of light through the windows and the folds of cloth, and between the viscous oozings on a slide and blood on a pavement. These pattern-recognitions function throughout the film as a sort of prolepsis of his awful end.

Much has been written about the colour coding in the film, which is usefully summarised by Andrew Patch.[508] He quotes Anthony Richmond, the film's Director of Photography: 'Nic is very visual . . . he knew that taking the red out of everything except the dwarf's clothing and the little girl's mac, really played a very big part in the design and the costume design.'[509] This is a serious oversimplification, though. There are, in fact, hints of red elsewhere in the clothing, and they are all ineluctably linked to the themes of femininity and death. Laura (Julie Christie), who otherwise dresses exclusively in black, grey and silver, dons bright red boots and handbag after her two moments of apotheosis on the film, the vision of the blind sister and the love-making scene. These red accoutrements signal her re-entry into the world of femininity, which is also that of procreation and death. And John wears a scarf with a bright red pattern throughout. The red part of the plaid is consistently wound round his throat, and so acts as a covert reference to the slash which he will receive there, and which we witness in unnerving explicitness.

The textures of the costumes are important too. Laura and John wear tweed clothes throughout, which signal their class mobility and wealth. Tweed can never be a neutral fabric, and this was something which Galer developed in her subsequent work. But the difference between the colour of the couple's clothes is important. Laura wears grey herringbone tweeds; John wears browns and greens, which on a subliminal level mark him out as closer to nature. Yet the script positions him, in his work as architectural historian, as a man of culture too. And so he appears as the fulcrum of all. The power of the film resides in the summary way it dispatches this powerful figure. The man of culture and nature is easily destroyed, which creates an intolerable level of anxiety.

Don't Look Now deploys costume details in an extremely subtle manner. This is demonstrated by three shots of the brooch worn by one of the psychic sisters. John sees it first of all in the restaurant (Laura has her back turned to it). Later he picks it up from the dressing-table of the sisters, cradles it on the palm of his hand, and clearly has some kind of preternatural moment of vision. Lastly, it appears to him in his death throes, in a swift montage of images of love, ecstasy and loss.

The brooch itself represents Melusina, a figure from Celtic myth. Melusina is a water-goddess, sometimes presented as a sprite or faery. She can bewitch men by her beauty, but her essentially double nature is destructive to them. For a while she can have legs, flanks, feet like any other, but she also secretly has fishy scales and a tail, which return to bring destruction to her lovers. This brooch functions as a condensed and over-determined symbol in the film. It embodies that double aspect of femininity which is at the heart of Western culture: desirable and deadly,

Figure 11 *Don't Look Now*

mother and destroyer. The brooch itself is adorned in a significant way. On the tail there are three stones. A lesser designer would have made these red. Instead, they are blue, and moreover the *exact* shade of blue of John's coat, thus linking him with the deathly tail. And hanging from that same tail are three pearls, symbol of tears. But pearls come from oysters, whose vulval/vaginal significance is legendary too. Thus we can see that costume symbolism can work with great power when thoroughly integrated into the overall schema of the production.

Editing

British editing practices in the 1970s were markedly different from those of earlier periods. In the 1950s, continuity editing had been carefully deployed, so that (for example) a protagonist would be seen opening a door and would then be seen on the other side, with an 'invisible' cut conferring fluidity on to the action.[510] Such techniques, though they lent coherence to the narrative, were abandoned with increasing rapidity during the 1960s, such that by the 1970s, more direct cutting was the norm. Roy Perkins and Martin Stollery have documented this shift, noting the ways in which veterans such as Ralph Kemplen and Anne Coates adapted their practices to the newer, faster styles.[511] Rapid cuts and ellipses, which would have been viewed as non-sequiturs to a previous generation of editors, became the fashionable norm. Such trends were exaggerated in the films of Ken Russell, where Stuart Baird's editing on *Lisztomania* and *Tommy* anticipated the dizzying juxtapositions of MTV. But rapid editing was increasingly used in action adventures like the Bond films too. Here John Glen and John Grover were instrumental in re-energising the casual style of Roger Moore's early Bonds; Hollywood blockbusters set the standard for fast-paced action in the second half of the decade.

Various reasons have been adduced for the transformation of British editing in the 1970s: the dominance of television discourses, the influence of the French New Wave, the Hollywood renaissance.[512] Whatever its causes, the effects of this transformation were visible in a wide range of films, from commercial to avant-garde productions. But with the latter, editing became political, rather than a device to make the story spin along. *Nightcleaners* was originally intended to be shown as a linear narrative, but was reconstituted in the cutting room into a radically deconstructed text, jagged and challenging on a formal level.[513] Of course, such radical techniques were Brechtian in their desire to strip away the audience's certainties and to work with the *Verfremdungseffekt* which ensued. And one director in particular, Lindsay Anderson, brought Brechtian aesthetics into mainstream cinema, with remarkable consequences.

Editing was an area of particular emotional tension for Anderson and, apart from the shooting itself, was the place where he thought the film artist should have most control. Writing with hindsight in 1988, he argued:

> The real attachment, as far as I'm concerned, comes in the time of editing, the time of intimate and scrupulous work on the material, when one's whole effort and concentration and feeling goes into the rhythmic ordering, the exact pointing by juxtaposition of every film that we have shot. It is at this stage that film most closely corresponds to Pater's dictum that 'all art constantly aspires to the condition of music.'[514]

Doubtless his experiences with the editing of *O Lucky Man!* had been crucial in refining Anderson's views.[515] The film was a picaresque tale of a young coffee salesman (Malcolm McDowell), who undergoes various vicissitudes on his road to a Zen-type enlightenment; he is blown up, interrogated, almost used for animal/human transplant surgery, employed as a money launderer, imprisoned, attacked by vagrants, suckled by a stranger and becomes a film star. Such a potentially shapeless narrative had to be given unity and structure, and this was achieved by the editing, and by the song-cycle composed and performed by Alan Price.

David Gladwell, who had worked on *If. . .* and whose elliptical and sharp style fitted the demands of that film, was again chosen by Anderson to edit.[516] But the requirements of *O Lucky Man!* were quite different, since it did not have *If. . .*'s narrative closure. Rather, its episodic structure required a type of editing which Gladwell was unable or unwilling to provide. Anderson's diaries record his famously choleric temperament, but they are also an index of the difficulty of finding an appropriate method for the picaresque narrative. First of all Anderson fell out with Karel Reisz, who was advising on the film and whose status as a theorist of editing was then unassailable; Anderson found him 'stale', 'square' and insufficiently intuitive.[517] Next, Anderson became disillusioned with Gladwell, finding his editing style slow and cumbersome and the whole editing team 'dolts'.[518] In September 1972, Anderson resolved to bring in Tom Priestley as editor. The diaries show some very fancy footwork by Anderson, alternately flattering, cajoling and criticising both Gladwell and Priestley, in order to get the editing rhythm he wanted. Anderson even reinserted scenes and shots rejected by Gladwell and smuggled them in under Priestley's nose.[519]

The final cut of *O Lucky Man!* is a virtuoso example of editing, in that every sequence – based on the separate vicissitudes of the hero – has a slightly different rhythm in terms of shot length. The hospital sequence, for example, alternates short with relatively lengthy shots, which has the effect of lulling and then intensifying the protagonist's anxieties. The pastoral sequence with breast-feeding has a much slower pace, with equally balanced and lengthier shots. This practice gives the film a varied pace. What provides an overall framework and *leitmotif* to the film is the series of songs performed by Alan Price. These are interspersed at regular intervals and mark each twist and turn of the narrative. And since they express a similar mood – worldly-wise and ironic – they create an impressive coherence of tone.

John Izod and his colleagues have demonstrated that Anderson

Figure 12 *O Lucky Man!*

constructed the film around the ideas and emotions expressed by Price, for whom he entertained a savage and unreciprocated *tendresse*.[520] The persistence of that intense but unrequited desire – a pattern repeated in Anderson's life – gives a sort of emotional scaffolding to the film. Price's songs are delivered with a throwaway elegance, and the chronic disengagement was clearly a source of both fascination and pain for the director. Price's performance and music operate as a sort of editing in themselves – a structure which both reveals and represses.

Of course, editing in commercial cinema is not just a matter of directorial desire, in the 1970s or at any other time. Warner Bros. had put up the money for *O Lucky Man!*, and they liked the 'hip' image which they thought Price would purvey. But when they saw the final cut, they were dismayed by its political radicalism and air of savage gloom, and so they demanded major reductions in two scenes: the Salvation Army scene, which invites viewers to disbelieve in human goodness, and the suicide of Mrs Richards, which utterly removed hope from the human condition.[521] Anderson protested, but to no avail, and the first-release version was shown with these and other cuts, which were reinstated on later release.[522]

Conclusion

At the beginning of this chapter we suggested that, if it were possible to conceive of the films of a period sharing a particular tone, then evidence of this was to be found in an analysis of visual style. Having undertaken that analysis, we are now in a position to make some speculative observations about the issue of tone or manner. It may be useful here to distinguish in the first instance between those production practices which constitute *mise en scène* (cinematography and lighting, set and costume design) and post-production procedures (editing and music). Both sets of practices reveal the fault-lines in creative agency which are characteristic of British film production in the 1970s. We have examined cases where these struggles were played out by directors and their creative teams working with relative freedom on location: *The Duellists*, *Barry Lyndon* and *Don't Look Now*. But rifts existed in post-production too. In our analysis of *O Lucky Man!* we noted how the score served to orchestrate tensions evident in the editing process and ultimately to resolve them. This may appear to be an exceptional case, but music was also a significant factor in the resolution of post-production struggles over the editing of *Performance* and *The Wicker Man*. In these cases studio intervention was instrumental in radically reshaping the films before release. These examples reveal the sometimes strained relations between production workers and their distant, but powerful, distributors. When Paramount Chairman Barry Diller viewed the rough-cut of *The Man Who Fell To Earth* he told British Lion's Michael Deeley in no uncertain terms: 'This is not the movie Paramount bought. The picture we bought is linear, and this isn't.'[523]

Such disputes serve to highlight the matter of narrative coherence. Classical narrative conventions are maintained by two sets of practices: the harmonious arrangement and lighting of elements within the frame (composition), and the smooth trajectory of the edit (montage). Observed together, these practices ensure their own self-effacement in the service of narrative realism. British cinema of the 1970s produced a remarkable number of films wherein these practices were either applied inconsistently, or deliberately subverted. It would be easy to attribute inconsistency to budgetary constraints, incompetence, or the kind of creative tensions illustrated above. But there is another explanation to consider also: a radical shake-up of attitudes to the materials of culture in the visual field. What do we mean by this?

Transformations in visual culture, and challenges to erstwhile secure boundaries between high and popular arts in the late 1960s, had a profound effect upon the symbolic function of objects in the cinema of the 1970s. Certain signifiers are made to bear an immense weight of meaning (the red mac in *Don't Look Now*, the giant pinballs in *Tommy*). But equally, as Robert Hughes remarked of *A Clockwork Orange*, we are assaulted by 'cultural objects cut loose from any power to communicate'.[524] It is hyper-signification versus meaninglessness. What are the conditions whereby such radical ambivalence can obtain?

This has to do not simply with the objects themselves, but with their anchorage. It depends upon their place within the frame (composition) and their frequency of iteration (montage). In both cases this is commonly disproportionate to their narrative function – a tendency which serves to undermine the objective correlative of the fictional world, and to promote a subjective manner which is self-referential and ironic. Irony is the most potent expression of the contingent nature of reality, of the world turned upside down. British cinema of the 1970s is, above all, a cinema of contingency. This noncommittal attitude carries with it not only a sort of moral relativism, but moreover a continual postponement of resolution. Nothing is ever settled, life is always elsewhere, meaning is perpetually deferred. This predominant tone is expressed in films across the spectrum of 1970s British cinema, from *Barry Lyndon* to *Alfie Darling*, from *Up Pompeii* to *Radio On*. It is an expression of disavowal which bears the imprimatur of post-modernity.

If this attitude can be perceived on such a widespread scale in the rendition of the material world of objects, it may also be evident in the visual field at large. For what is it about the filmic depiction of social space which denies objects within the visual field meaningful anchorage? In order to answer this question we shall turn next to the matter of performance style and the boundaries of personal and social space.

CHAPTER 12

Social Space

This chapter deals with the issue of social space, and asks whether 1970s British cinema constructs a dynamic field of power, in which human figures are placed within the social landscape in an innovatory way. We need to distinguish too between physical and mythical spaces. Film constructs physical spaces which can either liberate or limit its inhabitants. But it also relies on mythical spaces – those shared mental landscapes which operate as explanatory models for the whole culture. In this regard, cinema can present society's holy objects – the cross, the ankh, the unicorn – and its holy places – Avalon, heaven, the Sacred Grove. It has a double function, of both displaying and sanctifying those practices which bond society together in a coherent way. By the 1970s cinema's status had changed, and therefore it performed a range of different cultural tasks, and presented different models of social space. In interpreting these models, much depends on the means whereby we adduce a film's attitude to the everyday – to those objects which patrol the boundaries of the known world, and which function as symbols of interdiction or desire.

It is useful here to follow the aesthetic lead of R. G. Collingwood. In his neglected but remarkable *The Principles of Art*, Collingwood argues for the gnomic function of art, and distinguishes three degrees of representation: firstly, the naive and non-selective; secondly, the selective; and thirdly, the non-literal type which concentrates on 'an emotional representation'.[525] This affective function, according to Collingwood, is manifested in art-works whose symbols stimulate us to experience afresh the world we know. They do this by making us feel sensations akin to the material world. It is this affective function which we think is so crucial in British cinema of the decade. In film after film, the viewer is invited to experience what the world of everyday life feels like and, more crucially, what radical change would feel like too. In this way, the film culture contributes to a sense of the subjective and its relationship to the social world.

In this chapter we shall consider how subjectivity is dealt with in the context of social space. To do this, we need to distinguish between geographical and personal space. As we highlighted in the previous chapter, geographical space was predominately constructed through the creative adaptation of location in the cinema of this period, though this certainly did not make it a social realist cinema. We showed how a number of film-makers were particularly imaginative in the ways in which they transformed 'found' locations. Here, we need to undertake a more structured analysis of types of geographical space, in which we will explore the functions of the rural and urban settings where the human dramas are located. Personal space in cinema is defined by performative style, and body language is a historically specific discourse to which the cinema is particularly sensitive.

The first section below establishes the difference between those films in which geographical space is motivated by narrative function, and those in which there is a high level of redundancy in the visual field. It then proceeds to explore a range of films in which motivated space is deployed in distinctive ways, according to the intentions of the film-makers. The second section follows a different method. It covers a broader range of films, and discusses the construction of subjectivity by proposing an index of new performance types.

Geographical Space

In the 1970s, many low-budget films which might in earlier periods have been studio-bound, were filmed on location. In the television spin-offs, for example, there is a sharp distinction between foreground and background, between dramatic action and its location. Frequently, framing is so casual as to imply a shared belief in the solidity of the fictional world beyond the margins of the screen. Yet even these unmotivated spaces have something to tell: they illustrate what is, ideologically, taken as read. Whether it be beach or countryside, metropolis or provinces, these unmotivated landscapes are drab, windswept and suburban. They are the consequences of economic and aesthetic contingency, and have little dramatic function.

Films in which geographical space has a highly motivated function are more common, and fall into distinct types. A minority strand evokes the Pathetic Fallacy through landscape; there is a smooth coherence between the setting and the emotional landscape of the protagonists. In *Kidnapped* (1971), *The Railway Children*, *The Optimists of Nine Elms* (1973) and *Black Jack*, the natural world has a sympathetic function. In other geographically motivated films, the physical world is inimical to the human figures: for example, in *Ryan's Daughter*, *The Virgin and the Gypsy* (1970), *The Go-*

Between and *The Duellists*. In these films there is a disjunction between the visual space and the dramatic action. But these strands have only a minor presence in British cinema of the period. The majority of films in which geographical space is motivated fall into three broad categories: realism, naturalism and the mythic.

Realism

In Chapter 9 we suggested that realism was in decline. Few realist films of the period construct the metropolitan landscape in a comprehensive and coherent way. More often than not, urban spaces are viewed as an agglomeration of private discourses and diverse communities. For example, *Sunday Bloody Sunday*, *Pressure* and *Nighthawks* present the insularity of suburban life and the concerns of particular communities. In her work on *Babylon* in Chapter 6, Shaw shows how black communities were represented in terms of their specific social dynamics and cultural geographies.

This concern with fragmented communities and private discourses meant that realist cinema constructed geographical space in new ways. *Get Carter* was adapted from Ted Lewis's novel *Jack's Return Home*. Director Mike Hodges and producer Michael Klinger eschewed the Humberside location of the source novel in favour of Gateshead, which Hodges recalled from his national service: 'The visual drama of the place took my breath away. Seeing the great bridges crossing the Tyne, the waterfront, the terraced houses stepped up each side of the deep valley, I knew that Jack was home.'[526]

The social space of Tyneside achieves its intensity through the cinematography of Wolfgang Suschitzky. The terraced houses, local pubs, betting shops and clubs are at once depressingly familiar and menacingly strange. Fluid camera movement and point-of-view shots construct the subjective perception of the protagonist's homecoming. The film-makers assembled a cityscape where Victorian slum poverty persisted alongside the worst excesses of 1960s urban planning. This adapted environment served to locate the dubious relationships between local enterprise and criminal activity which the film presents.

The realist function of this regional landscape is most memorably achieved in the film's climactic scene. Following a chase along a colliery railway pier, Michael Caine's Jack Carter exacts his revenge upon Eric Paice (Ian Hendry), dumping his body in one of the hoppers which carry pit spoil out to sea. This grim, inhuman mechanism, which scars the coastal landscape at Blackhall Beach, County Durham, is the perfect metaphor for the gangster's callous tradings in human life. Hodges himself, on first seeing this stretch of coastline, remarked that it seemed an 'absolute vision of hell'.[527] The film's geographical space juxtaposes decaying infrastructure and entrepreneurial modernity, suggesting that this is a community trapped between the old world and the new. And it is important to recognise the almost perfunctory manner in which realist constructions of geographical spaces are internalised in the lives of their protagonists. Another crime film of the decade which operates in this way is *The Long Good Friday*. Here London is presented piecemeal as the gangland province of Harold Shand (Bob Hoskins); the undeveloped docklands, viewed from his Thames motor-yacht, are his own parish and constitute the landscape of his entrepreneurial ambitions. It is symbolic that IRA bombs physically destroy the East End of Shand's imagination. The geographical motivation of space in realist films of the 1970s goes beyond the urban crime genre, however. A coastal landscape functions in a similar way in the psychological drama, *Something to Hide*.

Naturalism

Naturalism is a documentary mode which combines an inclusive, democratic spirit with a rigorous attention to the surface of everyday life. As noted in Chapter 9, this visual mode was a narrow but significant field in the 1970s, attracting support in particular from the BFI Production Board. Although this field includes work by a range of film-makers with different interests, they share an attention to the minutiae of the past at a social or personal level. Their work is concerned with the anchorage of objects within a precise material world.

Like *Get Carter*, Bill Douglas's autobiographical trilogy is also set specifically in a regional landscape blighted by coal. It also offers a subjective view of that world. Yet its concerns and manner are entirely different. The trilogy comprises *My Childhood* (1972), *My Ain Folk* (1973) and *My Way Home* (1978). In these films, an austere documentarism is imbued with a poetic sensitivity rooted in personal memory. However, subjective though this vision is, it is never sentimental. One of the most powerful aspects of the trilogy is the vivid depiction of the characters' relations to their surroundings. *My Childhood* offers a number of examples: the boys going out to meet their fathers returning from the pit, kids scavenging for coal on the slag heaps, Jamie's grandmother arriving at the school gate to fetch him, and his mother eating an apple in her hospital bed. As producer Mamoun Hassan recalled in interview, the emotional truth of these moments was conveyed firstly in the visual imagination of the script itself, but secondly in the *mise en scène*. And often this emotional intensity was achieved at the expense of period authenticity, which was clearly of only secondary interest to Douglas's pursuit of the emotional truth of their experience. As Hassan comments:

> You can write whatever you like in a script and say, there is an intense scene, but you don't get the intense [sic], you just get the scene . . . The artist can create intensity – in the *mise en scène* . . . You can have another person and say, 'It's a medium shot.' But with Bill Douglas, it's a unique shot.[528]

In *My Childhood* this intensity is frequently created by the careful framing of a medium shot with maximum depth of field, and then holding the shot without additional camera movement or cutting-in for longer than convention dictates. A stillness descends upon the scene, momentarily, which seems to alienate the human figures from their surroundings. But then, the action of the characters within the frame suddenly revitalises their dramatic relation to the physical space, and breaks the stasis of the sustained moment. In this way, their actions, however apparently ordinary, carry a moral weight that is born of their own alienation from the landscape. When Jamie (Stephen Archibald) is summoned from school by his grandmother (Jean Taylor-Smith), she waits in front of the building for him, and the white line at the edge of the playground becomes a threshold she is unable to cross. The shot is held in real time, imbuing the reason for her summons with a profound moral charge.

During his tenure at the BFI's Production Board, Mamoun Hassan also sponsored Kevin Brownlow and Andrew Mollo's *Winstanley* (1975). Unlike Douglas, Brownlow and Mollo were highly preoccupied with the achievement of period authenticity. Brownlow's premise was to recreate historical circumstance: 'Despite the mass of admirable English historical films there are hardly any which give you the feeling of having lived through the event. We will try to ensure that this film provides the experience.'[529] To this end, they researched and made period costumes, scouted for unspoiled locations and seventeenth-century buildings, collected accurate farming implements and rare animal breeds, and even researched the right kind of seed to sow in their re-creation of the Diggers' encampment on St George's Hill. They enlisted the help of the Sealed Knot for the Civil War battle scenes, and borrowed authentic armour from the Master of Armouries at the Tower of London. Peasant shoes were manufactured based upon a 'single model extant in Northampton Shoe Museum'.[530] Brownlow even insisted that the hens' wings should not be clipped – a principle which had disastrous consequences when a cockerel flew the coop and was eaten by a local fox.[531]

Figure 13 *Winstanley*

Although the shoot was originally scheduled for eight weeks, for Brownlow it became 'abundantly clear that we needed the seasons – we needed to grow our own crops and to see their growth, culminating in the harvest. The seasons, and the weather, played a far more important part in the lives of seventeenth-century people than they do today.'[532] Such naturalist imperatives made for a very difficult shoot, presenting all kinds of personnel and continuity problems. Despite Ernest Vincze's superb monochrome photography, which does indeed bear witness to the changes in the landscape with the turning of the seasons, the film overlooks the fact that an audience must have emotional empathy with the lives of the characters. And it is at the level of script and characterisation that the imbalance in *Winstanley*'s creative resources is most marked. Partly this is due to Brownlow and Mollo's preference for amateur actors; partly it can be attributed to their radical departure from David Caute's own script of his source novel. Eric Porter, who turned down the offer of a leading role, summarised the film's essential problem: 'I would have said that a closer focus on a more intimate area (by which I mean the whole situation and events worked through and seen through the lives, actions and reactions of one family group) would have resulted in a more sympathetic engagement of an observer's interest.'[533] The film avoids the conventions of psychological realism. David Caute, on viewing the finished film, complained that 'it oscillates between very stylized language, mood and naturalism, and this doesn't work'.[534] This kind of extreme naturalist experiment attempts to construct a material world in which objects can be anchored without having any symbolic resonance. Subjectively, it denies the possibility of imaginative transformation.

There were also other kinds of naturalism. *Akenfield* (1974), Peter Hall's adaptation of Ronald Blyth's novel, manifests the same attention to period detail and rural specificity as *Winstanley*, but its prevailing romantic sensibility is rooted in the subjective experience of a First World War soldier returning to his Suffolk village. There is a palpable sense of loss evoked by the immutability of the natural landscape and the relationships between stories of human destiny and social change. Because of its grander scale, and the way it invokes deeper myths about ruralism and nationhood, this personal narrative has an affective power quite different from Bill Douglas's autobiographical trilogy. It is nostalgic, but never sentimental. *Akenfield* is thus a naturalist text which taps into national myths about place in a profound way. David Gladwell's *Requiem for a Village* (1975) was also set in rural Suffolk and, like *Akenfield*, mixes topographical essay and pastoral myth. But other texts of the period approach the mythic in an altogether different manner.

Myth

Our third category provides evidence of some of the most groundbreaking imaginative landscapes in the cinema of the period. The culture of the 1970s witnessed a revival of interest in alternative mythologies, which encouraged belief in the numinous. This cultural ratification of the mysterious provided fertile ground for some film-makers. They gave visual expression to whole mythical systems and allowed themselves to be led by their hearts and eyes rather than by their rational minds. To return to Collingwood, we want to argue that mythical texts offer an 'emotional representation', which has particular cultural currency in this period.

We have already argued that John Boorman's *Zardoz* showed an enormous range and imaginative flexibility. His other films of the period ushered the viewer into alternative systems of belief, and it is interesting to speculate how his Tolkien film might have turned out, given adequate funding. But other film-makers too wanted to live mythically, artistically speaking. The work of Roeg should be interpreted in this light. *The Man Who Fell To Earth* is a coherent vision which offers an imaginative commentary upon the strangeness of those on the margins of the familiar, and *Don't Look Now* can be interpreted as a narrative about a secret esoteric world which lies concealed beneath the world we know. Derek Jarman's work of the decade, particularly *Jubilee*, is mythic in tendency. And certainly the work of Ken Russell can be read in this way too, since he always portrays characters in the grip of certainties which are at odds with convention; the extreme flamboyance of his style ensues from an absolute belief in Romantic subjectivity.

Of course, 1970s mythic cinema contained appalling turkeys. *The Final Programme* should be obligatory viewing for anyone who thinks it is easy to maintain mythical coherence. The final sequence is a piquant reminder, if any were needed, that one can look very silly even while feeling magnificent. The 'lost world' cycle produced by John Dark and directed by Kevin Connor – *The Land That Time Forgot* (1975), *At the Earth's Core* and the rest – had an emotional and mythical coherence but were discredited by poor settings and performances.[535] And Stephen Weekes directed *Gawain and the Green Knight* (1973), starring Murray Head, whose casting illustrated the counter-cultural currency of Arthurian revivalism. None of these is an important film on its own, but together they demonstrate that it is in the mythic cinema of the period that the really significant innovations took place.

The Wicker Man, Robin Hardy and Anthony Shaffer's tale of pagan revivalism, combines scattered locations in South-West Scotland to create the mythical Summerisle, imbuing the landscape with a coherent belief system which conceals economic failure and challenges the rule of law. The power of this conceit is derived in part from the mythic potential in the discovered landscape. Consider, for example, how the Old Church at Anwoth is presented as a relic of Pagan desecration. Here, the hapless Sergeant Howie (Edward Woodward), who is investigating the disappearance of a missing child, clambers among broken apple boxes (the island's failed export crop) and ancient gravestones. The subjective camera focuses upon a skull and crossbones emblazoned on a stone coffin and discovers a young woman breast-feeding her baby while holding an egg in her up-turned palm. This is a powerfully evocative location because its malevolence and strangeness are found as much as staged. The film draws upon a residual spiritual potency in the landscape itself and its ancient relics, but the intensity is heightened by the selection of the human figure, its accoutrements, expression and framing.

Another 1970s film which transforms the Scottish landscape into sublime myth is *Monty Python and the Holy Grail* (1974). The Pythons were inspired in part by Pasolini's *Canterbury Tales* (1971), which, accord-

Figure 14 *The Wicker Man*

ing to Michael Palin, modelled a 'style and quality of shooting [required] to stop it being just another *Carry On King Arthur*'.[536] Much of the film's humour emanates from the juxtaposition of Arthurian legend with a conspicuous awareness of the impossibility of rendering historical reality in film. Co-directors Gilliam and Jones 'both had the idea of doing an antidote to the Hollywood vision of the Middle Ages . . . really dirty'.[537] Location filming in Glencoe, on Loch Tay and at Doune Castle achieved a certain bleak authenticity, which was assisted by budgetary constraints (old film stock bought cheaply), faulty equipment, impractical set-ups and novice co-direction.[538]

Despite these constraints, in the film's most evocative scenes the natural landscape is imbued with a dark, menacing quality which owes something to the work of Brueghel, while Gilliam's animated sequences draw in equal measure upon the stylisation of medieval illuminated manuscripts and the surreal allegories of Hieronymus Bosch. Although their meagre budget militated against bravura set pieces, 'Bring out your dead', the witch-ducking scene, the wedding at the castle, and the Bridge of Death share something visually of this spirit. And the film's climax, as the ship crosses Loch Leven through the mist, is genuinely cinematic, as Michael Palin noted in his diary: 'The boat that takes them across to the Castle Aaargh! looks really magical. It will give the film just the right kind of atmosphere and build-up to make the non-ending work.'[539]

The 'non-ending' comprises a sustained visual joke about film-as-form, expressed in a range of self-reflexive gestures and structuring devices. As the armed French hordes gather on the hillside, a despondent Arthur and Sir Bedevere (Jones) wade ashore (having somehow crossed Loch Leven) to be met by a twentieth-century police convoy with sirens wailing. The officer in charge proceeds to arrest the film's stars and approaches the cameraman, in a gesture of *cinéma-vérité*, to shut the film down. The film's subversive *dénouement* represents the ultimate transcendence of realism. This comic fantasy utterly transforms the dimensions of real geographical space and produces an imaginative landscape which plays fast and loose with the world of material objects and historical order.

So far, we have suggested that British films of the 1970s employed motivated geographical space to create a series of atomised, almost tribal, communities governed by discrete discursive formations. We now need to examine the ways in which the cinema dealt with identity and subjectivity through the development of a substantially new set of performance styles.

Personal Space

The portrayal of subjectivity is complex, and hedged around by issues of psychological realism. Subjectivity is not beyond history, but determined by it and saturated with it. There is a fashion in feelings, and each historical period has its own emotional range; certain types of expression will be encouraged, and others consigned to taboo. Sarah Ahmed's work on subjectivity and culture has usefully alerted us to the changing value which accrues to certain types of expression and she notes, 'the affective economies, whose feelings do not reside in subjects of objects, but are produced as effects of circulation'.[540] We want to argue that the 1970s was a period in which, *pacē* the transformations taking place on the social and sexual level, the emotional landscape was undergoing an acute transformation also. Cinema had its part to play in the process.

But it is through the body that feelings are expressed. Body language is a discourse which audiences intuitively read; styles of movement, gaze and proxemic convention are the building blocks of that subliminal understanding which forms the basis of the communicative interaction. Cinematic body language is notoriously different from that of (say) the theatre or the pantomime, due to the facility of the close-up in intensifying intimacy. Jennifer Barker mounts an argument that tactility and texture are key indices of subjectivity in the cinema, and this is an attractive idea.[541] But the problem is that such a model does not provide an explanation for the changing ways in which subjectivity is expressed, or the industrial constraints upon them.

What is needed is an approach to subjectivity and social space which takes cognisance of the conflicting agencies at work in film production, and which attempts to decide which narrative codes are qualitatively new. For the purposes of our argument, something may be learned if we differentiate between a range of distinct performance types, attempting to locate their discrete body language, and relating these to the social spaces being constructed. We propose to explore five types of self-presentation: self-containment, self-disclosure, damage, disavowal and awkwardness. This does not purport to provide a comprehensive account of the performance repertoire of the cinema of the period. Rather, it suggests the continuity of certain established performance types and the emergence of distinctive new ones.

Self-containment

A range of male actors in the decade displayed a performative style which was extremely self-contained. They tended to specialise in action films, and made a virtue of giving very little away. Their careers did not originate in the theatre, but they came to prominence in the cinema of the 1970s. Oliver Tobias, Edward Fox, Robert Powell and others exemplify an acute self-possession. The impassivity of these actors is combined with a social and sexual disengagement which is manifested in their body language. Their performances show that they are at ease with the world of goods, yet they paradoxically appear to have little memory of objects; they live in a perpetually illuminated present.

Powell manifests this self-contained style with increasing intensity as the decade progresses. His work on *Tommy* and *Mahler* exhibits a degree of expressivity, but his performance in *Jesus of Nazareth* (1977), a television mini-series directed by Zeffirelli, was clearly influential in the construction of that limpid emptiness which became his specialism. Powell appeared in *The Four Feathers* and *The Thirty Nine Steps*. In the former, he is the blinded hero Jack Durrance, played in the 1930s with great expressivity by Ralph Richardson. By contrast, Powell's Durrance exudes an uncanny confidence. In his performance in *The Thirty Nine Steps*, Powell critiques the Hannays of Robert Donat and Kenneth More. In their acting styles, they were sensitive to social and sexual nuance. Powell, however, plays Hannay with an unprecedented *sang-froid*. He wears his face like a mask, with all the musculature relaxed so as to give nothing away. Throughout the film he hardly blinks, and the saurian image is intensified by his erotic coolness; there are scarcely any two-shots of him with the heroine, and whenever they are together in frame, there

Figure 15 Robert Powell in *The Thirty Nine Steps*

is a lateral space between them in which nothing is going on. Powell has physical resolve, flexibility and strength (enough to turn back the hand of time in the Big Ben scene), but these rely on no exchange of power, or communication with others.

This avoidance of interiority can be seen in the performances of Edward Fox also, except that the facial musculature and physical carriage are held rigid instead of relaxed. In *Day of the Jackal*, he can kill or fornicate with ease, and he is presented mainly alone in centre frame. The same impassive purposefulness can be seen in the work of Oliver Tobias. In *The Stud* his style is impermeable and penetrative. Tobias's performance in *Arabian Adventure* references but rejects the high romance and responsiveness of John Justin's role in *The Thief of Bagdad* (1940). Tobias is physically lissom but emotionally null. He can perform the actions without experiencing the feelings which traditionally accompanied them, and his position in the frame is isolated; with the heroine (Emma Samms) or the fabled Rose of Elil, he rarely approaches the object of desire. It looks as though the self-containment ensues from distance and distaste.

Sean Connery's performance style shifts markedly in this decade. In the 1960s Bond films, he exhibited a degree of expressivity – brutal and unreflecting, to be sure, but flexible in the face of social and sexual exigencies. In the 1970s, Connery's style – in films by a range of directors – became more stolid and emotionally intransigent, and has much in common with other 'self-contained' types. In *Zardoz*, *Murder on the Orient Express* and *The Man Who Would be King*, Connery played characters who require space. Their impassive strength is a consequence of self-confidence and a mistrust of others, just like the heroes played by Powell.

How are we to account for the emergence of this style of self-presentation in 1970s cinema? Characters in this new category of self-containment avoid emotional rawness at all costs. It is a defensive strategy, cutting through the problems produced by the new sexual order. It is a conservative approach, which presents male vitality as unsullied by the newer fluid social conditions, and able to present an impervious exterior. It is significant that there is no discernible female style of self-containment in films of this period. Film culture was clearly suggesting that males could present a wounded but self-sufficient subjectivity, and that women were the problem, rather than the solution.

Self-disclosure

Some actors in the period practise a more expressive performance style. Actors such as Peter Finch, Albert Finney, Michael Caine and James Mason, who had honed their acting skills in previous periods, were able to doff and assume disguises at will. In the 1970s, this extreme flexibility of acting style was rare in the film culture overall. It is not 'character' acting, but develops out of long personal experience of empathy.

Peter Finch's homosexual Jewish doctor in *Sunday Bloody Sunday* was a multi-layered performance, which worked by subtly reducing bodily signals. A slightly lowered timbre, a glance infinitesimally lowered, a smile so fleeting that the audience almost misses it, are Finch's stock-in-trade. Doubtless Schlesinger's own homosexuality intensified his investment in the role, and he appreciated Finch's Negative Capability: 'Peter plunged right into his part and there was no time to talk it over with him. He knew the character in some way without, I think, ever having experienced any of it.'[542] This ability to deploy a repertoire was also evident in Albert Finney's work in the decade. His work in *Gumshoe* (1971) displayed an uncanny ability to embody the *noir* style. In *Murder on the Orient Express* he worked at distinguishing his patterns of gaze and body language from those of his co-actors, so that an inconsistent set of social relationships was constructed. James Mason, whose work had become more nuanced, turned in a remarkable performance in *Spring and Port Wine* (1970). It deals with the patriarchal Rafe Crompton (Mason), his exercise of familial tyranny, the challenges to it, and his eventual capitulation. The process of internal and familial change is carried by Mason's physical style. He maintains order in two ways. He does this, firstly, by facial expression; with each authoritative pronouncement he draws his lower lip down, displaying teeth, and then sharply brings it up and swiftly compresses the jaw. Secondly, he uses movement; he always takes the initiative, moving towards people before they can, such that the family's social space is his. Once he capitulates and softens, it is his cheek muscles which are brought into play, and this has the effect of lengthening the face and making the eyes appear to smile. Simultaneously, the 'new' Crompton moves less, and his bodywork invites the family to move into his space and make it their own.

In Michael Caine's 1970s work we see self-disclosure at its most expansive. In *Get Carter*, the subtlety of the performance resides in its minimalism. The separate discourses of voice, gaze and movement are organised so that they take turns at being expressive. In *The Man Who Would be King*, Caine plays the Cockney foil to Connery's blustering king. Blind, stranded and alone, he exploits both the comedy and the vulnerability of the role; he escapes, and carries the king's severed head in his knapsack. The manner in which he displays this trophy – both triumphant at his own resourcefulness and rueful at his friend's hubris – is a masterpiece of empathy. In *The Romantic Englishwoman*, Caine was not Losey's first choice for the anguished, cuckolded novelist Lewis – that was Dirk Bogarde. The latter rejected the role, which he thought 'pretty dreary . . . One of those yearning dullards full of patience and very little guile. He has no range, no rage, no true dimensions . . . hard to flesh out.'[543] Caine did 'flesh out' Lewis, bringing such a degree of ambiguity to the role that it was never clear whether his wife's liaison in the lift actually happened, or was the product of his fevered imagination. All Lewis's personal spaces are constrained – the study, the club, the car – and the only scene where he has spatial mastery over his environment is when he reclaims his wife (Glenda Jackson) in the modernist hotel. Losey's directorial control may well have determined Caine's management of space, but Caine's own account of his performance suggests that he had some latitude.[544]

It is crucial to recognise that this group of assured stylists, who interiorised their roles so that they purveyed complex sensibilities, represented a dying breed in 1970s British cinema. They had substantial professional experience, were without mannerisms, and disclosed emotions in a controlled but powerful way. Significantly, there were few female actors in this period who worked in this way. Roles for women in this period did not accord them this kind of expressive control. The cultural function of these 'self-disclosers' is to present men as competent for the social task in hand; this is masculinity *before* crisis.

Damage

Psychotic protagonists played a small but significant role in British cinema in previous periods: the damaged war veteran in the 1940s, or the juvenile delinquent in the 1950s. In 1970s British cinema, a qualitatively new persona emerges: the violent maverick. Actors of both sexes play such roles, but the deviants are differently nuanced according to gender. In *Performance*, James Fox's gangster is emotionally displaced. Because of his physical stillness, he generates a large space round himself. The same obtains for Stacey Keach, whose style in *The Duellists*, *Conduct Unbecoming* and *The Squeeze* is volatile but balanced. Due to his careful management of space and movement, we intuit the roots of his malaise. Malcolm McDowell's acting style in *A Clockwork Orange*, *O Lucky Man!*, *Royal Flash* and *Caligula* (1979) works by displaying a naive puzzlement at his own predicament, and by constantly making mistakes which are emotionally expensive; he has no mastery over his own space, and suffers for it. The best example of the damaged male in this decade is Oliver Reed, whose fury was always motivated. Reed glowered through a range of 1970s films, but the stillness and social isolation he displayed as early as *Women in Love* (1969) make for a spatial balance between himself and other protagonists. Reed's management of eye and glance encouraged audience sympathy, and made his dangerous energy seem poignant. In *The Devils*, *The Triple Echo* and *Royal Flash*, Reed's poise made his anger appear motivated.

This new category of damaged, psychotic individuals also contains females. But these are differently presented. The violent females in the decade are rarely contextualised; their crimes never have alibis. Consider the roles played by Sheila Keith in Pete Walker's horror trilogy. Her characters are vengeful, violent and paranoid, and the sheer excess of her physical style makes empathy impossible. The narrative function and behaviour of other bloodthirsty females in this period is exactly the same. Ingrid Pitt in *Countess Dracula*, Joan Collins in *The Bitch*, and the vulpine, cannibalistic predators in *Jubilee* are directly comparable. They too appear motiveless, and they all transgress normal boundaries, invading others' personal space.

The gender difference in this new 'damaged' category is of the greatest interest. The roles written for women, and the performance style exacted from them, suggest that they are far more dangerous to society than men, because they are unfathomable. Violent deviance is explicable in men; in women, it is condemned because it is unmotivated. Inwardness is a quality reserved for males.

Disavowal

Another new performance style in this period is that of ironic disavowal. An extremely mannered acting style emerges, which is restricted to certain female types and to camp or gayish roles. This style uses minimal shifts in facial expression or vocal tone to imply that the material or the proposition is not worth taking seriously. There is a knowingness and a jokiness in a whole range of performances, and this resides in a range of genres, production contexts, acting abilities and character types; there is a perceptible gap between the role and the subjectivity of the performer. The performances of Joan Collins, for example, in *Tales from the Crypt* (1972) and *Tales That Witness Madness* (1973) are masterpieces of insouciance, and in *I Don't Want to Be Born*, she hints at the absurdity of the material with a slightly raised eyebrow. Her work in these films has an ironic patina. The same can be said of a very different actress, Beryl Reid, who made a specialism of appearing to disbelieve in the characters she played. In *The Beast in the Cellar*, *Psychomania* and *Joseph Andrews*, Reid acted in a style that was simultaneously impassive and poised. To be sure, she imagined her characters' backgrounds and did the research,[545] but by little *moues* and sideways glances, she constructs a distance between herself and them.

Even Julie Christie gave some performances in the disavowal mode. In *The Go-Between*, for example, her acting has a modernist edge. Her portrayal of the 'innocent' heroine has, as Sian Barber argues, an archness which subverts the intentions of the script. Barber notes that her interlocutionary delivery – 'Am I?', 'Was I?', 'Did I?' – suggests a worldly experience.[546] Christie delivers these questions with a rising tone, and her knowingness invites the viewer to question the probity of her character. This self-reflexivity involves a whole repertoire of incongruously contemporary mannerisms which call into question the solidity of the period narrative.

This mask of disavowal is evident in some male performances also. Murray Melvin, for example, excels in a downward gaze and a raised pitch, and the effect of his acting in *The Boy Friend*, *Joseph Andrews* and *Barry Lyndon* is to make the audience disbelieve the script's assertions of his heterosexuality. Roger Moore's style in the 1970s Bond films can confidently be termed 'camp'. A raised eyebrow, a knowing look and an unnecessarily mellifluous tone invite the viewer to suspect the vigour of the desire which he professes. Ralph Bates too, though also heterosexual, turned in performances in Hammer films which were extremely 'knowing'. By deploying an obviously *faux* smoothness, his hero in *The Horror of Frankenstein*

(1970) is light-years away from those of Peter Cushing, and in *Dr. Jekyll and Sister Hyde* (1971), Bates overplays both the masculine and feminine self, thus suggesting that sexual identity is easily doffed and assumed. His performance in *Lust for a Vampire* (1970) is the most interesting. His mincing scholar becomes a tornado of deviant lust once the secret Carmilla is discovered. Bates and the other male 'disavowers' share the same bodily set – a fluid style of movement which invites other protagonists to share a socially extensive space, in which the physical constraints of the everyday can be challenged.

There are many more examples of disavowal in style and delivery: Vincent Price in the *Dr. Phibes* films, Tim Curry in *The Rocky Horror Picture Show*, Toyah Willcox in *The Tempest*. How can we account for this phenomenon, across such a range of production contexts and generic types? It clearly has a crucial cultural task. The disavowers' style of movement, and the social spaces they adumbrate, suggest to the audience that everything – even sexual identity – is up for negotiation. Nothing is fixed, nothing is what it seems; that which is circumscribed by social custom can be subverted. These modes of disavowal hint at a subliminal world where boundaries can be safely transgressed and pleasures extended. In classic Freudian analysis, disavowal is a defensive mode: a response, on a symbolic level, to a crisis of faith in authority figures. To assert simultaneously that something is, and is not, is only possible in situations of dire cultural emergency.

Awkwardness

This too is a new performance style, which only emerges in the 1970s. A range of mainly non-professional male actors offer performances which have in common an uncoordinated body language and a presentation of social space as chaotic. As explained in Chapter 10, David Bowie's physical behaviour in *The Man Who Fell To Earth* prefigures both the familiar and the alien. He acts in an abstracted manner: an unfocused gaze, long gaps between words, an inconsistent response to others' personal space. These traits emerge in the self-presentation of other 'amateurs'. Roger Daltry, for example, in *Tommy* and *Lisztomania*, though physically competent – performing all his own stunts – is clearly intended to be emotionally incompetent; he cannot judge others' boundaries or police his own. Similarly, Alan Price's performance in *Alfie Darling* displays someone who is at a loss. Lacking the insouciance of the Michael Caine original, Price is vulnerable. Rather than deploying searching movements, he actually uses very few at all, and the narrow repertoire enforces a sort of emotional candour. It also encourages the audience to empathise with him, since he is so patently incompetent in social and sexual codes. These qualities of awkwardness and spatial misalignment can also be seen in the performance of Robin Askwith in the *Confessions* films.[547] Askwith is ungainly – hunched and lop-sided – and his sexual encounters, which are often cross-class, are clumsy and ill coordinated.

One explanation for these awkward performances might be the actors' lack of professional training, but there is more to it than that. All of them are working-class by origin, and all play either aliens or proletarians. Their physical display and their organisation of space draw the audience into their world, and evoke sympathy for them. This procedure is a million miles away from the social function of the Angry Young Man in late 1950s British cinema. There, the proletarian heroes evoked at best a grudging admiration for their flair. Their energy was well organised, whereas these 1970s heroes are flailing among the world of goods, choosing the wrong thing or the wrong person, and their helplessness evokes sympathy.

But there is another kind of awkwardness in 1970s cinema, and that is predicated on gender rather than class. Glenda Jackson, in *The Romantic Englishwoman*, is physically wooden. This awkwardness can be partially attributed to Jackson's relationship with Losey. She remarked that Losey provided 'a lot of theory, but no space' – he did not allow her room to manœuvre.[548] This sense of entrapment is compounded by the narrative, which ultimately condemns the quixotic behaviour of the errant Elizabeth (Jackson). Losey's films all expressed a clear discomfort with female autonomy. Jackson, however, was a committed feminist, and her physically jagged body language in this performance should be interpreted as a (probably unconscious) critical response to the role she had to play. In her more sexual roles, in *The Music Lovers* and *Bequest to the Nation* (1973), there is always an edginess and a sense of spatial constraint. Elsewhere, in *The Triple Echo*, *The Maids* (1974), *Stevie* (1978) and *The Class of Miss MacMichael* (1978), she plays characters who are politically forthright, and her style in these films is smoother and more coherent.

Overall, it is clear that there was a profound shift in the vocabulary of self-presentation and subjectivity in the 1970s. It is remarkable how few balanced types there are. This should not, however, be adduced as 'evidence' of imbalance in society as a whole. Rather, we should see it as a cultural response to a series of social stresses, and that is of course predicated on the resources, predilections and autonomy of a whole range of agents –

Figure 16 Michael Caine and Glenda Jackson in *The Romantic Englishwoman*

producers, directors and of course the actors themselves. What is certain is that each of these fictional groupings – the disavowers, the damaged goods and the rest – satisfies different social hungers and performs discrete social tasks. The residual 'self-expressive' group probably provided reassurance for those viewers ill at ease with the new dispensation. But the other, more heavily populated groups encouraged both film-makers and audiences to come to terms with an uncertain world, in which the very landscape of meaning seemed unfixed.

Conclusion

In this chapter we have examined two kinds of social space: geographical space and personal space. We have observed that many films of the 1970s explore dynamic relations between motivated landscapes and alienated types of performance. These are such that actors frequently evince a lack of certainty about the fictional worlds they inhabit. Even in the social spaces constructed in realist and naturalist films, the relations between interior and exterior, between subjective and objective realities, are called into question. Mythical landscapes, by contrast, present alternative systems of meanings, and the prevalence of this type in the period is itself significant. These films construct imaginative spaces wherein their sacred objects and their iconic figures can carry a range of new meanings.

Our analysis has suggested that the delineation of subjectivity across a range of film types in the decade is acutely fractured by the emergence of qualitatively new kinds of performance style. Performances which confound or exceed narrative function make a virtue of expressivity for its own sake. This affective function, *pacē* Collingwood, is surely significant. It is possible to argue that the cinema of the period expresses a new sort of individualism which, in its varied and fractured forms, releases objects from their familiar anchorage in the everyday, and enables the materials of culture to be reshaped afresh.

CHAPTER 13

Cross-over

Popular cultural production of any period is subject to cycles of stasis and renewal. Patterns of innovation rely upon the relative vitality of different media forms and their institutional strengths. But cultural shifts are also dependent upon the relations between different media, and the extent to which their boundaries are contested or permeable. Flows of capital within and between media industries are, of course, important but capital is not the sole determinant of creativity. What is also required are institutional conditions which foster confidence, enabling creative artists to make their own interventions. An institution which is in the ascendancy will need to satisfy the demands of its market with a healthy supply of creative talent, thus promoting innovation and allowing greater flexibility on its boundaries. Conversely, an institution which is economically weak will offer limited and more unpredictable opportunities to creative talent, and will not foster innovation to the same extent. Its boundaries will be less secure, although it may also be dependent for its survival, financially and creatively, upon relations with other stronger media partners. This paradox may go some way to explain the relationships between British cinema and other media in the 1970s.

British cinema's institutional frailty, which has already been established, encouraged some producers to seek alliances with the music industry and with television. As Allen has shown in Chapter 8, popular music's institutional buoyancy and diversity of innovative practice prompted it to exploit the cinematic potential of music stars and soundtracks. But its financial investment in film production extended beyond specific marketing strategies, and some music impresarios invested more speculatively also. As Forster has established in Chapter 7, television was also a medium in its prime in the 1970s. Its industrial dominance led some broadcasters to establish film subsidiaries, and television's most popular genres provided familiar product for many cinematic spin-offs.

Another area of financial and cultural cross-over was between the commercial film industry and the burgeoning avant-garde. In Chapter 3, Allen examined a range of avant-garde and independent film-making practice which was stimulated by new sources of public funding. These new creative practices, their co-operatives, workshops and collectives, existed largely outside the markets of industrial production, and their artisanal methods were oppositional in character. Because the aesthetic and political imperatives of such work remained peripheral to the commercial logic of mainstream cinema, instances of cross-over were rare. However, the depleted cultural status of the commercial cinema was such that the prolific work on the margins of moving image culture gained considerable purchase during the decade.

This chapter will explore two different kinds of cross-over relationship. Firstly, cinema entered into a form of exchange with the media of popular music and television from which both, to a limited extent, profited. Secondly, avant-garde practices made limited incursions into mainstream cinema, with mixed results. We want to examine the dynamics of these relationships and to assess their impact upon the film culture at large.

Popular Music

The pop music industry, unlike British cinema, was in rude commercial health at the start of the decade. As Allen has shown, the music industry's dominance allowed it to exploit the diversity of emerging musical genres and their discrete fan cultures, as well as drawing upon a new preoccupation with pop music's own history. Screenwriter Ray Connolly observed that the film industry's recognition of this potential had been slow in coming:

> Although you and I may have known for years that the people who buy records in large numbers tend to be the very same people who enjoy going to the pictures, it appears to have come as a recent revelation to the film industry . . . For 20 years, while rock has been establishing itself as the contemporary music form of the second half of this century, film-makers have continued to view it with suspicion and not a little distaste.[549]

Whereas, in the 1960s, the cinema had found it difficult to keep pace with rapid developments in popular music, the new emphasis on nostalgia for the roots of rock & roll offered more attractive opportunities for cinematic treatments. This development was also bound up with the personal histories of the new generation of film producers who were inspired by the musical narratives of their youth. As Allen notes, Ray Connolly and David Puttnam's *That'll Be the Day* is a prime example. Indeed, at the beginning of the film, the father's midnight return from the forces was a deliberate recreation of Puttnam's own family story, and it is no coincidence that his own son, Sacha, was cast as the child Jim.

Puttnam and Lieberson's Goodtimes Enterprises gained half their production funding for *That'll Be the Day* from EMI, but also brokered an innovative deal with American record label, Ronco, to produce a soundtrack album. Ronco's popular reissues of recordings from the 1940s and 1950s coincided with a wave of musical retrospectives, which saw their compilation albums promoted on television commercials and sold in supermarkets.[550] As *Variety* loudly trumpeted: 'The UK is a self-sufficient and highly profitable disk market which helps to make such domestic pix [sic] as *That'll Be The Day*, when sold in association with an album, viable propositions.'[551] This film and *Stardust* featured rising pop star David Essex, who, alongside Ringo Starr and Billy Fury, represented three generations of pop performers. This added to the nostalgic patina and the self-conscious air of the film.[552]

These qualities mobilise aspects of the past in order to engage with contemporary concerns. This is particularly evident in the film's attitudes to sex. Whilst the novice Jim's bravado allows him to maintain a pretence of sexual experience, his holiday-camp conquest, Sandra (Deborah Watling), betrays her own pretence of innocence by asking, 'Do you always come so quick?' In this recreation of 1958, young women are liberated, initiated and savvy. Having slept with his wife's best friend on his stag night, Jim is questioned by his wife about his infidelity. He lies, but she replies, 'I wouldn't have minded. I'd just like to know, that's all.' Again, this anachronistic remark is evidence that the film is addressing attitudes about sex in the 1970s in a manner which presents them as moral choices rather than imperatives.

It was not only independent young film-makers who were interested in the potential of pop music cross-overs. Some music moguls were interested in the possibilities presented by cinema. Robert Stigwood extended his substantial interests in musical theatre by underwriting Ken Russell's adaptation of the Who's rock opera *Tommy*. As *Variety* reported: 'Stigwood, after *Jesus Christ Superstar* . . . now heads a whole corps of music industry personnel who are looking to get into films.'[553] And theatrical impresario, Michael White, ensured that the successful *Rocky Horror Show* was transferred to the cinema screen by brokering a deal with Twentieth Century Fox. Essentially, this was the entrepreneurialism of expedience; each producer identified a known product in which he already had a significant investment and exploited its success through cinema, reselling it to an existing audience.

Other music industry interventions were equally pragmatic. In order to finance their second feature film, *Quadrophenia*, the Who's management arranged a deal with their German-based record label, Polygram, whereby the record company would back the film in return for the band renegotiating their music contracts. Such arrangements gave considerable autonomy to the film-makers because the money-men remained at a disinterested distance, satisfied that their investment would be recouped by record sales, if not cinema receipts. As Allen has established, *Quadrophenia* successfully promoted a mod revival in the late 1970s. In fact, the narrative eschewed both the period recreation of rock & roll films like *That'll Be the Day* and the Pop Art quotation of musicals like *Tommy* and *Grease*. By contrast, the period anachronisms in the realist narrative of *Quadrophenia* show that the interests of the film-makers lie not in the accurate representation of the past but in revivifying the rites-of-passage myth for a 1970s audience. This elision is achieved largely through characterisation rather than *mise en scène*; no attempt is made to suppress the contemporary pop personae of Sting and Toyah Willcox. As Kevin Donnelly relates, this casting is indicative of efforts to articulate mod culture 'along lines that could be understood by a late-1970s punk-influenced audience'.[554] The formerly subversive sub-culture is thus reconstituted in *Quadrophenia* as a sanctuary from the tedium of the everyday.

These concerns were evident at the film's conception. First-time director Franc Roddam was chosen by producers Roy Baird and Bill Curbishley (the Who's manager) ahead of established names such as Ken Russell (*Tommy*). Roddam, noted for his documentary work on television, explained: 'We didn't want it to be just a nostalgia film about 1964 . . . I want it to have some relevance to today . . . What I didn't want to do, is make a stylised film like *Tommy*, where the music carried the narrative.'[555]

The music industry also had an influence upon cinema in less conspicuous and more idiosyncratic ways. Michael White was also approached when the Monty Python team were endeavouring to put together a deal to finance their second feature, *Monty Python and the Holy Grail*. Eventually, their record producer at Charisma, Tony Stratton-Smith – who was already investing personally in the project – managed to enlist some high-profile Python fans from the ranks of Led Zeppelin and Pink Floyd, who were only too pleased to offset against tax some of their considerable wealth by contributing to a project in which they shared a personal interest.[556] Similarly, ex-Beatle George Harrison came to the aid of the Pythons' follow-up feature, *Life of Brian*, when EMI's chief Bernard Delfont got cold feet over potential blasphemy allegations. Harrison had ventured into film production with Apple's backing of *Little Malcolm* before launching

Figure 17 *Quadrophenia*

HandMade Films, with his business partner Denis O'Brien, which went on to rescue *The Long Good Friday* when Lew Grade abandoned it.

Such notable interventions were, however, unusual. Most cross-over business was securely based upon the market awareness which Ray Connolly so shrewdly identified. In this way, big-budget American pop films such as *Saturday Night Fever* and *Grease* were duly accompanied by soundtrack albums; the films were essentially a promotional tool for the records. Similarly, commercial agents were quick to exploit the star potential of their high-profile clients in feature films. Donovan, David Essex, Mick Jagger, David Bowie, Toyah Willcox, Hazel O'Connor and Sting all had film roles. As we noted in the previous chapter, those pop performers who lacked professional acting skills brought a new kind of charisma to their screen roles in terms of performance style. Their *tabula rasa* personae were extensions of their pop music images, in that they invited the audience to project its own desires upon their unfinished performances. In this respect, the pop performers embodied a cult of Romantic individualism, often rooted, as Allen observed, in established music sub-cultures.

Cinema provided a useful medium not only for expressing rock & roll nostalgia, but also for amplifying the specific style markers and attributes of a range of new music taste-communities: northern soul, disco, mod-revival, punk, techno, prog-rock and reggae. More broadly, cinema in the 1970s hailed the youth audience via its preoccupations with visual style, self-image and identity. It permitted, frequently through identification with star protagonists, the imaginative exploration of new social and sexual freedoms. This trend is apparent in films as qualitatively different as *Rocky Horror Picture Show*, *The Man Who Fell To Earth* and *Quadrophenia*. As we shall see, in the hands of experimental film-makers such as Derek Jarman (*Jubilee*) and Chris Petit (*Radio On*), new music sub-cultures were also sites for exploring the moment of rupture, of cultural discontinuity, which grass-roots youth culture encapsulated so defiantly. For the makers of *Babylon*, music money from the Chrysalis label was instrumental in getting the project off the ground. But furthermore, the music sub-text became a means by which the political radicalism at the heart of the narrative might be marketed to a wider audience, and a willingness to brand it as a pop music film was key to its obtaining a British circuit release, as Shaw has shown. In the late 1970s, such radical interpretations of popular music sub-culture surfaced only as a result of struggles, both financial and political. On the whole, however, cinema's engagement with popular music was less confrontational, but more anodyne, than this. Film drew upon the vitality and variety of popular music culture and its distinctive taste-communities, but rarely engaged creatively with either. Most films simplified the complex pleasures provided by the music culture.

Television

In the 1970s, television played an increasingly major role in the cultural life of the country. Indeed, Hugh Jenkins, Minister for the Arts from 1974 to 1976, estimated that it constituted 23 per cent of people's leisure time, as opposed to 1 per cent of the traditional arts – theatre, museums and so on.[557] Forster has suggested in Chapter 7 that television was culturally focused, adequately funded and innovatory on the levels of form and content; this made it an extremely confident medium. In the 1970s, television drama, sitcoms and other programmes profited by being in a pre-regulatory period.[558] Not only metropolitan but also regional television was engaged in risk-taking, visionary films made specifically for the medium: BBC Birmingham's *Penda's Fen*, for example. And television encouraged the flowering of writers such as Jack Rosenthal, Dennis Potter, Jim Allen and Alan Bennett, as well as directors such as John McGrath, Clive Donner and Horace Ové. The television of the 1970s challenged established genres. *The Cheviot, the Stag and the Black, Black Oil* transformed the practice of committed drama; *Days of Hope* and *I, Claudius* were qualitatively new historical drama; *Pennies from Heaven* (1978) was a new type of musical.[559] The cinema, by contrast, had a much more uneven progress and profile.

Some television executives intervened directly in sponsoring film production. Lew Grade's ACC launched a raft of British international films (funded by his profitable ATC corporation), as noted in Chapter 9. On the domestic front, Grade formed the subsidiary Black Lion Films in order to produce feature films for television. This company sought to emulate the success of television crime dramas (such as Euston Films' *The Sweeney*) by backing *The Long Good Friday* initially for television broadcast. This project was planned as the third in a three-picture package which included *Bloody Kids* (ATV, 1979) and *Very Like a Whale* (ATV, 1980). The package was designed to boost the production slate of ATC in the sensitive run-up to the ITV franchise renewals in 1978.[560] Grade got cold feet over the film's IRA terrorist theme and dropped the project, which eventually gained a cinema release through the support of HandMade. Another television drama reject was Alan Clarke's *Scum*, which was banned by the BBC. Don Boyd intervened in this case, and the project was remade as a feature film.

There was a more consistent pattern of cross-over between television and film in situation comedy. Substantial money was made by these spin-offs, and some performed well at the box-office.[561] But at no level were the spin-offs innovatory; rather, they were retrospective, both formally and socially. They did differ from each other, though, and in important ways. Some established film production companies deployed their expertise in TV spin-offs. Hammer Films had made a specialism of marketing pre-sold material since the late 1940s, with films based on popular radio plays, and continued to be conservative in its selection of source material, though adapting it in a stylish manner. In the 1970s, though, as Ede has explained, Hammer's horror status was diminished by the decline of the gothic mode. In 1971, Roy Skeggs, Hammer's accountant, was promoted to production supervisor and then to producer, and had a hand in the reorientation of the studio to TV spin-offs. The studio made *On the Buses*, *Mutiny on the Buses* and *Holiday on the Buses*, which were extremely successful. The first of these was Hammer's most profitable film of all, and came second in the overall box-office listings for the year.[562]

Hammer producers had long been uninterested in artistic status, and continued that with the *Buses* films, suggesting that the poster headlines be 'From Telly Laughs to Belly Laughs'.[563] They chose to make a film of the series because it had 'toppled Coronation Street from the ratings more than once'.[564] The scriptwriters were Chesney and Wolfe, who had written the TV originals, and they claimed that the film sedulously avoided overlap, since 'otherwise we'd have been cheating the public.'[565] Where the films differed from the sit-com was in the intensity of their anxiety about women. The television series, which ran from 1969 to 1974, was preoccupied with male desire, and expended much screen time on abusing the hapless Olive (Anna Karen), whose chief crime was to wear spectacles and to answer back. But the film makes a double attack on women. Female bus drivers (gorgons all) are imported and threaten the heroes' overtime; simultaneously, Olive becomes pregnant. Chesney and Wolfe linked the two events, by claiming that they wanted to 'expand' the story and 'enlarge' Anna Karen.[566] This 'enlargement' precipitates a defensive panic in the film. Olive is portrayed as subject to unsavoury cravings (pickled onions) and unattractive foibles (curlers and face cream). The birth itself is prefaced by an extraordinary scene, in which her huge body is tightly wedged by the males into a motorcycle sidecar. Comic though it is, the scene should be read as an attempt, on a symbolic level, to reposition Olive herself back into the womb, where she can embarrass no one. This intense preoccupation with the dangers posed by females is carried through into the other films, except that the location is broadened beyond the home and the bus depot.

Hammer made *Love Thy Neighbour* (1973), in which other differences, racial this time, were minimised from the original television series. Again employing the same scriptwriting team as the series (Vince Powell and Harry Driver), the film provided a far more emollient account of contradictions, and smoothed over, rather than exacerbated, the racial issue. It looks as though the TV spin-offs gave Hammer producers freedom to concentrate on troublesome women, warn about their liberation and reposition them where they belonged. Other spin-off producers did the same.

Nat Cohen at EMI had already decided to include in his schedule some cheaper films which were not star vehicles:

> The public is not interested in whether a film costs 1 million or 50 million dollars, they are interested in the entertainment they want . . . I rate the director very high; I rate the story, the subject matter very high, and the rest follows.[567]

Accordingly, he gave tried-and-tested stories some priority in his schedules. Both *Steptoe and Son* and *Steptoe and Son Ride Again* were scripted by Galton and Simpson, who wrote the television series. But the films intensified the sexual distaste of the original. In the first film, Harold marries a stripper, who seems well intentioned but abandons her child, and commits adultery and (worse) miscegenation. In the second, the extremely buxom charms of Diana Dors impel Harold into a frenzy of sexual terror. Even EMI's *Up Pompeii* intensifies the sexual themes, with Frankie Howerd even more lascivious, and the women more lubricious, than in the television series.

EMI's *The Likely Lads* (1976) is qualitatively different from both its television incarnations, though scripted by the same pair, Clement and La Frenais. The film was produced after the last of the broadcast sitcoms in 1974, and is valedictory in tone, presiding over the demolition of the old working-class spaces. *The Likely Lads* predictably did much better in the North-East than in the metropolis, and both Paul Williams and Phil Wickham argue that the way the film connected with regional structures of memory accounts for its success.[568] What is remarkable too is the way the film allows the women to articulate their discontents. The television series presented Thelma as a querulous, illogical threat to male bonding, but the film shows her and Terry's girlfriend as entirely justified and moderate. The film accords the women the moral high ground in the shifting morass of social and sexual change. *The Likely Lads* proposes one of the most unpalatable possibilities of all: that women are right, and men are wrong.

Bless This House (1972) came from Rank and was directed and produced by Gerald Thomas and Peter Rogers of *Carry On* fame. Dave Freeman scripted both the film and the original TV sitcom, but again the film has markedly different sexual politics. The sitcom expressed a mild bewilderment at the separate tribe of the young, whereas the film focused unerringly on masculine predicaments. It was sold as an innocuous alternative to sex films.[569] The film works in this way until about the last 20 minutes when, in a dramatic change of pace and style, it develops into a maelstrom of masculine ineptitude. The defences of two respectable neighbours (Sid James and Terry Scott) are breached in a café brawl, when they are smothered in raw egg and cream. On the day of the marriage of their children, their discomfiture is intensified by an explosion in their amateur still, and, in their wedding regalia, they are singed by fire and soaked by water. Damaged by dirt, slime, fire and water, they pretend that nothing has happened, whereas the female protagonists express a reasonable consternation. Yet again, the film deploys an established format to show men on the edge.

The American majors also invested in sitcom adaptation. Columbia/ Warners financed *The Alf Garnett Saga* (1972), which was far more culturally insecure than either the television original or the earlier film, *Till Death Us Do Part* (1969), which was backed by British Lion. *The Alf Garnett Saga* was very unsure of its ground (the presentation of Alf's experiences on LSD was a strategic error), and it was only coherent when showing Alf with residual figures like Arthur Askey and Max Bygraves. Speight (who scripted both the TV and film versions) had argued that Alf's racism had a bracing effect on television audiences, in that it forced them to confront their worst fears about themselves.[570] But the 1972 film presented a white working-class man as a very poor alternative to the sleek black singer with whom Alf's daughter elopes.

Columbia also supported the film of *Dad's Army* (1971), which again had the same scriptwriters as the TV sitcom. This pattern was repeated in films produced by other outfits: *Ooh . . . You Are Awful*, *Please Sir!* (1971) and *Porridge*. In every case, the narrative extends the social space of the original, focuses on hapless male protagonists, and returns them, grateful, to their point of origin. They are secure in their cages. These films clearly offered a rueful settlement to their male viewers, but the audience position they offered to the females is more ambiguous.

We have suggested that, beneath the surface, the film comedies adumbrated a conservative response to sexual change. However, other television dramas spawned feature films of a different complexion. *Sweeney!* (1977), for example, was not concerned with masculinity under threat. It was the first film produced by Euston Films, founded specifically to market crime series for television. Euston's mode of procedure was, to use Graham Murdoch's terminology, one of 'operational' rather than 'allocative' control, since it had a high degree of policy and artistic autonomy.[571] To make TV series in an older format – 16mm – also made for far greater flexibility in working practices. *Sweeney*, like Euston's other projects, worked exclusively with freelancers, which led to major problems with the unions. The television *Sweeney* was a commodity made to precise specifications, according to producer Ted Childs.[572] The pace, narrative structure and politics were all determined by the producer, who tried to pair up scriptwriters with directors so that they could play to each others' strengths.[573]

Figure 18 *Sweeney!*

It was a new departure for Euston to make a feature film. *Sweeney!* was made relatively cheaply for £250,000, shooting 4 minutes a day as compared to the 5 minutes a day shot on the TV series.[574] Director David Wickes had little room for authorial manœuvre; in one key scene, he regretted that 'it has to be done in one shot, as we've only got one car and we've got to get it right'.[575] As in the TV series, all production staff were employed on a freelance basis, and there was considerable job overlap. Ted Childs also acted as script editor, and wanted to import cinematic (rather than televisual) pace and narrative colour into the script; he argued that 'the producer is the steersman and very significantly in dominance in the production team'.[576] Childs had had serious problems with Ian Kennedy Martin, who wrote the pilot for the television series; they had parted company on the issue of realism, since Childs was in favour of a more modulated and structured approach to social reality.[577] Accordingly, Childs worked with Ranald Graham on the film script, presumably since the latter had some *Sweeney* experience but no acrimonious previous history.

The film was recognised by quality critics as a feature film in its own right, compared to the more opportunistic TV spin-offs such as *On the Buses*, which had received short critical shrift. It was the breadth of *Sweeney*'s social and political spread which distinguished it from the competition: 'there is throughout the picture a sympathetic resonance with certain levels of present-day society which is too strong to overlook or disregard'.[578] The film's political landscape was broader than the TV series, dealing with international intrigue and the consequences of shifts in the oil market, and this rooted its analysis far more firmly in contemporary events and offered a radical take on politics. But when Euston made a second film, *Sweeney 2*, in 1978, the broader geographical canvas – with which television could not compete – had less honourable motivation. Troy Kennedy Martin suggested that 'It was a good little script . . . But they all wanted to go and have a holiday in Malta, so I had to write in all these Malta scenes, which really ruined the thing.'[579]

Sweeney!, however, had quite a distinct sexual politics from the television series. Its version of masculinity was far less abashed, and more confrontational, than that of other TV sitcoms. Protagonist John Thaw argued that 'What we're really doing is an urban Western, as it were, about two guys clearing up the town.'[580] But there was more to it than that: the *Sweeney!* males enacted a thoroughly old-fashioned, brutal version of patriarchy in their relations with women. They meted out disgust and desire in equal measure to all females, in a manner which made the Women's Movement worse than irrelevant – it made it invisible. Both the heroines are prostitutes. Society metes out punishment to them: death and humiliation, without any compensating compassion.

Most of the television spin-offs were undertaken in a spirit of desperation by established film companies, and the films they made, which often had an ad hoc, accidental air about them, operated as a playground for the rehearsal of fears about new female freedoms. In the sitcom films, the male protagonists were both worried and incompetent (rather like their producers, in fact), but the *Sweeney* films were a different case. Made by a highly structured company, whose producers were confident in both media, the films expressed a straightforward contempt for those women who perturbed society and whose venality challenged the patriarchal order.

The Avant-garde

We saw in the previous two sections that British producers were financially inventive in the 1970s, usually out of sheer need. They invited investment from the popular music business, which resulted in films which addressed the diversity and vibrancy of youth sub-cultures but which tempered their pleasures with an admonitory tone. Music films also embraced pop's new preoccupation with its own history but transformed it into cautionary tales of the consequences of hedonism. Film producers' relationship to the television industry was equally conservative. They imitated and adapted televisual forms in a profitable way, but usually modified them in a conservative manner in terms of gender debates, and were unable to match the formal innovation or social fleet-footedness of the television originals. From these examples it is possible to suggest that the power and sources of innovation provided by the music and television industries provided stimulus to the film industry, but that this was moderated in a cinema which was insecure about its own cultural boundaries.

As Allen has shown in Chapter 3, British avant-garde film culture was incredibly rich and varied in the 1970s. Incursions from the avant-garde into the mainstream were, however, rare. This was for ideological reasons. The commercial film industry viewed the avant-garde largely as an irrelevance, while many avant-garde practitioners were exercised by the venality of mainstream cinema. They preferred to retain absolute control over their own unorthodox procedures of production and distribution, and to defend the purity of their radical aesthetics. Some of them – Le Grice and others – hated even the idea of narrative. Others – Jane Arden, Laura Mulvey and Sally Potter – were then constructing a feminist experiment with form which brooked no engagement with patriarchal discourses. As both Allen and Porter have shown, the avant-garde was fostered by both the educational establishment and an increase in public arts funding. The BFI Production Board's sponsorship of feature films marked a clear development in the aspirations of the independent sector. Yet this financial support, for filmmakers like Kevin Brownlow, would never have been forthcoming from the commercial industry at that time. It is impossible to imagine *Winstanley* being shown at the Odeons, or indeed to speculate about what kind of audience response it would have received there. This serves to illustrate the gulf between the avant-garde and the market for commercial cinema. The two were wholly divided on the matter of audience pleasure. The avant-garde was premised on intellectual labour and distanciation. Commercial cinema, as ever, placed pleasure high in its pantheon, but in the 1970s was unsure about how it was constituted or how to achieve it.

It was not until the 1980s that Peter Greenaway was able to make films for the art-house circuit such as *The Draughtsman's Contract* (1982) and *The Cook, The Thief, His Wife and Her Lover* (1989). Later still, Sally Potter was able to turn her debates about pleasure, formal experiment and gender into the major international film *Orlando* (1992). In general, the 1970s British film industry was too inflexible to provide the funding or the appropriate cultural permission for such films. There were two exceptions, however. The first was Derek Jarman, whose films tiptoed around the mainstream and transformed it. We have already discussed *Sebastiane* and *Jubilee*, both of which used history to provide remarkable treatments of sexual and social marginality. But Jarman also directed *The Tempest*, which was an astonishingly inventive account of Shakespeare's play, advancing notions of adaptation and authorship, and creating a world which was both accessible yet challenging.

The second exception was the former *Time Out* film critic, Chris Petit. His *Radio On* received backing from the BFI Production Board, and the personal endorsement of the German director, Wim Wenders, whose own company, Road Movies Filmproduktion, co-financed this Anglo-German co-production. A deliberate attempt to challenge the social realist tradition of British film-making, Petit's script eschewed plot and characterisation in favour of process – the process being a journey from London to Bristol by car. Influenced not only by Wenders's own *Kings of the Road* (1976), but also Monte Hellman's *Two-Lane Blacktop* (1971), Petit describes his point of departure as 'a soundscape accompanied by visuals'.[581] Indeed, the addition of a contemporary popular music soundtrack (which incorporated the generous services of notables such as David Bowie, Sting, Kraftwerk, Reckless Eric and Ian Dury) was an imperative Petit found curiously missing from British cinema of the period, unlike the new German cinema he so much admired. The car radio/cassette provides the necessary diegesis for the music; the ability to employ it as an editorial device which is controlled by the main protagonist, the enigmatic Robert B. (David Beames). Petit's film is innovatory visually too. Its grainy, monochrome texture evinces a sparse, European quality rare in British cinema. And it is unique in the British cinema of the 1970s in celebrating the codes of pleasure of popular music culture.

Like Jarman's contemporary essay, *Jubilee*, *Radio On* is a journey away from the metropolis and into the provincial past. Petit's film explores the subjective past of the protagonist who is investigating the mysterious disappearance of his brother. And, like Jarman's, Petit's topographical survey of England combines disillusionment with nostalgia, and combines alienation with sympathy. As the film-maker has acknowledged, this is the suburban hinterland of J. G. Ballard and Iain Sinclair.[582] *Radio On*'s haunting 35mm black-and-white photography, and its attention to neglected remnants of British architectural modernism, elevate the narrative beyond mere documentarism, creating instead a poetic meditation upon landscape and loss. Unusually for a film of avant-garde provenance, *Radio On* works at the level of affect, and transforms an everyday search into a quest of mythic scale.

Avant-garde film of the decade was characterised by artisanal practices and energised by a revolutionary zeal. This powerful combination of forces promoted a quasi-Romantic notion of artistic autonomy and integrity. The refusal of these film-makers to compromise on matters of principle and technique meant that considerable intellectual effort was expended in defending the boundaries of their field of cultural production.

Conclusion

In the 1970s, British cinema's position of cultural centrality had been undermined by its economic frailty. In order to shore up its fragility, it sought alternative sources of institutional funding and cultural stimulus. These marriages of convenience had uneven effects upon the film culture, since the constitutional conservatism of the film industry hindered a radical transformation of cultural capital. The alliances with the music industry and television were exploited for their populist, commercial potential, at the expense of the cinema's more traditional alliances with literature and the theatre. This choice had the effect of widening the gulf between high- and low-brow production in the moving image culture of the decade, and this polarisation effectively destroyed the middle ground in cinema. In previous periods, the buffering effect of middle-brow cultural production had led to an easy stratification of the cultural hierarchy. In the 1970s everything changed. The fragmentation of film culture resulted in deep ideological rifts and the vigorous policing of the boundaries of pleasure and taste. One thing shared by popular music, television and the avant-garde sector was an attention to the needs of niche taste-communities, which the commercial cinema was slow to define. Its efforts to recognise its changing markets will be the subject of the next chapter.

CHAPTER 14

Audiences and Reception

There is a dearth of evidence about popular film taste in the 1970s, which makes a comprehensive survey of this territory difficult to achieve. In a decade when, as we have shown, the structure of the British film industry was weakened by financial hardship, and its cultural status was reduced relative to other entertainment media, it is unsurprising that evidence about popular taste is thin. Conversely, the 1970s saw a burgeoning critical film culture almost in apposition to cinema's declining popularity. This is a paradox which this chapter will seek to address. The first section provides an analysis of some quantitative data, which will help us to draw a provisional map of cinema-going and see what may be deduced from this about popular film tastes. The second section then undertakes a qualitative analysis of a range of contemporary critical writing about film, which will furnish us with evidence about the variety of discourses about film culture in the period.

Cinema-going and Popular Taste

The sources of evidence from which this analysis is derived may be found in the Appendices. Appendix I contains tables with box-office data, attendance figures, statistics for cinema conversions and closures, and related material. Appendix II presents Sian Barber's interpretation of attendance figures based on cinema registers for the Odeon Southampton. Appendix III presents evidence drawn from local press listings for Portsmouth; the full dataset, compiled by Peri Bradley, can be found at www.1970sproject.co.uk. These enable us to make some tentative conclusions about regional market variations in popular tastes, based upon patterns of distribution and exhibition.

During the 1970s, the popularity of cinema as a social pastime continued its downward trend. Its market decline resulted in the outright closure, or screen division, of many exhibition sites. Annual admissions fell from 192 million in 1970 to 83 million by 1981. However, while admissions fell, per capita visits halved (from 3.79 in 1970 to 1.85 in 1980) and cinemas did close, the number of screens actually increased, from 1,629 in 1970 to 3,391 in 1980. While box-office receipts (by dint of increased ticket prices) grew, if one takes inflation into account, their real value fell from £213 million in 1970 to £135.7 million in 1980 (1980 prices). But equally, the real costs of film hire depreciated by about a third during the decade. On the supply side, the overall number of films released in UK cinemas fell from 389 in 1970–1971 to 282 in 1980–1981. However, the number of films registered as British halved between 1970 (85) and 1979 (40) (see Table 3).

The explanations for the decline in admissions are familiar: specifically, increasing competition from television, and generally, the draw of other domestic and social consumption. Table 4 shows the growth in ownership of television sets, and Table 5 reveals that import figures for domestic video recorders rose from 1975. However, analyses carried out by *Screen Digest* during the 1970s wisely caution against straightforward correlations between television and video on the one hand and cinema-going on the other. Additionally, cinema was competing against a wider range of personal and domestic entertainments; for example, there was a continued rise in record sales and equipment during the decade. For other explanations we need to look more closely at cinema itself.

In August 1970 Terry McGrath, the general manager of the Theatre Division of Rank Leisure Services, warned that, in facing increasing competition from alternative entertainment products, the market for cinema 'will continue to fragment into distinct buyer groups . . . with different requirements'.[583] In order to cater for these diverse tastes he advocated a 'system of multi-auditoria', which would 'allow us to offer choice'.[584] The multi-screening of many cinema sites during the decade is evidence of the perceived fragmentation in the audience constituency. Yet the trade press showed that only rarely were these new screens filled (and then mostly with the US blockbusters which, from 1975, briefly revived cinema attendance). In addition, restrictive practices of film distribution militated against the kind of exhibition flexibility which McGrath proposed.

Rank and EMI continued to dominate the exhibition sector during the 1970s, though by the end of the decade Odeon had only 75 cinemas with 194 screens, while ABC had 107 sites and 287 screens.[585] The Monopolies and Mergers Commission remained concerned about the power of this duopoly, but fell short of recommending the establishment of a third, 'independent', circuit. The expansion of Tony Tenser's Tigon Group led to the purchase of the Classic and the Essoldo chains. Essoldo was rapidly subsumed within the Classic brand, and was bought out by Lew Grade's ACC for a sum approaching £13 million in 1980.[586] In practice, these three vertically integrated conglomerates offered relatively limited consumer choice in terms of film product. There were two main reasons for this. Firstly, uncertainty about audience preferences caused the major distributors to copy one another rather than diversify. Secondly, the continuation of the long-established rental practices of barring and block-booking allowed local cinema managers little flexibility in programming.

National Taste Patterns

In order to investigate the tastes of McGrath's 'distinct buyer groups', we need to look elsewhere. There are a number of clues to be found in box-office popularity charts and local cinema differentiation. A *Screen Digest* report of December 1976 predicted: 'As the cinema contracts, there appear to be two poles towards which it can be attracted. It either becomes dominated by aggressively commercial material, be it disaster movies or porn, or it becomes more introspective and national.'[587]Actually, the empirical evidence suggests that it moved in both directions, but in neither did it move particularly far or fast. What is also clear is that genres like the disaster movie were characteristic of the big-budget Hollywood event movie, while the 'introspective and national' qualities might be more readily found in comedies and thrillers which either were direct TV spin-offs, or owed much of their residual values and parochial aesthetics to television drama.

A more refined model of popularity may be obtained from an analysis of those genres and film titles which appear most frequently in the annual top ten box-office lists each year. Box-office figures show that war films, crime thrillers, musicals and action films are the highest international scorers, while children's films and comedies provide the most successful domestic fare (see Table 6). These results offer a more nuanced picture, which challenges assumptions about adult tastes derived from the high number of 'X' certificate films passed by the censor (see Table 2 in Chapter 2). While there was certainly a significant audience for 'X'-rated films (and some, like *A Clockwork Orange*, *Straw Dogs*, *The Exorcist* and *Emmanuelle*, were big box-office hits), the most popular films are always in other categories. What this analysis reveals is not so much the emergence of niche taste-communities (though this was an audience phenomenon of the period), but rather the rise of the event movie. As Linda Wood observes, 'The box office blockbusters were isolated incidents which depended on the attractiveness of individual films – unfortunately, they did not lead to the re-establishment of any regular pattern of cinema going so essential for any long-term improvement.'[588]

In the 1970s there was a widening gap between the regular cinema-goer (a much-diminished category) and the new 'event movie' audience, which suggests that cinema was being used by popular audiences in new ways. A closer scrutiny of the types of film which were box-office hits during the decade reveals a trend away from *Screen Digest*'s 'introspective' subjects, towards those with more international scope. As Table 7 shows, up to 1973, British productions were successful in the genres of costume, comedy, war and fantasy, with significant showings in the top twenty films. For example, in 1970, British features accounted for ten of the top seventeen films at the box office. In the following year, nine out of the top fifteen were British. From 1974 onwards, not only does the number of British films in the top box-office table diminish, but there is also a notable decline in the 'introspective' or domestic subject. This category is typified by the TV comedy spin-off (*On the Buses*, *Steptoe and Son*, *Dad's Army* and *Love Thy Neighbour*), but it also embraces sex comedies (*There's a Girl in My Soup* and *Percy*), costume dramas aimed at the family audience (*The Railway Children* and *Tales of Beatrix Potter*) and historical films (*Mary, Queen of Scots* and *Young Winston*).

There are economic explanations for this pattern in the first half of the decade. Many of the bigger-budget British successes of the early years of the decade had been financed at the turn of the 1960s by the Hollywood majors: *Women in Love*, *The Battle of Britain*, *Anne of the Thousand Days*, *Cromwell* and the Bond films. The Americans' hasty retrenchment left a vacuum which was filled by more domestic fare; TV spin-offs, in particular, could be produced relatively quickly and cheaply, and appealed directly to a ready market. But, equally, the financial crisis also opened up a cultural space which was filled by opportunistic independent auteurs (such as Losey, Russell and Roeg), whose modestly budgeted art films of this period had an exposure they might not have achieved in healthier economic climes. For example, it is possible to argue that the success of Ken Russell's films in the first half of the 1970s provide evidence not of an increase in the market for art-house films, but of the attractiveness to popular tastes of their sexual liberalism.

By 1974, only four British titles appeared in the top nineteen films at the box office: *Don't Look Now*, *Confessions of a Window Cleaner*, *Stardust* and *Gold*. However, the first two titles vied for the top box-office place, which is indicative of a profound divergence in popular tastes. This diversity in popular tastes was short-lived. Hereafter, films which did well at the British box office were often more international in their scope; even

Figure 19 *The Man with the Golden Gun*

the comedy genre took on a new cosmopolitanism with the Pink Panther films.

The exception to this rule was the Bond franchise, which had always enjoyed international appeal but performed unevenly at the box office in the 1970s. This was for a number of reasons. Firstly, the transition from Sean Connery's reign to Roger Moore's tenure received mixed responses. Secondly, the first six Bond films were now sold to television, which undermined the brand's cinematic exclusivity. Thirdly, Guy Hamilton's attempts to link Bond with popular trends in contemporary US cinema (*Live and Let Die* as blaxploitation, *The Man with the Golden Gun* as martial arts) only succeeded in exaggerating further the comic self-referentiality which Moore had brought to the role. Thereafter, as James Chapman notes, the introduction of Lewis Gilbert at the helm for *The Spy Who Loved Me* and *Moonraker* marked a much more patriotic retreat and a return to more serious militaristic themes around Cold War détente and the nuclear threat.[589] After the relative failure of *Golden Gun* at the box office, this limited retrenchment reveals that, in changing times, domestic audiences preferred their hero to present a more unambiguous version of the national mythology.

Aside from the Bond franchise, other British international genres achieved some notable box-office success. These were in the realms of costume drama (*Murder on the Orient Express* and *Death on the Nile*), war adventure (*The Wild Geese* and *The Eagle Has Landed*), the family film (*The Slipper and the Rose* and *Bugsy Malone*) and fantasy (*At the Earth's Core* and *Warlords of Atlantis*). Towards the end of the decade the domestic film is represented in the top box-office tables by only occasional hits (*Sweeney!*, *Quadrophenia* and *Porridge*). The international film, on the other hand, culminates in the popularity of the *Superman* and *Alien* series, and thereafter is subsumed by Hollywood.

But is this observable return to Hollywood dominance only an economic phenomenon? After all, the divergence amongst British film producers between domestic and international product dates back to the 1930s; it is hardly unique to the 1970s. And a comparison between top British successes at the domestic box office and the American rentals earnings of British films of the period reveals a direct correspondence (see Table 8). However, broader analysis of the most popular titles of the decade (British and American) suggests, perhaps, that a deeper cultural change is afoot. Let us think for moment about gender discourses as a means of exploring the shifting boundaries of British audience taste.

As we have established in previous chapters, the brief impact of the British domestic film in the early part of the decade served either to problematise male sexuality through humour and dysfunction, or to hark back nostalgically to worlds where sexual politics were blissfully repressed. And, as noted above, the prominent art films of this period made explicit a palpable uncertainty surrounding gender distinctions and sexual preferences. The most popular American films in Britain in the same period tended to be those by younger directors of the 'New Hollywood'. Such films explored masculine anxieties through narratives of power, alienation and violence (*Soldier Blue*, *The Godfather*, *Dirty Harry*, *Death Wish*, *Rollerball*, *The Outlaw Josey Wales*, *All the President's Men*). In the second half of the decade some of these issues were displaced on to science-fiction fantasies (*Star Wars* and *Close Encounters*). There was also a return to the solidly reactionary action hero (in *The Towering Inferno*, *Earthquake*, *Jaws* and *Rocky*). While female sexuality was demonised in *The Exorcist* and *Carrie*, musicals directed squarely at the female market (*Funny Girl*, *Hello Dolly!*, *Mary Poppins*, *The Sound of Music*, *Grease* and *Abba – The Movie*) were uniformly conservative in ideological terms. It looks from this survey as if British audiences had different expectations of, and sought different kinds of pleasure from, Hollywood films of the period. But furthermore, there appears to have been a marked shift in taste patterns in mid-decade. We have noted a brief period between 1971 and 1974, when popular tastes diversified and in which a variety of challenging films enjoyed popular success alongside residual, domestic fare. The year 1975 saw the re-emergence of something approaching popular consensus of taste, with the return to box-office dominance of the Hollywood majors in the second half of the decade. But whilst this view about shifts in popular taste can be derived from national box-office data, this is rather different from the film provision that audiences in local cinemas experienced.

Local Taste Patterns

It will be useful to compare the findings above with two sets of data about South Coast cinemas in the 1970s. Barber's analysis (Appendix II) of a single cinema in Southampton during the 1970s furnishes us with some attendance figures and, though limited to a single Odeon site, crucially includes takings of films shown, derived from cinema ledgers. This not only offers a model of local Rank distribution during the decade, but also suggests something about local popular tastes. There are no comparative data for other cinemas in Southampton, so any conclusions drawn from this evidence must be limited by the unknown competition factor. But Barber's study does enable us to make some comparisons between this Odeon cinema located at Eastern Docks, and the one in Portsmouth's North End.

Narrow though they may be, Barber's data are rich in certain respects. Firstly, they reveal something of the taste-community which Rank had worked so hard to cultivate in its provincial cinemas. Exploitation fare of the period is under-represented in this cinema, and the most popular examples nationally (the *Confessions* films) do only modest trade. Barber reveals that *Confessions of a Window Cleaner* (nationally the top-grossing British film of 1974) played for only a week at the Southampton Odeon; by contrast, it was held over for ten weeks in Portsmouth and showed at both Odeon cinemas (in North End and Southsea). Secondly, the local policy of screening the new Roger Moore Bond releases, *Live and Let Die* and *The Man with the Golden Gun*, as double-bill packages with older Sean Connery Bonds seems to have backfired in terms of box office. By contrast, the Odeon at Portsmouth held over *Live and Let Die* for eight weeks in 1973, while *The Man with the Golden Gun* also played for two months, being paired with a returning *Live and Let Die* in December 1975. Thirdly, genre pictures with an international scope otherwise did very well at Southampton's Odeon. *Don't Look Now*, *Gold*, *A Bridge Too Far* and *The Revenge of the Pink Panther* were all in the top flight behind the decade's Hollywood blockbusters, *Star Wars*, *Close Encounters* and *The Empire Strikes Back*. Finally, the local audience's preference for fantasy adventures is clear, whether it had the youth appeal of Southampton-born

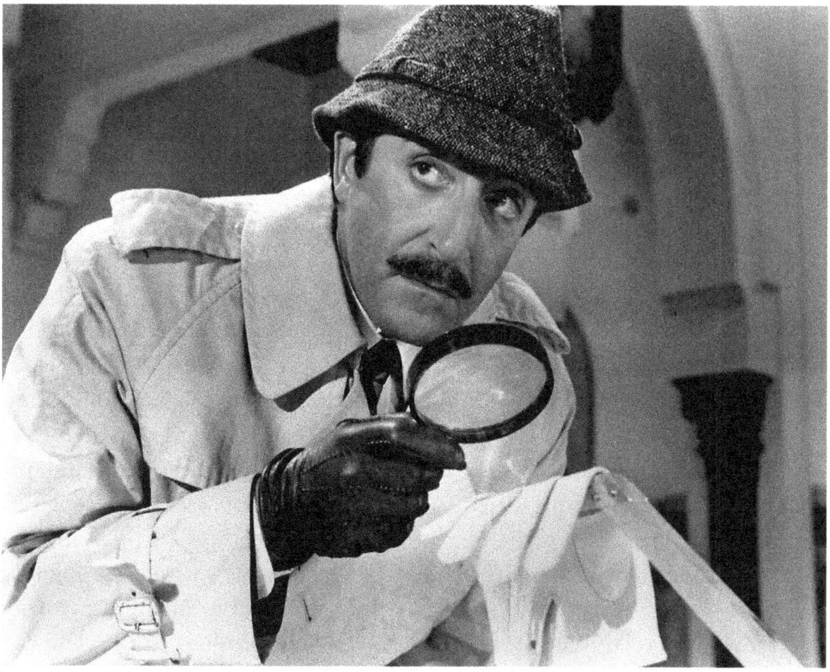

Figure 20 *Return of the Pink Panther*

Ken Russell (*Tommy*), or the family attraction of Disney's *Island at the Top of the World* and *The Rescuers*. Moreover, as Barber's table indicates, from mid-decade the Odeon cashed in on Disney's back catalogue too, so the enduring popularity of these classic animations palpably involved a strong element of nostalgia for local audiences. By contrast, Portsmouth's Odeon only screened *Island at the Top of the World* for two weeks in 1974–1975, and while *The Rescuers* was held over for a month in 1977, its box-office standing at Southampton was far higher. Whilst we must be cautious with these data about reading too much into the taste preferences of Odeon cinema-goers in Southampton, what is clear is that the local cinema manager of the day, James Tilmouth, exercised significant personal judgements about film programming when compared with the Odeons in Portsmouth and Southsea.

The weekly cinema listings from *The News* (compiled by Peri Bradley) provide two kinds of information relevant to film consumption (www.1970sproject.co.uk). Firstly, they reveal a pattern of changes in cinema provision during the decade (cinema closures and multi-screen conversions) which is not untypical of any provincial city in this period. Secondly, they offer a different model of local distribution (from the national popularity by box-office index, and from Southampton Odeon data), which allows us to interpret something about the predilections of the local clientele.

Portsea Island comprises a number of separate but adjacent demographic constituencies. Whilst the socio-economic character of these communities varied considerably in the 1970s, the close proximity of several cinemas (and the effective local transport infrastructure), in conjunction with the disappearance of the regular cinema audience of days gone by, meant that cinema choice was more likely to be based upon films shown rather than other factors.[590] However, by mid-decade, Portsmouth's cinema provision had contracted along lines not untypical of the period. From a situation where three localities each offered neighbourhood choices between a circuit major and a smaller independent, by 1976 only a single ABC and two rival Odeons remained. And the Rank circuit was always in the lead. From 1973 its three screens in North End replaced the choices previously provided by three cinemas, and throughout the rest of the decade its sister site in Southsea frequently showed completely different films.[591] Arguably, the ABC only survived at all by dint of its central Commercial Road location. However, independent cinema had not been entirely eradicated in Portsmouth. As a naval town, with the Royal Naval Dockyard still by far the largest local employer in this period, it is not surprising that Portsmouth also boasted two regular venues which showed exclusively 'X'-rated films for adult audiences. These were the euphemistically named Palace Continental in Commercial Road (the central shopping district) and The Tatler in Kingston Road. The former was a commercial venue showing 'X'-rated films on general release; the latter was a private members' club which showed non-certificated pornographic films. Popular titles included *The Sexy Dozen*, *Midnite Plowboy* and *Overdose of Degradation.* Significantly, until the advent of home video and licensed sex shops, these independents held their own throughout the 1970s.

Apart from the enduring appeal of strictly adult fare, it is difficult to gain any nuanced picture of local taste patterns simply from the titles of films shown. This information alone tells us nothing about their relative popularity. However, a crude measure might be provided by looking at those titles which were held over, or were screened at more than one venue, or were shown without a supporting feature, and to compare these with national box-office trends. The Portsmouth data is at first sight unsurprising in this regard. Those films which were held over for more than a week, or ran concurrently in more than one cinema in the city, are predominantly the same titles which topped the box office nationally. As

Table 12 shows, the top twelve titles which appear in the decade listings fifteen times or more are as follows, in rank order: *Star Wars* (25), *Close Encounters of the Third Kind* (20), *Paint Your Wagon* (19), *Confessions of a Window Cleaner* (18), *Magnum Force* (18), *Butch Cassidy and the Sundance Kid* (17), *Where Eagles Dare* (17), *Live and Let Die* (16), *Soldier Blue* (16), *Blazing Saddles* (16), *Anne of the Thousand Days* (15) and *Moonraker* (15). So, to that extent, it appears that popular tastes in Portsmouth were not unusual. However, it is often the middle ground in such rankings which offers a more nuanced picture of local preferences. The tranche of titles appearing between ten and fifteen times reveals a strong predilection for action adventures, war films and thrillers, intelligent comedies, Disney and musicals. In all cases (perhaps with the exception of the locally shot *Tommy*), generic and gender coding is unambiguous.

But there is also a further aspect to these programme data which is interesting: the trends in film provision over time. Of course, as has been noted, this cannot be related directly to popularity. None the less, the shift in the local film culture during the decade (on the basis of the type of material screened) is profound. In part this is due to the contraction of the market, as explained above, but that itself must be seen as a reflection (rather than a cause) of changing patterns in taste. The gradual diminution of exploitation fare (even in the context of its local Portsmouth appeal) is consistent with broader trends in this area. This is further evidence of the increasing internationalism and conservatism of popular tastes as the decade progresses. The popularity of New Hollywood titles alongside both more radical and parochial British fare in the first four years of the decade was eclipsed by more predictable material. It is also clear that film provision in Portsmouth in the first half of the 1970s was sustained by a significant proportion of films made in the previous decade. One of the recourses of cinemas in the face of the economic crisis of 1971–1974 was to rescreen older material; another was towards more eclectic offerings catering to very different niche taste-communities.

What we find in surveying British film distribution and exhibition during the 1970s is evidence of the deep cultural fault-lines in the film tastes of the period, and the decline in the popularity of the independent film in mainstream cinema. This is noteworthy, since it must be remembered that the 1970s marked the end of the long period when cinema was the dominant arena of film consumption. We can tentatively conclude from evidence about popular taste that it responded in a quite immediate way to recent changes in the film market and that the hitherto stable generic patterns of popularity (such as obtained up until the 1960s) were disrupted. We saw that the popularity of small-scale domestic films, intimately tied in to British preoccupations, was short-lived, and gave way to a marked audience preference for big-budget international event movies in which the individual was shaken free from the parochialism of ideological constraints. We also saw that the preference for films which contained an unprecedented amount of sex or violence declined in popularity from mid-decade. This can be interpreted as a reinstatement of boundaries of permission which had been temporarily breached from the late 1960s.

Popular film tastes may be seen as revealing a new kind of cultural eclecticism which privileged consumer choice and personal pleasure. Such patterns in popular taste can be interpreted as a rapid response to changes in cultural provision, as well as in society at large. Here is where we can see the emergence of a major contradiction in film culture. Popular tastes were predicated on immediacy, personal pleasures and the disposability of the object of desire. Critical tastes, on the other hand, were predicated on issues of quality, status and intellectual labour. The major film journals, alongside popular magazine, television and radio reviews, played an increasingly important role in debates about cinema.

Critical Discourse and High-Brow Taste

Up until the 1960s, British film criticism was thoroughly coherent in its modes of address, but in the 1970s, that coherence no longer obtained. There were two reasons for this. The first was the expansion of critical writing and media programmes about film. The second was the increased rivalry between film publications. There arose conflicting 'parishes of belief' evinced by various film magazines and their fierce rivalries about the methods of film criticism obscured popular visual culture.

To be sure, mainstream journalists plied their trade as before, and were an integral part of the cultural mechanism of the newspapers for which they worked. Hence critics such as Dilys Powell, Derek Malcolm, David Robinson, John Russell Taylor and Alexander Walker had two functions: to inform their readers about the latest mainstream film provision, and to express the distinctiveness of their own tastes. The film recommendations in *Time Out* addressed a specific audience – the younger London intelligentsia – but were still structured by the weekly availability of films and the need to publicise them. *Time Out*'s intervention in film culture was at a consistently high level; its writings were thorough and occasionally eccentric, though always with a slightly academic gloss. Television films and cinema releases were carefully previewed, and readers were informed about the buying policies of TV companies, which determined the films they could see.[592] Occasionally, the journal would make a direct intervention in film history in a distinctively 'cultish' manner. In 1975, for example, *Time Out* championed the cultural significance of lost 'B' features, with an essay by their chief film critic, Chris Petit, and a taxonomy of significant films by him and David Pirie.[593] The magazine's letter pages contain passionate engagements with film issues, and often are fiercely critical of National Film Theatre programming, as well as mainstream provision.

As Forster notes in Chapter 7, film criticism in the 1970s gained a greater prominence from television programmes. Granada/LWT screened *Cinema* (Fridays 10.30), hosted by Russell Davies from *The Observer*, which considered films on recent release. *Film Night* was released by BBC2 (Thursdays 11.45), chaired by Tony Bilbow and Philip Jenkinson, and *Film*, presented by Barry Norman, was produced by BBC1 and shown on Fridays at 10.45. In addition, there was Granada's *Clapperboard* for young audiences, which was chaired by Chris Kelly on Friday afternoons. This all meant that there were informed discussions about recent films, featuring interviews with key directors and stars, across the schedules. Thus television provided British critics and intellectuals with an expanded platform on which to debate ideas about film in the very period when the British industry itself was in financial and cultural crisis.

The specialist monthly or quarterly film magazines were different, and they provide evidence of a radical fragmentation of intellectual taste-communities. *Films and Filming* was an important mainstream journal. Edited by journalist Robin Bean, and part of the publishing stable which produced *Art and Artists* and *Dance and Dancers*, the journal marked out a middle ground between high-brow aficionados and popular fandom. *Films and Filming* was replete with film stills, often of scantily clad females, which the editor defended from readers' criticism by noting, 'If what we print arouses you, you should see what we leave out.'[594] The journal presented a varied diet, featuring transcripts of interviews with stars and directors, and British and non-British workers.[595] Attention was paid to the pantheon of cinema history,[596] to film finance,[597] and to production/distribution relations.[598]

Films and Filming was the only serious journal to give positive attention to popular British cinema.[599] It was also rare in the praise it gave to Ken Russell. Gordon Gow, a regular writer, presciently found *Tommy* 'a milestone in British cinema, which will go down as either the film which stopped the slide into mediocrity and mindlessness, or it may turn out to be the lone, gloriously defiant stand against apathy and indifference'.[600] *Films and Filming* also had a positive attitude to films on television, and

Allen Eyles's articles presented televised films as an alternative to the straitjacket imposed by cinema distribution practices. The journal located itself as a liberal alternative to the coteries of *Sight and Sound* and *Movie*.[601]

So *Films and Filming* provided access to middle-of-the-road critical tastes. But uniquely in the period, it also provided insights into its readers' cultural needs, and responded to them in detail. In late 1971, the editor extended the letter page and transferred it to the beginning of the journal. The letters are approximately 98 per cent male. Three leitmotifs dominate the letter pages. Firstly, the distribution system: letter after letter bewails the narrow provision in the provinces, and the practice of blind-booking.[602] Secondly, the issue of censorship preoccupies many letter-writers, who take a universally critical line on the liberalism of the BBFC.[603] Thirdly, there is a robust rejection of over-intellectual criticism and excessive Freudianism.[604] On the controversies over violence, one writer says it is 'better to be depraved and corrupted by the likes of Kubrick, Russell, Peckinpah and others, than be reduced to automatic laughing machines for television transplants'.[605] For many readers, the TV spin-offs mark the boundaries of debates about taste. One correspondent argues that film should simply

> satisfy its chosen audience . . . I'm not so naive as to assume that just because Godard and Renoir are packing 'em in in the common room that they'll ensure full houses in the ABC in the High Street (particularly if there's a TV spin-off in competition).[606]

Another reader praises *Confessions of a Window Cleaner* as 'an accurate and inspiring picture of the life of the average British working lad' and finds it preferable to Antonioni's *The Passenger*.[607] For another, Robin Askwith's 'commonness' makes him into 'a modern-day counterpart of George Formby'.[608] Some letter-writers took risks. One argued, astutely, that critics misunderstood *Zardoz*, which 'debunks as it edifies', that Boorman 'laughs at what he is doing', and that he tends to 'lead us, through parody and uncertainty, into a genuinely serious and intelligent conclusion'.[609]

In addition, *Films and Filming* inaugurated a 'Question and Answer' feature by David McGillivray. This is extremely revealing about what readers want to know. They ask about George Segal, about the soundtrack of *The Last Picture Show*, about the locations in *Barry Lyndon*, about books on Laurel and Hardy, about the sets in *Gawain and the Green Knight* and the peacock cloak in *Samson and Delilah*. They want to know if Robert Redford did his own ski stunts, and the dates of Elizabeth Taylor's weddings and divorces. The 'For Sale/Wanted' columns are also instructive. Readers want to buy material on Burgess Meredith, *any* scripts, and signed photos of the stars. Such marginalia indicate the sheer intractability of fan tastes, even among middle-of-the-roaders.

Films and Filming was a journal without sponsors or affiliations, and it expressed a coherent liberal position. Other journals were more extreme. *Movie* had a little financial support from the BFI, so was not altogether independent; it was edited by Ian Cameron, with V. F. Perkins, Robin Wood and Jim Hillier playing key roles. *Movie*'s pre-1975 period was an apologia for American cinema. Its tone was unremittingly combative, with Hitchcock's *Topaz* being preferred because all other film journals had been 'short-sighted' in its interpretation.[610] The early *Movie* espoused an auteurism derived from those heady days of *Cahiers du cinéma* before it was tainted by Marxism. The problem with the *auteur* theory is that it can seem obvious if unskilfully deployed, and Robin Wood's reference for Kazan, for example, was lamely expressed: 'He is always at his best . . . when he has no Big Theme, no Message, no Protest, when his material forces an ambivalent response.'[611] *Movie*'s rationale was influenced by Perkins's *Film as Film*, which championed visual style as the ultimate criterion of taste. He argued for visual pleasure above all, and poured scorn on 'the old notion that virtue consists in hardship, and that what's pleasant must be regarded with suspicion'.[612] This was unexceptionable in itself, but problematical when combined with a reluctance to consider film's relationship to society.

So far, so anodyne; but *Movie* was transformed when it was relaunched in Spring 1975. The editorial reaffirmed the importance of *mise en scène* and located its own critical position carefully. *Movie* was now thoroughly focused on a struggle with *Screen* and *Sight and Sound.* Robin Wood reaffirmed his own and the journal's position thus:

> I do rely on my sense of belonging to a cultural tradition and respecting it, whereas so much writing centred on *Screen* and Semiology tends to be based on a kind of revolutionary politics which sees its aim as simply opposing that tradition, attacking it, labelling it with names like bourgeois ideology.[613]

In 1978–1979, *Movie* dedicated a whole number to an attack on *Screen*'s 'avant-garde intellectual terrorism', noting that it had 'performed a feat which must be the envy of other serious film magazines: it has communicated its influence even to those who have not read it'.[614] The number contained a piece by Andrew Britton which is a robust rebuttal of *Screen.* Britton had understood Althusser, Lacan and Barthes, and his flaying of the modish beatification of these figures is a *pièce de résistance*. His rebuttal of the idea of suture is incisive.[615] *Movie*'s relatively narrow tastes put it in an extremely exposed position. There is, after all, nothing wrong in liking

Raoul Walsh. But, instead of refining its own views about visual pleasure, *Movie* spent too much of its time trying to thrust a poniard between the ribs of its enemies.

Films and Filming and *Movie* also excoriated the organs of the BFI: *Monthly Film Bulletin* and *Sight and Sound*. Why was this? Its tastes, after all, were not so very different from theirs: quality films, auteurist directors, clever scripts, elegant visuals. But *Sight and Sound* was bound to foster jealousy. It was very well supported financially and institutionally, but more importantly, it was able to function hegemonically, in that it expressed the confident taste of an intelligentsia with a particularly British trait: they actually trusted cultural authorities like the BFI. Throughout the 1970s, *Sight and Sound* was edited with a firm hand by Penelope Houston, who took no intellectual prisoners. Under her reign, the journal combined sumptuous production values with a range of policies: information on recent government initiatives, interviews with key directors, attention to European cinemas, and reviews of recent films.

Sight and Sound provides evidence about the aesthetic mind-set of intellectuals who wished to assert their own sense of distinction. Hence the overweening concentration on the more abstruse aspects of cinema: Dostoevski's influence on Bresson, for example.[616] *Sight and Sound* allowed space for bilious attacks on the commercial industry: 'The people who run the industry have always been frightened. They have always avoided important themes . . . The cinema has been whoring long enough, living off immoral dollar earnings.'[617] Such views were unlikely to be welcomed by beleaguered producers, but were doubtless music to the ears of those who constituted an important aesthetic caucus at this time. *Sight and Sound*'s letter-pages differed significantly from those of *Film and Filming*, since they gave voice mainly to those who created or supported the tradition.[618] Its letter-pages are not the site where ideas are forged; they are asserted.

Throughout the decade, by far the majority of *Sight and Sound*'s articles focused on European film-makers: Chabrol, Bertolucci, Godard, Makavejev, Fassbinder, Truffaut, Resnais, Ophuls, Rivette, Syberberg, Dreyer. It is piquant to wonder how film aficionados in the Hebrides or Truro would have responded to these apothegms, given dire distribution conditions outside London. But it was a crucial aspect of *Sight and Sound*'s taste-repertoire to favour European films, and an uncharitable interpretation might be that they were harder to consume and often even harder to see, and thus conferred kudos on those who saw them. When it came to British films, the magazine seemed at a loss. The reviewer of *Performance* noted: 'I do not pretend to understand (or really worry about) certain aspects of the film.'[619] Another thought that *Get Carter*'s 'iconography is wrong. It's not a patch on Melville.'[620] The only British films that tended to be praised were self-referential films which, like *Gumshoe*, stimulated a love for the cinema 'instead of the self-love that emerges via the works of Ken Russell'.[621] Even *O Lucky Man!* had 'an unappealingly sanctimonious edge'.[622]

Such critiques are not due to cussedness, but proceed from a belief in expositionary criticism. Richard Roud's review of *The Go-Between* is a case in point. He effectively tells the story, re-enacting the emotions evoked by the film, and shows where its tastes coincide poignantly with his own.[623] The majority of reviewers use this unmethodical but mannerly technique, and it is tempting to imagine that this ramshackle approach operated as a sort of stimulus to *Screen* to develop a critique which avoided the expression of personal taste.

Sight and Sound's position was that British cinema, unlike the European ones, had become fatally alienated from its own sense of national identity. Until that was restored, according to John Russell Taylor in a key article, British cinema would be 'dead as the dodo'. Contemporary funding structures blurred national boundaries, and since a film like *Sunday Bloody Sunday* was funded by Americans, he had 'no feeling of its being in any sense a British film. It is not an American film either.'[624] In the same number, David Wilson noted of Mamoun Hassan that 'it is no small irony that . . . such confidence in the Britishness of British cinema is voiced by a Saudi Arab'.[625] Thus in a prolix, querulous way, *Sight and Sound* wound a skein around itself.

What ran through many of *Sight and Sound*'s judgements is the sense of a great tradition *à la* Leavis, unsullied by commerce or excess. Its Top Ten Films, which appeared in 1971–1972, was virtually the same list as that of ten years before, contained no British films, and was headed by *Citizen Kane*, *La Règle du Jeu* and *Battleship Potemkin*.[626] This belief in a tradition, into which British cinema had to be inserted (by force if necessary), was what gave the journal its confidence.

Monthly Film Bulletin was published by the BFI but was a distinct operation from *Sight and Sound*. *Monthly Film Bulletin*'s aim was to provide a monthly digest of all films released; a range of professional and academic writers provided a précis and critique of each film. On the whole, *Monthly Film Bulletin*'s taste was fairly close to that of *Sight and Sound*. It had a predilection for foreign films, and only praised British films unreservedly if they fell into the art-house category: 'no synopsis could adequately convey the wealth of imaginative incident which fills *Jubilee* with a textual and theoretical richness quite extraordinary in the field of British (and especially British independent) production.'[627] British films like *Gumshoe* which contested traditional genres had a favourable response.[628] Ken Russell met with particular opprobrium. *The Boy Friend* was thought to be too ready 'to bring it *all* on, all the *time*',[629] and *Tommy* had 'every sequence characteristically pitched at a hit-or-miss fortissimo'.[630]

Monthly Film Bulletin reviewers reserved their most biting irony for the sex films, which was rather like shooting fish in a barrel. The reviews of *What Are you Doing After the Orgy?*[631] and *Madame Bovary* (aka *Play the Game or Leave the Bed*)[632] are masterpieces of satire. But the reviews are useful for scholars when they quote from the scripts of sex films which are no longer available, thus evoking the gamy flavour of a vanished culture. Lines quoted by *Monthly Film Bulletin* reviewers from the scripts of sex films include: 'I haven't eaten butter since seeing *Last Tango in Paris,*'[633] 'Guests are reminded that all umbrellas and bras to be left in the hall'[634] and, from an Australian sex marathon, 'The day will come when I'm gonna stick my dick in the heart of the earth . . . and the bang'll be heard in Alaska!'[635] However, *Monthly Film Bulletin*'s ironic tone did not attract the venom of *Movie* and *Screen* in the way that *Sight and Sound* did. Throughout the decade, *Screen* was engaged in an assault on the great tradition, such that the very idea of personal taste was anathema.

As Porter has outlined in Chapter 4, *Screen* developed originally as a product of SEFT.[636] When Sam Rohdie became editor from Spring 1971, the journal's policy was transformed into an explicitly revolutionary one. Throughout the decade, the tenets of Marxism, semiotics and psychoanalysis inspired this radical zeal. The journal expended much energy attacking realism and the 'classic realist text' because it was ideologically compromised – an uncomfortable conclusion, since that was the form most beloved by the masses, whose tolerance of distanciation was bound to be limited.[637] By the time Rohdie stood down as editor in 1974, he thought that *Screen* had effectively destroyed 'forms of impressionistic and intuitive criticism'.[638] Certainly, the readership had been encouraged to enter into those sunlit uplands beyond personal taste.

The majority of the editorial board resigned in Summer 1976, on the grounds that the journal had become too obscure, too estranged from educational matters, and too wedded to the code-breaking avant-garde: 'a sectarian atmosphere developed, where dissent and scrutiny were seen as lack of good faith.'[639] Increasingly, *Screen* became self-referential and self-promoting, allowing huge spaces for its favourites and very little for its opponents.

The problem was that *Screen*'s intentions were forensic and analytical. Crucial to its enterprise was the notion that the validation of individual taste, which had hitherto played such a prominent role in film criticism, was fatally compromised by its ideological position. This meant that the journal had the profoundest problems with pleasure, and presented it as a conspiracy. The pleasures of cinema were foisted on unwitting spectators, and *Screen*'s task was to tear the veil from their eyes and make them witness their own duped exploitation. Laura Mulvey's 'Visual pleasure and narrative cinema' should be interpreted as the apotheosis of *Screen*'s 1970s work, since it is both inductive and puritanical – inductive in that it deploys a rigid theoretical framework to 'explain' films, and puritanical in that it is predicated on a fear of *jouissance*. Here, indeed, are the Boundaries of Pleasure, and we enter that barren country where intellectuals fear the unruly pleasures of that working class to which (politically at least) they are committed.

Conclusion

In earlier chapters we have suggested that, due to the economic and cultural crisis in the British film industry, the market for popular cinema was profoundly unstable. We want to argue that this instability was partially responsible for the dramatic schism between popular and critical taste, and the polarised relationship between the two. Patterns of popular taste in the 1970s – as in every other period – are an index of cycles of consumption, and are subject to the immediacy and availability of the product. But in the 1970s, taste was more fragmented than before. In the early part of the decade, as we have shown, there was a marked but short-lived preference for domestic films and radical sexual politics. This gave way, in mid-decade, to a preference for more conservative and internationalist films, led by the resurgence of the Hollywood event film. It can be argued that the increase in popular film criticism across the media contributed to this realignment of popular taste. Critical or academic taste, on the other hand, was in this period predicated on what was not easily available. The high brow film journals we have surveyed here encouraged the construction of an alternative film history – one in which *On the Buses* was pushed to the periphery by the discovery of hitherto neglected films by Bresson or Dziga-Vertov.

The map of popular taste in the 1970s appears to be predicated on the desire to choose from a range of available pleasures, according to personal preference. High-brow cultural critics objected profoundly to such a notion of consumer choice, since its very eclecticism was seen as a symptom of its dependence upon the market. In response to the cultural crisis in the British film market, high-brow critics intervened by according cultural value to certain kinds of film. Paradoxically, the film as an object of attention increasingly disappeared amidst the competing voices of critical discourse. These critics argued, with varying degrees of zealotry, for the establishment of a new film order – often construed as oppositional – constructed in the image of its own particular orthodoxies. In the 1970s, despite the continued decline in cinema attendance and the unpredictability of the market, there was no diminution in the range and intensity of popular pleasures which film afforded. Indeed, we have shown that the growth of varied discourses *about* film were evidence of the contested space it occupied in the culture.

Conclusion

At the outset of this book, we suggested that the particular challenges of 1970s British film culture demanded an innovative approach. The Portsmouth project produced a range of work which focused on discrete aspects of the period. Some of this work is represented in Part I of the book. These chapters provide evidence about the conflicting agendas of different interest groups which characterised the film culture of the period. Traditional spheres of influence (government policy, censorship, film design) were augmented by new interventions (from the avant-garde, educational establishments, racial minorities, television and popular music). As the authors of Part I have shown, each of these fields, whether old or new, was riven by internal conflicts. But additionally, as shown in Part II, there were tensions in the relations between these interest groups. These complex disjunctions gave rise to an unusually conflicted cultural field.

In our Introduction we raised a number of key questions about British film culture in the 1970s. We are now in a position to return to these. To begin with, we sought to identify the determinants on artistic innovation in a period of economic uncertainty. We suggested that the relations between production, distribution and exhibition in the film industry were disrupted by financial crisis. The 'old guard' of producers and directors was unable to adapt to new circumstances. The rise of new producers (often from non-industry backgrounds) injected new kinds of cultural capital and drew upon fresh sources of finance. This was a precarious market, in which the lines of communication between capital and artistic production were often remote and sometimes stretched to the limit, creating conditions of unpredictability and risk. This resulted in a commercial film culture characterised by extremes: on the one hand, a cinema of clumsiness, and on the other hand, one of sublime innovation.

These circumstances gave directorial opportunities to some lesser creative talents who might have struggled to find a place in the old studio structures. But they also allowed the emergence of some directors who were able to respond in a sensitive way to upheavals in the visual culture, and who felt free to push the boundaries of commercial film practice. Additionally, this period witnessed the flourishing of avant-garde film and video, which extended the definition and creative possibilities of those media on the cultural margins. These radical practices, often fostered by the educational establishment, were diverse and insular in character during the 1970s, but had a greater prominence and coherence in the 1980s.

We also raised the question of how British cinema of the 1970s engaged with aspects of social change. We argued that cinema does not reflect historical change in any straightforward manner, though it often engages with contemporary concerns. British cinema in the 1970s did not respond in a direct way to socio-political transformations, in part due to its diminished place within the culture at large. Rather, it engaged obliquely with some social issues and not at all with others. For example, the 'Troubles' in Northern Ireland and Britain's entry into the Common Market, both of which dominated politics and the media throughout the decade, were scarcely visible in feature film. Similarly, the oil crisis and industrial disputes were only directly referenced in television spin-offs, as indices of topicality. The disregard for these pressing political matters suggests that commercial film-makers were reluctant to deal directly with some sensitive contemporary issues which were given considerable coverage in other media.

Patterns of class representation were distinctive in 1970s British cinema. The aristocracy no longer occupied the dominant narrative and symbolic space that it was formerly accorded. And authority figures were frequently mocked and undermined. Many films placed outsiders at centre-stage, and *parvenus*, *picaros* or *déraciné* characters often set the stories in motion. These itinerants were rarely defined by conventional class markers, and they enjoyed the right to roam in middle-class territory. Traditional middle-class fractions were less sharply delineated than in previous periods. Hence the centre ground, in class terms, appeared to be more open to incursion. But there was an important exception to this. In the television spin-offs and other low-brow comedies, class boundaries were much more clearly defined. Thus the full spectrum of the social order is radically reorganised in this cinema, and its social arrangements are divided between those empowered figures who are mobile and those powerless ones whose place is fixed.

Race politics was an important issue in the 1970s, and received some direct if limited treatment on film, largely through new creative opportunities for black film-makers. These films were ground-breaking in terms of agency and self-determination, and their radicalism was predicated on youth sub-culture and codes of masculinity. But beyond their appeal to black audiences and political sympathisers, these films made a significant contribution to emergent discourses about diversity and sub-cultural identities. Otherwise, residual representations of ethnic minorities in film and television continued to rely on well-worn stereotypes and comic caricatures.

Sexual politics in the 1970s underwent vigorous transformation, with the Women's Movement and Gay Liberation in the vanguard. Film culture was partisan and intense in its response to developments in the gender field. With a couple of notable exceptions, lesbian and gay sexuality was scarcely addressed in mainstream cinema, and appeared in camp and butch guises in low-brow comedies and TV spin-offs. But the upheavals attendant upon the broader sexual revolution had widespread expression in commercial film culture. While many films exploited relaxations in censorship to present the female body for the sexual pleasure of men, most also expressed anxiety about sexually empowered women. A significant number of films addressed sexuality more ambiguously, and their anxieties and equivocations were often expressed ironically. This manner may be interpreted as an attempt to deal with profound transformations in the sexual field candidly, and without risk. Irony enables two contradictory attitudes – fear and desire – to be expressed simultaneously. Culturally speaking, this mode is a way of marking the boundary between the sacred and the profane; of assuming, and then doffing at will, a mask of identity. This attitude presents sexual identity as contingent, and sexual pleasure as a commodity – a matter of lifestyle choice. In foregrounding this attitude, 1970s British cinema can be seen to have contributed to the new vocabulary of sexuality.

We discovered that contingency and irony were not confined to attitudes in the sexual field in the films of the period. Attention to visual style revealed these modes to be more prevalent generally. Film style in the decade underwent significant reformation as a result of changes in production practices. We have noted examples of imbalance in the orchestration of lighting, editing, music and performance style, such that certain elements within the *mise en scène* either carry a burden of meaning beyond their narrative function, or have a high level of redundancy. Such unevenness runs right across the film culture and is evident in films of markedly different provenance. In many cases, these visual practices accentuated the primacy of subjective response, disturbed narrative coherence, and threw into question the place of objects within the visual field.

Our analysis of social space revealed that, in a range of film types, the relations between subjective and objective realities were disrupted. This meant that motivated spaces were set in a dynamic relation to methods of characterisation. From the taxonomy of new performance styles which we proposed, it emerged that there was a wider range than in previous periods and that the emotional landscape of the cinema was fragmented. What D. H. Lawrence called 'the old stable ego of the self' was profoundly in question in the cinema of this period. The new subjectivity was without a centre but full of expressivity; this is consonant with cinematic worlds full of ambiguous objects.

We have suggested that the cinema of the period performed a range of discrete cultural tasks. This was due in part to its beleaguered status, and to its creation of separate taste-communities. The fragmentation of the market was caused by disrupted relations between production, distribution and exhibition. But in addition, the challenges to cultural hierarchies in the previous decade intensified the division between commercial and art-house cinema; this, in turn, stimulated critical controversy about the nature of film as a medium and the cultural function of cinema. Market fragmentation was so intense that it fostered a sort of tribalism, in which distinct taste-communities were constructed, whose boundaries were rigorously policed.

The aim of this book has been to draw a map of film culture in 1970s Britain. We have tried to interpret these terms mindfully, and it now looks as though each of them is complex in its own way. To begin with, the 'film culture' underwent a series of transitions. The economic crisis which beset the industry in both the production and exhibition sectors was a cause of concern for successive governments, who responded with piecemeal policy initiatives. Declining attendance and cinema closures reduced the cultural status of cinema; the dominance of television, and the rise of home video towards the end of the decade, extended the sites of film consumption. The technological innovation of video also created a hiatus in the practices of censorship, which had been a matter of public and political concern earlier in the decade. Extreme material, which had prompted high-profile controversies in the first half of the decade, did not diminish as a result of censorship. Rather, exploitation fare was accommodated by unregulated home video and licensed sex-shops. Thus the film market became increasingly segmented, with separate exhibition arrangements obtaining for both ends of the taste spectrum – pornography and the avant-garde. Consequently, in the second half of the decade, the commercial centre-ground became dominated by Hollywood event movies with broad appeal, and by British films which catered for a range of youth sub-cultures. The diminished status of mainstream cinema paradoxically stimulated a wide range of critical discourses about film, from television magazine programmes to erudite film journals and university courses. A steady increase in government funding for the BFI also provided an important stimulus to the independent production sector, which raised the status of experimental work on the cultural margins. These various developments decentred the film culture, making it more diffuse than it had been in the 1960s.

On the face of it, 'the 1970s' is a decade like any other, but the caveat that cultural history rarely fits into neat decades has proved especially true in this case. From the outset, it was clear that the crisis in film funding which marked the decade was precipitated by the withdrawal of American capital at the end of the 1960s. Moreover, it seems to us that the narratives of 1970s British cinema were determined by the cultural transformations of 1968, particularly in the area of sexuality, and that this goes some way towards accounting for the prevalent tone of irony and disavowal. The full effects of the funding crisis were felt most acutely in the period 1971–1974. The financial vacuum and the increased impetus of the counter-culture produced a polarised and insular cinema dominated by TV spin-offs and radical *causes célèbres*. There followed, however, a break in cultural practice and in cinematic taste, which took place about 1974. The second half of the decade was marked by the further decline of British cinema attendance and by a downturn in British film production, while there was a new settlement around the hegemony of the Hollywood blockbuster.

From 1977, the year of the Queen's Silver Jubilee, there was a notable return in British films to matters of national identity. Partly, this was predicated upon more conservative interpretations of that individualism which had been explored in alternative ways earlier in the decade. The radical utopianism of earlier experiments in film was increasingly replaced by a more materialist conception of individual identity.

'British' is always a fluid term in cultural criticism, but it is particularly so in the case of the cinema of the 1970s. Only in television spin-offs and low-brow comedies was national identity addressed consistently and in a straightforward manner. Even the Bond franchise began the decade uncertainly, though its later offerings returned to a more solidly patriotic tone. Most films before 1977 did not confront national identity head-on, but made allusion to it via modes of displacement such as fantasy, regionalism and the historical. Although these were indirect modes of address, they permitted some film-makers to explore radical ideas about society. A handful of innovative films suggested the unthinkable: that patriarchy could be overturned (*Zardoz*), that society could be constructed on the basis of unfettered desire (*The Wicker Man*), that private property could be abolished (*Winstanley*). These variously dystopian and utopian visions were isolated examples. However, they can be seen as a manifestation of a broader concern with imagined communities rooted in primal myths of the culture.

Films such as *Akenfield*, *Requiem for a Village* and the historical elements in *Jubilee* presented an elegiac celebration of a vanished culture. Such films commemorated, in a nostalgic manner, an organic relationship between the individual and the natural environment – an English *Heimat*. This consonance was presented as a lost idyll, and the idea of national 'wholeness' was central to their project, but it was predicated upon a conception of Albion – a mythic history of English (rather than British) unity. This kind of history was a minority strand in the film culture of the period, and remained on the cultural margins thereafter.

By the end of the 1970s, British national identity was addressed with a new contemporary directness and in a solidly realist manner. *The Long Good Friday* marked a return to familiar, consensual symbols of national identity (the Thames and Tower Bridge). Its direct manner asserted proto-Thatcherite values, placing entrepreneurial individualism at the heart of the national interest – an interest which was threatened by violence from the margins.

To conclude, we need to consider the broader issue of the relationship between the film culture of this period and changes in consciousness. This fragmented film culture, with its de-centred practices and its insecure position, was able to articulate an unusually wide range of responses to social change, albeit in a chaotic and often oblique way. Arguably, its most important innovations occurred on the cultural margins. Yet film as a medium could still be a crucial vehicle for the articulation of fundamental fears and desires. We have suggested that this was a cinema of contingency and disavowal. Its dominant manner of irony enabled some film-makers to express deep anxieties, to think the unthinkable, or to imagine the world turned upside down. In the second half of the decade there was an ideological rupture in consciousness which witnessed a new settlement around more conservative notions of individualism, against the backdrop of a fragmented social order. Some films tapped into the new structures of feeling and presented a bleak world, in which the only consolation was the personal freedom to fashion oneself anew. Many British films of the 1970s extended the boundaries of pleasure in unprecedented ways. From mid-decade, there was a significant retreat from them. Thereafter, the cinema reasserted the dominance of the world of material goods over the world of ideas and desires.

Endnotes

Notes to Introduction

1. Eric Hobsbawn, *The Age of Extremes: The Short Twentieth Century 1914–91* (London: Michael Joseph, 1994), Arthur Marwick, *The Sixties: Cultural Revolution in Britain, France, Italy and the United States, c.1958–c.1974* (Oxford: Oxford University Press, 1998), Richard Weight, *Patriots: National Identity in Britain 1940–2000* (London: Macmillan, 2002).
2. Christopher Booker, *The Seventies: Portrait of a Decade* (Harmondsworth: Penguin, 1980).
3. Howard Sounes, *Seventies: The Sights, Sounds and Ideas of a Brilliant Decade* (London: Simon & Schuster, 2006).
4. Dave Haslam, *Not ABBA: The Real Story of the 1970s* (London: HarperPerennial, 2005).
5. Francis Wheen, *Strange Days Indeed: The Golden Age of Paranoia* (London: Fourth Estate, 2009), p. 9.
6. Alwyn Turner, *Crisis? What Crisis? Britain in the 1970s* (London: Aurum, 2008).
7. Andy Beckett, *When the Lights Went Out: Britain in the Seventies* (London: Faber & Faber, 2009).
8. Mark Garnett, *From Anger to Apathy: The British Experience since 1975* (London: Jonathan Cape, 2009).
9. Dominic Sandbrook, *State of Emergency: The Way We Were: Britain, 1970–1974* (London: Allen Lane, 2010), p. 346.
10. Laurel Forster and Sue Harper (eds), *British Culture and Society in the 1970s: The Lost Decade* (Newcastle: Cambridge Scholars, 2010).
11. Alexander Walker, *National Heroes: British Cinema in the Seventies and Eighties* (London: Harrap, 1985), Alexander Walker, *Hollywood, England: The British Film Industry in the 1960s*, 2nd edn (London: Harrap, 1986).
12. John Walker, *The Once and Future Film: British Cinema in the Seventies and Eighties* (London: Methuen, 1985), David Docherty, David Morrison and Michael Tracey, *The Last Picture Show: Britain's Changing Film Audiences* (London: BFI, 1987). Negative views of the decade have also been provided by James Park, *British Cinema: The Lights That Failed* (London: Batsford,

1990) and George Perry, *The Great British Picture Show* (London: Pavilion/ Michael Joseph, 1985).
13. Andrew Higson, 'A diversity of film practices: renewing British cinema in the 1970s', in Bart Moore-Gilbert (ed.), *The Arts in the 1970s: Cultural Closure?* (London: Routledge, 1994), pp. 216–39.
14. Pamela Church Gibson and Andrew Hill, '"Tutte e macchio!": excess, masquerade and performativity in 70s Cinema', in R. Murphy (ed.), *The British Cinema Book*, 2nd edn (London: BFI, 2000), pp. 263–9.
15. Leon Hunt, *British Low Culture: From Safari Suits to Sexploitation* (London: Routledge, 1998), p. 1.
16. Peter Hutchings, *Hammer and Beyond: The British Horror Film* (Manchester: Manchester University Press, 1993), Steve Chibnall, *Making Mischief: The Cult Films of Pete Walker* (Guildford: FAB, 1998), David McGillivray, *Doing Rude Things: The History of the British Sex Film 1958–1981* (London: Sun Tavern Fields, 1992).
17. John Baxter, *An Appalling Talent: Ken Russell* (London: Michael Joseph, 1973), Gene D. Phillips, *Ken Russell* (Boston: Twayne, 1979), Joseph A. Gomez, *Ken Russell: The Adaptor as Creator* (London: Frederick Muller, 1976). Neil Sinyard, *The Films of Nicolas Roeg* (London: Letts, 1991), John Izod, *The Films of Nicolas Roeg: Myth and Mind* (London: Macmillan, 1992), Scott Salwolke, *Nicolas Roeg Film by Film* (Jefferson: McFarland, 1993). Alexander Walker, *Stanley Kubrick Directs* (London: Davis-Poynter, 1972), Mario Falsetto (ed.), *Perspectives on Stanley Kubrick* (New York: G. K. Halt, 1996), Mario Falsetto, *Stanley Kubrick: A Narrative and Stylistic Analysis*, 2nd edn (London: Praeger, 2001).
18. A. L. Rees, *A History of Experimental Film and Video: From the Canonical Avant-Garde to Contemporary British Practice* (London: BFI, 1999), David Curtis, *A History of Artists' Film and Video in Britain, 1897–2004* (London: BFI, 2006), Michael O'Pray (ed.), *The British Avant-Garde Film 1926 to 1995* (Luton: John Libbey Media, 1996), Margaret Dickinson (ed.), *Rogue Reels: Oppositional Film in Britain 1945–90* (London: BFI, 1999).
19. Robert Shail (ed.), *Seventies British Cinema* (London: Palgrave Macmillan, 2008), Paul Newland (ed.), *Don't Look Now: British Cinema in the 1970s* (Bristol: Intellect, 2010).

Notes to Chapter 1

20. Ernest Betts, *The Film Business* (London: George Allen & Unwin, 1973), Margaret Dickinson and Sarah Street, *Cinema and State: The Film Industry and the British Government 1927–1984* (London: BFI, 1985), Bill Baillieu and John Goodchild, *The British Film Business* (Chichester: John Wiley, 2002).
21. Dickinson and Street, *Cinema and State*, p. 237, M. Dickinson, 'The state and the consolidation of monopoly', in James Curran and Vincent Porter (eds), *British Cinema History* (London: Weidenfeld & Nicholson, 1983), p. 92.

22. Lawrence Napper, 'A despicable tradition? Quota quickies in the 1930s', in R. Murphy (ed.), *The British Cinema Book* (London: BFI, 2001), Steve Chibnall, *Quota Quickies: The Birth of the British 'B' Film* (London: BFI, 2007), Steve Chibnall and Brian McFarlane, *The British 'B' Film* (London: BFI/Palgrave Macmillan, 2009).
23. Napper, 'A despicable tradition?', p. 47.
24. See Sue Harper and Vincent Porter, *British Cinema of the 1950s: The Decline of Deference* (Oxford: Oxford University Press, 2003), pp. 5–17.
25. See Dickinson and Street, *Cinema and State*, p. 231.
26. Linda Wood (ed.), *British Films 1971–1981* (London: BFI Library Services, 1983), p. 144.
27. British Film Fund Agency Committee Minutes, National Archives (NA): BT 383/14 – BT 383/23.
28. Ibid.
29. Alan Lovell, *The British Film Institute Production Board* (London: BFI, 1976), p. 5.
30. Ibid., p. 1.
31. See Christophe Dupin, 'The BFI and British independent cinema in the 1970s', in Shail (ed.), *Seventies British Cinema*, pp. 159–74.
32. D. Todd, 'Freedom for the flicks', *Kinematograph Weekly*, 19 December 1970, pp. 3–4.
33. Letter to Editor from Lindsay Anderson et al., 'Financial support for film-makers', *The Times*, 5 August 1971, p. 13.
34. Roy Mason, Hansard (Commons) 821, 15 July 1971, p. 876.
35. Dickinson and Street, *Cinema and State*, p. 241.
36. *National Film Finance Corporation Annual Report*, HMSO, 1972, p. 1.
37. K. Courte, 'No longer the kindly money lenders', *Today's Cinema*, 3 September 1971, p. 10.
38. Figures taken from *National Film Finance Corporation Annual Reports*, 1969–1980.
39. Ibid.
40. *National Film Finance Corporation Annual Report*, 1974, p. 4.
41. *National Film Finance Corporation Annual Report*, 1978, p. 7.
42. *Film Co-production Agreement Between the Government of the United Kingdom of Great Britain and Northern Ireland and the Government of the French Republic*, 21 September 1965, Cmd 2781, p. 2.
43. Ibid.
44. FPA, *Co-production Guide to the Anglo-French and the Anglo-Italian Co-production Treaties* (London: Film Producers Association of Great Britain, 1971), pp. 1–13.
45. Ibid.
46. Ibid.
47. S. Caulkin, 'Movie moguls look to Brussels for fresh aid', *The Times*, 19 April 1972, p. 23.

48. Losey Papers, Box JL/22, Special Collections, BFI Library.
49. Ibid.
50. 'Nationalising the film industry', *ACTT Report*, August 1973, pp. 5–35.
51. NA: ED 245/54, CFC Report.
52. Film Producers Association *Annual Report*, 1974–1975, p. 19.
53. Ibid., p. 3.
54. Don Boyd, interview with the authors, 13 November 2008.
55. Written question from Mr Faulds, Hansard (Commons) 867, 21 January 1974, p. 212.
56. Estimated costs from Gwyneth Dunwoody from her speech in Hansard (Commons) 871, 4 April 1974, p. 1586.
57. Des Freeman, *Television Policies of the Labour Party, 1951–2001* (London: Frank Cass, 2003), p. 49, Peter Goodwin, *Television under the Tories: Broadcasting Policy 1979–1997* (London: BFI, 1998), p. 16.
58. Harold Wilson, Hansard (Commons) 892, 17 June 1975, p. 395.
59. National Film Finance Corporation, *Annual Report*, 1976, p. 7.
60. *Future of the British Film Industry: Report of the Prime Minister's Working Party*, Cmd 6372.
61. Ibid.
62. Ibid.
63. Ministers' Special Meeting of the Cinematograph Films Council to discuss the Terry Report dated 26 January 1976, NA: FV 81/95.
64. NA: FV 81/95.
65. Michael Meacher, Hansard (Commons) 959, 27 November 1978, p. 4.
66. Ibid., 969, 2 July 1979, p. 884.
67. Ibid., 983, 25 April 1980, p. 859.
68. Ibid., pp. 859–60.
69. Ibid., p. 867.
70. Clinton Davis, MP for Hackney, ibid., p. 868.
71. Figures compiled from British Film Fund Agency Committee Minutes, NA: BT 383/14 – BT 383/23.

Notes to Chapter 2

72. James C. Robertson, *The Hidden Cinema: British Film Censorship 1913–1972* (London: Routledge, 1989). See also Guy Phelps, *Film Censorship* (London: Victor Gollancz, 1975), p. 69.
73. Anthony Aldgate and James C. Robertson, *Censorship in the Theatre and the Cinema* (Edinburgh: Edinburgh University Press, 2005).
74. Written answer to a question from Mr Harold Walker, Hansard (Commons) 856/857, 24 May 1974, p. 117, Written answer to a question from Mr Michael McNair-Wilson, Hansard (Commons) 911, 20 May 1976, Written answer to a question from Mr Hugh Jenkins, Hansard (Commons) 917, 21 October 1976, Debate on power of local

authorities with regard to censorship, Hansard (Commons) 915, 22 July 1976, p. 2219.

75. NA: HO 300/166, memo dated 29 February 1975.
76. NA: HO 265/2, submission of the BBFC to the Williams Committee.
77. BBFC file for *Vampire Circus.*
78. Anon., 'Murphy must go', *Cinema TV Today*, 11 March 1972, p. 1.
79. Peter Waymark, 'Film makers rally to support censor', *The Times*, 15 March 1972.
80. Aldgate and Robertson, *Censorship in the Theatre and the Cinema*, p. 177.
81. Enid Wistrich, *'I don't mind the sex, it's the violence': Film Censorship Explored* (London: Marion Boyars, 1978), p. 26 and p. 108.
82. *Minutes of Fire Services and Public Control Committee Meetings 1971–1974*, Books CCM1/54 and CCM1/55, Portsmouth City Archives.
83. Ibid.
84. Some examples would be *Carry On England*, *Carry On Dick*, *Vampire Circus* and *10 Rillington Place.*
85. Alexander Walker, *Evening Standard*, 25 November 1971, F. Cashin, *The Sun*, 7 January 1972.
86. BBFC file for *Straw Dogs.*
87. Ibid.
88. BBFC files for *The Abominable Dr. Phibes* and *House of Whipcord.* See also files on *The Oblong Box* and *Dr. Jekyll and Sister Hyde.*
89. Examples of films which deliberately negotiated higher classification include *Percy*, *The Beast Must Die* and *Confessions from a Holiday Camp.*
90. BBFC file for *Confessions of a Window Cleaner.*
91. BBFC file for *Confessions from a Holiday Camp.*
92. For further evidence of the way in which producers Tony Tenser, Harrison Marks and Stanley Long clashed with the BBFC, see BBFC files for *The Wife Swappers*, *Zeta One*, *Groupie Girl*, *Naughty!*, *Come Play with Me* and *Oh Calcutta!*
93. BBFC file for *The Beast Must Die.*
94. Ibid.
95. BBFC file for *Vampire Circus.*
96. BBFC file for *The Go-Between.*
97. BBFC file for *Stardust.*
98. John Trevelyan, *What the Censor Saw* (London: Michael Joseph, 1973).
99. For examples of this process, see BBFC files for *Carry On Camping*, *Carry On Dick* and *Carry On Abroad.*
100. BBFC file for *Carry On Emmannuelle.*
101. Ibid.
102. Ibid.
103. See extensive material on the BBFC file for Michael Winner's *Scorpio.*
104. BBFC file for *The Long Good Friday.*
105. Ibid.

106. Ibid.
107. BBFC file for *Oh Calcutta!*
108. Ibid. The film was re-examined in 1975 and subsequently passed with no cuts as an 'X' certificate in 1978.
109. BBFC file on *Monty Python's Life of Brian.*
110. Ibid.
111. Ibid.
112. BBFC file for *Quadrophenia.*
113. BBFC file for *Stardust.*
114. Ibid.
115. Ibid.
116. Ibid.

Notes to Chapter 3

117. Peter Wollen, 'The two avant gardes', in *Studio International*, Vol. 190, No. 978, November/December 1975, pp. 171–5, P. Adams Sitney, *Visionary Film: The American Avant-Garde 1943–1978* (Oxford: Oxford University Press, 1979), Malcolm Le Grice, *Abstract Film and Beyond* (London: Studio Vista, 1977), Philip Drummond (ed.), *Film as Film: Formal Experiment in Film 1910–1975* (London: Hayward Gallery / Arts Council of Great Britain, 1979), Peter Gidal, *Materialist Film* (London: Routledge, 1989), A. L. Rees, *A History of Experimental Film and Video: From the Canonical Avant-Garde to Contemporary British Practice* (London: BFI, 1999), Scott MacDonald, *Avant-Garde Film: Motion Studies* (Cambridge: Cambridge University Press, 1993), Michael O'Pray (ed.), *The British Avant-Garde Film 1926 to 1995* (Luton: John Libbey Media, 1996).
118. Malcolm Le Grice, 'The history we need', in Drummond, *Film as Film*, p. 113.
119. Malcolm Le Grice, in 'Filmographies 1940–1975', in ibid., p. 142.
120. Le Grice, *Abstract Film and Beyond*, p. 7.
121. http://studycollection.co.uk/hiddenhistorybfi.html.
122. Rees, *A History of Experimental Film and Video*, p. 77.
123. Barry Miles, *London Calling: A Countercultural History of London since 1945* (London: Atlantic, 2010), p. 237.
124. Malcolm Le Grice, at http://studycollection.co.uk/hiddenhistorybfi.html.
125. Miles, *London Calling*, pp. 238–9.
126. Ibid., p. 289.
127. http://studycollection.co.uk/hiddenhistorybfi.html.
128. Miles, *London Calling*, pp. 291–3.
129. Raymond Durgnat, at http://studycollection.co.uk/hiddenhistorybfi.html.
130. Tanya Leighton, 'I – histories and revisions', in T. Leighton (ed.), *Art and the Moving Image* (London: Tate/Afterall, 2008), p. 49.

131. Deke Dusinberre, 'The avant-garde attitude in the Thirties', in O'Pray (ed.), *The British Avant-Garde Film*, p. 65.
132. Christopher Finch, *Image as Language: Aspects of British Art 1950–1968* (Harmondsworth: Penguin, 1969), p. 156.
133. Peter Wollen, 'The two avant gardes'.
134. Leighton, 'I – histories and revisions', p. 52.
135. Le Grice, *Abstract Film and Beyond*, p. 20.
136. Jonathan Walley, 'Modes of film practice in the avant garde', in Leighton (ed.), *Art and the Moving Image*, p. 184.
137. Annabel Nicolson et al., 'Woman and the formal film', Drummond, in *Film as Film*, p. 118.
138. Margaret Tait: http://www.luxonline.org.uk/artists/t.html.
139. Le Grice, *Abstract Film and Beyond*, p. 87.
140. See, for example, Anne Anderson, Robert Meyrick, Peter Nahum, *Ancient Landscapes, Pastoral Visions, Samuel Palmer to the Ruralists* (Woodbridge: Antique Collectors' Club, 2008), Jerrold Northrop Moore, *The Green Fuse: Pastoral Visions in English Art* (Woodbridge: Antique Collectors Club, 2007), Peter Woodcock, *This Enchanted Isle: The Neo-Romantic Vision from William Blake to the New Visionaries* (Glastonbury: Gothic Image, 2000).
141. Peter Ackroyd, *Albion: The Origins of the English Imagination* (London: Chatto & Windus, 2002), p. 433.
142. I completed the final draft of this chapter on the day when *The Guardian* announced that Alexandra Harris had won the newspaper's 'first book award' (and £10,000) for her *Romantic Moderns: English Writers, Artists and the Imagination from Virginia Woolf to John Piper.* Their feature included an extract with the title 'Rural Art as Wartime Propaganda' (2 December 2009, p. 23).
143. Annabel Nicolson, 'Expanded cinema', in Hayward Gallery, *Perspectives on British Avant-Garde Film* (London: Arts Council of Great Britain, 1977), numbered papers.
144. A. L. Rees, 'Conditions of illusionism', *Screen*, Vol. 3, No. 18, Autumn 1977, pp. 41–54.
145. Le Grice, 'The history we need', in Drummond, *Film as Film*, p. 113.
146. Lis Rhodes, 'Woman and the formal film', Drummond, *Film as Film.*
147. Philip Dodd, 'Modern Stories', in Philip Dodd and Ian Christie, *Spellbound: Art and Film* (London: Hayward Gallery/BFI, 1996), p. 32.
148. Ibid., p. 40.
149. Richard Cork, *Everything Seemed Possible: Art in the 1970s* (New Haven: Yale University Press, 2003).
150. Ibid., p. 46.
151. Ibid., p. 58.
152. Ibid., pp. 149–53.
153. Hayward Gallery, *Perspectives on British Avant-Garde Film.*
154. Ibid., Introduction.

155. Cork, *Everything Seemed Possible*, p. 150.
156. Ibid., p. 152.
157. Ibid., p. 153.
158. Anne Seymour, 'Introduction', in Hayward Gallery, *The New Art* (London: Arts Council of Great Britain, 1972), p. 7.

Notes to Chapter 4

159. Michael Stringer, quoted in Terence St John Marner (ed.), *Film Design* (London: Tantivy, 1973), p. 9.
160. John Russell Taylor, 'Background to the fore', *The Times*, 22 March 1969, p. 16.
161. Michael Stringer (1973), publicity booklet for the Guild of Film Art Directors, p. 1, held at BFI Library.
162. Ibid.
163. Richard Levin, *Television by Design* (London: Bodley Head, 1961), p. 141.
164. Tim O'Brien, 'Design for movement', *The Times*, 21 September 1960, p. 16.
165. Alexander Vetchinsky, interviewed by Mark Yonge in 1977. Quoted from the microfiche on Alexander Vetchinsky at the BFI Library.
166. Assheton Gorton, quoted in S. Bancroft, 'Set pieces', *AIP & Co*, January–February 1986, p. 16.
167. Peter Rogers, quoted in *The Times*, 5 November 1959, p. 16.
168. Peter Rogers, quoted in the Sydney *Daily Telegraph*, 13 September 2006, p. 71.
169. Location-spotting is a favourite hobby of the *Carry On* enthusiast. Further details of *Carry On* location shoots can be found in fannish books such as K. Snelgrove and P. Dayman-Johns, *The Carry On Book of Statistics: Taking the Carry Ons into a New Century* (Somerset: KAS, 2003).
170. Further details of Hammer financing during the 1970s can be found in C. Koetting, 'Hands across the water: the Hammer-Seven Arts alliance', *Little Shoppe of Horrors*, April 1994, pp. 41–5.
171. Letter from Iain Moncrieffe to *The Spectator*, 10 April 1971, p. 509.
172. Press book for *Dracula A.D. 1972* held at the BFI Library. Other production details are drawn from Item 11 in the Hammer Film Productions Special Collections file, BFI Library.
173. Guy Hamilton, quoted in *Cinema TV Today*, 24 August 1974, p. 9.
174. Ken Adam, quoted in J. Delson, 'Art directors: Ken Adam', *Film Comment*, January 1982, p. 40. See also Christopher Frayling, *Ken Adam and the Art of Production Design* (London: Faber & Faber, 2005), pp. 172–91.
175. See *Screen International*, 12 February 1977, p. 10.
176. Ken Adam, conversation with the author, 30 April 2007.
177. Robin Wood, 'New criticism?', *Definition*, Winter 1960/61, p. 10.
178. Molly Plowright, review of *Just Like a Woman*, *Films and Filming*, November 1966, p. 51.

179. Robert Fuest, quoted in C. Koetting, 'Mr. Fuest rises again', *Fangoria*, October 1988, p. 19.
180. Robert Fuest, quoted in the publicity materials for *The Abominable Dr. Phibes*, BFI Library.
181. See Gordon Gow, 'Shock treatment', *Films and Filming*, May 1972, p. 24.
182. Ken Russell, quoted in the press materials for *The Boy Friend* (1971), BFI Library.
183. Ken Russell, quoted in Gow, 'Shock treatment', p. 8.
184. Ken Russell, quoted in G. D. Phillips, 'Fact, fantasy, and the films of Ken Russell', *Journal of Popular Film*, July 1976, p. 201.
185. Derek Jarman, *Dancing Ledge* (London: Quartet, 1984), p. 100.
186. Box 6, Anne Skinner Papers, Special Collections, BFI Library.
187. Ken Russell, quoted in *Sight and Sound*, October 1997, p. 69.
188. John Barry, quoted in St John Marner (ed.), *Film Design*, p. 129.
189. Ibid., p. 161.
190. John Barry, in ibid., p. 128.
191. Ibid., p. 128. See also the press book for *A Clockwork Orange*, BFI Library.
192. Stanley Kubrick, quoted in *Take One*, May–June 1971, p. 28.

Notes to Chapter 5

193. Susan Crosland, *Tony Crosland* (London: Jonathan Cape, 1982), pp. 147–8, Patricia Hollis, *Jennie Lee: A Life* (Oxford: Oxford University Press, 1997), p. 293.
194. Department of Education and Science (DES), *A Plan for Polytechnics and Other Colleges: Higher Education in the Further Education System* (London: HMSO, 1966).
195. Hollis, *Jennie Lee: A Life*, p. 280.
196. M. D. A. Freeman, 'Lloyd, Dennis, Baron Lloyd of Hampstead (1915–1992)', *Oxford Dictionary of National Biography* (Oxford: Oxford University Press, 2009), online edition, Lawrence Goldman (ed.), http://www.oxforddnb.com/view/article/51187, accessed 18 January 2011.
197. Department of Education and Science, *Report of a Committee to Consider the Need for a National Film School* (London: HMSO, 1967), pp. 46–7.
198. Ibid., p. 43.
199. Hollis, *Jennie Lee: A Life*, p. 281.
200. Sir Robin Darwin, 'National Film School plan', *The Times*, 24 June 1969, p. 9.
201. Hollis, *Jennie Lee: A Life*, p. 282.
202. Ibid., p. 282, Films Act 1970, ss. 6 (1) (d) and 6 (2).
203. Colin Young, interview with Alan Sapper: *BECTU Tape 256*, 19 July 1992, BFI Library.
204. Anon., 'Film School Head chosen', *The Times*, 12 March 1970, p. 2.
205. Young, interview with Alan Sapper.

206. Ibid.
207. DES, *National Film School*, p. 37.
208. Ibid., p. 36.
209. Vincent Porter, 'A degree course in the photographic arts', *Industrial and Commercial Photographer*, Vol. 11, No. 2, February 1971, pp. 51–5.
210. David Robinson, 'Film schools: active and passive', *Sight and Sound*, Vol. 44, No. 3, Summer 1975, pp. 166–9.
211. Colin Young, 'National Film School', *Sight and Sound*, Vol. 41, No. 1, Winter 1971/1972, p. 6.
212. Ibid.
213. David Robinson, 'Film schools: active and passive', p. 167, House of Commons, *British Film Fund Agency, Nineteenth Annual Report and Statement of Accounts for the Fifty-Two Weeks Ended 25 September 1976* (London: HMSO, 1977), p. 6.
214. David Robinson, 'Film schools: active and passive'.
215. Ibid.
216. Hugh Jenkins, *The Culture Gap: An Experience of Government and the Arts* (London: Marion Boyars, 1978), p. 134.
217. House of Commons, *British Film Fund Agency, Annual Report and Statement of Accounts for the Fifty-Two Weeks Ended 20 September 1980* (London: HMSO, 1981), p. 7.
218. David Robinson, 'Edinburgh: a festival that gets the films', *The Times*, 29 August 1974, p. 10.
219. David Robinson, 'The view of the first generation', *The Times*, 13 December 1974, p. 11.
220. David Robinson, 'In search of the elixir of youth', *The Times*, 14 February 1975, p. 13.
221. David Robinson, 'National Film School films', *Sight and Sound*, Vol. 46, No. 2, Spring 1977, pp. 126–7.
222. Colin Young and Karol Kulik, 'After school', *Sight and Sound*, Vol. 46, No. 4, Autumn 1977, pp. 201–4.
223. Anon., 'Cinemas still required to support the British film industry', *The Times*, 7 June 1980, p. 3.
224. Walter James, 'Opposing views on design education', *The Times*, 22 August 1970, p. 11.
225. Anon., 'Artists in the Polytechnic web', *The Times*, 30 October 1970, p. 13.
226. Anon., 'Planned merger "will not change art education"', *The Times*, 21 June 1973, p. 4.
227. DES, *National Film School*, p. 33.
228. Joost Hunningher, 'Film schools, and how they function', *Movie Maker*, June 1982, p. 345.
229. www.veraneubauer.com.
230. Christopher Frayling, *Art and Design: 100 Years at the Royal College of Art* (London: Collins & Brown, 1999), p. 306.

231. Ibid.
232. David Curtis, *Experimental Cinema: A Fifty Year Evolution* (London: Studio Vista, 1971), Peter Gidal, *Structural Film Anthology* (London: BFI, 1976).
233. Michael Mazière, *Institutional Support for Artists' Film and Video in England, 1966–2003*, AHRB Centre for British Film and Television Studies, British Artists Film and Video Collection, 2008, http://www.studycollection.co.uk, Section 4.2.
234. Ibid., Section 4.3.
235. Central Advisory Council for Education (England), *Half Our Future: A Report of the Central Advisory Council for Education* (London: HMSO, 1963), paragraph 474.
236. Roger Watkins, 'Film and television: a main subject course at Bulmershe College of Education', *Screen*, Vol. 10, No. 1, January/February 1969, pp. 34–41.
237. Elfreda Symonds, 'The development of film study at Hammersmith College for Further Education', *Screen*, Vol. 10, No. 1, January/February 1969, pp. 42–65.
238. Terry Bolas, *Screen Education: From Film Appreciation to Media Studies* (Bristol: Intellect, 2009), p. 99.
239. Roger Watkins, *CSE Examinations in Film* (London: BFI Education Department / SEFT, 1969), p. 1.
240. Ibid., pp. 1–2.
241. David Lusted, *A CSE Course in Film* (London: BFI Education Department, 1971).
242. Paddy Whannel, 'Film education and film culture', *Screen*, Vol. 10, No. 3, May/June 1969, p. 49.
243. Ibid., p. 51.
244. Ibid., p. 52.
245. British Film Institute Governors' Minutes (20 April 1971), 5338-5344, cited by Bolas (2009), *Screen Education*, p. 182.
246. Screen Editorial Board, *Screen*, Vol. 12, No. 1, Spring 1971, p. 4.
247. See also John Ellis, Foreword to *Screen Reader 1: Cinema/Ideology/Politics* (London: SEFT, 1977).
248. Jill Forbes, 'Film and French Studies', in Christine Gledhill (ed.), *Film and Media Studies in Higher Education: Papers from a Conference Organized in 1979 by the BFI and London University Institute of Education* (London: BFI Education, September 1981), p. 72.
249. Richard Collins, 'A diploma course in film study at the Polytechnic of Central London', *Screen Education Notes*, No. 9, Winter, 1973/1974, p. 11.
250. PCL (advertisement), 'Postgraduate Diploma in Film Studies', *Sight and Sound*, Vol. 43, No. 3, Summer, 1974, p. iii.
251. Colin McArthur, 'Foreword', in Julian Petley, *BFI Distribution Library Catalogue* (London: BFI, 1977).

252. John Corner, 'BFI Distribution Library Catalogue', *Screen Education*, No. 24, Autumn 1977, pp. 60–2.
253. Philip Simpson, 'Film and media studies in higher education 1977–79', in Gledhill (ed.), *Film and Media Studies in Higher Education*, pp. 153–60.
254. Philip Simpson, 'Institutions and course structures', in Gledhill (ed.), *Film and Media Studies in Higher Education*, pp. 45–6.
255. Philip Simpson, 'Film and media studies in higher education 1977–79', p. 155.
256. Ibid., p. 157.
257. The PCL authors were Nicholas Garnham, Richard Collins, Christopher Williams and Vincent Porter.
258. Ben Brewster, 'Film history in film studies teaching', in Gledhill (ed.), *Film and Media Studies in Higher Education*, p. 139.
259. Christopher Williams, 'Film-making and film theory', in ibid., p. 91.
260. Philip Hayward, *16+ Syllabuses in Film, Television and Media Studies: A Survey* (London: BFI Education, 1985), pp. 21–5.
261. V. F. Perkins, *Film as Film: Understanding and Judging Movies* (Harmondsworth: Penguin, 1972), p. 7.

Notes to Chapter 6

262. Recent writing on 1970s black British film includes Paul Newland, 'We know where we're going, we know where we're from: *Babylon*', in P. Newland (ed.), *Don't Look Now: British Cinema in the 1970s* (Bristol: Intellect, 2010), pp. 93–104, and Josie Dolan and Andrew Spicer, 'On the margins: Anthony Simmons, *The Optimists of Nine Elms* and *Black Joy*', in Newland (ed.), *Don't Look Now: British Cinema in the 1970s*, pp. 79–92. See also Jim Pines, 'The cultural context of black cinema', in Mbye Cham and Claire Andrade-Watkins (eds), *Black Frames: Critical Perspectives on Black Independent Cinema* (cambridge, MA: MIT Press, 1988), pp. 26–36.
263. Horace Ové, interview with the author, 23 June 2009.
264. Ibid.
265. Ibid.
266. Jamie Medhurst, 'Competition and change in British television', in M. Hilmes (ed.), *The Television History Book* (London: BFI, 2003), p. 40.
267. Norman Beaton, *Beaton but Unbowed* (London: Methuen, 1986), p. 190.
268. Andrew Spicer, 'The production line: reflections on the role of the film producer in British cinema', *Journal of British Cinema and Television*, Vol. 1, No. 1, 2004, p. 33.
269. Ibid.
270. Ibid.
271. Sean Burke, 'The ethics of signature', in S. Burke (ed.), *Authorship – From Plato to Postmodern – a Reader* (Edinburgh: Edinburgh University Press, 1995), p. 285.

272. Jenny Craven, 'Jenny Craven on location with *Babylon*', *Films and Filming*, Vol. 26, No. 8, May 1980, pp. 40–1.
273. Franco Rosso, quoted in Chris Salewicz, *Land of Sour Milk and Sus*, www.uncarved.org/dub/babylon/nme.html, accessed 14 September 2007.
274. Robert Murphy (ed.), *Directors in British and Irish Cinema – A Reference Guide Companion* (London: BFI, 2006), p. 525.
275. Chris Salewicz, *Land of Sour Milk and Sus.*
276. Institute of Race Relations, *Police Against Black People*, Race and Class Pamphlet 6 (London: IRR, 1979), p. 10.
277. Commission for Racial Equality, *Annual Report*, 1977, p. 33.
278. Peter Fryer, *Staying Power – The History of Black People in Britain* (London: Pluto, 1984), p. 397.
279. Ibid.
280. Ibid.
281. Ambalavaner Sivanandan, *A Different Hunger – Writings on Black Resistance* (London: Pluto, 1982), p. 132.
282. The Runnymede Trust and the Radical Statistics Race Group, *Britain's Black Population* (London: Heinemann Education, 1980), p. 44.
283. Sivanandan, *A Different Hunger*, p. 132.
284. Ibid.
285. Margaret Thatcher, interview, *World in Action* (Granada Television, broadcast 27 January 1978).
286. Martin Kettle and Lucy Hodges, *Uprising! The Police, The People and the Riots in Britain's Cities* (London: Pan, 1982), p. 30.
287. Ibid.
288. Craven, 'Jenny Craven on location with *Babylon*', p. 40.
289. Osiris Films Presents *Babylon* (Press Book, 1980), p. 4. Gavrik Losey Papers, Bill Douglas Centre (BDC), University of Exeter, File 6/1/2/3 Babylon.
290. Ibid.
291. Martin Stellman, memo to Franco Rosso, File 7/12/1979, Gavrik Losey Papers, BDC, File 6/1/2/16.
292. Osiris Films Presents *Babylon* (Press Book, 1980), p. 4.
293. Craven, 'Jenny Craven on location with *Babylon*', p. 40, and Salewicz, *Land of Sour Milk and Sus.*
294. Mamoun Hassan, unpublished, undated interview with Don Boyd, Don Boyd Papers, BDC.
295. Mamoun Hassan, letter to Rosso and Stellman, 8 November 1979.
296. Ernest Cashmore, *Rastaman – The Rastafarian Movement in England* (London: Allen & Unwin, 1982), pp. 167–8.
297. Eden Charles, 'No war in this Babylon', *Race Today Review*, January 1981, p. 90.
298. Gavrik Losey in 'Jenny Craven on location with Babylon', *Films and Filming*, Vol. 26, No. 8, 1980, p. 40.
299. Gavrik Losey in Vivian Goldman, 'The brethren in Babylon', *Time Out*, 7 November 1980, p. 13.

300. Gavrik Losey, letter to Don Smith, 14 March 1980, Gavrik Losey Papers, BDC.
301. Goldman, 'The brethren in Babylon', p. 12.
302. Gavrik Losey, letter to James Ferman, 11 June 1980, Gavrik Losey Papers, BDC.
303. James Ferman, letter to Gavrik Losey, 2 October 1980, Gavrik Losey Papers, BDC.
304. Ibid.
305. Ibid.
306. Charles, 'No war in this Babylon'.
307. Spicer, 'The production line', p. 33.

Notes to Chapter 7

308. Memo sent 5 February 1968, BBC Written Archives, Caversham. Ref: Drama Memos 1968–1970, T5/782/5.
309. Raymond Williams, *Television: Technology and Cultural Form* (London: Routledge, 1974), p. 7.
310. Ibid., p. 14.
311. Helen Wheatley, 'ITV 1955–89: populism and experimentalism', in Michele Hilmes (ed.), *The Television History Book* (London: BFI, 2003), p. 79.
312. Sylvia Harvey, 'Channel Four television: from Annan to Grade', in Ed Buscombe (ed.), *British Television: A Reader* (Oxford: Oxford University Press, 2000), pp. 95–105.
313. Wheatley, 'ITV 1955–89', p. 79.
314. Ibid.
315. Ed Buscombe, 'All bark and no bite: the film industry's response to television', in John Corner (ed.), *Popular Television in Britain: Studies in Cultural History* (London: BFI, 1991), p. 198.
316. Ibid., p. 198.
317. Colin McArthur, *Television and History* (London: BFI, 1978), p. 40.
318. Lez Cooke, *British Television Drama: A History* (London: BFI, 2003), pp. 113–18.
319. Winston Fletcher, *Powers of Persuasion: The Inside Story of British Advertising 1951–2000* (Oxford: Oxford University Press, 2008), pp. 93, 110.
320. Most TV advertising was for food, drink, household goods, toiletries and cars. Expenditure on British television grew from £137,589 in 1968 to £412,550 in 1979. Brian Henry (ed.), *British Television Advertising: The First Thirty Years* (London: Century Benham, 1986), pp. 515–17.
321. Fletcher, *Powers of Persuasion*, p. 129.
322. Sue Harper and Vincent Porter, 'Beyond media history: the challenge of visual style', *Journal of British Cinema and Television*, 2005, Vol. 2, No. 1, pp. 1–17 and p. 8.

323. Dave Rolinson, 'The last studio system: a case for British television films', in Paul Newland, *Don't Look Now: British Cinema in the 1970s* (Bristol: Intellect, 2010), pp. 171–4.
324. John McGrath, in Cooke, *British Television Drama*, p. 105.
325. Ibid., p. 108.
326. David McQueen, '1970s current affairs: a golden age?', in Laurel Forster and Sue Harper (eds), *British Culture and Society in the 1970s: The Lost Decade* (Newcastle upon Tyne: Cambridge Scholars, 2010), pp. 76–92.
327. David Morley, *Television, Audiences and Cultural Studies* (London: Routledge, 1992), pp. 75–130.
328. Julian Matthews, '"And finally . . . news for children": an insight into the institutional development of the BBC children's news programme, *John Craven's Newsround*', in Laurel Forster and Sue Harper (eds), *British Culture and Society in the 1970s*, pp. 164–74.
329. Laura Stempel Mumford, 'Feminist theory and television studies', in Christine Geraghty and David Lusted (eds), *The Television Studies Book* (London: Arnold, 1998), p. 115.
330. Ibid., p. 117.
331. David Self, *Television Drama: An Introduction* (Basingstoke: Macmillan, 1984), p. 39.
332. Irene Shubik, *Play for Today: The Evolution of Television Drama* (London: Davis-Poynter, 1975), p. 125.
333. Cooke, *British Television Drama*, p. 91.
334. Ken Loach, in Graham Fuller (ed.), *Loach on Loach* (London: Faber & Faber, 1998), pp. 13–14.
335. Shubik, *Play for Today*, p. 77.
336. Ibid., p. 23.
337. Cooke, *British Television Drama*, p. 95.
338. Ibid., pp. 94–5.
339. Self, *Television Drama*, p. 40.
340. Rolinson, 'The last studio system', p. 167.
341. Fuller, *Loach on Loach*, pp. 32–64.
342. BBC Written Archives, Caversham. Ref: The Wednesday Play R78/1, 919/1.
343. Ibid. Ref: Drama, Wednesday Play 1968–9, TS/695/4.
344. Dave Rawlinson, 'Introduction to Play for Today', http://www.britishtelevisiondrama.org.uk/?page_id=858, accessed 9 November 2010.
345. Richard Eyre, quoted in Self, *Television Drama*, pp. 40, 42.

Notes to Chapter 8

346. Nik Cohn, *Awopbopaloobopalopbamboom: Pop from the Beginning* (London: Pimlico, 1969).

347. Ibid., p. 1. The broad definition of popular music is not unproblematic and is addressed regularly by academics, notably through the journal *Popular Music* since its first edition in 1981 and especially in a virtual symposium with contributions from the International Advisory Editors of the journal, in *Popular Music*, Vol. 24, No. 1, 2005, pp. 133–45.
348. Cohn, *Awopbopaloobopalopbamboom*, p. 1.
349. See, for example, Theodor Adorno, 'Perennial fashion – jazz', in *Prisms* (Cambridge, MA: MIT Press, 1967).
350. Joni Mitchell's song 'Woodstock' from the album *Ladies of the Canyon* (1970).
351. For example, Mike Evans and Paul Kingsbury (eds), *Woodstock: Three Days that Rocked the World* (New York: Sterling, 2009) or Pete Fornatle, *Back to the Garden: The Story of Woodstock and How it Changed a Generation* (New York: Touchstone, 2009).
352. Tom Ewing, 'Upfront, on music', in *The Guardian Film & Music*, 28 January 2011, p. 2.
353. For example, Stanley Cohen, *Folk Devils and Moral Panics* (London: MacGibbon & Kee, 1972) and Dick Hebdidge, *Subculture: The Meaning of Style* (London: Routledge, 1979).
354. *The Times*, Fashion Section 1–3, 1 September 2010.
355. The phrase 'Swinging London' came to prominence following the publication of an article in the American magazine, *Time*. See P. Halasz, 'You can walk across it on the grass', *Time*, 15 April 1966, pp. 30–4.
356. Dave Allen, 'A public transition: acoustic and electric performances at the Woodstock Festival', in A. Bennett (ed.), *Remembering Woodstock* (Aldershot: Ashgate, 2004), pp. 111–26.
357. Robert Young, *Electric Eden: Unearthing Britain's Visionary Music* (London: Faber & Faber, 2010).
358. Ibid., p. 413.
359. Dave Allen, 'How high the moon? Science fiction and popular music', in G. Harper, R. Doughty and J. Eisentraut (eds), *Sound and Music in Film and Visual Media, An Overview* (New York: Continuum, 2009), pp. 231–49.
360. See, for example, Stephen Colegrave and Chris Sullivan, *Punk: A Life Apart* (London: Cassell, 2001).
361. Barry Miles, *London Calling: A Countercultural History of London Since 1945* (London: Atlantic, 2010), p. 374.

Notes to Chapter 9

362. See Michael Deeley, with Matthew Field, *Blade Runners, Deer Hunters and Blowing the Bloody Doors Off: My Life in Cult Movies* (London: Faber & Faber, 2008), p. 112.
363. Tony Klinger, quoted by Andrew Spicer, 'An impossible task? Scripting "The Chilian Club"', in Jill Nelmes (ed.), *Analysing the Screenplay* (London: Routledge, 2011), pp. 71–88.

364. Steve Gerrard, 'What a Carry On! The decline and fall of a great British institution', in Shail (ed.), *Seventies British Cinema*, pp. 36–45.
365. Bryan Forbes, *Notes for a Life* (London: Everest, 1974), p. 375.
366. Walker, *National Heroes*, pp. 25–8.
367. Deeley, *Blade Runners*, p. 110.
368. Harper and Porter, *British Cinema of the 1950s*, p. 111.
369. Walker, *National Heroes*, p. 120.
370. Allan Brown, *Inside 'The Wicker Man': The Morbid Ingenuities* (London: Sidgwick & Jackson, 2000), pp. 3 and 28.
371. Ibid., p. 114.
372. See Robert Shail, *Stanley Baker: A Life in Film* (Cardiff: University of Wales Press, 2008), p. 113.
373. Deeley, *Blade Runners*, p. 113.
374. Ibid., p. 134.
375. Ibid., p. 183.
376. Ibid., p. 187.
377. See Walker, *National Heroes*, Chapter 3 (on Puttnam) and Chapter 6 (on Boyd).
378. Sandy Lieberson, interview with the authors, 6 March 2008.
379. See Walker, *National Heroes*, pp. 61–4.
380. Lieberson, interview with the authors.
381. Andrew Yule, *Enigma: David Puttnam, The Story so Far* (Edinburgh: Mainstream, 1988), p. 88.
382. Lieberson, interview with the authors.
383. Ibid.
384. Ibid.
385. Ibid.
386. Ibid.
387. See Walker, *National Heroes*, p. 66.
388. Ibid., p. 166.
389. See Dan North, 'Don Boyd: the accidental producer', in Shail (ed.), *Seventies British Cinema*, pp. 139–49 and Nigel Tutt, *The Tax Raiders: The Rossminster Affair* (London: Financial Training Publications, 1985).
390. Interview with Sian Barber, *1970s British Film: Capital, Culture and Creativity* (Unpublished PhD thesis, University of Portsmouth, 2009), p. 357.
391. Letter from Boyd to T. J. Evans, 11 September 1980. DB 009, Don Boyd Papers, BDC.
392. Interview with Sian Barber, *1970s British Film: Capital, Culture and Creativity*, p. 359. Documents in the Boyd Papers on the casting and the distribution indicate the intensity of Boyd's involvement with the minutiae of production: see DB 303 and DB C18.
393. Ibid.
394. The files on *Agatha* in Gavrik Losey Papers, BDC, reveal the personality clashes and organisational problems which beset this production.

395. For a complete list of Brabourne's institutional activities see Vincent Porter, 'Knatchbull, John Ulick, Seventh Baron Brabourne of Brabourne [John Brabourne], (1924–2005)', *Oxford Dictionary of National Biography* (Oxford: Oxford University Press, 2009), Online edition, Lawrence Goldman (ed.), http://www.oxforddnb.com/view/article/96042, accessed 30 March 2010.
396. Sarah Street, 'Heritage crime: the case of Agatha Christie', in Shail (ed.), *Seventies British Cinema*, p. 110.
397. Harper and Porter, *British Cinema of the 1950s*, p. 173.
398. See Justin Smith, 'Une entente cordiale? – A brief history of the Anglo-French Film Co-Production Agreement, 1965–1979', in Lucy Mazdon and Catherine Wheatley (eds), *Je t'aime . . . moi non plus: Franco-British Cinematic Relations* (Oxford and New York: Berghahn, 2010), pp. 51–66.
399. Andrew Spicer, 'The precariousness of production: Michael Klinger and the role of the film producer in the British film industry during the 1970s', in Forster and Harper (eds), *British Culture and Society in the 1970s*, p. 107.
400. Sian Barber, *1970s British Film: Capital, Culture and Creativity*, pp. 199–211.
401. Spicer, 'The precariousness of production', pp. 197–8.
402. John Hamilton, *Beasts in the Cellar: The Exploitation Film Career of Tony Tenser* (Guildford: FAB, 2005), p. 223.
403. Steve Chibnall, *Making Mischief*, p. 35.
404. For an account of Walker's scripting methods, see David McGillivray, *Doing Rude Things*.
405. See Chibnall, *Making Mischief*, p. 137.
406. See David Hemmings, *Blow-Up and Other Exaggerations* (London: Robson, 2004), p. 239, for a list of their activities in the later 1960s and early 1970s.
407. Ibid., pp. 251, 214.
408. Kenneth Courte, 'Big blow-up in the Hemdale group', *Today's Cinema*, No. 9831, 14 August 1970, p. 6. See also 'The Hemdale row is dissolved', *Today's Cinema*, No. 9856, 13 November 1970, p. 2.
409. See Andrew Spicer's entry for Daly in the *New Oxford Dictionary of National Biography*, forthcoming.
410. 'Major film distribution company announces its new programme', *Screen International*, No. 52, 4 September 1976, pp. 15, 17.
411. John Austin, 'Big US/UK tie-up', ibid., No. 44, 10 July 1976, p. 1.
412. Anon., 'Marketing that gets results', ibid., No. 174, 27 January 1979, p. 16.
413. See Jake Eberts and Terry Illot, *My Indecision is Final: The Rise and Fall of Goldcrest Films* (London: Faber & Faber, 1990).
414. Carol Reed, *International Film Festival of San Sebastian* (Pamplona: Filmoteca Española, 2000, bilingual edition), p. 189.
415. See Bruce Babbington, *Launder and Gilliat* (Manchester: Manchester University Press, 2002), pp. 185–7.
416. See Alan Burton, Tim O'Sullivan and Paul Wells (eds), *The Family Way: The Boulting Brothers and British Film Culture* (Trowbridge: Flicks, 2000), pp. 249–50.

417. Lieberson, interview with the authors.
418. Steve Chibnall, *J. Lee Thompson* (Manchester: Manchester University Press, 2000), pp. 324–6.
419. Brian McFarlane, *An Autobiography of British Cinema* (London: Methuen, 1997), pp. 510–13.
420. Ibid., p. 513.
421. See John Schlesinger Papers, Box JRS/7/19, Special Collections, BFI Library.
422. See interview with Sharp, *Filmfax*, February/March 1998, pp. 111–14, 122–6.
423. See his autobiography, *So You Want to Be in Pictures?* (London: Reynolds & Hearn 2001).
424. Ken Annakin, National Film Theatre Programme, 1998, p. 24.
425. See John Williams, 'Michael Tuchner, Likely Lad', *Films Illustrated*, Vol. 5, No. 53, January 1976, p. 183.
426. See the Gavrik Losey Papers on *Agatha*, which show Apted's difficulties on set, BDC.
427. *Sunday Times Colour Supplement*, 5 September 1976. See also Ray Connolly, *Stardust Memories* (London: Pavilion, 1985), pp. 227–40.
428. Christopher Koetting, 'On beyond Phibes', *Fangoria*, No. 178, November 1998, pp. 15, 18.
429. For an account of *Juggernaut*, see Neil Sinyard, *Richard Lester* (Manchester: Manchester University Press, 2010), pp. 97–110.
430. For a consideration of realism in films of the period, see James Leggott, 'Nothing to do around here: British realist cinema in the 1970s', in Shail (ed.), *Seventies British Cinema*, pp. 94–104.
431. Attributed to Pauline Kael by Stephen Pizzello, DVD review, *American Cinematographer*, Vol. 84, No. 3, March 2003, p. 18.
432. Scott interviewed in 'Duelling Directors: Ridley Scott and Kevin Reynolds' (Dir. Charles de Lauzirika, US, Paramount Pictures, 2002), DVD Special Feature.

Notes to Chapter 10

433. See Laurel Forster, 'Printing liberation: the women's movement and magazines in the 1970s', in Forster and Harper (eds), *British Culture and Society in the 1970s*, pp. 93–106.
434. See Jo Turney, 'Sex in the sitting room: renegotiating the fashionable British domestic interior for the post-permissive generation', in ibid., pp. 263–74.
435. Dominic Sandbrook, *White Heat: A History of Britain in the Swinging Sixties* (London: Little Brown, 2006), pp. 262–3.
436. Geoffrey Gorer, *Sex and Marriage in England Today: A Study of the Views and Experiences of the Under-45s* (London: Nelson, 1971), p. 204.
437. Weight, *Patriots*, p. 377. See also Wheen, *Strange Days Indeed*, p. 128.

438. Notable titles included: Germaine Greer's *The Female Eunuch* (1970), Sheila Rowbotham's *Hidden from History* (1972), Juliet Mitchell's *Woman's Estate* (1971) and Ann Oakley's *Gender and Society* (1972).
439. Beckett, *When the Lights Went Out*, pp. 226–7.
440. Ibid., pp. 224–5.
441. Frank Pakenham, Earl of Longford, *Pornography: The Longford Report* (London: Coronet, 1972).
442. Turner, *Crisis? What Crisis*, pp. 254–5.
443. BBFC file on *Countess Dracula*, letter from Trevelyan to Sasdy, 3 July 1970.
444. BBFC file on *Countess Dracula*, Reader's Report (ADF), 19 June 1970.
445. Note from Trevelyan in file, 18 December 1970.
446. Philip Strick, 'Interview with John Boorman', *Sight and Sound*, Vol. 42, No. 2, April 1974, p. 75.
447. Ibid., p. 77.
448. Boorman, interview with Michel Ciment, *John Boorman* (London: Faber & Faber, 1986), p. 144.
449. Ibid., p. 148.
450. Ibid., p. 153.
451. 'Script of *Riddles of the Sphinx*', *Screen*, Vol. 18, No. 2, July 1977, pp. 61–77.
452. Jarman Papers, Box 3, Item 2b, Jarman's notes.
453. Ibid.
454. A complete run of costs is given in the Jarman Papers, Box 26, Item 26.
455. In Jarman Papers, Box 3. See also Box 29, Item 4, Notebook, containing original research for the film.
456. Jarman Papers, Box 23, Notebook, entries for 16 and 17 April 1975.
457. Ibid., entry for February 1975.
458. BBFC file on *Sebastiane*, Examiner's report, 6 September 1976.
459. Deeley, *Blade Runners*, p. 107.
460. *Cinema TV Today*, No. 10110, 23 November 1974.
461. Pete Walker quoted in Chibnall, *Making Mischief*, p. 132.
462. May Routh interviewed in 'Watching the Alien' (Dir. David Gregory, US, Blue Underground Inc./Anchor Bay Entertainment, 2002), DVD Special Feature.
463. Ibid.
464. Nicolas Roeg, quoted in interview with Jason Wood, 'His brilliant career', *The Guardian*, Friday 3 June 2005. See http://film.guardian.co.uk/hay2005/story/0,,1497877,00.html, accessed 15 September 2005.
465. Ibid.
466. Frank and Judy Vermorel, '1976: Julie: he's got a lot to answer for', in Hanif Kureishi and Jon Savage (eds), *The Faber Book of Pop* (London: Faber & Faber, 1995), pp. 458–9.

Notes to Chapter 11

467. Interview with Walter Lassally, *American Cinematographer*, Vol. 56, No. 2, February 1975, pp. 174–6. Interview with Geoffrey Unsworth, *American Cinematographer*, Vol. 58, No. 4, April 1977, pp. 372–3, 396–7 and 428–31.
468. Interview with John Boorman, *American Cinematographer*, Vol. 56, No. 3, March 1975, p. 285.
469. Interview with Peter Suschitzky, *American Cinematographer*, Vol. 57, No. 2, February 1976, pp. 225–9.
470. Interview with Peter Suschitzky, *American Cinematographer*, Vol. 58, No. 11, November 1977, pp. 1134–41.
471. Interview with Ken Russell, ibid., pp. 1141 and 1164.
472. Ibid., p. 1164.
473. David Samuelson, 'The "Panaflex" camera: a new concept in design', *Film and Television Technician*, February 1973, pp. 22–3.
474. 'The Arriflex 35BL camera', *American Cinematographer*, Vol. 51, No. 12, December 1970, pp. 1176–7.
475. Ed DiGiulio, 'Two special lenses for *Barry Lyndon*', *American Cinematographer*, Vol. 57, No. 3, March 1976, pp. 276–7, 318, 336–7.
476. David Samuelson, 'Cinematographers view new camera equipment', *Film and Television Technician*, May 1970, pp. 24–5, 27.
477. Lewis Macleod, 'Exposure meters today', *Film and Television Technician*, March 1970, pp. 14–15.
478. 'Thorn Lighting introduces hot restrike CSI lamps', *American Cinematographer*, Vol. 56, No. 9, September 1975, pp. 1040, 1084.
479. Lewis Macleod, 'Introducing the new Eastman colour negative', *Film and Television Technician*, February 1974, pp. 15, 20.
480. L. B. Happé, 'New developments in the film laboratory', *Film and Television Technician*, August 1970, pp. 8–10. See also Vic Margutti, 'The value of opticals in film making', *Film and Television Technician*, August 1970, pp. 12–13, and Harry Waxman, 'Improvements in process projection systems', *Film and Television Technician*, November 1973, pp. 18–20.
481. 'Moviola's new editing console', *American Cinematographer*, Vol. 51, No. 12, December 1970, pp. 1194–5, 1230–1.
482. Duncan Petrie, *The British Cinematographer* (London: BFI, 1996), p. 58.
483. Ibid.
484. Scott interviewed in 'Duelling Directors: Ridley Scott and Kevin Reynolds'.
485. Ibid.
486. Ibid.
487. Ibid.
488. Ibid.
489. Ibid.

490. See, for example, Tom Milne, '*The Duellists*', *Monthly Film Bulletin*, Vol. 44, No. 527, December 1977, p. 258, and Mosk, *The Duellists*, *Variety*, 1 June 1977, p. 18.
491. Sue Summers, 'I'm glad I had to wait for *The Duellists*, says Ridley Scott', *Screen International*, 22 May 1977, p. 39.
492. Scott interviewed in 'Duelling Directors: Ridley Scott and Kevin Reynolds'.
493. Ciment, *Kubrick: The Definitive Edition* (London: Faber & Faber, 2001), p. 170.
494. Undated note from A. J. Maxstead to Kubrick: on the latter's instructions, one worker has been rejected as 'too much a studio kind of name and no good in the field'. Stanley Kubrick Archive, University of the Arts, London, SK/14/2/15.
495. For further views on location shooting, see Ken Adam interview in *American Cinematographer*, Vol. 58, No. 5, May 1977, p. 553, interview with Adam in Ciment, *Kubrick: The Definitive Edition*, p. 205.
496. Gene Phillips and Rodney Hill, *The Encyclopedia of Stanley Kubrick* (New York: Checkmark, 2002), Adam section, p. 1.
497. John Baxter, *Stanley Kubrick: A Biography* (London: HarperCollins, 1997), p. 291.
498. Ken Adam Location notes. Stanley Kubrick Archive, SK/14/2/1/1/1.
499. Breakdown papers for filming in Ireland. Stanley Kubrick Archive, SK/14/3/10.
500. Script changes dated 20 August 1973 which locate the point-of-view shots precisely in relation to the windows. Note here the precise age chart for every character in the film. Stanley Kubrick Archive, SK 14/3/10.
501. Stanley Kubrick Archive, SK 14/2/15/1.
502. 'Photographing *Barry Lyndon*', *American Cinematographer*, Vol. 57, No. 3, March 1976, pp. 268–77, 320–1, 338.
503. Ken Adam interview in Ciment, *Kubrick: The Definitive Edition*, p. 289.
504. Ibid., p. 205. See also interview with Ken Adam in Vincent LoBrutto, *By Design: Interviews with Film Production Designers* (London: Praeger, 1992), p. 44.
505. See interviews with Emma Porteus in David Richardson, 'Aliens and beyond: costumes', *Starburst*, October 1994, pp. 50–1, and Jane Killick and Howard Maxford, 'Almost an Angel/Talking Pictures/A Switch in Time/Dred', *Starburst*, 31 December 1995, pp. 57–62.
506. Jocelyn Rickards, *The Painted Banquet: My Life and Loves* (London: Weidenfeld & Nicolson, 1987), pp. 125–34.
507. Interview with Shirley Russell in *Films and Filming*, Vol. 24, No. 1, October 1977, pp. 12–16.
508. Andrew Patch, 'Beneath the surface: Nicolas Roeg's *Don't Look Now*', in Newland (ed.), *Don't Look Now*, pp. 258–9.
509. Ibid., p. 259.

510. See Karel Reisz, *The Technique of Editing* (London: Focal [1953], 1958), pp. 48–56.
511. Roy Perkins and Martin Stollery, *British Film Editors: The Heart of the Movie* (London: BFI, 2004), pp. 138–9.
512. Ibid., pp. 140–2.
513. Claire Johnston and Paul Willemen, 'Brecht in Britain: the independent political film', *Screen*, Vol. 16, No. 4, December 1975, pp. 101–18.
514. Lindsay Anderson Diaries, 3 October 1988: LA 2/7/2/6/61, Lindsay Anderson Papers, University of Stirling.
515. See John Izod, Karl Magee, Kathryn Mackenzie and Isabelle Gourdin, 'What is there to smile at?': Lindsay Anderson's *O Lucky Man!*', in Newland (ed.), *Don't Look Now*, pp. 215–28.
516. David Gladwell, 'Editing Anderson's *If. . .*', *Screen*, Vol. 10, No. 1, January 1969, p. 24.
517. Lindsay Anderson Diaries, 20 July 1972: LA 6/1/64/191.
518. Lindsay Anderson Diaries, 5 September 1972: LA 6/1/64/236. See also 21 July 1972: LA 6/1/64/192, 27 July 1972: LA 6/1/64/197.
519. Lindsay Anderson Diaries, 28 September 1972: LA 6/1/64/259–260, 4 October 1972: LA 6/1/64/264, 22 October 1972: LA 6/1/64/280, 23 October 1972: LA 6/1/64/281.
520. John Izod, Karl Magee, Kathryn Mackenzie and Isabelle Gourdin, 'Music/industry/politics: Alan Price's roles in *O Lucky Man!*', in Laurel Forster and Sue Harper (eds), *British Culture and Society in the 1970s*, pp. 201–12.
521. Lindsay Anderson, personal communication, 11 July 1973: LA 1/7/3/12/3.
522. Lindsay Anderson, personal communication (undated): LA 1/7/3/2/1–66.
523. Quoted by Michael Deeley, *Blade Runners*, p. 125.
524. Robert Hughes, 'The décor of tomorrow's hell', in M. Falsetto (ed.), *Perspectives on Stanley Kubrick*, pp. 185–6.

Notes to Chapter 12

525. R. G. Collingwood, *The Principles of Art* (Oxford: Oxford University Press [1936], 1958), pp. 54–6.
526. Mike Hodges, quoted in Mark Adams, *Mike Hodges* (Harpenden: Pocket Essentials, 2001), p. 22.
527. Mike Hodges, quoted in Steve Chibnall, *Get Carter* (London: I. B. Tauris, 2003), p. 86.
528. Mamoun Hassan, interview with the authors, 7 October 2009.
529. Kevin Brownlow, BFI Production Board Files, Box 3, Special Collections, BFI Library
530. Kevin Brownlow, *Winstanley: Warts and All* (London: UKA, 2009), p. 75.
531. BFI Production Board Files, Box 3, Special Collections, BFI Library.

532. Brownlow, *Winstanley: Warts and All*, p. 68.
533. Eric Porter (letter to Brownlow of 4 February 1972), cited in ibid., p. 103.
534. Ibid., p. 235.
535. See James Chapman, 'From Amicus to Atlantis: the lost worlds of 1970s British cinema', in Shail (ed.), *Seventies British Cinema*, pp. 56–64.
536. Michael Palin, *Diaries 1969–1979: The Python Years* (London: Orion, 2007), pp. 163–4.
537. Terry Jones, *The Pythons' Autobiography by the Pythons* (London: Orion, 2003), p. 239.
538. Michael Palin, ibid., p. 200.
539. Michael Palin, ibid., p. 190.
540. Sarah Ahmed, *The Cultural Politics of Emotion* (New York: Routledge, 2004), p. 8. See also p. 50.
541. Jennifer Barker, *The Tactile Eye: Touch and the Cinematic Experience* (Berkeley: University of California Press, 2009), p. 38.
542. Elaine Dundy, *Finch, Bloody Finch* (London: Michael Joseph, 1980), p. 309.
543. Letter from Bogarde to Losey, 14 April 1974, Production files for *The Romantic Englishwoman*, Item 22, Joseph Losey Papers, Special Collections, BFI Library.
544. Michael Caine, *What's It All About?* (London: Arrow, 1992), pp. 383–5.
545. *ABC Film Review*, February 1970, p. 7.
546. Sian Barber, *1970s British Film: Capital, Culture and Creativity*, p. 139.
547. See Sian Barber, 'The pinnacle of popular taste?: the importance of *Confessions of a Window Cleaner*', *Scope*, Issue 18, October 2010, www.scope.nottingham.ac.uk. See also Robin Askwith, *The Confessions of Robin Askwith* (London: Ebury, 1999).
548. Glenda Jackson, interview with the authors, 15 November 2007. See also Letter from Losey to Tom Stoppard, 21 August 1974, Production Files for *The Romantic Englishwoman*, Joseph Losey Papers, Special Collections, BFI Library.

Notes to Chapter 13

549. Ray Connolly, 'Tommy', *Time Out*, No. 265, 28 March 1975, p. 10.
550. Lieberson, interview with the authors.
551. *Variety*, 15 May 1974.
552. See John Mundy, *The British Musical Film* (Manchester: Manchester University Press, 2007), p. 225.
553. Ibid.
554. K. J. Donnelly, *Pop Music in British Cinema: A Chronicle* (London: BFI, 2001), p. 59.
555. Franc Roddam interviewed by Colin Vaines, 'The mods and the movie', *Screen International*, No. 166, 25 November 1978, p. 26.

556. Michael Palin, *Diaries 1969–79*, p. 166.
557. Hugh Jenkins, *The Culture Gap: An Experience of Government and the Arts*, p. 104.
558. Dave Rolinson, 'The last studio system: a case for British television films', pp. 165–6.
559. Cooke, *British Television Drama*, pp. 90–127.
560. Sophie Belhatchet, *AIP & Co*, No. 28, September 1980, p. 3.
561. Adrian Garvey, 'Pre-sold to millions: the sitcom films of the 1970s', in Newland (ed.), *Don't Look Now*, pp. 181–3.
562. Ibid., pp. 182–3. For details of the way the film broke various records, see *Today's Cinema*, 20 August 1971, p. 2.
563. Press Book for *On the Buses*, BFI Library.
564. Ibid.
565. Ibid.
566. Ibid.
567. *Today's Cinema*, 18 December 1970, p. 10. See also Cohen's views on entertainment in ibid., 26 March 1971.
568. Paul Williams, 'Class, nostalgia and Newcastle: contested space in *The Likely Lads*', in Newland (ed.), *Don't Look Now*, pp. 189–90, Phil Wickham, *The Likely Lads* (London: BFI, 2008), p. 18.
569. *Bless This House* publicity material, BFI Library.
570. See Gavin Schaffer, 'Race on the television: the writing of Johnny Speight in the 1970s', in Forster and Harper (eds), *British Culture and Society in the 1970s*, pp. 107–18.
571. Manual Alvarado and John Stewart (eds), *Made for Television: Euston Films Limited* (London: BFI, 1985), pp. viii–ix.
572. James Donald, 'Anxious moments: *The Sweeney* in 1975', in ibid., pp. 118–19.
573. Alvarado and Stewart, *Made for Television*, p. 65.
574. Richard Paterson, '*The Sweeney*: a Euston Films product', *Screen Education*, No. 20, Autumn 1976, p. 6.
575. Rory Pickard, 'My day on location with *The Sweeney*', *Photoplay*, Vol. 27, No. 8, August 1976, p. 12.
576. Paterson, '*The Sweeney*: a Euston Films product', p. 8.
577. Donald, 'Anxious moments: *The Sweeney* in 1975', p. 120.
578. *Films and Filming*, April 1977, p. 43. See also *Monthly Film Bulletin*, No. 512, September 1976, p. 200.
579. Interview with Troy Kennedy Martin, *Movie*, Winter 1989, p. 38.
580. Quoted by Rory Pickard, 'My day on location with *The Sweeney*', p. 12.
581. *Radio On*, DVD interview.
582. Ibid.

Notes to Chapter 14

583. Terry McGrath, 'The market place changes – so must we', *Kinematograph Weekly*, 29 August 1970, p. 7.
584. Ibid., p. 9.
585. Allen Eyles, 'Exhibition and the cinema-going experience', in R. Murphy (ed.), *The British Cinema Book*, 2nd edn (London: BFI, 1997), p. 167.
586. Walker, *National Heroes*, pp. 281–2.
587. 'CTV report', *Screen Digest*, December 1976, p. 222.
588. Wood, *British Films 1971–1981*, p. 3.
589. James Chapman, *Licence to Thrill: A Cultural History of the James Bond Films* (London: I. B. Tauris, 1999), p. 178.
590. See Ron Brown, *Cinemas and Theatres of Portsmouth from Old Photographs* (Stroud: Amberley, 2009).
591. By contrast, Southampton's Odeon was a single-screen cinema which was not doubled until relatively late (1979).
592. *Time Out*, 27 June 1975, p. 13.
593. Ibid., 7 November 1975, pp. 14–15.
594. *Films and Filming*, August 1971, p. 4.
595. *Films and Filming* interviews were extensive: see, for example, Jules Dassin (February 1970, pp. 22–6 and March 1970, pp. 66–70), Peter Rogers (June 1970, pp. 70–3), Ken Russell (July 1970, pp. 8–12), Raymond Stross (March 1971, pp. 18–22), Dirk Bogarde (May 1971, pp. 40–50), Nicolas Roeg (January 1972, pp. 18–25), Ann-Margret (January 1976, pp. 12–16).
596. Ibid., June 1974, pp. 56–60, and September 1974, p. 4.
597. See, for example, Michael Wakeley, 'Situation hopeless but not serious', in ibid., May 1970, pp. 6–9.
598. See a survey on foreign films on British screens, in ibid., June 1970, pp. 18–26.
599. See the piece on *Carry On Camping* in January 1970, p. 37. See an important piece by Mike Sarne, 'What's wrong with the British public?', in ibid., February 1973, pp. 32–3. See the very positive review of *Carry On Henry* in ibid., October 1971, p. 64.
600. Ibid., May 1975, p. 35. See also the account of the visual patterns in *Women in Love* (which no one else noticed) in January 1970, pp. 49–50. See ibid., October 1972, pp. 12–14, for a very balanced account of Russell's critics. There is (unusually) a very good review of *Mahler* in May 1974, pp. 41–2.
601. See Raymond Durgnat, 'Shoot-out in Dean Street', in ibid., February 1972, pp. 41–2.
602. Ibid., January 1971, p. 6, June 1971, p. 4, August 1971, p. 4, January 1972, p. 4, July 1972, p. 6, November 1972, p. 4, May 1973, p. 4, June 1973, p. 4, July 1975, p. 4, August 1975, p. 4, January 1976, p. 4, April 1976, p. 6, May 1976, p. 4, November 1976, p. 4, March 1977, p. 4. All these aggrieved letters come from outside London.

603. Ibid., May 1971, p. 8, August 1971, p. 4, December 1971, p. 4, July 1972, p. 4, October 1972, p. 6, December 1972, p. 6, February 1973, p. 4, February 75, p. 4. See the response by Stephen Murphy in the March number, p. 4. For other letters critical of relaxed censorship, see December 1975, p. 4, March 1976, p. 4, February 1977, p. 4.
604. See ibid., March 1971, p. 4, April 1971, p. 4, July 1971, p. 6, October 1971, pp. 4–5.
605. Ibid., February 1973, p. 4.
606. Ibid., March 1973, p. 4.
607. Ibid., October 1975, p. 4.
608. Ibid., September 1976, p. 4.
609. Ibid., July 1974, p. 4.
610. Michael Walker, 'The old age of Alfred Hitchcock', *Movie*, No. 18 (Winter 1970/1971), pp. 10–13.
611. Robin Wood, 'The Kazan problem', *Movie*, No. 19 (Winter 1970/1971), p. 31.
612. V. F. Perkins, *Film As Film: Understanding and Judging Movies* (Harmondsworth: Penguin, 1972), p. 136.
613. *Movie*, No. 20, Spring 1975, p. 21.
614. *Movie*, No. 26, Winter 1978/9, p. 1. For an earlier nasty attack by *Screen* on *Movie*, see Steve Neale, 'The re-appearance of *Movie*', *Screen*, Vol. 16, No. 3, Autumn 1975, pp. 112–15.
615. Andrew Britton, 'The ideology of *Screen*', *Movie*, No. 26, Winter 1978/1979, pp. 2–28. To elaborate Britton's critical position, see Barry Keith Grant (ed.), *Britton on Film: The Complete Film Criticism of Andrew Britton* (Detroit: Wayne State University Press, 2009).
616. Eric Rhode, 'Dostoievski and Bresson', *Sight and Sound*, Vol. 39, No. 2, Spring 1970, pp. 82–3.
617. *Sight and Sound*, Autumn 1970, pp. 175–6. The first sentence is by Kevin Brownlow, and the second by James Clark.
618. See letter from Lotte Eisner in Autumn 1973, from Michael Balcon in Spring 1976, from Basil Wright in Autumn 1976 and from Edgar Anstey in Spring 1979.
619. Ibid., Spring 1971, pp. 67–8.
620. Ibid., pp. 107–8.
621. Ibid., Winter 1971–1972, p. 47. For a really savage review of *The Boy Friend*, see Spring 1972, pp. 111–12, where Russell is lambasted for not being a proper *auteur*.
622. Ibid., Summer 1973, p. 128.
623. Ibid., Summer 1971, pp. 158–9.
624. John Russell Taylor, 'Tomorrow the world: some reflections on the unevenness of British films', ibid., Vol. 43, No. 2, Spring 1974, pp. 80–3.
625. David Wilson, 'Images of Britain', ibid., Vol. 43, No. 2, Spring 1974, pp. 84–6.

626. Ibid., Winter 1971–1972, pp. 12–16.
627. *Monthly Film Bulletin*, April 1978, p. 66.
628. Ibid., January 1972, p. 8.
629. Ibid., March 1972, p. 48.
630. Ibid., April 1975, p. 89.
631. Ibid., February 1972, p. 36
632. Ibid., March 1972, p. 54.
633. Review of *The Amorous Milkman*, in ibid., February 1976, p. 27.
634. Review of *Die Nackte Gräfin*, in ibid., March 1972, p. 55.
635. Review of *Dick Down Under*, in ibid., January 1978, p. 6.
636. See also Terry Bolas, *Screen Education*.
637. See the editorial by Geoffrey Nowell-Smith on realism in ibid., Vol. 18, No. 1, Spring 1977, p. 5.
638. Ibid., Vol. 15, No. 3, Autumn 1974, p. 6.
639. Ed Buscombe, Christine Gledhill, Alan Lovell and Christopher Williams resigned (*Screen*, Vol. 17, No. 2, Summer 1976, pp. 106–9). Ben Brewster, Stephen Heath, Colin McCabe and others held the field: see their reply on pp. 110–16.

APPENDIX I

Cinema Statistics, Box Office and Related Data

Justin Smith

Table 3 Cinema attendance and related statistics, 1972–1980

	1972	1973	1974	1975	1976	1977	1978	1979	1980
Cinema sites	1,314	1,269	1,176	1,100	1,057	1,005	985	978	942
No. of cinema screens	1,531	1,600	1,590	1,576	1,562	1,547	1,563	1,582	1,576
Total admissions (millions)	163	142	143	124	107	108	127	112	102
Gross box office (£millions)	59.4	58	69.3	71.2	75.8	85.5	118.2	126.8	143
Payments to British Film Fund Agency (£millions)	4.2	3.7	4.4	4.9	4.8	5.4	7.2	7	5.8
Average admission charge (p)	38	43	50	61	73	83	94	113	141
Films registered	386	380	402	341	338	318	286	274	257
British features	89	80	78	70	64	42	50	40	41
Visits per year	2.89	2.47	2.54	2.14	1.91	1.9	2.31	2.05	1.85

Sources: *Business Monitor*, *Screen Digest* 'British Cinema and Film Statistics', 1990, p. 1

Table 4 UK television deliveries, 1971–1975

Year	Colour		Monochrome	
	Units (000s)	£000s	Units (000s)	£000s
1971	824	115,583	1,538	61,009
1972	1,446	203,971	1,473	59,102
1973	2,076	292,952	941	36,947
1974	1,770	267,156	574	23,602
1975	1,326	221,178	504	23,475

Source: *Screen Digest*, May 1976, p. 81

Table 5 UK video recorder imports, 1975–1979

Year	Period	Units	£ total	£ average per unit
1975	Q1	965	715,519	741.47
	Q2	1,150	1,902,527	1,654.37
	Q3	1,235	1,113,482	901.60
	Q4	1,861	916,413	492.43
	Year	5,211	4,647,941	891.95
1976	Q1	2,374	1,104,591	465.29
	Q2	2,687	2,069,108	770.04
	Q3	2,984	2,002,005	670.91
	Q4	4,663	4,090,985	877.33
	Year	12,708	9,266,689	729.20
1977	Q1	4,074	2,902,878	712.54
	Q2	5,441	4,023,347	739.45
	Q3	5,251	3,894,459	741.66
	Q4	7,047	3,127,612	443.82
	Year	21,813	13,948,296	611.42
1978	Q1	8,026	5,487,000	683.65
	Q2	16,225	7,679,000	473.28
	Q3	22,240	9,516,000	427.88
	Q4	49,135	17,502,000	362.67
	Year	95,626	40,184,000	423.55
1975–1978		136,358	60,046,926	501.36

Source: *Screen Digest*, April 1979, p. 74

Table 6 Top box-office titles, 1970–1979, by Gifford genre. British titles are shown in bold

Title	Distributor	Gifford genre	Total films in genre	Genre percentage share of total	No. British in genre
The Poseidon Adventure	Fox	Adventure			
The Three Musketeers	Fox	Adventure			
Robin Hood	Disney	Adventure			
Island at the Top of the World	Disney	Adventure			
The Four Musketeers	Fox	Adventure			
When the North Wind Blows	Unknown	Adventure			
The Adventures of the Wilderness Family	Unknown	Adventure			
		Adventure count	7	3.87%	0
The Lady and the Tramp	Disney	Children's			
The Aristocats	Disney	Children's			
The Railway Children	Associated British	Children's			
Tales of Beatrix Potter	Anglo-EMI	Children's			
Bedknobs and Broomsticks	Disney	Children's			
Sleeping Beauty	Disney	Children's			
Snow White and the Seven Dwarfs	Disney	Children's			
Golden Voyage of Sinbad	Columbia	Children's			
Jungle Book	Disney	Children's			
Bambi	Disney	Children's			
Sinbad and the Eye of the Tiger	Columbia	Children's			
One Hundred and One Dalmatians	Disney	Children's			
Bugsy Malone	Rank	Children's			
The Rescuers	Disney	Children's			
Candleshoe	Disney	Children's			
Watership Down	Avco Embassy	Children's			
Pete's Dragon	Disney	Children's			
The Cat from Outer Space	Disney	Children's			
Lord of the Rings	United Artists	Children's			
		Children's count	19	10.50%	5
Carry On Up the Jungle	Rank	Comedy			
Every Home Should Have One	Columbia-British Lion	Comedy			
On the Buses	Anglo-EMI	Comedy			
There's a Girl in My Soup	Ascot Productions	Comedy			

Table 6 (continued)

Title	Distributor	Gifford genre	Total films in genre	Genre percentage share of total	No. British in genre
Percy	Anglo-EMI	Comedy			
Up Pompeii	Anglo-EMI	Comedy			
Dad's Army	Columbia	Comedy			
Steptoe and Son	Anglo-EMI	Comedy			
What's Up, Doc?	Warner Bros	Comedy			
Mutiny on the Buses	Anglo-EMI	Comedy			
Please, Sir!	Rank	Comedy			
Up the Chastity Belt	Anglo-EMI	Comedy			
Love Thy Neighbour	Anglo-EMI	Comedy			
Herbie Rides Again	Disney	Comedy			
Blazing Saddles	Warner Bros	Comedy			
Monty Python and the Holy Grail	EMI	Comedy			
Return of the Pink Panther	United Artists	Comedy			
Adventures of a Taxi Driver	ITC	Comedy			
The Pink Panther Strikes Again	United Artists	Comedy			
Revenge of the Pink Panther	United Artists	Comedy			
Herbie Goes to Monte Carlo	Disney	Comedy			
Heaven Can Wait	Paramount	Comedy			
National Lampoon's Animal House	Universal	Comedy			
Porridge	ITC	Comedy			
		Comedy count	24	13.26%	18
On Her Majesty's Secret Service	United Artists	Crime			
When 8 Bells Toll	Rank	Crime			
Diamonds Are Forever	United Artists	Crime			
The Godfather	Paramount	Crime			
The French Connection	Fox	Crime			
Dirty Harry	Warner Bros	Crime			
Shaft	MGM	Crime			
Klute	Warner Bros	Crime			
Live and Let Die	United Artists	Crime			
The Day of the Jackal	Universal	Crime			
Fear is the Key	Anglo-EMI	Crime			
Superfly	Warner Bros	Crime			
Fuzz	United Artists	Crime			

Table 6 (continued)

Title	Distributor	Gifford genre	Total films in genre	Genre percentage share of total	No. British in genre
The Sting	Universal	Crime			
Chinatown	Paramount	Crime			
The Man with the Golden Gun	United Artists	Crime			
Murder on the Orient Express	EMI	Crime			
Death Wish	Paramount	Crime			
Freebie and the Bean	Warner Bros	Crime			
The Spy Who Loved Me	United Artists	Crime			
The Enforcer	Warner Bros	Crime			
Sweeney!	EMI	Crime			
The Gauntlet	Warner Bros	Crime			
Moonraker	United Artists	Crime			
Death on the Nile	EMI	Crime			
The 39 Steps	Rank	Crime			
The Warriors	Paramount	Crime			
		Crime count	27	14.91%	13
Midnight Cowboy	United Artists	Drama			
Women in Love	United Artists	Drama			
The Devils	Warner Bros	Drama			
Straw Dogs	ABC	Drama			
The Go-Between	EMI-MGM	Drama			
Papillon	Allied Artists	Drama			
The Great Gatsby	Paramount	Drama			
The Way We Were	Columbia	Drama			
Don't Look Now	British Lion	Drama			
Gold	Hemdale	Drama			
Last Tango in Paris	United Artists	Drama			
American Graffiti	Universal	Drama			
The Towering Inferno	Fox	Drama			
Earthquake	Universal	Drama			
Airport '75	Universal	Drama			
One Flew Over the Cuckoo's Nest	United Artists	Drama			
It Shouldn't Happen to a Vet	EMI	Drama			
All the President's Men	Warner Bros	Drama			
Barry Lyndon	Warner Bros	Drama			
Airport '77	Universal	Drama			

Table 6 (continued)

Title	Distributor	Gifford genre	Total films in genre	Genre percentage share of total	No. British in genre
Rocky	United Artists	Drama			
Annie Hall	United Artists	Drama			
Convoy	EMI/United Artists	Drama			
The Goodbye Girl	MGM/ Warners	Drama			
Julia	Fox	Drama			
International Velvet	MGM	Drama			
Midnight Express	Columbia	Drama			
		Drama count	27	14.91%	8
A Clockwork Orange	Warner Bros	Fantasy			
The Land that Time Forgot	Lion International	Fantasy			
Rollerball	United Artists	Fantasy			
Death Race 2000	De Laurentis	Fantasy			
At the Earth's Core	**Amicus**	Fantasy			
King Kong	De Laurentis	Fantasy			
Star Wars	Fox	Fantasy			
Close Encounters of the Third Kind	Columbia	Fantasy			
Warlords of Atlantis	EMI	Fantasy			
Spiderman Strikes Back	Columbia	Fantasy			
Superman	Columbia-EMI-Warner	Fantasy			
Alien	Fox	Fantasy			
Battlestar Galactica	Universal	Fantasy			
		Fantasy count	13	7.18%	5
The Lion in Winter	Avco Embassy	Historical			
Nicholas and Alexandra	Columbia	Historical			
Mary, Queen of Scots	Universal	Historical			
Young Winston	Columbia	Historical			
Lady Caroline Lamb	Anglo-EMI	Historical			
Anne of the Thousand Days	Rank-Universal	Historical			
Cromwell	Columbia	Historical			
		Historical count	7	3.87%	6
The Exorcist	Warner Bros	Horror			

Table 6 (continued)

Title	Distributor	Gifford genre	Total films in genre	Genre percentage share of total	No. British in genre
Jaws	Universal	Horror			
The Omen	Fox	Horror			
Exorcist II: The Heretic	Warner Bros	Horror			
Carrie	United Artists	Horror			
The Deep	EMI/ Columbia	Horror			
Jaws 2	Universal	Horror			
		Horror count	7	3.87%	1
King Boxer	Warner Bros	Martial Arts			
Enter the Dragon	Warner Bros	Martial Arts			
The Way of the Dragon	Golden Harvest	Martial Arts			
		Martial Arts count	3	1.66%	0
Paint Your Wagon	Paramount	Musical			
Funny Girl	Columbia	Musical			
Oliver	Columbia	Musical			
Woodstock	Warner Bros	Musical			
Hello, Dolly!	Fox	Musical			
Fiddler on the Roof	United Artists	Musical			
Cabaret	ABC	Musical			
That'll Be the Day	Anglo-EMI	Musical			
Lady Sings the Blues	Paramount	Musical			
Lost Horizon	Columbia	Musical			
Alice's Adventures in Wonderland	Fox-Rank	Musical			
The Great Waltz	MGM	Musical			
Mary Poppins	Disney	Musical			
Stardust	EMI	Musical			
Tommy	Hemdale	Musical			
The Sound of Music	Fox	Musical			
A Star is Born	First Artists	Musical			
Grease	Paramount	Musical			
Saturday Night Fever	Paramount	Musical			
Abba – The Movie	Warner Bros	Musical			
Quadrophenia	Brent Walker	Musical			
		Musical count	21	11.60%	6
Ryan's Daughter	MGM	Romance			

Table 6 (continued)

Title	Distributor	Gifford genre	Total films in genre	Genre percentage share of total	No. British in genre
The Slipper and the Rose	Universal	Romance			
Gone with the Wind	MGM	Romance			
Every Which Way But Loose	Warner Bros	Romance			
		Romance count	4	2.21%	2
Emmanuelle	Columbia	Sex			
Confessions of a Window Cleaner	Columbia	Sex			
Emmanuelle 2	Paramount	Sex			
The Stud	Brent Walker	Sex			
The Bitch	EMI	Sex			
		Sex count	5	2.76%	3
The Battle of Britain	United Artists	War			
*M*A*S*H*	Fox	War			
Where Eagles Dare	MGM	War			
Too Late the Hero	ABC	War			
The Last Valley	ABC	War			
Tora! Tora! Tora!	Fox	War			
Shout at the Devil	Hemdale	War			
A Bridge Too Far	United Artists	War			
The Eagle Has Landed	ITC	War			
The Wild Geese	Rank	War			
The Deer Hunter	EMI/ Universal	War			
		War count	11	6.08%	6
Butch Cassidy and the Sundance Kid	Fox	Western			
Soldier Blue	Avco Embassy	Western			
Little Big Man	Fox	Western			
High Plains Drifter	Universal	Western			
The Outlaw Josey Wales	Warner Bros	Western			
		Western count	6	3.31%	0

Source: P. Swern and M. Childs, *The Guinness Book of Box Office Hits* (Enfield: Guinness, 1995), Denis Gifford, *British Film Catalogue: Fiction Film 1895–1994*, Vol. 1, 3rd edn (London: Fitzroy Dearborn, 2001)

Table 7 Top box-office titles, 1970–1979, by year, including Gifford genre. British titles are shown in bold

Year	Title	Distributor	Gifford genre	Total films in genre	British films in genre
1970	***The Battle of Britain***	United Artists	War		
	Paint Your Wagon	Paramount	Musical		
	On Her Majesty's Secret Service	United Artists	Crime		
	*M*A*S*H*	Fox	War		
	Funny Girl	Columbia	Musical		
	Midnight Cowboy	United Artists	Drama		
	Butch Cassidy and the Sundance Kid	Fox	Western		
	Oliver	Columbia	Musical		
	Anne of the Thousand Days	Rank-Universal	History		
	Cromwell	Columbia	History		
	Where Eagles Dare	MGM	War		
	Women in Love	United Artists	Drama		
	Carry On Up the Jungle	Rank	Comedy		
	Every Home Should Have One	Columbia-British Lion	Comedy		
	The Lion in Winter	Avco Embassy	Historical		
	Woodstock	Warner Bros	Musical		
	Hello, Dolly!	Fox	Musical		
				17	10
1971	*The Aristocats*	Disney	Children's		
	On the Buses	Anglo-EMI	Comedy		
	Soldier Blue	Avco Embassy	Western		
	There's a Girl in My Soup	Ascot Productions	Comedy		
	Percy	Anglo-EMI	Comedy		
	The Railway Children	Associated British	Children's		
	Too Late the Hero	ABC	War		
	Tales of Beatrix Potter	Anglo-EMI	Children's		
	Up Pompeii	Anglo-EMI	Comedy		
	The Last Valley	ABC	War		
	Butch Cassidy	Fox	Western		
	When 8 Bells Toll	Rank	Crime		
	Tora! Tora! Tora!	Fox	War		
	Dad's Army	Columbia	Comedy		
	Little Big Man	Fox	Western		
				15	9
1972	***Diamonds Are Forever***	United Artists	Crime		
	The Godfather	Paramount	Crime		
	Fiddler on the Roof	United Artists	Musical		
	Bedknobs and Broomsticks	Disney	Children's		
	The Devils	Warner Bros	Drama		
	Steptoe and Son	Anglo-EMI	Comedy		
	The French Connection	Fox	Crime		
	Nicholas and Alexandra	Columbia	Historical		

Table 7 (continued)

Year	Title	Distributor	Gifford genre	Total films in genre	British films in genre
	Ryan's Daughter	MGM	Romance		
	Dirty Harry	Warner Bros	Crime		
	Mary, Queen of Scots	Universal	Historical		
	A Clockwork Orange	Warner Bros	Fantasy		
	What's Up, Doc?	Warner Bros	Comedy		
	Straw Dogs	ABC	Drama		
	Shaft	MGM	Crime		
	Klute	Warner Bros	Crime		
	Young Winston	Columbia	Historical		
	The Go-Between	EMI-MGM	Drama		
	Mutiny on the Buses	Anglo-EMI	Comedy		
	Sleeping Beauty	Disney	Children's		
	Please, Sir!	Rank	Comedy		
	Up the Chastity Belt	Anglo-EMI	Comedy		
				22	12
1973	***Live and Let Die***	United Artists	Crime		
	The Godfather	Paramount	Crime		
	A Clockwork Orange	Warner Bros	Fantasy		
	Snow White and the Seven Dwarfs	Disney	Children's		
	The Poseidon Adventure	Fox	Adventure		
	Last Tango in Paris	United Artists	Drama		
	Cabaret	ABC	Musical		
	The Day of the Jackal	Universal	Crime		
	Lady Caroline Lamb	Anglo-EMI	Historical		
	That'll Be the Day	Anglo-EMI	Musical		
	Lady Sings the Blues	Paramount	Musical		
	Lost Horizon	Columbia	Musical		
	High Plains Drifter	Universal	Western		
	Fear is the Key	Anglo-EMI	Crime		
	Love Thy Neighbour	Anglo-EMI	Comedy		
	Alice's Adventures in Wonderland	Fox-Rank	Musical		
	Superfly	Warner Bros	Crime		
	King Boxer	Warner Bros	Martial Arts		
	Fuzz	United Artists	Crime		
	The Great Waltz	MGM	Musical		
				20	8
1974	*The Sting*	Universal	Crime		
	The Exorcist	Warner Bros	Horror		
	Enter the Dragon	Warner Bros	Martial Arts		
	The Three Musketeers	Fox	Adventure		
	Papillon	Allied Artists	Drama		

Table 7 (continued)

Year	Title	Distributor	Gifford genre	Total films in genre	British films in genre
	Herbie Rides Again	Disney	Comedy		
	Robin Hood	Disney	Adventure		
	The Great Gatsby	Paramount	Drama		
	Mary Poppins	Disney	Musical		
	The Way We Were	Columbia	Drama		
	Golden Voyage of Sinbad	Columbia	Children's		
	Don't Look Now	British Lion	Drama		
	Chinatown	Paramount	Crime		
	The Way of the Dragon	Golden Harvest	Martial Arts		
	Blazing Saddles	Warner Bros	Comedy		
	Confessions of a Window Cleaner	Columbia	Sex		
	Stardust	EMI	Musical		
	Gold	Hemdale	Drama		
	Last Tango in Paris	United Artists	Drama		
	American Graffiti	Universal	Drama		
				19	4
1975	*The Towering Inferno*	Fox	Drama		
	The Exorcist	Warner Bros	Horror		
	The Man with the Golden Gun	United Artists	Crime		
	Emmanuelle	Columbia	Sex		
	Earthquake	Universal	Drama		
	Airport '75	Universal	Drama		
	Murder on the Orient Express	EMI	Crime		
	Papillon	Allied Artists	Drama		
	Stardust	EMI	Musical		
	Island at the Top of the World	Disney	Adventure		
	Confessions of a Window Cleaner	Columbia	Sex		
	Tommy	Hemdale	Musical		
	Blazing Saddles	Warner Bros	Comedy		
	The Land that Time Forgot	Lion International	Fantasy		
	Death Wish	Paramount	Crime		
	The Four Musketeers	Fox	Adventure		
	Freebie and the Bean	Warner Bros	Crime		
	The Lady and the Tramp	Disney	Children's		
	Monty Python and the Holy Grail	EMI	Comedy		
	Rollerball	United Artists	Fantasy		
				20	7
1976	*Jaws*	Universal	Horror		
	One Flew Over the Cuckoo's Nest	United Artists	Drama		

Table 7 (continued)

Year	Title	Distributor	Gifford genre	Total films in genre	British films in genre
	Jungle Book	Disney	Children's		
	Return of the Pink Panther	United Artists	Comedy		
	Emmanuelle	Columbia	Sex		
	Rollerball	United Artists	Fantasy		
	The Omen	Fox	Horror		
	It Shouldn't Happen to a Vet	EMI	Drama		
	The Outlaw Josey Wales	Warner Bros	Western		
	All the President's Men	Warner Bros	Drama		
	The Slipper and the Rose	Universal	Romance		
	Death Race 2000	De Laurentis	Fantasy		
	Bambi	Disney	Children's		
	Shout at the Devil	Hemdale	War		
	Tommy	Hemdale	Musical		
	Gone with the Wind	MGM	Romance		
	The Sound of Music	Fox	Musical		
	At the Earth's Core	Amicus	Fantasy		
	Adventures of a Taxi Driver	ITC	Comedy		
	Barry Lyndon	Warner Bros	Drama		
				20	8
1977	***The Spy Who Loved Me***	United Artists	Crime		
	A Star is Born	First Artists	Musical		
	When the North Wind Blows	Unknown	Adventure		
	The Pink Panther Strikes Again	United Artists	Comedy		
	A Bridge Too Far	United Artists	War		
	Sinbad and the Eye of the Tiger	Columbia	Children's		
	The Omen	Fox	Horror		
	King Kong	De Laurentis	Fantasy		
	Airport '77	Universal	Drama		
	The Adventures of the Wilderness Family	Unknown	Adventure		
	One Hundred and One Dalmatians	Disney	Children's		
	The Enforcer	Warner Bros	Crime		
	Jaws	Universal	Horror		
	Sweeney!	EMI	Crime		
	The Eagle Has Landed	ITC	War		
	Emmanuelle 2	Paramount	Sex		
	Bugsy Malone	Rank	Children's		
	Exorcist II: The Heretic	Warner Bros	Horror		
	Carrie	United Artists	Horror		
	Rocky	United Artists	Drama		
				20	6

Table 7 (continued)

Year	Title	Distributor	Gifford genre	Total films in genre	British films in genre
1978	*Star Wars*	Fox	Fantasy		
	Grease	Paramount	Musical		
	Close Encounters of the Third Kind	Columbia	Fantasy		
	Saturday Night Fever	Paramount	Musical		
	Revenge of the Pink Panther	United Artists	Comedy		
	The Rescuers	Disney	Children's		
	Abba – The Movie	Warner Bros	Musical		
	The Gauntlet	Warner Bros	Crime		
	Herbie Goes to Monte Carlo	Disney	Comedy		
	The Stud	Brent Walker	Sex		
	The Deep	EMI/Columbia	Horror		
	Annie Hall	United Artists	Drama		
	Convoy	EMI/United Artists	Drama		
	The Wild Geese	Rank	War		
	Warlords of Atlantis	EMI	Fantasy		
	Candleshoe	Disney	Children's		
	The Goodbye Girl	MGM/Warners	Drama		
	Spiderman Strikes Back	Columbia	Fantasy		
	Heaven Can Wait	Paramount	Comedy		
	Julia	Fox	Drama		
	International Velvet	MGM	Drama		
				21	5
1979	***Moonraker***	United Artists	Crime		
	Superman	Columbia-EMI-Warner	Fantasy		
	Jaws 2	Universal	Horror		
	Every Which Way But Loose	Warner Bros	Romance		
	Alien	Fox	Fantasy		
	Watership Down	Avco Embassy	Children's		
	The Deer Hunter	EMI/Universal	War		
	Grease	Paramount	Musical		
	Quadrophenia	Brent Walker	Musical		
	Pete's Dragon	Disney	Children's		
	Midnight Express	Columbia	Drama		
	National Lampoon's Animal House	Universal	Comedy		
	Death on the Nile	EMI	Crime		
	Porridge	ITC	Comedy		
	The Cat from Outer Space	Disney	Children's		
	Battlestar Galactica	Universal	Fantasy		
	The 39 Steps	Rank	Crime		
	The Bitch	EMI	Sex		

Table 7 (continued)

Year	Title	Distributor	Gifford genre	Total films in genre	British films in genre
	Lord of the Rings	United Artists	Children's		
	The Warriors	Paramount	Crime		
				19	9

Source: P. Swern and M. Childs, *The Guinness Book of Box Office Hits* (Enfield: Guinness, 1995), Denis Gifford, *British Film Catalogue: Fiction Film 1895–1994*, Vol. 1, 3rd edn (London: Fitzroy Dearborn, 2001)

Table 8 US rental earnings of British films, 1970–1979

Title	Rentals ($millions)
Superman (1978)	82.8
Alien (1979)	40.3
Moonraker (1979)	33.9
The Spy Who Loved Me (1977)	24.4
A Bridge Too Far (1977)	20.4
Return of the Pink Panther (1975)	20.2
The Pink Panther Strikes Again (1976)	19.8
Diamonds Are Forever (1971)	19.7
Murder on the Orient Express (1974)	19.1
Tommy (1975)	17.8
A Clockwork Orange (1971)	17.0
Live and Let Die (1973)	16.0
Dracula (1979)	10.7
Monty Python's Life of Brian (1979)	10.5
Barry Lyndon (1975)	9.2
Death on the Nile (1978)	8.8
The Day of the Jackal (1973)*	8.6
The Odessa File (1974)**	5.7
Monty Python and the Holy Grail (1975)	5.2
The Eagle Has Landed (1977)	4.2
Straw Dogs (1971)	4.0
Mary, Queen of Scots (1972)	3.6
The Man Who Fell To Earth (1976)	3.0
Scrooge (1970)	3.0
Women in Love (1970)	3.0

* Britain/France.
** Britain/West Germany.

Source: S. Street, *Transatlantic Crossings* (London: Continuum, 2002), p. 195

APPENDIX II

Cinema-going at the Southampton Odeon: Exhibition Data and Popular Taste

Sian Barber

One of the principal challenges of studying 1970s British cinema is to locate original data about distribution and exhibition. Recent work by Sue Harper, Mark Glancy and Robert James has demonstrated that exhibition data can offer unique insights into the world of the audience.[1] However, similar data for the 1970s are hard to unearth, and this makes the personal ledgers of James Tilmouth, who managed the Odeon cinema in Southampton throughout the 1970s, so important.

Tilmouth's personal records reveal which films were shown, how many people saw them, and how much money each film made. It is possible from this data to map the success of individual films and to speculate about popular taste. However, it is unwise to generalise using such sparse data. As well as the possible inaccuracies and omissions within the records, these accounts only offer an insight into films shown in a single cinema; they cannot be used to create a full picture of cinema-going in Southampton or, indeed, in Britain.

It is not my intention here to undertake the detailed analysis which these data deserves, but instead to highlight some of the trends revealed.[2] Yet before beginning, there are some important issues pertaining to the data which must be acknowledged. One of the principal concerns is the way that the data is recorded. Personal records, no matter how meticulously preserved, will always be subject to minor errors and inaccuracies. Additionally, the way in which the financial data are recorded also needs to be treated with appropriate caution. For example, from 1972 to 975, profits were recorded in net, whereas from 1975 onwards, they were recorded in gross.

Another significant issue with the data is that it does not run from one year's end to the next, nicely book-ending each year in easily comparable sections. Instead, it begins in October and end in September. This makes drawing comparisons between years complex. For example, the material pertaining to 1975/1976 might show several notable omissions,

Table 9 Films recording substantial admissions at the Southampton Odeon, 1972–1980

Admissions for individual films	Number of films to record these admissions
Over 6,000	24
Over 10,000	6
Over 15,000	11
Over 20,000	12
Over 30,000	3
Over 40,000	3
Over 60,000	2
Over 100,000	1

but this may be due to the fact that the films in question were released in late 1976 and so do not feature in the figures for this year. The data for Southampton only begin in 1972, when Tilmouth took over the management of the cinema. A significant break in the data reflects the splitting of the auditorium which took place in 1978/1979, when the cinema was closed for eight weeks.

Finally, wider 1970s economic fluctuations are evident within the admissions ledgers. Throughout the eight years, numerous price increases and occasional decreases are noted in the ledgers, reflecting the high rate of inflation and the rise in the cost of living which were such a critical part of the 1970s decade. These economic undercurrents would have had a significant impact on habits of cinema-going and need to be actively considered when offering conclusions about cinema attendance.

All of these issues problematise straightforward analysis of these data but are an inevitable aspect of this kind of work. Bearing all of these issues in mind, I now want to begin to consider what the data reveals. One of the most obvious things that the data reveals is the popularity of a few major films. As Table 9 illustrates, in a decade of declining cinema audiences, only nine films attracted admissions of over 30,000. This select group included *The Island at the Top of the World* (1974), *Jungle Book* (1967) and *A Bridge Too Far* (1977).

Star Wars was the clear box-office winner at the Odeon, with no other single film of the decade coming close in terms of admissions and total profits. The film played for eleven weeks, made over £85,000 in gross profit and recorded admissions of 108,134. Yet, following this film's release, box-office admissions for other films actually fell rather than increased. The only other film to do significant business in the same year was *Close Encounters of the Third Kind* (1977), which ran for nine weeks and made £56,980. No other films in the weeks that followed accrued significant profits. After *Star Wars* and *Close Encounters*, the highest-grossing films for 1977/1978 at the Odeon were *Revenge of the Pink Panther* (1978), which made £38,885, and *The Rescuers* (1977), which was released before *Star Wars* and made £22,370, its lower takings perhaps reflecting the reduced prices charged for children's admissions. If we look at the admissions for specific films across the decade, the pattern becomes clearer, with a discernible difference between the blockbuster films and the majority of the other releases, which could be deemed a major success if they captured audiences of 20,000.

The ledgers reveal that, with the exception of these four arguably atypical films, cinema-going for other lower-budget, non-blockbuster films remained at their pre-*Star Wars* levels, largely unaffected by the massive impact of the blockbuster, even in the years following 1977. For example, in the year following the screening of *Star Wars*, the futuristic *Alien* (1979) topped the box office with admissions of 24,807, while *Pete's Dragon* (1977), in second place, secured 22,316.

Impressive though these figures are, they fit comfortably within the parameters of popularity established by films screened at the Odeon before *Star Wars*. For example, in 1974/1975, the top-grossing films were *The Island at the Top of the World* with 34,148 admissions and *Tommy* (1975) with 30,480 admissions. In light of these figures, *Star Wars*, *Close Encounters* and *The Empire Strikes Back* must be seen as aberrations. Within the context of these data, they should be seen as successful films which attracted massive audiences, but are atypical and stand out from the rest of the data.

So what else stands out in the Southampton data? It is clear that the films which dominated this particular cinema are not the low-budget sex and horror films which are often considered 'typical' of 1970s British filmmaking.

Exploitation cinema in the 1970s has received a great deal of critical attention, notably from Leon Hunt and I. Q. Hunter, who have drawn attention to the difficulties of defining such a multi-faceted genre in this decade.[3] Films from the low-budget end of the spectrum took advantage of increasing permissiveness to use nudity, sex and horror to sell their films, with titles such as *The Happy Hooker* (1975), *Come Play with Me* (1977) and *And Now the Screaming Starts* (1973) indicating clearly to audiences what types of films they were. However, as Table 10 shows, exploitation films comprised a very small number of the total exhibited 'X'-rated films at the Odeon. Many low-budget exploitation films did very little business at the Odeon, with even the popular favourite, *Confessions of a Window Cleaner* (1974), only taking a modest £2,508. Although this was a reasonable showing, the film was not rebooked for another week, suggesting it

Table 10 Exploitation films and their recorded admissions at the Southampton Odeon, 1972–1980

Year	No. of 'X' films	No. of exploitation films	Total admissions for exploitation films
1972–1973	13	0	
1973–1974	17	1	2,303
1974–1975	14	2	6,888
1975–1976	10	1	13,022
1976–1977	11	2	9,381
1977–1978	15	3	454
1978–1979	13	5	26,306
1979–1980	21	5	18,623
TOTAL	114	19	76,977

was not strong enough to justify a further week's screening. Throughout the decade, individual exploitation films performed well, but there was no outright domination at this cinema by low-brow product from the horror and sex genres.

But what of James Bond? Did Bond prevail when sex and horror failed? Significantly, the ledgers demonstrate that the newly released Bond films of the 1970s made very little impact at the Odeon. In the years covered by the ledgers, four Bond films were produced, and it might be expected that *Live and Let Die* (1973), *The Man with the Golden Gun* (1974), *The Spy who Loved Me* (1977) and *Moonraker* (1979) would all feature prominently within these data. Yet this is not the case. Throughout these eight years, Bond films played for a total of only forty-eight days within the Odeon Southampton. The only Bond film to play for a full week as an individual feature was *Diamonds are Forever* (1971), which was shown in October 1972, a year after its nationwide release. Neither *The Spy who Loved Me* nor *Moonraker* features at all in the ledgers, while *Live and Let Die* and *The Man with the Golden Gun* were screened as part of double bills, alongside other Bond adventures. With the exception of *Diamonds are Forever*, all the Bond films shown at the cinema were screened as double-bill programmes. The highest-grossing weekly screenings were of *Diamonds are Forever/From Russia with Love* (1963), which made £2,540, and *Live and Let Die/On Her Majesty's Secret Service* (1969), which made £2,165, both in 1973/1974. These very modest sums were easily surpassed at the box office by the first-week runs of both *Gold* (1974) and *Don't Look Now* (1974), both of which went on to play for further weeks at the cinema. The information recorded demonstrates that Bond films were clearly not big box-office earners at the Southampton Odeon.

Table 11 Performance of Disney films which featured in the top ten annual films, 1972–1980

Name	Year produced	Year exhibited	Admissions
Robin Hood	1973	1973/74	51,651
Jungle Book	1967	1975/76	36,338
Island at the Top of the World	1974	1974/75	34,148
The Rescuers	1977	1977/78	31,391
101 Dalmatians	1961	1976/77	23,753
Pete's Dragon	1977	1978/79	22,316
Bambi	1942	1975/76	20,227
Escape to Witch Mountain	1975	1974/75	18,753
Bedknobs and Broomsticks	1971	1978/79	16,058
The Aristocats	1970	1979/80	15,579
Mary Poppins	1964	1972/73	12,810
Lady and the Tramp	1955	1974/75	12,184
Sword in the Stone	1963	1972/73	11,380
Cinderella	1950	1977/78	9,624
Bambi	1942	1978/79	8,717
Snow White and the Seven Dwarves	1937	1973/74	7,576
Song of the South	1946	1973/74	6,469
Jungle Book	1967	1977/78	4,548
TOTAL			343,522

So what does dominate? Unlike the 'X'-rated sex and horror films, it is the 'U'-certificated family film which is the unequivocal box office winner at the Odeon, perhaps unsurprisingly when considering the family values espoused by the Rank Organisation, owners of the Odeon chain. Over the course of this eight-year period, Disney films played at the Odeon for 377 days. In that time, the franchise admitted 365,580 people and made a massive £219,210 – double the amount of profit made by *Star Wars*. Although *Star Wars* was massively successful for a single film, it is the sustained performance of the Disney franchise which attests to the longevity of these films and to their continued box-office appeal in an era of declining cinema attendance.

Table 11 reveals the franchise's dominance in the years 1972–1980 at the Southampton Odeon and includes, for the sake of brevity, only those films which made it into the top ten most popular films of respective years.

While this data clearly reveals the extent to which Disney triumphed in terms of admissions, it is interesting to note that most of the films were older productions, yet still found a ready and enthusiastic audience.

Out of the nineteen Disney feature films identified here, only four – *Robin Hood* (1973), *The Island at the Top of the World*, *The Rescuers*

(1977) and *Escape to Witch Mountain* (1975) – were newly made features. Between them, these four films accounted for 135,943 of the total admissions within the eight-year period, an impressive figure but only a third of the total Disney admissions of this period. Although these four films occupy places near the top of the list, the older films also contributed significantly to the success of the franchise. In a period where many films struggled to do business, many of the older Disney features played for three or four weeks, often occupying the coveted Christmas period slot; *Jungle Book* and *101 Dalmatians* both played for five weeks in 1975 and 1976. Despite the long runs for these films, both continued to do significant business every week, with the lowest weekly admissions being 3,705 for *Jungle Book* and 2,458 for *101 Dalmatians*.

These figures are perhaps not surprising when considering the time period and the high number of children who were likely to attend the cinema during the holidays, yet what is significant is how these films successfully competed against other releases. *Jungle Book* outperformed contemporary releases in January 1976, such as *Carry on Behind* (1975), which secured admissions of 2,435 and played for only seven days, while only *A Bridge Too Far* and the *Pink Panther Strikes Again* (1976) performed better than *101 Dalmatians* during the entire financial year of 1976/1977.

So what can such observations tell us about cinema-going at the Southampton Odeon? While it is clear that blockbusters like *Star Wars* enjoyed huge success, neither this film nor any of the blockbusters which followed it prompted increased attendance for all other films. The dominance of Disney feature films at the Odeon is a trend which actively demonstrates the popularity of the franchise but also reveals a great deal about audience taste. This popularity becomes even more significant when considered alongside the low impact of 'adult' genres such as sex and horror. Not only were family films successful with younger audiences, but also they could guarantee to secure the cinema audience for four- or even five-week periods at a time, suggesting that they were catering to diverse audiences, not simply a juvenile one.

The frequent price increases, the splitting of the auditorium and the poor attendance for many screened features – all of which is documented in the ledgers – accords with broader patterns of cinema-going in the 1970s. It must be acknowledged that, while this snapshot is interesting, it only offers a very specific window on to the decade. What it does demonstrate, however, is that exhibition data offer a great deal to the researcher of film history and cinema. Much remains to be done, yet even this brief investigation has demonstrated that such data are invaluable and should be thoroughly analysed in order to increase understandings of cinema exhibition in this much-maligned decade.

Notes

1. R. James, 'Kinematograph Weekly in the 1930s: Trade Attitudes Towards Audience Taste', *Journal of British Cinema and Television*, Vol. 3, No. 2 (2006), pp. 229–43, M. Glancy, *When Hollywood Loved Britain: The Hollywood 'British' Film, 1939–45* (Manchester: Manchester University Press, 1999), S. Harper, 'A Lower-Middle-Class Taste Community in the 1930s: Admission Figures at the Regent, Portsmouth', *Historical Journal of Film, Radio and Television*, Vol. 24, No. 4 (2004), pp. 565–88, S. Harper, 'Fragmentation and Crisis: 1940's Admissions Figures at the Regent Cinema, Portsmouth, UK', *Historical Journal of Film, Radio and Television*, Vol. 26, No. 3 (2006), pp. 361–94.
2. This work has been undertaken in S. Barber, 'Beyond sex, Bond and *Star Wars*: exhibition data from the Southampton Odeon 1972–1980', *POST SCRIPT: Essays in Film and the Humanities* (forthcoming Spring/Summer 2011).
3. L. Hunt, *British Low Culture: From Safari Suits to Sexploitation* (London: Routledge, 1998), I. Q. Hunter, 'Take an easy ride: sexploitation in the 1970s', in Robert Shail (ed.), *Seventies British Cinema*, pp. 3–13.

APPENDIX III

Top Films Shown at Portsmouth Cinemas, 1970–1979

Peri Bradley

Table 12 Top films shown at Portsmouth cinemas, 1970–1979, by weekly screen event listing

Title	Country of origin	Year first released	Screen events
Star Wars	US	1977	25
Close Encounters of the Third Kind	US	1977	20
Paint Your Wagon	US	1969	19
Confessions of a Window Cleaner	UK	1974	18
Magnum Force	US	1973	18
Butch Cassidy and the Sundance Kid	US	1969	17
Where Eagles Dare	UK	1968	17
Live and Let Die	UK	1973	16
Soldier Blue	US	1970	16
Blazing Saddles	US	1974	16
Anne of the Thousand Days	UK	1969	15
Moonraker	UK	1979	15
A Bridge Too Far	UK	1977	14
Emmanuelle	FR	1974	14
Battle of Britain	UK	1969	13
Revenge of the Pink Panther	UK	1978	13
Monty Python and the Holy Grail	UK	1974	13
The Towering Inferno	US	1974	12
The Spy Who Loved Me	UK	1977	12
The Sound of Music	US	1965	12
Easy Rider	US	1969	12
The Return of the Pink Panther	UK	1974	11
The Man With the Golden Gun	UK	1974	11
Sinbad and the Eye of the Tiger	US	1977	11
Saturday Night Fever	US	1977	11
Hello, Dolly!	US	1969	11
Kelly's Heroes	US	1970	10
Percy	UK	1971	10
Bullitt	US	1968	10
Enter the Dragon	US/HK	1973	10

Table 12 (continued)

Title	Country of origin	Year first released	Screen events
Annie Hall	US	1977	10
Song of Norway	US	1970	10
Tommy	UK	1975	10
Waterloo	USSR/IT	1970	10
Aristocats	US	1970	10
Cromwell	UK	1970	10
Jaws	US	1975	10
Fist of Fury	HK	1972	10
*M*A*S*H*	US	1969	9
The Four Musketeers	PA/SP	1974	9
The Sting	US	1973	9
Pink Panther Strikes Again	UK	1976	9
Freebie and the Bean	US	1974	9
Confessions of a Driving Instructor	UK	1976	9
Confessions of a Pop Performer	UK	1975	9
Carrie	US	1976	9
Dirty Harry	US	1971	9
The Wild Bunch	US	1969	8
There's a Girl in my Soup	UK	1970	8
Vanishing Point	US	1971	8
What's Up, Doc?	US	1972	8
When Eight Bells Toll	UK	1971	8
The Golden Voyage of Sinbad	US	1973	8
The Island at the Top of the World	US	1973	8
The Devils	UK	1971	8
Bonnie and Clyde	US	1967	8
For a Few Dollars More	IT/SP	1965	8
Death Wish	US	1974	8
High Plains Drifter	US	1972	8
Oliver!	UK/US	1968	8
On the Buses	UK	1971	8
One Flew Over the Cuckoo's Nest	US	1975	8
Love Story	US	1970	8
Robin Hood	US	1973	8
Shout at the Devil	UK	1976	8
A Fistful of Dollars	IT/SP	1964	7
Alien	US	1979	7
The Rescuer	US	1977	7
And Now for Something Completely Different	UK	1971	7
Born to Run	US/AUS	1977	7
Carnal Knowledge	US	1971	7
Escape From the Planet of the Apes	US	1971	7
Flesh Gordon	US	1974	7
Gold	UK	1974	7

Table 12 (continued)

Title	Country of origin	Year first released	Screen events
Grease	US	1978	7
Mary Poppins	US	1964	7
Midnight Cowboy	US	1969	7
Papillon	US/FR	1973	7
Pete's Dragon	US	1977	7
Scrooge	UK	1970	7
Secrets of a Door to Door Salesman	UK	1973	7
Shivers	US	1974	7
Sleeper	US	1973	7
That'll Be the Day	UK	1973	7
The Exorcist	US	1973	7
The Omen	US/UK	1976	7
The Poseidon Adventure	US	1972	7

Source: *The News*, Portsmouth 1970–1979 (compiled by P. Bradley)

Bibliography

Official Sources

Government Published Document Sources (Date Order)

Commission for Racial Equality, *Annual Report*, 1977, p. 33.

Parliamentary Debates: House of Commons, Fifth Series (Hansard).

Great Britain: Central Advisory Council for Education (England), *Half Our Future: A Report of the Central Advisory Council for Education*. London: HMSO, 1963.

Great Britain: House of Commons, *Film Co-Production Agreement between the Government of the United Kingdom of Great Britain and Northern Ireland and the Government of the French Republic, 1965* (Cmd 2781).

Great Britain: Department of Education and Science, *A Plan for Polytechnics and Other Colleges: Higher Education in the Further Education System*. London: HMSO, 1966.

Great Britain: Department of Education and Science, *Report of a Committee to Consider the Need for a National Film School*. London: HMSO, 1967.

Great Britain: Prime Minister's Working Party, *Future of the British Film Industry: Report of the Prime Minister's Working Party, 1976* (Cmd 6372).

Great Britain: House of Commons, *British Film Fund Agency. Nineteenth Annual Report and Statement of Accounts for the Fifty-Two Weeks Ended 25 September 1976*. London: HMSO, 1977.

Great Britain: House of Commons, *British Film Fund Agency: Annual Report and Statement of Accounts for the Fifty-Two Weeks Ended 20 September 1980*. London: HMSO, 1981.

Film Industry Reports

ACTT Report. *Nationalising the Film Industry*, August 1973.

Cinematograph Films Council, *Report* (NA: ED 245/54).

Film Production Association. *Annual Report*, 1974–1975.

—. *Co-production Guide to the Anglo-French and the Anglo-Italian Co-production Treaties*. London: Film Production Association of Great Britain, 1971.
National Film Finance Corporation. *Annual Report*. London: HMSO, 1972.
—. *Annual Report*. London: HMSO, 1974.
—. *Annual Report*. London: HMSO, 1976.
—. *Annual Report*. London: HMSO, 1978.

Archival / Unpublished Sources

Public Record Office, Kew, London (PRO)

British Film Fund Agency. *British Film Fund Agency Committee Minutes 1970* (BT 383/14–BT 383/23).
—. *British Film Fund Agency Committee Minutes* (BT 383/14–BT 383/23).
Home Office. *Submission to the Williams Committee by the BBFC, 1977* (HO 265/2).
—. *Memo* (300/166).
Ministers' Special Meeting of the Cinematograph Films Council. *The Terry Report* (FV 81/95).

British Film Institute, London (BFI)

Special Collections

Derek Jarman Papers; Joseph Losey Papers; David Puttnam Papers: John Schlesinger Papers; Anne Skinner Papers.
BFI Production Board Files; Hammer Films Production Files.

BFI Library

Vetchinsky, Alexander. *Interview with Mark Yonge, London* (1977). Held on microfiche.
BECTU Oral History Recordings: Val Guest, Alan Sapper.

Internal Memoranda

British Film Institute. *Governors' Minutes*. 20 April 1971 (5338–5344).

BBC Written Archives Centre, Caversham, Reading (BBC)

Drama Memos 1968–1979 (T5/782/5).
The Wednesday Play 1968–1969 (R78/1, 919/1).

British Board of Film Classification, London

Range of individual film files, referenced in end-notes.

Bill Douglas Centre, University of Exeter

Don Boyd Papers; Gavrik Losey Papers.

University of the Arts, London

Stanley Kubrick Archive.

University of Stirling

Lindsay Anderson Papers.

Portsmouth City Archives

Meetings, Fire Services and Public Control Committee. *Minutes 1971–74* (Books CCM1/54 and CCM1/55).

Theses

Barber, Sian, *1970s British Film: Capital, Culture and Creativity* (Unpublished PhD thesis, University of Portsmouth, 2009).

Interviews

Adam, Ken. Interviewed by Laurie Ede, 30 April 2007.
Boyd, Don. Interviewed by Sue Harper and Justin Smith, 13 November 2008.
Hassan, Mamoun. Interviewed by Sue Harper and Justin Smith, 7 October 2009.
Jackson, Glenda. Interviewed by Sue Harper and Justin Smith, 15 November 2007.
Lieberson, Sandy. Interviewed by Sue Harper and Justin Smith, 6 March 2008.
Ové, Horace. Interviewed by Sally Shaw, 23 June 2009.
Winner, Michael. Interviewed by Sian Barber and Sue Harper, 15 July 2008.

Chapters in Edited Books and Journal Articles

Adam, Ken, Interview, *American Cinematographer*, Vol. 58, No. 5, May 1977, p. 553.
Allen, Dave, 'How high the moon? Science fiction and popular music', in G. Harper, R. Doughty and J. Eisentraut (eds), *Sound and Music in Film and Visual Media: An Overview* (New York: Continuum, 2009), pp. 231–49.
—, 'A public transition: acoustic and electric performances at the Woodstock Festival', in A. Bennett (ed.), *Remembering Woodstock* (Aldershot: Ashgate, 2004), pp. 111–26.

Anderson, Lindsay et al., 'Financial support for film-makers', *The Times*, 5 August 1971, p. 13.

Ann-Margret, Interview, *Films and Filming*, January 1976, pp. 12–16.

Anon, 'Film School Head chosen', *The Times*, 12 March 1970, p. 2.

—, 'Artists in the Polytechnic web', *The Times*, 30 October 1970, p. 13.

—, 'The Arriflex 35BL camera', *American Cinematographer*, Vol. 51, No. 12, December 1970, pp. 1176–7.

—, 'Moviola's new editing console', *American Cinematographer*, Vol. 51, No. 12, December 1970, pp. 1194–5, 1230–1.

—, 'Murphy must go', *Cinema TV Today*, 11 March 1972, p. 1.

—, 'Planned merger "will not change art education"', *The Times*, 21 June 1973, p. 4.

—, 'Thorn Lighting introduces hot restrike CSI lamps', *American Cinematographer*, Vol. 56, No. 9, September 1975, pp. 1040, 1084.

—, 'Photographing Barry Lyndon', *American Cinematographer*, Vol. 57, No. 3, March 1976, pp. 268–77, 320–1, 338.

—, 'Major film distribution company announces its new programme', *Screen International*, No. 52, 4 September 1976, pp. 15, 17.

—, 'CTV report', *Screen Digest*, December 1976, p. 222.

—, 'Marketing that gets results', *Screen International*, No. 174, 27 January 1979, p. 16.

—, 'Cinemas still required to support the British film industry', *The Times*, 7 June 1980, p. 3.

Austin, John, 'Big US/UK tie-up', *Screen International*, No. 44, 10 July 1976, p. 1.

Bogarde, Dirk, Interview, *Films and Filming*, May 1971, pp. 40–50.

Boorman, John, Interview, *American Cinematographer*, Vol. 56, No. 3, March 1975, p. 285.

Britton, Andrew, 'The ideology of *Screen*', *Movie*, No. 26, Winter 1978/1979, pp. 2–28.

Burke, Sean, 'The ethics of signature', in Sean Burke (ed.), *Authorship – from Plato to Postmodern – A Reader* (Edinburgh: Edinburgh University Press, 1995), pp. 285–91.

Buscombe, Ed, 'All bark and no bite: the film industry's response to television', in John Corner (ed.), *Popular Television in Britain: Studies in Cultural History* (London: BFI, 1991), pp. 197–208.

Carpenter, Gary, and Paul Newland, 'Folksploitation: charting the horrors of the British folk music tradition in *The Wicker Man*', in Shail (ed.), *Seventies British Cinema*, pp. 119–28.

Caulkin, S., 'Movie moguls look to Brussels for fresh aid', *The Times*, 19 April 1972, p. 23.

Chapman, James, 'From Amicus to Atlantis: the lost worlds of 1970s British cinema', in Shail (ed.), *Seventies British Cinema*, pp. 56–64.

Charles, Eden, 'No war in this Babylon', *Race Today Review*, January 1981, pp. 89–90.

Church Gibson, Pamela, and Andrew Hill, '"Tutte e macchio!": excess, masquerade and performativity in 70s Cinema', in Murphy (ed.), *The British Cinema Book*, pp. 263–9.

Collins, Richard, 'A diploma course in film study at the Polytechnic of Central London', *Screen Education Notes*, No. 9, Winter 1973/1974, p.11.

Connolly, Ray, 'Tommy', *Time Out*, No. 265, 28 March 1975, p. 10.

Corner, John, 'BFI Distribution Library Catalogue', *Screen Education*, No. 24, Autumn 1977, pp. 60–2.

Courte, Kenneth, 'Big blow-up in the Hemdale group', *Today's Cinema*, No. 9831, 14 August 1970, p. 6.

—, 'The Hemdale row is dissolved', *Today's Cinema*, No. 9856, 13 November 1970, p. 2.

—, 'No longer the kindly money lenders', *Today's Cinema*, 3 September 1971, p. 10.

Craven, Jenny, 'Jenny Craven on location with *Babylon*', *Films and Filming*, Vol. 26, No. 8, May 1980, pp. 40–1.

Darwin, Sir Robin, 'National Film School plan', *The Times*, 24 June 1969, p. 9.

Dassin, Jules, Interview, *Films and Filming*, February 1970, pp. 22–6 and March 1970, pp. 66–70.

Delson, J., 'Art directors: Ken Adam', *Film Comment*, January 1982, p. 40.

Dickinson, Margaret, 'The state and the consolidation of monopoly', in James Curran and Vincent Porter (eds), *British Cinema History* (London: Weidenfeld & Nicholson, 1983), pp. 74–95.

DiGiulio, Ed, 'Two special lenses for *Barry Lyndon*', *American Cinematographer*, Vol. 57, No. 3, March 1976, pp. 276–7, 318, 336–7.

Dodd, Philip, 'Modern stories', in Philip Dodd and Ian Christie, *Spellbound: Art and Film* (London: Hayward Gallery/BFI, 1996), pp. 32–41.

Dolan, Josie, and Andrew Spicer, 'On the margins: Anthony Simmons, *The Optimists of Nine Elms* and *Black Joy*', in Newland (ed.), *Don't Look Now*, pp. 79–92.

Donald, James, 'Anxious moments: *The Sweeney* in 1975', in Manuel Alvarado and John Stewart (eds), *Made for Television: Euston Films Limited* (London: BFI, 1985), pp. 117–35.

Donnelly, Kevin, 'British punk films: rebellion into money, nihilism into innovation', *Journal of Popular British Cinema*, No.1 (1998), pp. 101–14.

Dupin, Christophe, 'The BFI and British independent cinema in the 1970s', in Shail (ed.), *Seventies British Cinema*, pp. 159–74.

Durgnat, Raymond, 'Shoot-out in Dean Street', *Films and Filming*, February 1972, pp. 41–2.

Dusinberre, Deke, 'The avant-garde attitude in the Thirties', in Michael O'Pray (ed.), *The British Avant-Garde Film 1926 to 1995* (Luton: John Libbey Media, 1996), pp. 65–85.

Eyles, Allen, 'Exhibition and the cinema-going experience', in R. Murphy (ed.), *The British Cinema Book* (London: BFI, 1997), pp. 217–25.

Forbes, Jill, 'Film and French Studies', in Christine Gledhill (ed.), *Film and Media Studies in Higher Education. Papers from a Conference Organized in 1979 by the BFI and London University Institute of Education* (London: BFI Education, 1979), pp. 71–81.

Forster, Laurel, 'Printing liberation: the women's movement and magazines in the 1970s', in Forster and Harper (eds), *British Culture and Society in the 1970s*, pp. 93–106.

Frith, Simon et al., 'Can we get rid of the "popular" in popular music? A virtual symposium with contributions from the International Advisory Editors of *Popular Music*', *Popular Music*, Vol. 24, No. 1, 2005, pp. 133–45.

Garvey, Adrian, 'Pre-sold to millions: the sitcom films of the 1970s', in Newland (ed.), *Don't Look Now*, pp. 177–86.

Gerrard, Steve, 'What a Carry On! The decline and fall of a great British institution', in Shail (ed.), *Seventies British Cinema*, pp. 36–45.

Gladwell, David, 'Editing Anderson's *If . . .*', *Screen*, Vol. 10, No. 1, January 1969, pp. 24–33.

Goldman, Vivian, 'The brethren in Babylon', *Time Out*, 7 November 1980, pp. 12–13.

Gorton, Assheton, 'Set pieces', *AIP & Co.*, January–February 1986, p.16.

Gow, Gordon, 'Shock treatment', *Films and Filming*, May 1972, p. 24.

Happé, L. B., 'New developments in the film laboratory', *Film and Television Technician*, August 1970, pp. 8–10.

Harper, Sue, and Vincent Porter, 'Beyond media history: the challenge of visual style', *Journal of British Cinema and Television*, Vol. 2, No. 1, 2005, pp. 1–17.

Harvey, Sylvia, 'Channel Four television: from Annan to Grade', in Ed Buscombe (ed.), *British Television: A Reader* (Oxford: Oxford University Press, 2000), pp. 95–105.

Higson, Andrew, 'A diversity of film practices: renewing British cinema in the 1970s', in Bart Moore-Gilbert (ed.), *The Arts in the 1970s: Cultural Closure?* (London: Routledge, 1994), pp. 216–39.

Hughes, Robert, 'The décor of tomorrow's hell', in M. Falsetto (ed.), *Perspectives on Stanley Kubrick* (New York: G. K. Halt, 1996), pp. 185–6.

Hunningher, Joost, 'Film schools, and how they function', *Movie Maker*, June 1982, pp. 344–5.

Hunter, I. Q., 'Take an easy ride: sexploitation in the 1970s', in Shail (ed.), *Seventies British Cinema*, pp. 3–13.

Izod, John et al., 'Music/industry/politics: Alan Price's roles in *O Lucky Man!*', in Forster and Harper (eds), *British Culture and Society in the 1970s*, pp. 201–12.

—, '"What is there to smile at?": Lindsay Anderson's *O Lucky Man!*', in Newland (ed.), *Don't Look Now*, pp. 215–28.

James, Walter, 'Opposing views on design education', *The Times*, 22 August 1970, p. 11.

Killick, Jane, and Howard Maxford, 'Almost an Angel/Talking Pictures/A Switch in Time / Dred', *Starburst*, 31 December 1995, pp. 57–62.

Johnston, Claire and Paul Willemen, 'Brecht in Britain: the independent political film', *Screen*, Vol. 16, No. 4, December 1975, pp. 101–18.

Koetting, Christopher, 'Hands across the water: the Hammer-Seven Arts alliance', *Little Shoppe of Horrors*, April 1994, pp. 41–5.

—, 'Mr. Fuest rises again', *Fangoria*, No. 177, October 1998, pp. 12–19.

—, 'On beyond Phibes', *Fangoria*, No. 178, November 1998, pp. 15–20.

Lassally, Walter, Interview, *American Cinematographer*, Vol. 56, No. 2, February 1975, pp. 174–6.

Le Grice, Malcolm, 'The history we need', in Philip Drummond (ed.), *Film as Film: Formal Experiment in Film 1910–1975* (London: Hayward Gallery/Arts Council of Great Britain, 1979), pp. 113–17.

Leggott, James, 'Nothing to do around here: British realist cinema in the 1970s', in Shail (ed.), *Seventies British Cinema*, pp. 94–104.

Leighton, Tanya, 'I – histories and revisions', in Tanya Leighton (ed.), *Art and the Moving Image* (London: Tate/Afterall, 2008), pp. 49–53.

Macleod, Lewis, 'Exposure meters today', *Film and Television Technician*, March 1970, pp. 14–15.

—, 'Introducing the new Eastman colour negative', *Film and Television Technician*, February 1974, pp. 15, 20.

Margutti, Vic, 'The value of opticals in film making', *Film and Television Technician*, August 1970, pp. 12–13.

Martin, Troy Kennedy, Interview, *Movie*, Winter 1989, p. 38.

Matthews, Julian, '"And finally . . . news for children": an insight into the institutional development of the BBC children's news programme, *John Craven's Newsround*', in Forster and Harper (eds), *British Culture and Society in the 1970s*, pp. 164–74.

McGrath, Terry, 'The market place changes – so must we', *Kinematograph Weekly*, 29 August 1970, p. 7.

McQueen, David, '1970s current affairs: a golden age?', in Forster and Harper (eds), *British Culture and Society in the 1970s*, pp. 76–92.

Medhurst, Jamie, 'Competition and change in British television', in Michele Hilmes (ed.), *The Television History Book* (London: BFI, 2003), pp. 40–4.

Millar, Gavin, 'A Passion to Shock', *The Listener*, 24 June 1982.

Milne, Tom, '*The Duellists*', *Monthly Film Bulletin*, Vol. 44, No. 527, December 1977, p. 258.

Mosk, '*The Duellists*', *Variety*, 1 June 1977, p. 18.

Mulvey, Laura, and Peter Wollen, 'Script of *Riddles of the Sphinx*', *Screen*, Vol. 18, No. 2, July 1977, pp. 61–77.

Mumford, Laura Stempel, 'Feminist theory and television studies', in Christine Geraghty and David Lusted (eds), *The Television Studies Book* (London: Arnold, 1998), pp. 114–30.

Neale, Steve, 'The re-appearance of *Movie*', *Screen*, Vol. 16, No. 3, Autumn 1975, pp. 112–15.

Newland, Paul, 'We know where we're going, we know where we're from: *Babylon*', in Newland (ed.), *Don't Look Now*, pp. 93–104.

Nicolson, Annabel, 'Expanded cinema', in Hayward Gallery (ed.), *Perspectives on British Avant-Garde Film* (London: Arts Council of Great Britain, 1977), numbered papers.

Nicolson, Annabel et al., 'Woman and the formal film', in Philip Drummond (ed.), *Film as Film: Formal Experiment in Film 1910–1975* (London: Hayward Gallery/Arts Council of Great Britain, 1979), p. 118.

North, Dan, 'Don Boyd: the accidental producer', in Shail (ed.), *Seventies British Cinema*, pp. 139–49.

O'Brien, Tim, 'Design for movement', *The Times*, 21 September 1960, p. 16.

Patch, Andrew, 'Beneath the surface: Nicolas Roeg's *Don't Look Now*', in Newland (ed.), *Don't Look Now*, pp. 253–64.

Paterson, Richard, '*The Sweeney*: A Euston Films product', *Screen Education*, No. 20, Autumn 1976, pp. 6–9.

Petit, Chris, and David Pirie, 'Bye Bye B Films', *Time Out*, 27 November 1975, pp. 14–15.

Phillips, Gene D., 'Fact, fantasy, and the films of Ken Russell', *Journal of Popular Film*, Vol. 5, No. 3–4, July 1976, pp. 200–10.

Pickard, Rory, 'My day on location with the Sweeney', *Photoplay*, Vol. 27, No. 8, August 1976, pp. 12–13.

Pines, Jim, 'The cultural context of black cinema', in Mbye Cham and Claire Andrade-Watkins (eds), *Black Frames: Critical Perspectives on Black Independent Cinema* (Cambridge, MA: MIT Press, 1988), pp. 26–36.

Pizzello, Stephen, 'DVD review of *The Duellists*', *American Cinematographer*, Vol. 84, No. 3, March 2003, p. 18.

Plowright, Molly, 'Review of *Just Like a Woman*', *Films and Filming*, November 1966, p. 51.

Porter, Vincent, 'A degree course in the photographic arts', *Industrial and Commercial Photographer*, Vol. 11, No. 2, 1971, pp. 51–5.

Rees, A. L. 'Conditions of illusionism', *Screen*, Vol. 18, No. 3, Autumn 1977, pp. 41–54.

Rhode, Eric, 'Dostoievski and Bresson', *Sight and Sound*, Vol. 39, No. 2, Spring 1970, pp. 82–3.

Richardson, David, 'Aliens and beyond: costumes', *Starburst*, October 1994, pp. 50–1.

Robinson, David, 'Edinburgh: a festival that gets the films', *The Times*, 29 August 1974, p. 10.

—, 'The view of the first generation', *The Times*, 13 December 1974, p. 11.

—, 'In search of the elixir of youth', *The Times*, 14 February 1975, p. 13.

—, 'Film schools: active and passive', *Sight and Sound*, Vol. 44, No. 3, March 1975, pp. 166–9.

—, 'National Film School films', *Sight and Sound*, Vol. 46, No. 2, Spring 1977, pp. 126–7.
Roeg, Nicolas, Interview, *Films and Filming*, January 1972, pp. 18–25.
Rogers, Peter, Interview, *Films and Filming*, June 1970, pp. 70–3.
Rolinson, Dave, 'The last studio system: a case for British television films', in Newland (ed.), *Don't Look Now*, pp. 163–76.
Russell, Ken, Interview, *Films and Filming*, July 1970, pp. 8–12.
—, Interview, *American Cinematographer*, Vol. 58, No. 11, November 1977, pp. 1141, 1164.
Russell, Shirley, Interview, *Films and Filming*, Vol. 24, No. 1, October 1977, pp. 12–16.
Samuelson, David, 'Cinematographers view new camera equipment', *Film and Television Technician*, May 1970, pp. 24–5, 27.
—, 'The "Panaflex" camera: a new concept in design', *Film and Television Technician*, February 1973, pp. 22–3.
Sarne, Mike, 'What's wrong with the British public?', *Films and Filming*, February 1973, pp. 32–3.
Schaffer, Gavin, 'Race on the television: the writing of Johnny Speight in the 1970s', in Forster and Harper (eds), *British Culture and Society in the 1970s*, pp. 107–18.
Seymour, Anne, 'Introduction' in Hayward Gallery, *The New Art* (London: Arts Council of Great Britain, 1972), pp. 1–15.
Sharp, Don, Interview, *Filmfax*, February/March 1998, pp. 111–14, 122–6.
Simpson, Philip, 'Film and media studies in higher education 1977–79', in Christine Gledhill (ed.), *Film and Media Studies in Higher Education. Papers from a Conference Organized in 1979 by the BFI and London University Institute of Education* (London: BFI Education, 1979), pp. 153–60.
Smith, Justin, 'Une entente cordiale? – A brief history of the Anglo-French Film Co-Production Agreement, 1965–1979', in Lucy Mazdon and Catherine Wheatley (eds), *Je t'aime . . . moi non plus: Franco-British Cinematic Relations* (Oxford and New York: Berghahn, 2010), pp. 51–66.
Spicer, Andrew, 'The production line: reflections on the role of the film producer in British cinema', *The Journal of British Cinema and Television*, Vol. 1, No. 1, 2004, pp. 33–50.
—, 'The precariousness of the producer: Michael Klinger and the role of the film producer in the British film industry during the 1970s', in Forster and Harper (eds), *British Culture and Society in the 1970s*, pp. 188–200.
—, 'An impossible task? Scripting "The Chilian Club"', in Jill Nelmes (ed.), *Analysing the Screenplay* (London: Routledge, 2011), pp. 71–88.
Street, Sarah, 'Heritage crime: the case of Agatha Christie', in Shail (ed.), *Seventies British Cinema*, pp. 105–16.
Strick, Philip, Interview with John Boorman, *Sight and Sound*, Vol. 42, No. 2, April 1974, pp. 73–7.
Summers, Sue, 'I'm glad I had to wait for *The Duellists*, says Ridley Scott', *Screen International*, 22 May 1977, p. 39.

Suschitzky, Peter, Interview, *American Cinematographer*, Vol. 57, No. 2, February 1976, pp. 225–9.

—, Interview, *American Cinematographer*, Vol. 58, No. 11, November 1977, pp. 1134–41.

Symonds, Elfreda, 'The development of film study at Hammersmith College for Further Education', *Screen*, Vol. 10, No. 1, January/February 1969, pp. 42–65.

Taylor, John Russell, 'Background to the fore', *The Times*, 22 March 1969, p. 16.

—, 'Tomorrow the world: some reflections on the unevenness of British films', *Sight and Sound*, Vol. 43, No. 2, Spring 1974, pp. 80–3.

Todd, D., 'Freedom for the flicks', *Kinematograph Weekly*, 19 December 1970, pp. 3–4.

Turney, Jo, 'Sex in the sitting room: renegotiating the fashionable British domestic interior for the post-permissive generation', in Forster and Harper (eds), *British Culture and Society in the 1970s*, pp. 263–74.

Unsworth, Geoffrey, Interview, *American Cinematographer*, Vol. 58, No. 4, April 1977, pp. 372–3, 396–7, 428–31.

Vaines, Colin, 'The mods and the movie', *Screen International*, 25 November 1978, p. 26.

Vermorel, Frank, and Judy Vermorel, '1976: Julie: he's got a lot to answer for', in Hanif Kureishi and Jon Savage, *The Faber Book of Pop* (London: Faber & Faber, 1995), pp. 458–9.

Wakeley, Michael, 'Situation hopeless but not serious', *Films and Filming*, May 1970, pp. 6–9.

Walker, Michael, 'The old age of Alfred Hitchcock', *Movie*, No. 18, Winter 1970/1971, pp. 10–13.

Walley, Jonathan, 'Modes of film practice in the avant-garde', in Tanya Leighton (ed.), *Art and the Moving Image: A Critical Reader* (London: Tate/Afterall, 2008), pp. 182–99.

Watkins, Roger, 'Film and television: a main subject course at Bulmershe College of Education', *Screen*, Vol. 10, No. 1, January/February 1969, pp. 34–41.

Waxman, Harry, 'Improvements in process projection systems', *Film and Television Technician*, November 1973, pp. 18–20.

Whannel, Paddy, 'Film education and film culture', *Screen*, Vol. 10, No. 3, May/June 1969, pp. 49–59.

Wheatley, Helen, 'ITV 1955–89: populism and experimentalism', in Michele Hilmes (ed.), *The Television History Book* (London: BFI, 2003), pp. 76–80.

Williams, John, 'Michael Tuchner, Likely Lad', *Films Illustrated*, Vol. 5, No. 53, January 1976, p. 183.

Williams, Paul, 'Class, nostalgia and Newcastle: contested space in *The Likely Lads*', in Paul Newland (ed.), *Don't Look Now: British Cinema in the 1970s* (Bristol: Intellect, 2010), pp. 189–98.

Wilson, David, 'Images of Britain', *Sight and Sound*, Vol. 43, No. 2, Spring 1974, pp. 84–7.

Wollen, Peter, 'The two avant gardes', *Studio International*, Vol. 190, No. 978, November/December 1975, pp. 171–5.
Wood, Jason, 'His brilliant career', *The Guardian*, Friday 3 June 2005.
Wood, Robin, 'The Kazan problem', *Movie*, No. 19, Winter 1970/1971, p. 31.
Young, Colin, 'National Film School', *Sight and Sound*, Vol. 41, No. 1, Winter 1971/1972, pp. 5–8.
—, and Karol Kulik, 'After school', *Sight and Sound* , Vol. 46, No. 4, Autumn 1977, pp. 201–4.

Books

Adams, Mark, *Mike Hodges* (Harpenden: Pocket Essentials, 2001).
Aldgate, Anthony, and James C. Robertson, *Censorship in the Theatre and the Cinema* (Edinburgh: Edinburgh University Press, 2005).
Alvarado, Manuel, and John Stewart, *Made for Television: Euston Films Limited* (London: BFI, 1985).
Askwith, Robin, *The Confessions of Robin Askwith* (London: Ebury, 1999).
Baillieu, Bill, and John Goodchild, *The British Film Business* (Chichester: John Wiley, 2002).
Baxter, John, *An Appalling Talent: Ken Russell* (London: Michael Joseph, 1971).
—, *Stanley Kubrick: A Biography* (London: HarperCollins, 1997).
Beaton, Norman, *Beaton but Unbowed* (London: Methuen, 1986).
Beckett, Andy, *When the Lights Went Out: Britain in the 1970s* (London: Faber & Faber, 2009).
Betts, Ernest, *The Film Business* (London: George Allen & Unwin, 1973).
Bolas, Terry, *Screen Education: From Film Appreciation to Media Studies* (Bristol: Intellect, 2009).
Booker, Christopher, *The Seventies: Portrait of a Decade* (Harmondsworth: Penguin, 1980).
Brown, Allan, *Inside 'The Wicker Man': The Morbid Ingenuities* (London: Sidgwick & Jackson, 2000).
Brown, Ron, *Cinemas and Theatres of Portsmouth from Old Photographs* (Stroud: Amberley, 2009).
Brownlow, Kevin, *Winstanley: Warts and All* (London: UKA, 2009).
Burton, Alan, Tim O'Sullivan and Paul Wells, *The Family Way: The Boulting Brothers and British Film Culture* (Trowbridge: Flicks, 2000).
Caine, Michael, *What's It All About?* (London: Arrow, 1992).
Cashmore, Ernest, *Rastaman – The Rastafarian Movement in England* (London: Allen & Unwin, 1982).
Chapman, James, *Licence to Thrill: A Cultural History of the James Bond Films* (London: I. B. Tauris, 1999).
Chibnall, Steve, *Making Mischief: The Cult Films of Pete Walker* (Guildford: FAB, 1998).

—, *J. Lee Thompson* (Manchester: Manchester University Press, 2000), pp. 324–6.
—, *Get Carter* (London: I. B. Tauris, 2003).
—, and Brian McFarlane, *The British 'B' Film* (London: BFI/Palgrave Macmillan, 2009).
Ciment, Michel, *John Boorman* (London: Faber & Faber, 1986).
—, *Kubrick: The Definitive Edition* (London: Faber & Faber, 2001).
Cohen, Stanley, *Folk Devils and Moral Panics* (London: MacGibbon & Kee, 1972).
Cohn, Nik, *Awopbopaloobopalopbamboom: Pop from the Beginning* (London: Pimlico, 1969).
Colegrave, Stephen, and Chris Sullivan, *Punk: A Life Apart* (London: Cassell, 2001).
Connolly, Ray, *Stardust Memories* (London: Pavilion, 1985).
Cooke, Lez, *British Television Drama: A History* (London: BFI, 2003).
Cork, Richard, *Everything Seemed Possible: Art in the 1970s* (New Haven: Yale University Press, 2003).
Crosland, Susan, *Tony Crosland* (London: Jonathan Cape, 1982).
Curtis, David, *Experimental Cinema: A Fifty Year Evolution* (London: Studio Vista, 1971).
—, *A History of Artists' Film and Video in Britain, 1897–2004* (London: BFI, 2006).
Deeley, Michael, and Matthew Field, *Blade Runners, Deer Hunters and Blowing the Bloody Doors Off: My Life in Cult Movies* (London: Faber & Faber, 2008).
Margaret Dickinson (ed.), *Rogue Reels: Oppositional Film in Britain 1945–90* (London: BFI, 1999).
—, and Sarah Street, *Cinema and State: The Film Industry and the British Government 1927–1984* (London: BFI, 1985).
Docherty, David, David Morrison and Michael Tracey, *The Last Picture Show: Britain's Changing Film Audiences* (London: BFI, 1987).
Dodd, Philip, and Ian Christie, *Spellbound: Art and Film* (London: Hayward Gallery, BFI, 1996).
Donnelly, Kevin, *Pop Music in British Cinema: A Chronicle* (London: BFI, 2001).
—, *British Film Music and Film Musicals* (Basingstoke: Palgrave, 2007).
Drummond, Philip, *Film as Film: Formal Experiment in Film 1910–1975* (London: Hayward Gallery/Arts Council of Great Britain, 1979).
Dundy, Elaine, *Finch, Bloody Finch* (London: Michael Joseph, 1980).
Eberts, Jake and Terry Illot, *My Indecision is Final: The Rise and Fall of Goldcrest Films* (London: Faber & Faber, 1990).
Falsetto, Mario, *Stanley Kubrick: A Narrative and Stylistic Analysis*, 2nd edn (London: Praeger, 2001).
Fletcher, Winston, *Powers of Persuasion: The Inside Story of British Advertising 1951–2000* (Oxford: Oxford University Press, 2008).
Forbes, Bryan, *Notes for a Life* (London: Everest, 1974).

Forster, Laurel and Sue Harper (eds), *British Culture and Society in the 1970s: The Lost Decade* (Newcastle: Cambridge Scholars, 2010).
Frater, Charles, *Sound Recording for Motion Pictures* (London: Tantivy and A. S. Barnes, 1979).
Frayling, Christopher, *Art and Design: 100 Years at the Royal College of Art* (London: Collins & Brown, 1999).
—, *Ken Adam and the Art of Production Design* (London: Faber & Faber, 2005).
Freeman, D., *Television Policies of the Labour Party 1951–2001* (London: Frank Cass, 2003).
Fryer, Peter, *Staying Power – The History of Black People in Britain* (London: Pluto, 1984).
Fuller, Graham (ed.), *Loach on Loach* (London: Faber & Faber, 1998), pp. 13–14.
Garnett, Mark, *From Anger to Apathy: The British Experience since 1975* (London: Jonathan Cape, 2009).
Gidal, Peter, *Structural Film Anthology* (London: BFI, 1976).
—, *Materialist Film* (London: Routledge, 1989).
Gifford, Denis, *British Film Catalogue: Fiction Film 1895–1994*, Vol. 1, 3rd edn (London: Fitzroy Dearborn, 2001).
Gomez, Joseph A., *Ken Russell: The Adaptor as Creator* (London: Frederick Muller, 1976).
Goodwin, Peter, *Television under the Tories: Broadcasting Policy 1979–1997* (London: BFI, 1998).
Gorer, Geoffrey, *Sex and Marriage in England Today: A Study of the Views and Experiences of the Under-45s* (London: Nelson, 1971).
Grant, Barry Keith (ed.), *Britton on Film: The Complete Film Criticism of Andrew Britton* (Detroit: Wayne State University Press, 2009).
Guest, Val, *So You Want to Be in Pictures?* (London: Reynolds & Hearn, 2001).
Hamilton, John, *Beasts in the Cellar: The Exploitation Film Career of Tony Tenser* (Guildford: FAB, 2005).
Harper, Sue, *Women in British Cinema: Mad, Bad and Dangerous to Know* (London: Continuum, 2000).
—, and Vincent Porter, *British Cinema of the 1950s: The Decline of Deference* (Oxford: Oxford University Press, 2003).
Haslam, Dave, *Not ABBA: The Real Story of the 1970s* (London: HarperPerennial, 2005).
Hayward Gallery (ed.), *Perspectives on British Avant-Garde Film* (London: Arts Council of Great Britain, 1977).
Hayward, Philip, *16+ Syllabuses in Film, Television and Media Studies: A Survey* (London: BFI Education, 1985).
Hebdige, Dick, *Subculture: The Meaning of Style* (London: Routledge, 1979).
Hemmings, David, *Blow-Up and Other Exaggerations* (London: Robson, 2004), p. 239.
Henry, Brian (ed.), *British Television Advertising: The First Thirty Years* (London: Century Benham, 1986), pp. 515–17.

Hollis, Patricia, *Jennie Lee: A Life* (Oxford: Oxford University Press, 1997).
Hunt, Leon, *British Low Culture: From Safari Suits to Sexploitation* (London: Routledge, 1998).
Hutchings, Peter, *Hammer and Beyond: The British Horror Film* (Manchester: Manchester University Press, 1993).
Institute of Race Relations, *Police Against Black People*, Race and Class Pamphlet 6 (London: IRR, 1979).
Izod, John, *The Films of Nicolas Roeg: Myth and Mind* (London: Macmillan, 1992).
Jarman, Derek, *Dancing Ledge* (London: Quartet, 1984).
Jenkins, Hugh, *The Culture Gap: An Experience of Government and the Arts* (London: Marion Boyars, 1978).
Jones, Terry, *The Pythons' Autobiography by the Pythons* (London: Orion, 2003).
Kettle, Martin, and Lucy Hodges, *Uprising! The Police, the People and the Riots in Britain's Cities* (London: Pan, 1982).
Le Grice, Malcolm, *Abstract Film and Beyond* (London: Studio Vista, 1977).
LoBrutto, Vincent, *By Design: Interviews with Film Production Designers* (London: Praeger, 1992).
Lovell, Alan, *The British Film Institute Production Board* (London: BFI, 1976).
Lusted, David, *A CSE Course in Film* (London: BFI Education Department, 1971).
MacDonald, S., *Avant-Garde Film: Motion Studies* (Cambridge: Cambridge University Press, 1993).
Marner, Terence St John, *Directing Motion Pictures* (London: Tantivy, 1972).
—, *Film Design* (London: Tantivy, 1973).
McArthur, Colin, *Television and History* (London: BFI, 1978).
McFarlane, Brian, *An Autobiography of British Cinema* (London: Methuen, 1997).
McGillivray, David, *Doing Rude Things: The History of the British Sex Film 1958–1981* (London: Sun Tavern Fields, 1992).
Miles, Barry, *London Calling: A Countercultural History of London since 1945* (London: Atlantic, 2010).
Moore-Gilbert, Bart (ed.), *The Arts in the 1970s: Cultural Closure?* (London: Routledge, 1994).
Morley, David, *Television, Audiences and Cultural Studies* (London: Routledge, 1992).
Mundy, John, *The British Musical Film* (Manchester: Manchester University Press, 2007).
Murphy, Robert (ed.), *Directors in British and Irish Cinema – A Reference Guide Companion* (London: BFI, 2006).
Newland, Paul (ed.), *Don't Look Now: British Cinema in the 1970s* (Bristol: Intellect, 2010).
Pakenham, Frank, Earl of Longford, *Pornography: The Longford Report* (London: Coronet, 1972).
Palin, Michael, *Diaries 1969–1979: The Python Years* (London: Orion, 2007).

Perkins, Roy, and Martin Stollery, *British Film Editors: The Heart of the Movie* (London: BFI, 2004).
Perkins, V. F., *Film as Film: Understanding and Judging Movies* (Harmondsworth: Penguin, 1972).
Petrie, Duncan, *The British Cinematographer* (London: BFI, 1996).
Phelps, Guy, *Film Censorship* (London: Victor Gollancz, 1975).
Phillips, Gene, *Ken Russell* (Boston: Twayne, 1979).
—, and Rodney Hill, *The Encyclopedia of Stanley Kubrick* (New York: Checkmark, 2002).
Reed, Carol, *International Film Festival of San Sebastian* (Pamplona: Filmoteca Española, 2000, bilingual edition), p. 189.
Rees, A. L., *A History of Experimental Film and Video: From the Canonical Avant-Garde to Contemporary British Practice* (London: BFI, 1999).
Rickards, Jocelyn, *The Painted Banquet: My Life and Loves* (London: Weidenfeld & Nicolson, 1987).
Robertson, James C., *The Hidden Cinema: British Film Censorship 1913–1972* (London: Routledge, 1989).
Runnymede Trust and the Radical Statistics Race Group, *Britain's Black Population* (London: Heinemann Education, 1980), p. 44.
Salwolke, Scott, *Nicolas Roeg Film by Film* (Jefferson: McFarland, 1993).
Sandbrook, Dominic, *State of Emergency: The Way We Were: Britain, 1970–1974* (London: Allen Lane, 2010).
Self, David, *Television Drama: An Introduction* (Basingstoke: Macmillan, 1984).
Shail, Robert (ed.), *Seventies British Cinema* (London: Palgrave Macmillan, 2008).
—, *Stanley Baker: A Life in Film* (Cardiff: University of Wales Press, 2008).
Shubik, Irene, *Play for Today: The Evolution of Television Drama* (London: Davis-Poynter, 1975).
Sinyard, Neil, *The Films of Nicolas Roeg* (London: Letts, 1991).
—, *Richard Lester* (Manchester: Manchester University Press, 2010), pp. 97–110.
Sivanandan, Ambalavaner, *A Different Hunger – Writings on Black Resistance* (London: Pluto, 1982).
Smith, Justin, *Withnail and Us: Cult Films and Film Cults in British Cinema* (London: I. B. Tauris, 2010).
Snelgrove, K., and P. Dayman-Johns, *The Carry on Book of Statistics: Taking the Carry Ons into a New Century* (Somerset: KAS, 2003).
Sounes, Howard, *Seventies: The Sights, Sounds and Ideas of a Brilliant Decade* (London: Simon & Schuster, 2006).
Stempel, Tom, *Screenwriting* (San Diego: A. S. Barnes, 1982).
Swern, P., and M. Childs, *The Guinness Book of Box Office Hits* (Enfield: Guinness, 1995).
Trevelyan, John, *What the Censor Saw* (London: Michael Joseph, 1973).
Turner, Alwyn W., *Crisis? What Crisis? Britain in the 1970s* (London: Aurum, 2008).

Tutt, Nigel, *The Tax Raiders: The Rossminster Affair* (London: Financial Training Publications, 1985).

Walker, Alexander, *Stanley Kubrick Directs* (London: Davis-Poynter, 1972).

—, *National Heroes: British Cinema in the Seventies and Eighties* (London: Harrap, 1985).

—, *Hollywood, England: The British Film Industry in the 1960s*, 2nd edn (London: Harrap, 1986).

Walker, John, *The Once and Future Film: British Cinema in the Seventies and Eighties* (London: Methuen, 1985).

Watkins, Roger, *CSE Examinations in Film* (London: BFI Education Department/ SEFT, 1969).

Wheen, Francis, *Strange Days Indeed: The Golden Age of Paranoia* (London: Fourth Estate, 2009).

Wickham, Phil, *The Likely Lads* (London: BFI, 2008).

Williams, Raymond, *Television: Technology and Cultural Form* (London: Routledge, 1974).

Wistrich, Enid, *'I Don't Mind the Sex, It's the Violence': Film Censorship Explored* (London: Marion Boyars, 1978).

Wood, Linda (ed.), *British Films 1971–1981* (London: BFI, 1983).

Wymer, Roland, *Derek Jarman* (Manchester: Manchester University Press, 2005).

Young, Robert, *Electric Eden: Unearthing Britain's Visionary Music* (London: Faber & Faber, 2010).

Yule, Andrew, *Enigma: David Puttnam, The Story So Far* (Edinburgh: Mainstream, 1988).

Internet Sources

Barber, Sian, 'The pinnacle of popular taste? The importance of *Confessions of a Window Cleaner*', *Scope*, Issue 18, October 2010, http://www.scope.nottingham.ac.uk.

British Artists Film and Video Study Collection, London, 2008, AHRB Centre for British Film and Television Studies, http://studycollection.co.uk/hiddenhistorybfi.html.

LUX, 'LUXOnline', London, 2011, http://www.luxonline.org.uk.

Freeman, M. D. A., 'Lloyd, Dennis, Baron Lloyd of Hampstead (1915–1992)', *Oxford Dictionary of National Biography* (Oxford: Oxford University Press, 2009), online edition, Lawrence Goldman (ed.), http://www.oxforddnb.com/view/article/51187, accessed 18 January 2011.

Mazière, Michael, 'Institutional Support for Artists' Film and Video in England 1966–2003', London, 2008, AHRB Centre for British Film and Television Studies, British Artists Film and Video Collection, http://www.studycollection.co.uk.

Porter, Vincent, 'Knatchbull, John Ulick, Seventh Baron Brabourne of Brabourne [John Brabourne], (1924–2005)', *Oxford Dictionary of National Biography*

(Oxford: Oxford University Press, 2009). Online edition, Lawrence Goldman (ed.), http://www.oxforddnb.com/view/article/96042, accessed 30 March 2010.

Rolinson, Dave, 'Play for Today', Stirling, 2010, *British Television Drama*, University of Stirling, http://www.britishtelevisiondrama.org.uk/?page_id=858, accessed 22 February 2011.

Salewicz, Chris, 'Land of Sour Milk and Sus', *New Musical Express*, *Uncarved*, http://www.uncarved.org/babylon/?page_id=73, accessed 22 February 2011.

Filmography

This contains all the British films cited in the book which were released between 1970 and 1980.

Italicised abbreviations:
d: director (last name, first name)
prod: production company

The Abominable Dr. Phibes (1971). *d*: Fuest, Robert, *prod*: American International Productions (England) Ltd.

Aerial (1974). *d*: Tait, Margaret, *prod*: Ancona Films.

Agatha (1978). *d*: Apted, Michael, *prod*: Sweetwall Productions, Casablanca FilmWorks, First Artists Productions, Warner Bros.

Akenfield (1974). *d*: Hall, Peter, *prod*: Angle Films.

The Alf Garnett Saga (1972). *d*: Kellett, Bob, *prod*: Associated London Films, Virgin Films, Columbia Pictures.

Alfie Darling (1975). *d*: Hughes, Ken, *prod*: Signal Films, EMI.

All Coppers Are . . . (1971). *d*: Hayers, Sidney, *prod*: Rank Film Distributors, Peter Rogers Productions.

And Then There Were None (1974). *d*: Collinson, Peter, *prod*: Filibuster Films, Corona-Filmproduktion (Munich), Coralta Cinematografica (Rome), Talia Films (Madrid), Comeci (Paris).

Anti-Clock (1979). *d*: Arden, Jane, *prod*: Kendon Films, Jack Bond Films.

Arabian Adventure (1979). *d*: Connor, Kevin, *prod*: Badger Films Ltd.

Assault (1970). *d*: Hayers, Sidney, *prod*: Rank Film Distributors, Peter Rogers Productions.

At the Earth's Core (1976). *d*: Connor, Kevin, *prod*: Burrowing Productions Inc., American International Pictures, Samuel Z. Arkoff, Amicus, Midcore Ltd.

Babylon (1980). *d*: Rosso, Franco, *prod*: National Film Trustee Company Ltd, National Film Finance Corporation.

Barry Lyndon (1975). *d*: Kubrick, Stanley, *prod*: Warner Bros., Peregrine Productions, Hawk Films.

The Beast in the Cellar (1970). *d*: Kelly, James, *prod*: Tigon British Productions Ltd, Leander Films.
The Beast Must Die (1974). *d*: Annett, Paul, *prod*: Amicus.
Behind the Rent Strike (1974). *d*: Broomfield, Nicholas, *prod*: National Film School.
The Belstone Fox (1973). *d*: Hill, James, *prod*: Independent Artists.
Bequest to the Nation (1973). *d*: Jones, James Cellan, *prod*: Universal.
The Big Sleep (1978). *d*: Winner, Michael, *prod*: Winkast Film Productions.
The Bitch (1979). *d*: O'Hara, Gerry, *prod*: Spritebowl Productions.
Black Beauty (1971). *d*: Hill, James, *prod*: Tigon British Productions Ltd, Chilton Film & Television Enterprises Ltd.
Black Jack (1979). *d*: Loach, Ken, *prod*: Kestrel Films.
Black Joy (1977). *d*: Simmons, Anthony, *prod*: National Film Trustee Company Ltd, West One Film Producers, Winkast Programming Ltd, NFFC.
Bless This House (1972). *d*: Thomas, Gerald, *prod*: Peter Rogers Productions.
Blood on Satan's Claw (1970). *d*: Haggard, Piers, *prod*: Tigon British Productions Ltd, Chilton Film & Television Enterprises Ltd.
Bloody Kids (1979). *d*: Frears, Stephen, *prod*: Black Lion Films, ITC Entertainment.
The Body (1971). *d*: Battersby, Roy, *prod*: Kestrel Films.
Born to Boogie (1972). *d*: Starr, Ringo, *prod*: Apple Films.
The Boy Friend (1971). *d*: Russell, Ken, *prod*: MGM-EMI, Russflix.
A Bridge Too Far (1977). *d*: Attenborough, Richard, *prod*: Joseph E. Levine Productions.
Broken English: Three Songs by Marianne Faithfull (1979). *d*: Jarman, Derek, *prod*: Blue Mountain Films/Island Record Films.
Bronco Bullfrog (1970). *d*: Platts-Mills, Barney, *prod*: Maya Films.
Brother Sun, Sister Moon (1972). *d*: Zeffirelli, Franco, *prod*: Euro International/VIC.
The Brute (1976). *d*: O'Hara, Gerry, *prod*: Trigon Productions.
Bugsy Malone (1977). *d*: Parker, Alan, *prod*: National Film Trustee Company Ltd, Rank, Goodtimes Enterprises, NFFC, Bugsy Malone Productions.
The Call of the Wild (1972). *d:* Annakin, Ken, *prod:* Massfilms.
Captain Kronos: Vampire Hunter (1974). *d*: Clemens, Brian, *prod*: Hammer.
Caravan to Vaccares (1974). *d*: Reeve, Geoffrey, *prod*: Crowndale Holdings Limited, Geoff Reeve Productions, S. N. Prodis (Paris).
Carry On Abroad (1972). *d*: Thomas, Gerald, *prod*: Rank.
Carry On Behind (1975). *d*: Thomas, Gerald, *prod*: Rank.
Carry On Dick (1974). *d*: Thomas, Gerald, *prod*: Rank.
Carry On Emmannuelle (1978). *d*: Thomas, Gerald, *prod*: National Film Trustee Company Ltd.
Carry On England (1976). *d*: Thomas, Gerald, *prod*: Rank.
Carry On Henry (1971). *d*: Thomas, Gerald, *prod*: Rank.
Carry On Loving (1970). *d*: Thomas, Gerald, *prod*: Rank.
Carry On Up The Jungle (1970). *d*: Thomas, Gerald, *prod*: Rank.

Chato's Land (1971). *d*: Winner, Michael, *prod*: Scimitar Films.
Children (1976). *d*: Davies, Terence, *prod*: BFI Production Board.
The Class of Miss MacMichael (1978). *d*: Narizzano, Silvio, *prod*: Moonbeam Productions, Kettledrum Productions, Brut Productions.
A Clockwork Orange (1971). *d*: Kubrick, Stanley, *prod*: Warner Bros., Polaris Productions, Hawk Films.
Concert for Bangladesh (1972). *d*: Swimmer, Saul, *prod*: Apple Films, Twentieth Century Fox.
Conduct Unbecoming (1975). *d*: Anderson, Michael, *prod*: Lion International, Crown Production Company.
Confessions from a Holiday Camp (1977). *d*: Cohen, Norman, *prod*: Columbia, Swiftdown.
Confessions of a Pop Performer (1975). *d*: Cohen, Norman, *prod*: Columbia, Swiftdown.
Confessions of a Window Cleaner (1974). *d*: Guest, Val, *prod*: Columbia, Swiftdown.
Countess Dracula (1970). *d*: Sasdy, Peter, *prod*: Hammer, Rank.
Creatures the World Forgot (1971). *d*: Chaffey, Don, *prod*: Hammer.
Cromwell (1970). *d*: Hughes, Ken, *prod*: Irving Allen Ltd, Columbia.
Daddy (1973). *d*: Whitehead, Peter and Niki de St Phalle, *prod*: Narcis Films.
Dad's Army (1971). *d*: Cohen, Norman, *prod*: Columbia (British) Productions, Norcon Film Productions.
Day of the Jackal (1973). *d*: Zinnemann, Fred, *prod*: Warwick Film Productions, Paris Universal Productions France.
Dead Cert (1974). *d*: Richardson, Tony, *prod*: Woodfall Film Productions.
Dear Mr. Barber, I'd Like to Swim the Channel (1974). *d*: Lewin, Ben, *prod*: National Film School.
Death on the Nile (1978). *d*: Guillermin, John, *prod*: EMI.
A Delicate Balance (1973). *d*: Richardson, Tony, *prod*: American Express Films, Ely Landau Organisation, Cinevision Ltee, The American Film Theatre.
The Devils (1971). *d*: Russell, Ken, *prod*: Warner Bros., Russo Productions.
The Devil's Rain (1975). *d*: Fuest, Robert, *prod*: Sandy Howard Productions.
Diamonds Are Forever (1971). *d*: Guy, Hamilton, *prod*: United Artists.
The Disappearance (1977). *d*: Cooper, Stuart, *prod*: National Film Trustee Company Ltd, Trofar, Tiberius Film Productions, Canadian Film Development Corporation.
A Doll's House (1973). *d*: Garland, Patrick, *prod*: Elkins Productions, Freeward Films.
Don't Look Now (1973). *d*: Roeg, Nicolas, *prod*: D. L. N. Ventures Partnership, Casey Productions, Eldorado Films.
Doomwatch (1972). *d*: Sasdy, Peter, *prod*: Tigon British Productions Ltd.
The Double-Headed Eagle (1973). *d*: Becker, Lutz, *prod*: Visual Programme Systems, Goodtime Enterprises.
Dr. Jekyll and Sister Hyde (1971). *d*: Baker, Roy Ward, *prod*: Hammer, EMI.

Dr. Phibes Rises Again (1972). *d*: Fuest, Robert, *prod*: American International Productions (England) Ltd.

Dracula (1974). *d*: Curtis, Dan, *prod*: Dan Curtis Productions, Latglen Ltd.

Dracula A.D. 1972 (1972). *d*: Gibson, Alan, *prod*: Hammer.

The Duellists (1977). *d*: Scott, Ridley, *prod*: Paramount, Enigma, National Film Finance Corporation, Scott Free.

The Eagle Has Landed (1976). *d*: Sturges, John, *prod*: ITC Entertainment.

Endless Night (1972). *d*: Gilliat, Sidney, *prod*: National Film Trustee Company Ltd, British Lion Films, EMI Film Productions.

Eskimo Nell (1974). *d*: Campbell, Martin, *prod*: Salon Productions.

The Europeans (1979). *d*: Ivory, James, *prod*: National Film Trustee Company Ltd, Merchant Ivory.

Family Life (1971). *d*: Loach, Ken, *prod*: Kestrel Films, Anglo-EMI.

Fear Is the Key (1972). *d*: Tuchner, Michael, *prod*: Anglo-EMI.

Feelings (1974). *d*: Britten, Lawrence, *prod*: Playpont Films, Mara Company.

The Fifth Musketeer (1977). *d:* Annakin, Ken, *prod:* Sascha-Vien Films.

The Final Programme (1973). *d*: Fuest, Robert, *prod*: National Film Trustee Company Ltd, Goodtime Enterprises.

Fire in the Water (1977). *d*: Whitehead, Peter, *prod*: Fontglow.

Flame (1974). *d*: Loncraine, Richard, *prod*: Spouberry Ltd, Visual Programming Systems, Goodtimes Enterprises.

Follow Me! (1972). *d*: Reed, Carol, *prod*: Universal.

The Four Feathers (1978). *d*: Sharp, Don, *prod*: Southbrook International Programmes, Trident Films Ltd, Norman Rosemont Productions.

The Four Musketeers (1974). *d*: Lester, Richard, *prod*: Film Trust, Barcelona Este Films.

Free the Six (1974). *d*: Newsreel, Group, *prod*: National Film School.

Fright (1971). *d*: Collinson, Peter, *prod*: Amicus (Fantale Films), British Lion.

Frightmare (1974). *d*: Walker, Pete, *prod*: Peter Walker (Heritage) Ltd.

Gawain and the Green Knight (1973). *d*: Weeks, Stephen, *prod*: Sancrest.

Get Carter (1971). *d*: Hodges, Mike, *prod*: EMI, MGM.

The Go-Between (1971). *d*: Losey, Joseph, *prod*: EMI.

Gold (1974). *d*: Hunt, Peter, *prod*: Avton Film Productions.

The Great Rock 'n' Roll Swindle (1979). *d*: Temple, Julien, *prod*: Boyd's Company, Kendon Films Ltd, Matrixbest, Virgin Films.

Green Men, Yellow Woman (1973). *d*: Goldman, Thelma, *prod*: London Film School.

Gumshoe (1971). *d*: Frears, Stephen, *prod*: Memorial Enterprises, Columbia.

Hands of the Ripper (1971). *d*: Sasdy, Peter, *prod*: Hammer, Rank.

Hannie Caulder (1971). *d*: Kennedy, Burt, *prod*: Tigon British Productions Ltd, Curtwel Productions.

Hennessy (1975). *d*: Sharp, Don, *prod*: Hennessy Film Productions, American International Productions.

Holiday on the Buses (1973). *d*: Izzard, Bryan, *prod*: Hammer, Anglo-EMI, Nat Cohen.

The Horror of Frankenstein (1970). *d*: Sangster, Jimmy, *prod*: EMI Film Productions, Hammer Film Productions, Anglo-EMI Film Distributors Ltd, MGM-EMI Film Distributors Ltd.

House of Mortal Sin (1975). *d*: Walker, Pete, *prod*: Peter Walker (Heritage) Ltd, Columbia.

House of Whipcord (1974). *d*: Walker, Pete, *prod*: Peter Walker (Heritage) Ltd.

Hussy (1979). *d*: Chapman, Matthew, *prod*: Berwick Street Films 'D', Boyd's Company.

I Don't Want to Be Born (1975). *d*: Sasdy, Peter, *prod*: Rank.

I, Monster (1971). *d*: Weeks, Stephen, *prod*: Amicus, British Lion.

In Celebration (1974). *d*: Anderson, Lindsay, *prod*: AFT Distributing Corporation, The American Film Theatre, Ely Landau Organisation, Cinevision Ltee.

The Island of Dr. Moreau (1977). *d*: Taylor, Don, *prod*: American International Productions (England) Ltd.

Jabberwocky (1977). *d*: Gilliam, Terry, *prod*: National Film Trustee Company Ltd, Umbrella Entertainment, National Film Finance Corporation.

Joseph Andrews (1976). *d*: Richardson, Tony, *prod*: Woodfall Film Productions.

Jubilee (1977). *d*: Jarman, Derek, *prod*: Whaley-Malin Productions, Megalovision.

Kidnapped (1971). *d*: Mann, Delbert, *prod*: Omnibus Productions Ltd.

The Kids Are Alright (1979). *d*: Stein, Jeff, *prod*: The Who Films Ltd.

Lady Caroline Lamb (1972). *d*: Bolt, Robert, *prod*: Pulsar Productions Ltd, Anglo-EMI, GEC, Vides Cinematografica.

The Lady Vanishes (1979). *d*: Page, Anthony, *prod*: Rank, Hammer.

The Land That Time Forgot (1975). *d*: Connor, Kevin, *prod*: Amicus, Lion International.

Leo the Last (1970). *d*: Boorman, John, *prod*: Char-Wink-Boor Productions Inc., Caribury Films Ltd.

Let It Be (1970). *d*: Lindsay-Hogg, Michael, *prod*: Apple Films.

The Likely Lads (1976). *d*: Tuchner, Michael, *prod*: Anglo-EMI.

Lisztomania (1975). *d*: Russell, Ken, *prod*: Visual Programme Systems, Goodtime Enterprises.

Little Malcolm and His Struggle Against the Eunuchs (1974). *d*: Cooper, Stuart, *prod*: Subafilms, Apple Films.

Live and Let Die (1973). *d*: Hamilton, Guy, *prod*: Danjaq S.A., Eon Productions, United Artists.

The Long Good Friday (1979). *d*: MacKenzie, John, *prod*: Black Lion Films, Calendar Productions.

Loot (1970). *d*: Narizzano, Silvio, *prod*: Performing Arts, British Lion Films.

Love Thy Neighbour (1973). *d*: Robins, John, *prod*: Hammer.

Lust for a Vampire (1970). *d*: Sangster, Jimmy, *prod*: EMI, Hammer, Fantale Films.

The Magnificent Seven Deadly Sins (1971). *d*: Stark, Graham, *prod*: Tigon British Productions Ltd.
Mahler (1974). *d*: Russell, Ken, *prod*: Ken Russell Productions, Goodtimes Enterprises.
The Maids (1974). *d*: Miles, Christopher, *prod*: Ely Landau Organisation, Cinevision Ltee, Cine Films, The American Film Theatre.
Man Friday (1975). *d*: Gold, Jack, *prod*: Keep Films, ABC Entertainment, ITC.
The Man From O.R.G.Y. (1970). *d*: Hill, James, *prod*: United Hemisphere Productions, Delta Films International.
The Man Who Fell To Earth (1976). *d*: Roeg, Nicolas, *prod*: British Lion.
The Man with the Golden Gun (1974). *d*: Hamilton, Guy, *prod*: Danjaq S.A., Eon Productions.
The Mangrove Nine (1973). *d*: Rosso, Franco, *prod*: Franco Rosso / John La Rose Productions.
Mary, Queen of Scots (1971). *d*: Jarrott, Charles, *prod*: Universal.
Melody (1971). *d*: Hussain, Waris, *prod*: Hemdale/Sagittarius/Goodtimes.
Miner's Film (1974). *d*: Newsreal Group, *prod*: National Film School.
Miss Julie (1972). *d*: Phillips, Robin, and John Glenister, *prod*: Tigon British Productions Ltd, Sedgemoor Productions.
Monty Python and the Holy Grail (1974). *d*: Gilliam, Terry, and Terry Jones, *prod*: National Film Trustee Company Ltd, Python (Monty) Pictures, Michael White.
Monty Python's Life of Brian (1979). *d*: Jones, Terry, *prod*: Python (Monty) Pictures, HandMade Films.
Moonraker (1979). *d*: Gilbert, Lewis, *prod*: Danjaq S.A., Eon Productions, Les Productions Artistes Associés.
Murder on the Orient Express (1974). *d*: Lumet, Sidney, *prod*: EMI.
The Music Lovers (1970). *d*: Russell, Ken, *prod*: Russfilms.
Mutiny on the Buses (1972). *d*: Booth, Harry, *prod*: Hammer, Anglo-EMI.
My Ain Folk (1973). *d*: Douglas, Bill, *prod*: BFI Production Board.
My Childhood (1972). *d*: Douglas, Bill, *prod*: BFI Production Board.
My Way Home (1978). *d*: Douglas, Bill, *prod*: BFI Production Board.
Neither the Sea nor the Sand (1972). *d*: Burnley, Fred, *prod*: LMG Film Distributors, Portland Film Corporation, Tigon British Productions Ltd.
Nightcleaners (1975). *d*: Berwick Street Film Collective, *prod*: Berwick Street Film Collective.
The Nightcomers (1972). *d*: Winner, Michael, *prod*: Avco Embassy Pictures, Motion Picture and Theatrical Investments, Joseph E. Levine, Kastner-Ladd-Kanter, Scimitar Films.
Nighthawks (1978). *d*: Peck, Ron, *prod*: Nighthawks, Four Corners Films, Nashburgh.
Not Now Darling (1972). *d*: Croft, David, and Ray Cooney, *prod*: L.M.G., Sedgemoor Productions, Not Now Films.
O Lucky Man! (1973). *d*: Anderson, Lindsay, *prod*: Warner Bros.
The Odessa File (1974). *d*: Neame, Ronald, *prod*: Domino Productions, Oceanic

Filmproduktion, Houtsnede Maatschappij N.V., Columbia Pictures Corporation.

On the Buses (1971). *d*: Booth, Harry, *prod*: Hammer, EMI.

On the Mountain (1974). *d*: Tait, Margaret, *prod*: Ancona Films.

Ooh . . . You Are Awful (1972). *d*: Owen, Cliff, *prod*: National Film Trustee Company Ltd, Quintain, British Lion.

The Optimists of Nine Elms (1973). *d*: Simmons, Anthony, *prod*: Sagittarius Productions, Cheetah Films, West One Film Producers.

Overlord (1975). *d*: Cooper, Stuart, *prod*: Joswend.

Painted Eightsome (1970). *d*: Tait, Margaret, *prod*: Ancona Films.

Paper Tiger (1974). *d:* Annakin, Ken, *prod:* MacLean / Lloyd.

The Passage (1978). *d*: Thompson, J. Lee, *prod*: Hemdale Holdings, Passage Films, Monday Films.

Penthesilea: Queen of the Amazons (1974). *d*: Mulvey, Laura, and Peter Wollen, *prod*: Laura Mulvey–Peter Wollen.

Percy (1971). *d*: Thomas, Ralph, *prod*: Welbeck Films Ltd, Anglo-EMI.

Performance (1970). *d*: Cammell, Donald and Nicolas Roeg, *prod*: Warner Bros., Goodtimes Enterprises.

The Pied Piper (1971). *d*: Demy, Jacques, *prod*: Goodtimes Enterprises.

The Pink Panther Strikes Again (1976). *d*: Edwards, Blake, *prod*: United Artists.

Please Sir! (1971). *d*: Stuart, Mark, *prod*: LWI Productions, Rank.

Porridge (1979). *d*: Clement, Dick, *prod*: Black Lion Films, ITC Entertainment.

Pressure (1975). *d*: Ové, Horace, *prod*: BFI Production Board.

Psychomania (1972). *d*: Sharp, Don, *prod*: Benmar Productions Ltd.

Pulp (1972). *d*: Hodges, Mike, *prod*: United Artists, Three Michaels Film Productions Ltd.

The Punk Rock Movie (1977). *d*: Letts, Don, *prod*: Punk Rock Films, Notting Hill Studios.

Puttin' on the Ritz (1974). *d*: Starkiewicz, Antoinette, *prod*: London International Film School.

Quadrophenia (1979). *d*: Roddam, Franc, *prod*: The Who Films Ltd, Curbishley-Baird Enterprises, Polytel Films.

Rachel's Man (1975). *d*: Mizrahi, Moshe, *prod*: Loraglade.

Radio On (1979). *d*: Petit, Chris, *prod*: BFI Production Board, National Film Trustee Company Ltd, Road Movies Filmproduktion GmBH, National Film Finance Corporation.

The Raging Moon (1970). *d*: Forbes, Bryan, *prod*: EMI.

The Railway Children (1970). *d*: Jeffries, Lionel, *prod*: EMI, MGM.

Reggae (1970). *d*: Ové, Horace, *prod*: Bamboo Records.

Requiem for a Village (1975). *d*: Gladwell, David, *prod*: BFI Production Board.

Return of the Pink Panther (1974). *d*: Edwards, Blake, *prod*: Jewel Productions Ltd, Pimlico.

Revenge (1971). *d*: Hayers, Sidney, *prod*: Rank Film Distributors, Peter Rogers Productions.

Revenge of the Pink Panther (1978). *d*: Edwards, Blake, *prod*: Jewel Productions Ltd, Pimlico.

The Riddle of the Sands (1979). *d*: Maylam, Tony, *prod*: Worldmark Productions.

Riddles of the Sphinx (1977). *d*: Mulvey, Laura, and Peter Wollen, *prod*: BFI Production Board.

The Rocky Horror Picture Show (1975). *d*: Sharman, Jim, *prod*: Houtsnede Maatschappij N.V., Twentieth Century Fox Film Corporation, Michael White Productions.

Rogue Male (1976). *d*: Donner, Clive, *prod*: BBC, Twentieth Century Fox.

The Romantic Englishwoman (1975). *d*: Losey, Joseph, *prod*: National Film Trustee Company Ltd, Dial Films, Fox-Rank, Méric-Matalon.

Royal Flash (1975). *d*: Lester, Richard, *prod*: Two Roads Productions, Zeeuwse Maatschappij N.V.

Ryan's Daughter (1970). *d*: Lean, David, *prod*: Faraway Productions.

Satan's Slave (1976). *d*: Warren, Norman J., *prod*: Monumental Pictures.

Savage Messiah (1972). *d*: Russell, Ken, *prod*: MGM, Russ-Arts.

Scum (1979). *d*: Clarke, Alan, *prod*: Kendon Films, Berwick Street Films.

Sebastiane (1976). *d*: Humfress, Paul and Jarman, Derek, *prod*: Disctac.

The Shining (1980). *d*: Kubrick, Stanley, *prod*: Warner Bros., The Producer Circle Company, Hawk Films, Peregrine Productions.

The Shout (1977). *d*: Skolimowski, Jerzy, *prod*: National Film Trustee Company Ltd, Recorded Picture Company, National Film Finance Corporation, Rank.

Shout at the Devil (1976). *d*: Hunt, Peter, *prod*: Tonau Film Productions Ltd.

The Slipper and the Rose (1976). *d*: Forbes, Bryan, *prod*: Paradine Co-Productions.

Soft Beds, Hard Battles (1973). *d*: Boulting, Ray, *prod*: Charter Film Productions.

Something to Hide (1971). *d*: Reid, Alastair, *prod*: Avton Film Productions.

Spring and Port Wine (1970). *d*: Hammond, Peter, *prod*: Memorial Enterprises.

The Spy Who Loved Me (1977). *d*: Gilbert, Lewis, *prod*: United Artists.

The Squeeze (1977). *d*: Apted, Michael, *prod*: Martinat Productions, Warner Bros.

Stardust (1974). *d*: Apted, Michael, *prod*: EMI, Goodtime Enterprises.

Steptoe and Son (1972). *d*: Owen, Cliff, *prod*: Associated London Films.

Steptoe and Son Ride Again (1973). *d*: Sykes, Peter, *prod*: Associated London Films, Nat Cohen, Anglo-EMI Film Distributors.

Stevie (1978). *d*: Enders, Robert, *prod*: First Artists Productions, Grand Metropolitan, Bowden Productions.

The Stud (1978). *d*: Masters, Quentin, *prod*: Brent Walker Film Productions, Artoc Corporate Services.

Sunday Bloody Sunday (1971). *d*: Schlesinger, John, *prod*: Vectia Films, Vic Films (London), United Artists.

Swallows and Amazons (1974). *d*: Whatham, Claude, *prod*: Theatre Projects Films.

Swastika (1973). *d*: Mora, Philippe, *prod*: Visual Programme Systems, Goodtime Enterprises.

Sweeney! (1976). *d*: Wickes, David, *prod*: Euston Films.

Sweeney 2 (1978). *d*: Clegg, Tom, *prod*: Euston Films.

Sweet William (1979). *d*: Whatham, Claude, *prod*: Kendon Films, Berwick Street Film Collective, Boyd's Company.

Tales from the Crypt (1972). *d*: Francis, Freddie, *prod*: Metromedia Producers Corporation, Amicus Productions.

Tales of Beatrix Potter (1971). *d*: Mills, Reginald, *prod*: EMI, MGM.

Tales That Witness Madness (1973). *d*: Francis, Freddie, *prod*: World Film Services.

Taste the Blood of Dracula (1970). *d*: Sasdy, Peter, *prod*: Hammer.

The Tempest (1979). *d*: Jarman, Derek, *prod*: Boyd's Company.

That'll Be the Day (1973). *d*: Watham, Claude, *prod*: Goodtime Enterprises, Nat Cohen, Anglo-EMI FIlm Distributors.

There's a Girl in My Soup (1970). *d*: Boulting, Ray, *prod*: Ascot Productions.

The Thirty Nine Steps (1978). *d*: Sharp, Don, *prod*: Norfolk International Films.

The Three Musketeers (The Queen's Diamonds) (1973). *d*: Lester, Richard, *prod*: Film Trust.

Time for Loving (1971). *d*: Miles, Christopher, *prod*: London Screenplays / DeGrunwald.

To the Devil a Daughter (1976). *d*: Sykes, Peter, *prod*: Hammer.

Tommy (1975). *d*: Russell, Ken, *prod*: Robert Stigwood Organisation.

A Touch of the Other (1970). *d*: Miller, Arnold, *prod*: Global-Queensway.

The Triple Echo (1972). *d*: Apted, Michael, *prod*: Hemdale Holdings, Senta Productions.

Tower of Evil (1972). *d*: O'Connolly, Jim, *prod*: Grenadier Films, Fanfare Film Productions.

Twins of Evil (1971). *d*: Hough, John, *prod*: Hammer, Rank.

Under Milk Wood (1972). *d*: Sinclair, Andrew, *prod*: Tinton Films, Hugh French, Jules Buck.

Up Pompeii (1971). *d*: Kellett, Bob, *prod*: Anglo-EMI, Associated London Films, Virgin Films, Nat Cohen.

The Ups and Downs of a Handyman (1975). *d*: Sealey, John, *prod*: KFR Productions.

Valentino (1977). *d*: Russell, Ken, *prod*: United Artists, Aperture Films.

Vampire Circus (1971). *d*: Young, Robert, *prod*: Hammer, Rank.

Very Like a Whale (1980). *d*: Bridges, Alan, *prod*: Black Lion Films, ATV.

Villain (1971). *d*: Tuchner, Michael, *prod*: Anglo-EMI.

The Virgin and the Gypsy (1970). *d*: Miles, Christopher, *prod*: Patientia Anstalt, Kenwood Films.

Voices (1973). *d*: Billington, Kevin, *prod*: Warden.

Walkabout (1970). *d*: Roeg, Nicolas, *prod*: Max L. Raab-Si Litvinoff Films.

Warlords of Atlantis (1978). *d*: Connor, Kevin, *prod*: EMI.

When Eight Bells Toll (1971). *d*: Périer, Étienne, *prod*: Winkast Film Productions.

The Wicker Man (1973). *d*: Hardy, Robin, *prod*: British Lion.

The Wild Geese (1978). *d*: McLaglen, Andrew V., *prod*: Richmond Film Productions (West) Ltd.

The Wildcats of St. Trinian's (1980). *d*: Launder, Frank, *prod*: Wildcat Film Productions.
Winstanley (1975). *d*: Brownlow, Kevin, and Andrew Mollo, *prod*: BFI Production Board.
Yanks (1979). *d*: Schlesinger, John, *prod*: Joseph Janni-Lester Persky Productions, CIP Filmproduktion, United Artists.
Young Winston (1972). *d*: Attenborough, Richard, *prod*: Columbia Pictures, Open Road.
Zardoz (1973). *d*: Boorman, John, *prod*: Twentieth Century Fox Film Corporation, John Boorman Productions.

Television Broadcasts

Armchair Cinema: Regan, 4 June 1974 (Thames).
Armchair Theatre, 1956–1969 (ABC), 1970–1974 (Thames).
Bagpuss, 12 February–7 May 1974 (BBC1).
The Benny Hill Show, 19 November 1969–1 May 1989 (Thames).
The Black and White Minstrel Show, 1958–1978 (BBC1).
Citizen Smith, 3 November 1977–4 July 1980 (BBC1).
Colditz, 19 October 1972–1 April 1974 (BBC1).
Coronation Street, 1960– (Granada).
Crossroads, 2 November 1964–4 April 1988 (ATV).
Days of Hope 11 September–25 September 1975 (BBC1).
Dread, Beat an' Blood, 7 June 1979 (BBC1).
The Duchess of Duke Street, 4 September 1976–24 December 1977 (BBC1).
Edward and Mrs. Simpson, 8 November–20 December 1978 (Thames).
Edward the Seventh, 1 April–1 July 1975 (ATV).
Elizabeth R, 17 February–24 March 1971 (BBC 2).
Empire Road, 1978–1979 (BBC Birmingham).
The Fall and Rise of Reginald Perrin, 8 September 1976–24 January 1979 (BBC).
Fawlty Towers, 1975–1979 (BBC).
Film, 1972–1998 (BBC1).
The Fosters, 1976–1977 (LWT).
George and Mildred, 6 September 1976–25 December 1979 (Thames).
The Good Life, 4 April 1975–22 May 1977 (BBC1).
Houseparty, 1972–1980 (Southern).
I, Claudius, 20 September–6 December 1976 (BBC TV / London Films).
John Craven's Newsround, 1972–1989 (BBC1).
The Kenny Everett Video Show/Video Cassette, 3 July 1978–21 May 1981 (Thames).
Kisses at Fifty, 22 January 1973 (BBC1).
Late Night Line-Up, 1964–1972 (BBC).
Love Thy Neighbour, 13 April 1972–22 January 1976 (Thames).
Man About the House, 15 August 1973–7 April 1976 (Thames).

Mixed Blessings, 1978–1980 (LWT).
Monty Python's Flying Circus, 5 October 1969–5 December 1974 (BBC).
The Multi-Coloured Swap Shop, 2 October 1976–27 March 1982 (BBC1).
The Naked Civil Servant, 17 December 1975 (Thames).
Nationwide, 1969–1983 (BBC1).
New Scotland Yard, 22 April 1972–25 May 1974 (LWT).
Not the Nine O' Clock News, 16 October 1979–8 March 1982 (BBC).
The Old Grey Whistle Test, 1971–1987 (BBC2).
On the Buses, 28 February 1969–6 May 1973 (LWT).
The Onedin Line, 15 October 1971–25 October 1980 (BBC1).
The Pallisers, 19 January–2 November 1974 (BBC2).
Panorama, 1953– (BBC).
Pennies from Heaven, 7 March–11 April 1978 (BBC1).
Play for Today: Theatre Six Two Five, 1964–1968 (BBC).
Play for Today: Abigail's Party, 1 November 1977 (BBC1).
Play for Today: All Good Men, 31 January 1974 (BBC1).
Play for Today: The Cheviot, The Stag and the Black, Black Oil, 6 June 1974 (BBC1).
Play for Today: Edna the Inebriate Woman, 27 October 1971 (BBC1).
Play for Today: Hard Labour, 12 March 1973 (BBC1).
Play for Today: A Hole in Babylon, 29 November 1979 (BBC1).
Play for Today: Leeds – United!, 31 October 1974 (BBC1).
Play for Today: Penda's Fen, 21 March 1974 (BBC Birmingham).
Play of the Month, 1965–1983 (BBC1).
Poldark, 5 October 1975–18 January 1977 (BBC TV/London Films).
Pop Goes the Easel, 25 March 1962, for the BBC's *Monitor* programme.
Q, 1969–1982 (BBC).
Rising Damp, 13 December 1974– 9 May 1978 (Yorkshire).
Rock Follies, 24 February 1976–8 June 1977 (Thames).
Secret Army, 7 September 1977–15 December 1979 (BBC1/BRT Belgium).
The Six Wives of Henry VIII, 1 January–2 May 1970 (BBC2).
Special Branch, 1969–1974 (Thames).
The Stone Tape, 25 December 1972 (BBC2).
The Sweeney, 2 January 1975–28 December 1978 (Euston Films/Thames Television).
Take Three Girls, 1969–1971 (BBC1).
Target, 1977–1978 (BBC1).
Thirty Minute Theatre, 1966–1973 (BBC2).
TISWAS, 5 January 1974–3 April 1982 (ATV Network/Central TV).
Today, 1 December 1976 (Thames).
Top of the Pops, 1964–2006 (BBC1).
Upstairs, Downstairs, 10 October 1971–21 December 1975 (LWT).
The Wednesday Play, 1965–1970 (BBC1).
The Wednesday Play: The Big Flame, 19 February 1969 (BBC1).

The Wednesday Play: Up the Junction, 3 November 1965 (BBC1).
Weekend World, 1972–1988 (LWT).
The Wombles, 5 February 1973–24 October 1975 (BBC/Central TV/Film Fair Productions).
World in Action, 7 January 1963–7 December 1998 (Granada).
World in Action: Margaret Thatcher Interview, 27 January 1978 (Granada).

Index